PRAISE FOR *YOUNG THURGOOD*

"Gibson's thoroughly researched and insightful book about charismatic Thurgood Marshall is a must-read."

> —Elaine R. Jones, former president
> and director-counsel,
> NAACP Legal Defense and
> Educational Fund

"Gibson paints vivid pictures of the people, places, and events that molded the extraordinary lawyer with whom my father and I had the privilege of working."

> —James M. Nabrit III, civil rights lawyer

"The many photographs and other images throughout the book add an energetic dimension to Gibson's description of Marshall's world."

> —Ronald M. Shapiro, lawyer,
> negotiations expert,
> *New York Times*–bestselling author
> of *Dare to Prepare*

"Gibson's fascinating account of Marshall's early years gives us a better understanding of this extraordinary American, who was one of my personal heroes."

> —Vernon E. Jordan Jr., lawyer,
> business executive, civil rights leader

"Gibson succeeds where others have failed to help us appreciate the forces that shaped the man whose career helped shape the nation."

> —Kurt L. Schmoke, vice president and
> general counsel of Howard University

DATE DUE

APR 2 4 2018	

BRODART, CO.   Cat. No. 23-221

Young Thurgood

Young Thurgood
THE MAKING OF A SUPREME COURT JUSTICE

Larry S. Gibson
FOREWORD BY THURGOOD MARSHALL JR.

 **Prometheus Books**

59 John Glenn Drive
Amherst, New York 14228–2119

Published 2012 by Prometheus Books

Cover photo by James W. Murphy. Courtesy of James W. Murphy.
Cover design by Nicole Sommer-Lecht

Inquiries should be addressed to
Prometheus Books
59 John Glenn Drive
Amherst, New York 14228–2119
VOICE: 716–691–0133
FAX: 716–691–0137
WWW.PROMETHEUSBOOKS.COM

16 15 14 13   5 4 3

Library of Congress Cataloging-in-Publication Data

Gibson, Larry S., 1942–
    Young Thurgood : the making of a Supreme Court Justice / by Larry S. Gibson.
        p. cm.
    Includes bibliographical references and index.
    ISBN 978–1–61614–571–2 (cloth : alk. paper)
    ISBN 978–1–61614–527–9 (ebook)
    1. Marshall, Thurgood, 1908–1993. 2. United States. Supreme Court—Officials and employees. 3. Judges—United States—Biography. 4. United States. Supreme Court—History. I. Title.

KF8745.M34G55 2012
347.73'035092—dc23
[B]

2012027517

Printed in the United States of America on acid-free paper

To my wife, Diana Gibson,
and Thurgood's wife, Cecilia Marshall.

Contents

Foreword

Many works about my father have been assembled, ranging from formal works of scholarship to popular biographical profiles to children's books, movies, and documentaries. With this detailed and carefully crafted volume, Professor Larry S. Gibson has crafted a unique and engrossing portrait.

The photograph that graces the cover speaks volumes about the content of this book. The tall, striking, and confident figure is unmistakable, yet it is an image of Thurgood Marshall that is rarely if ever seen, even by those who have studied his life or who knew him well.

The cover photo is just one of countless treasures from my father's early and formative years that Professor Gibson has unearthed. Through the rich collection of childhood anecdotes; the insights into the colorful assemblage of relatives, mentors, and legal clients who shaped my father's development; and the recounting of the challenges and opportunities my father encountered in his local community and throughout our country, this book weaves together the events that formed the foundation for my father's career.

Professor Gibson's attention to detail and thorough research is apparent throughout this book. His sleuthing has led him to courthouses and clerk's offices as well as to professional and personal correspondence in many locales. That trove of information has enabled him to understand the ways in which my father applied his talent and skill and faced his own personal challenges.

Readers will see in this book the origins of my father's penchant for storytelling and his desire to act as an advocate for fairness on behalf of those who are marginalized in American society. Professor Gibson sets the stage with a gritty sense of the tone of the times when my father was born in Baltimore, which at that time was a segregated city not far from communities that often tilted toward vigilante justice instead of the rule of law.

This book brings to life the array of relatives and friends who surrounded my father as he grew up and demonstrates how an early focus on academics and debate honed his skills and determined his interests for a lifetime. With classmates like Cab Calloway and Langston Hughes, there was little room in his social circle for shrinking violets or backbenchers. And there was plenty of room for creative fun and mischief. Law school brought those experiences together in new ways and gave my father the tools he needed to live a life of consequence.

This book also details the breadth of my father's legal work. By the time my father began arguing cases before the US Supreme Court, he had already handled a diverse array of client interests that included divorces, simple assaults, and capital murder cases. Here, too, are chronicled my father's early involvement with politics, the civil rights movement, and the NAACP, as well as his early efforts to bring equality to education, voting, housing, and the fabric of American society. *Young Thurgood* provides that information in an enjoyable way, even to the point of letting us know about the kind of employment my father found after the workday was over to make ends meet.

Professor Gibson has given us a book that contains many new facts and insights and presents them in compelling prose. The result is as entertaining as it is unique, poignant, and informative.

Thurgood Marshall Jr.

Preface

"This had better be a criminal matter," Thurgood Marshall said as he opened the door to find my fellow attorney, Charles Curtis Lee, and me standing outside his Falls Church, Virginia, home around 11:00 p.m. on July 1, 1975. "No, Mr. Justice, it is not. It's about Baltimore," I replied. The justice, still in his bathrobe, invited us in.

After following Marshall into his study, we did not leave until 2:00 a.m. We had come to seek an emergency order in the case of our client— Dr. Roland N. Patterson, the superintendent of the Baltimore public schools—who was being fired from his job. I wanted the courts to block his removal until he received proper notice of the reasons for his dismissal and an adequate hearing.

Marshall was not the justice assigned to emergency matters from Maryland, yet he agreed to help us. He had adeptly managed the media throughout his career, and he realized that we wanted him to grant our motion so that we could buy a little time and obtain press coverage of the Patterson case. We talked about Patterson for less than twenty minutes; after that, Marshall asked us a little about our backgrounds and where we lived in Baltimore and then spent most of the next two and a half hours entertaining us with stories about our city. Marshall signed the temporary stay, but in the end—as expected—Dr. Patterson lost his job.

Until that summer night in 1975, I'd had no special knowledge of Thurgood Marshall. I had simply been proud of him, a fellow black Baltimorean, whose extraordinary legal career had led all the way to his becoming a US Supreme Court justice. My first meeting with Marshall destroyed some preconceived notions I had acquired over the years. Many had reported that he had turned into a curmudgeon. Yet, from the cheer and wit he displayed despite our having awakened him, I saw a different person. Also, according to popular belief, Marshall hated Baltimore.

However, while Marshall did have some bad memories of Baltimore's stifling racial segregation, he still spoke mainly with affection for the city where he was born and raised.

My next involvement with Marshall came three years later, in 1978. I was the faculty adviser to the Black American Law Students Association (BLSA; today the Black Law Student Association) at the University of Maryland School of Law, and the students wanted to name the school's new law library in honor of Justice Marshall. The administration did not welcome this proposal; they had planned to sell the name to a well-heeled donor. Yet BLSA pressed on and gained the support of a member of the university's board of regents.

A year after the naming initiative began, the university president wrote to Marshall asking for the justice's permission to name "a university building" in his honor. However, the president did not specify which campus or which building. Having recently read about some racial problems at the university's flagship campus in College Park, Marshall initially declined to give permission. Clarence M. Mitchell Jr., the NAACP lobbyist, intervened and explained to Marshall that it was the law students who wanted to name the new law library after him. Marshall consented and authorized Justice William Brennan to attend the ceremony on his behalf. Despite his acquiescence, the press gave the misleading impression that Marshall had rebuffed the efforts of the students and the school to honor him.

Thereafter, I began to notice that the media were continuing to perpetuate the myth that Marshall had applied for admission to the University of Maryland School of Law and been rejected. If Marshall had applied in 1930, he most certainly would have been rejected because the school had been racially segregated since 1891. But the fact was that Marshall, realizing that he would be rejected, did not apply.

This and other misimpressions that I encountered, as well the fact that Marshall had seemed so different from the man I had expected to meet during my late-night visit to his home, made me want to learn the truth about him. Researching his life in Baltimore was an obvious place to start. Marshall had been born and raised in my hometown, and many of his contemporaries were still living here. Between 1981 and 1985, I interviewed Marshall's Baltimore relatives, his classmates from elementary school and high school, his college roommate, who was also best man at his wedding, his neighbors, and two of his high school teachers. These interviews gave me insight into Marshall from people who knew him, and an image of Marshall as a person began to emerge. After a while, I felt that I had gathered sufficient information about Marshall's youth to satisfy my curiosity, and I turned my attention to other matters.

From time to time, I read books and articles about Marshall, such as Richard Kluger's prodigious work *Simple Justice*, published in 1976, and Bob Woodward's behind-the-scenes look at the Supreme Court, *The Brethren*, published in 1979.[1] Although I found this literature informative, I repeatedly encountered in it what I knew to be inaccuracies about Marshall. Nevertheless, I also understood that authors, who must rely heavily on interviews, can fall victim to their sources' imperfect memories.

My own inquiries had decisively dispelled in my mind some often-repeated notions about Marshall. Some writers understated Marshall's high intellect and energy while he was growing up and suggested that he was lazy at worst and an average student at best. Several writers depicted Marshall as something of a "late bloomer," whose intellectual prowess did not become evident until he was in law school. I knew that both of those notions were incorrect. Marshall's contemporaries described a bright boy who had been a top student in one of the best of Baltimore's segregated schools. He had skipped a grade in elementary school and had graduated, with academic honors, from high school at age 16—finishing almost two years ahead of his peers.

My interest in Marshall was heightened by a brief, humorous encounter in 1985, at the dedication of the Clarence M. Mitchell Jr. Courthouse in downtown Baltimore. During the luncheon, Marshall was chatting with Mitchell's widow, the civil rights firebrand Juanita Jackson Mitchell. I asked a bystander to take a photograph of me with the justice. As I stood next to Marshall while the photographer seemed to take forever to snap the photograph, Marshall turned to me and quipped, "So, what am I supposed to do, kiss you?"

Several years passed after that amusing encounter with Marshall before his retirement from the Supreme Court in 1991 triggered another wave of public interest and writing. Months later, commentaries compared Marshall's life and judicial philosophy with that of his replacement, Clarence Thomas.

Thurgood Marshall died two years later, and four major biographies of him appeared shortly thereafter. In 1993, journalist Carl T. Rowan published *Dream Makers, Dream Breakers: The World of Justice Thurgood Marshall.* In 1994, Michael Davis and Hunter Clark published an updated and revised edition of their 1992 work, *Thurgood Marshall: Warrior at the Bar, Rebel on the Bench.* Then in 1998, Howard Ball wrote *A Defiant Life: Thurgood Marshall and the Persistence of Racism in America* and Juan Williams published the most thorough and definitive biography of Marshall to date, and an invaluable resource for understanding Marshall's full career, *Thurgood Marshall: American Revolutionary.*[2] Although I differ from these writers on some details about Marshall's early years, I have benefited from studying their works, and several additional years of research since the publication of those volumes have understandably borne some new fruit.

"So, what am I supposed to do, kiss you?"

My early investigations convinced me that a clear understanding of Marshall required a close examination of his formative years before he joined the NAACP staff in New York. This early period of Marshall's life had shaped his personality, attitudes, priorities, and work habits. Even so, I was uncertain about what to do with this insight. Finally, at the urging of Karen Rothenberg, who was then dean of the University of Maryland School of Law, and my law partner, Paul Mark Sandler, I decided to write a book about the first thirty years of Marshall's life.

I have been well positioned (perhaps uniquely so) to write this book. Having taught law since 1971, with an emphasis on racial matters, has provided me with historical perspective. Other courses I have taught— on evidence, civil procedure, and election law—have helped me interpret Marshall's law practice. As a lifelong Baltimorean, I know the city and its history. Before beginning work on this book, I had already spent several years researching the lives and careers of Maryland's first one hundred black lawyers, of whom Marshall was one. Maryland State Archivist Dr. Edward Papenfuse, with whom I have, for more than a decade, taught a law school seminar called "Race and the Law: The Maryland Experience," gave me access to and assistance with voluminous state records. My friend John Oliver, publisher of the newspaper the *Afro-American*, made available to me the paper's morgue files containing materials about Marshall and his relatives, classmates, neighbors, and friends.

As my research continued, the year 2004 marked the fiftieth anniversary of *Brown v. Board of Education*, reigniting national interest in Marshall. During 2004, I joined many others in giving speeches about Marshall, answering questions from newspapers and television stations, and participating in symposia and presentations on Marshall's role in *Brown*.

I then embarked on another round of interviews. This process included a trip to Philadelphia to visit Howard Pindell, Marshall's earliest potential plaintiff in the teacher pay equalization campaign. Pindell possessed documents from Marshall that no one else had seen for decades. I also interviewed Philip and Rachel Brown at their home in Anne Arundel County, Maryland. The Browns, married for more than seventy years, had worked closely with Marshall while organizing the Anne Arundel County chapter of the NAACP. William H. Murphy Sr., one of the first blacks to graduate from the University of Maryland School of Law following *Murray v. Pearson*, the case that opened the doors of the University of Maryland School of Law to blacks and signaled the beginning of the end for de jure racial segregation in the United States, gave me much-needed information about the neighborhood where Marshall lived.

I interviewed Harold Arthur Seaborne, a man somewhat forgotten by history, whose application to the University of Maryland School of Law in 1933 helped pave the way for Donald Gaines Murray's lawsuit two years later. One of the most pleasant interviews took place in my office with the vibrant, seventy-three-year-old Esther McCready, who had gained admission to the University of Maryland School of Nursing due to the efforts of Marshall and others.

In Richmond, Virginia, I interviewed Oliver W. Hill, the legendary civil rights lawyer, who was Marshall's best friend during their years at Howard University School of Law. The family of Clarence M. Mitchell Jr. and Juanita Jackson Mitchell, who worked closely with Marshall, provided invaluable resources that they had assembled over the years. Lucille Scott, one of the potential plaintiffs in the Baltimore County High School desegregation litigation, still blushed when recounting how, seventy years earlier, "that handsome, young lawyer took our hands and walked us into court."

All of this was capped off by the cooperation of Thurgood Marshall's immediate and extended family. The Baltimore relatives were extremely cooperative, in some cases turning over to me files about Marshall that they had assembled through the years. The justice's widow, Cecilia Marshall, patiently tolerated many hours of my wife, Diana, and me probing around her home, asking her questions, and scanning items from files and family albums. Thurgood Marshall Jr. sent letters to Lincoln University and Howard University, thus opening up to me materials that would not otherwise have been available.

This book reconstructs Marshall's life from his birth; through grade school, high school, college, and law school; and, finally, through his first years as a lawyer. To give the reader a glimpse into Marshall's world, the book quotes from several letters and memoranda authored by Marshall. His different choices of words when writing to different persons provide valuable insight into his thoughts, attitudes, and relationships.

Marshall's papers document a strong work ethic and amazing stamina. He was extraordinarily busy and productive, usually working on several projects simultaneously. A remarkable discovery was that, while practicing law in Baltimore during the daytime, Marshall worked a night job as a clerk in a clinic for patients with sexually transmitted diseases. The assembled research shows a young lawyer with a mixed record of wins and losses in criminal and civil trials who found a path that would eventually take him to a position of national leadership.

One week after becoming a lawyer, Marshall was thrust into the political firestorm that followed the lynching of George Armwood on Maryland's Eastern Shore. A month later, he led an economic boycott of Baltimore stores that refused to hire black sales personnel. And by 1935,

Marshall was involved in the aforementioned *Murray v. Pearson*, the case that helped begin the process of dismantling de jure racial segregation in the United States.

As one examines Marshall's early years, a fascinating man emerges. He was a supremely confident and pragmatic person. He was a diplomat but could be brusque to those around him. He was gregarious, with a wry sense of humor, but could also have a sharp tongue. He sometimes made quick and unfair assessments of individuals or stretched the truth to achieve a laudable objective. He adapted his speech and mannerisms to suit the setting or the moment. There was also something charming about the young Thurgood Marshall. From an early age, he possessed a charisma that attracted bright people to his side, people who wanted to work with him and help him succeed.

The reader of this book will see Marshall learn to evaluate people and situations, correspond with colleagues and opponents, react to successes and disappointments, mature as a lawyer and a negotiator, and develop strategies that would guide his career. The reader will meet Marshall's key mentors from before and after he went to law school and will learn about the special impact his participation in competitive debating from the age of thirteen through college had upon him. This book also documents the beginnings of Marshall's relationships with Clarence Mitchell, Charles Houston, Walter White, Roy Wilkins, and other civil rights leaders. As the book ends, the reader witnesses Marshall's decision to spend the rest of his life using the law to combat racial discrimination.

More than thirty-five years have passed since my first encounter with Thurgood Marshall, late on that summer night in 1975. Hopefully, this book will increase understanding of and appreciation for a man who contributed so much to America.

Chapter 1

Is There an Investigation Taking Place?

"Is there an investigation taking place within the state police department?" Thurgood Marshall asked the governor of Maryland. On October 25, 1933, Marshall, only twenty-three years old and fresh out of law school, gathered with ten other black lawyers in the Baltimore office of Governor Albert C. Ritchie, looking for answers. They wanted to know what he was going to do about the brutal lynching of George Armwood in Somerset County.[1]

THE ARMWOOD LYNCHING

A few days earlier, an elderly white woman named Mary Dentson had claimed that she was attacked in Princess Anne, a small town on the southern end of Maryland's Eastern Shore. While the exact injury she suffered remains unknown, a young black man would pay for it with his life.

Dentson reported that George Armwood, considered "feeble minded" by the locals,[2] had jumped out from behind some bushes as she was walking to town. She claimed that he grabbed her, tore her dress, and frightened her. The local prosecutor, state's attorney John B. Robbins, wasted no time. He ordered Armwood's arrest and charged him with felonious assault. Despite such quick action from the prosecutor, many of Somerset County's white residents, impatient with what they perceived as the slow pace of justice, clamored for Armwood's swift punishment.

The desire of some locals to take the law into their own hands should not have come as a surprise to officials in Princess Anne. Two years earlier, a black farmhand named Euel Lee, who also went by the name "Orphan Jones," stood accused of murdering four members of a white family in the charming Eastern Shore town of Berlin. Concerned for his safety, Maryland authorities moved Lee across Chesapeake Bay to the Baltimore City Jail to prevent a lynching. The practice of transporting blacks to Baltimore "for safekeeping" when they were accused of crimes against whites dated back many years. Officials considered Baltimore to be the only place in Maryland where blacks accused of crimes against whites were safe from vigilante violence.[3]

By the time of George Armwood's arrest, the Euel Lee case had dragged on for two years, with multiple trials and appeals. In October 1933, the Euel Lee matter was coming to an end, with Lee awaiting execution in the Baltimore City Jail. However, his defense team, provided by the American Communist Party's International Labor Defense, continued its ultimately unsuccessful efforts to save Lee from the gallows.[4]

Racial tensions on the Eastern Shore had turned violent when Maryland's most recent lynching occurred in December 1931. A black man named Matthew Williams stood accused of fatally shooting his white employer before turning the gun on himself. Six members of a mob dragged the gravely wounded Williams from his hospital bed in Salisbury, fourteen miles north of Princess Anne, and pushed him out a window and into a crowd of three hundred people waiting below. The mob tripled in size as it dragged Williams to the courthouse lawn. Although he was probably already dead, the lynch mob hung Williams from a tree. A member of the crowd then dragged his body behind a truck to a black neighborhood, where the mob doused his body in gasoline and set it on fire.[5] Some Eastern Shore whites claimed that the Williams incident was a reaction to legal maneuvers by communist lawyers who were delaying the execution of Euel Lee for the murder of the Green family.[6]

With such a deadly precedent, local authorities had good reason to be concerned for Armwood's safety in October 1933. However, Somerset County officials appeared oblivious to the looming threat of mob violence. State's Attorney Robbins openly denied that Princess Anne residents would take the law into their own hands. According to the *Baltimore Sun*, "Mr. Robbins said he anticipated no trouble on the part of the populace. Their chief wish, he said, was to see justice done as soon as possible, and they understood the county authorities were making every effort for a speedy trial."[7] In rural Maryland, the circuit court judge was the most powerful governmental figure in most of the twenty-three counties. Judge Robert F. Duer—a resident of Princess Anne and the judge on the First Circuit Court, whose jurisdiction included Somerset County—agreed, and he predicted that there would be no trouble and that it would be "perfectly safe" to let the accused man remain in the Somerset County Jail.[8]

Governor Albert Ritchie was more realistic. At the urging of Captain Edward Johnson of the Maryland State Police, Ritchie dispatched twenty-four state troopers to provide safe escort for Armwood across Chesapeake Bay to the Baltimore City Jail.[9] The *Afro-American* prophetically captured the concurrence of events: "With the Euel Lee case still pending and the lynching of Matthew Williams still fresh in the memories of Marylanders, George Armwood, 28 year old laborer, was rushed to Baltimore Monday night to escape a mob of 2,000 bent on lynching him near the same spot where Williams was hanged and burned."[10]

However, Armwood would have a very short stay in Maryland's largest city. Robbins and Duer quickly ordered Armwood's return to Somerset County for arraignment. The newspapers and radio ominously released the itinerary for Armwood's trip back to Princess Anne, making it easy for the gathering mob to track Armwood's return. "Police Squads Escort Negro Back to Shore," read the headline in the *Baltimore Sun*. As the mob calling for Armwood's death grew, the *Sun* also listed the timetable of Armwood's return to Princess Anne: "The guard of State police taking George Armwood, Negro, from the Baltimore City Jail passed through Salisbury at 2:37 o'clock this morning. Princess Anne is about fourteen miles from Salisbury and the police expect to have Armwood in jail by 3:30."[11]

That night, Armwood's fate was sealed. The assault began a few hours after Armwood's arrival in Princess Anne. Accounts of the mob's size varied from one thousand to five thousand people. The mob smashed in the jailhouse door with a battering ram and dragged Armwood from his cell. As they carried him into the street, a teenager cut off one of his ears with a butcher knife. The sight of blood drove the crowd wild. Hundreds of frenzied men, women, and children pounced on Armwood. They punched, kicked, and dragged him through the streets before hanging him next door to Judge Duer's house. They then cut his body down from the tree and

One week after Marshall became a lawyer, George Armwood was taken from the Baltimore City Jail, returned to Somerset County, and lynched within twenty-fours hours. *Courtesy of* Afro-American *Newspaper Archives and Research Center.*

George Armwood's sister and mother mourn his death. *Courtesy of* Afro-American *Newspaper Archives and Research Center.*

dragged it through the streets again. They yanked gold fillings from his teeth and cut clothing and flesh from his body. The lynch mob hung Armwood's body again, this time from a telegraph pole. Finally, in an eerie repetition of the Williams lynching, they dumped his body in a lumberyard, poured gasoline on it, and set it on fire. Standing around the burning body, the men and women in the mob joined hands and sang "John Brown's Body" and

"Give Me Something to Remember You By." Afterwards, the members of the mob cut the rope used to hang Armwood into small pieces and chopped up the battering ram. The crowd took home the pieces of those grim instruments as souvenirs.[12]

The threat to Armwood was so obvious that two reporters, including rookie reporter Clarence M. Mitchell Jr., and a photographer from the *Afro-American* newspaper left Baltimore and headed toward Princess Anne as soon as they learned that Armwood was on his way back to Somerset County. Fearful of taking the more direct ferryboat route east across Chesapeake Bay during a period of high racial tensions, the black newspaper crew instead drove north, crossing the Susquehanna River near the Delaware border, and then south down the length of Maryland's Eastern Shore to Princess Anne. They arrived to find Armwood's charred corpse in the lumberyard with part of the noose still around his broken neck.

The *Afro-American* published its account with the banner headline "BURN" and a gruesome photograph of Armwood's mangled body. The macabre caption read, "George Armwood *a la* Maryland." Mitchell's article gave an account of how Armwood's body was found in a lumberyard by the *Afro-American* reporters at 6:30 a.m. "after 2,000 of Maryland's 'best' staged their 'barbecue' in front of the courthouse." Witnesses had told the reporters that members of the local fire department had sounded an alarm and brought out a fire truck to bring out the mob and begin the assault.[13]

THE "OLD LINE STATE"

Maryland—home of Chesapeake Bay, the nation's largest estuary—is known as the "Old Line State" because of its location on the Mason-Dixon Line. During the 1930s, the northern and western regions of Maryland— home to small farms, mills, railroads, and some mining operations— resembled similar regions in many northern states.

Baltimore was the nation's eighth-largest city, with a population of 804,000. An important industrial center, it was also the cultural and educational capital of the state of Maryland. Prior to the Civil War, it had the largest population of free blacks of any city in the United States. Yet in the 1930s, Southern mores still prevailed in Baltimore, and it was a very segregated place.

Three southern Maryland counties—Calvert, Charles, and Saint Mary's—and the entire Eastern Shore mirrored much of the Deep South, physically and socially. Their economies were built around agriculture and seafood, especially crabs and oysters. On the Eastern Shore, vegetable and fruit canneries and seafood-packing houses operated on seasonal schedules. Black Marylanders lacked significant political power outside Baltimore City and were at the bottom of the social and economic ladders. Many blacks lived in genuine fear for their lives at the hands of law enforcement officers and white civilians who were intent on keeping blacks subordinated.

Despite rigid segregation throughout the state, Maryland had been spared the widespread, wanton violence against blacks that had been rife in other parts of the country since the turn of the twentieth century.

RACIAL VIOLENCE IN AMERICA

From 1890 to 1940, nearly five thousand black Americans were lynched in the United States.[14] Before and after the Civil War, groups of vigilantes attacked and murdered blacks in the Deep South. Violence against blacks occurred not just in the South but throughout the United States. Almost always, the perpetrators acted with impunity.[15]

The violence against blacks included several mass killings. In April 1873, following a contested election in Louisiana, almost three hundred blacks lost their lives in what became known as the Colfax Massacre.

In July 1917, whites who were fearful of competition for jobs from black migrants fleeing the Deep South sparked the East Saint Louis Race Riots. Three thousand whites gathered downtown and began to beat and shoot blacks. Rioters torched black homes and businesses. The National Guard was called in to restore order, but many of the troops turned against the blacks and joined in the assaults. When the dust cleared, more than one hundred blacks had been killed and six thousand had been left homeless.

In the summer and early fall of 1919, a series of race riots known as the "Red Summer," a term coined by poet James Weldon Johnson, claimed hundreds of lives. Much of the violence was aimed at black veterans of World War I, some of whom were lynched while still in uniform. In the nation's capital, 6 blacks were killed and 150 injured in racial mob attacks. During five days of rioting in Chicago, 50 blacks were killed and hundreds of mostly black homes and businesses on the city's south side were burned to the ground. In Elaine, Arkansas, an altercation between white farmers and black sharecroppers led to the deaths of 5 whites and between 100 and 200 blacks.

In June 1920, three black circus workers in Duluth, Minnesota, were accused of raping a nineteen-year-old white girl at gunpoint. Although an examination by the girl's personal physician found no signs of rape or assault, a mob of five thousand to ten thousand surrounded the Duluth jailhouse, broke down the door with little resistance from the deputies on duty, dragged the three suspects into the street, and lynched them.

In 1915, acts of antiblack intimidation, violence, and murder such as these were glorified in the racist cinematic epic *The Birth of a Nation*. Directed by D. W. Griffith, the film was more than three hours long and cost $110,000 to make. The movie broke many budget and box office records of the day. The film portrayed the Ku Klux Klan as saviors of the white race and protectors of white women. Although many leaders condemned the film and some states banned it from movie theaters, President Woodrow Wilson praised the movie after a private White House screening.

Finally, in the spring of 1921, the Tulsa Race Riot was the deadliest of all. The riot began as the result of a never-substantiated rumor about an assault on a white, female elevator operator by a nineteen-year-old, black shoeshine boy. White rioters converged on a thirty-five-block area of North Tulsa known as the "Black Wall Street," which consisted of more than 1,200 residences and hundreds of businesses. By the time the riot was over, the Black Wall Street had been ravaged by fire, leaving more than three hundred people dead and ten thousand people homeless.

Maryland had not completely escaped the surge in racial violence that had taken place around the turn of the twentieth century. Between 1882 and 1930, Maryland ranked twenty-seventh out of the forty-eight states in the number of lynchings that occurred within its borders. Of the approximately 4,300 lynchings that had taken place across the country during that period, 33 had occurred in Maryland, with all but 3 of the victims being black. However, Maryland experienced a welcome lull in the violence for several years. By the time of the Matthew Williams lynching in 1931, the state had gone twenty years without a lynching. Maryland's last victim prior to Williams, a man by the name of King Davis, was hanged by a Baltimore mob on Christmas Day 1911.[16]

The preventable and horrific lynching of George Armwood produced demonstrations, rallies, and demands for new state and federal anti-lynching laws. *Courtesy of Afro-American Newspaper Archives and Research Center.*

Charles Houston and the president of the Washington NAACP joined demonstrations with nooses around their necks to protest lynchings. *Courtesy of Afro-American Newspaper Archives and Research Center.*

The news of the entirely preventable and gruesome lynching of George Armwood sent shockwaves through Maryland's black communities. Black and white citizens and leaders held antilynching rallies, signed petitions, agreed to form new organizations, proposed antilynching legislation, and demanded to meet with Governor Ritchie.[17]

In the wake of the Armwood lynching, new coalitions and new organizations were formed, but most of them did not last for long. At the urging of his high school teacher and debate coach, Gough McDaniels, Marshall participated in the early formation of the American League against War and Fascism; a broad, interracial coalition of intellectuals, peace activists, socialists, communists, labor leaders, and black leaders who were united by their opposition to fascism in Europe and to racial injustice in the United States. Marshall attended the League's first organizing meeting at Johns Hopkins University in Baltimore. The group resolved to perform a national assessment of the strengths of racial, labor, and progressive organizations with the goal of finding common interests among those groups. At a later conference in Washington, DC, Marshall joined the League's Commission on Minorities, which he immediately persuaded to focus on the issue of educational equality. Marshall argued that providing an inferior education to minorities made them less able to resist fascism. Lack of time and money curtailed Marshall's participation in the League, which became more involved in national political issues before dissolving in 1939.

MARSHALL JOINS THE BAR

Thurgood Marshall became a lawyer on October 8, 1933, one week before the Armwood lynching. He faced some sharp realities as he tried to find office space in downtown Baltimore. Most landlords refused to rent offices to black professionals. As a law student living in Baltimore, Marshall had risen at five o'clock in the morning each school day and had walked to the railroad station to catch the train to Howard University in Washington, DC. The reason for the long commute was simple—the University of Maryland School of Law in Baltimore did not admit blacks. But with a law license and office space in downtown Baltimore secured, Marshall was ready to begin his legal career.

To Baltimore's black community, Marshall's admission to the bar was a noteworthy event. Until 1885, a Maryland statute had restricted the practice of law to white males only. The law was successfully challenged and Everett J. Waring became Maryland's first black lawyer. Only sixty African Americans had been lawyers in Maryland before Thurgood Marshall, and half of them were still active. The *Afro-American* announced the bar admission of all new black attorneys, and its publisher, Carl Murphy, made sure that his newspaper gave special attention to Marshall. One article announced Marshall's completion of law school, another reported his passing the bar, and a third reported the opening of his law office.[18]

Throughout his career, Marshall had the good fortune to be associated with colleagues who wanted him to succeed and were willing to help him. With veteran attorney Warner T. McGuinn and Boston University law graduate William Alfred Carroll Hughes Jr. as his new office mates, Marshall entered the practice of law with colleagues who were already involved in civil rights.[19] McGuinn was approaching the end of a long and distinguished career. He had served several terms on the Baltimore City Council, had been an early organizer of the NAACP, and had been involved in almost every significant civil rights issue of the twentieth century. Al Hughes had been a lawyer for only two years, but he was already the lawyer for the Baltimore branch of the NAACP.

The morning after the Armwood tragedy, Marshall wrote to Charles Hamilton Houston, his former dean at the Howard University School of Law. After telling Houston the good news about his new office, Marshall wrote, "Everyone over here right now is talking about the lynching last night." In the letter, Marshall also made some political predictions. He wrote, "Something will come out of [the lynching]. . . . Judge Duer is a Republican and Ritchie is a Democrat. Ritchie has placed the blame on Duer, and he will in turn tell something about Ritchie."[20]

Subsequent events quickly proved Marshall prophetic. "Governor Blames Judge Duer and State's Attorney Robbins," reported the *Afro-American*.[21] "Immediately following the lynching, Governor Ritchie issued a statement that he was 'shocked beyond expression at this horrible lynching.' He announced he had been in constant touch with the situation in Princess Anne from 1 p.m. Wednesday until after the lynching was over. He placed direct blame for the affair on Judge Robert F. Duer and State's Attorney John B. Robbins."

The very public finger-pointing among Governor Ritchie, Judge Duer, and State's Attorney Robbins continued for several weeks.[22]

IN THE GOVERNOR'S OFFICE

The meeting with the governor had been arranged by Josiah F. Henry Jr., the well-connected Baltimore lawyer who was president of the Monumental City Bar Association, an organization for Baltimore's black lawyers. Marshall had persuaded Henry, one of the few Democratic black attorneys in Baltimore, to set up the audience. The senior lawyer in the delegation was Charles Houston, the dean of Howard University Law School. Joining him from Washington were Howard University law professor Leon A. Ransom and four recent Howard graduates: Edward P. Lovett, James G. Tyson, Frank W. Adams, and J. Byron Hopkins. Marshall and Henry brought with them two young Baltimore lawyers, Dallas F. Nicholas and Robert P. McGuinn.[23]

Before the meeting, the members of the delegation agreed that they would try to persuade the governor to issue a bold response to the brutal lynching. Houston read Governor Ritchie a petition signed by each of the lawyers that called for a state police investigation of the Armwood murder. The delegation urged the governor to support passage of a strong anti-lynching law, demanded "rigorous punishment of the principals" involved in the Armwood lynching, called for the removal and prosecution of government officials who had failed to protect Armwood, and requested ten thousand dollars in damages for Armwood's family.[24]

Albert Ritchie was finishing his fourth term as Maryland's governor and had twice sought the Democratic presidential nomination. Born in 1876 in Richmond, Virginia, Ritchie was a product of the post-Reconstruction South. He could not have imagined the changes that black citizens would demand of the nation, nor could he have imagined that sitting before him was a future associate justice of the US Supreme Court.

Although Marshall was the youngest lawyer in the room, he asked the most pointed question, using a poised assertiveness that would appear throughout his career. "Is there an investigation taking place in the state police department?" Marshall asked Ritchie. No one would have blamed Marshall if he had remained politely silent during the meeting. Such a demeanor was probably expected of him. Yet Thurgood Marshall spoke up and asked the governor a very direct question, providing an early glimpse of the advocate who would fundamentally alter American history. Governor

Marshall, Houston, Lovett, and seven other lawyers signed and presented to Governor Albert Ritchie a petition demanding that he order an investigation and take other strong actions. Marshall's signature is the eighth from the top. *Courtesy of Afro-American Newspaper Archives and Research Center. and Library of Comgress, NAACP Papers.*

Governor Albert L. Ritchie (Democrat) was completing his fourth term as governor of Maryland when the Armwood lynching occurred. *Courtesy of Maryland State Archives.*

Ritchie declined to answer Marshall's question, stating that he did not want to compromise ongoing law enforcement efforts. Clarence Mitchell reported the meeting and Marshall's question in the *Afro-American*; it was the first of many times that he would write about Marshall over the next three years.[25]

THE ANTILYNCHING CAMPAIGN

Justice proved elusive. The state impaneled a grand jury and temporarily detained some of the lynch mob's leaders.[26] Accusations flew back and forth as to who was most at fault. The American Civil Liberties Union offered a $1,000 reward for information leading to the conviction of any member of the lynch mob. Governor Ritchie sent a contingent of the Maryland National Guard to the Eastern Shore to arrest "ring leaders" of the mob. Four men were arrested and briefly held in Baltimore until the sheriff of Somerset County, armed with a writ of habeas corpus signed by Judge Duer, went to Baltimore and brought the four men back to Princess Anne. No formal charges were brought, and the men were released. In the end, no one was held accountable for Armwood's death.[27]

However, the antilynching efforts were not totally in vain, and George Armwood was the last person ever to be lynched in Maryland. Publicity about the events in Princess Anne added substantial energy to the national antilynching campaign that had come about in response to a recent, dramatic resurgence in lynchings in America. After a decade of decline, the number of lynchings nationwide rose from ten in 1932 to twenty-six in 1933. On January 4, 1934, Senator Edward P. Costigan of Colorado and Senator Robert F. Wagner of New York introduced legislation to make lynching a federal crime.[28]

Thurgood Marshall joined the efforts to obtain passage of the Costigan-Wagner Anti-Lynching Bill. At the request of Walter White, the executive secretary of the NAACP, Marshall assembled information about prior lynchings in Maryland. Marshall's research findings contradicted the widespread belief that most lynching victims were rape suspects. Blacks accused of minor offenses also faced death by lynching. In February 1934, Marshall's research provided the basis for White's testimony before a

US Senate subcommittee hearing on the Costigan-Wagner bill. Charles Houston, Clarence Mitchell, and Juanita Jackson also testified. Jackson, a dynamic youth leader, presented Costigan with a petition signed by thousands of Marylanders urging passage of the legislation.[29]

The battle over Costigan-Wagner continued into 1935, with a new bill introduced by the respective sponsors.[30] Marshall's approach became pragmatic. Although the US House of Representatives passed antilynching bills, the real battle was in the Senate, where all antilynching bills faced stiff opposition from Southern senators, who cited states' rights objections. Marshall decided to lobby Maryland's senior senator, Millard Tydings, who had not taken a public position on the proposed legislation. In the *Afro-American*, Clarence Mitchell covered every round of the Tydings–Marshall exchange.

> That Senator Millard E. Tydings (Dem., Md.) has not come to a definite conclusion as to just how he would vote on the Costigan-Wagner anti-lynching bill was indicated, this week, in the continued exchange of correspondence between the Congressman and Thurgood Marshall, local attorney. . . . Previous statements by Senator Tydings in a missive to Mr. Marshall had been interpreted as meaning that the Senator opposed the bill on the basis that it was a violation of the state's rights. The Senator stated that in his opinion the bill did not seem to get at the root of the trouble—improper functions of the court and long delay in bringing the guilty to trial, which disgusted the people.[31]

In response to one of Marshall's letters, Senator Tydings kept his options open:

> You write as though I had expressed myself as opposed to the pending anti-lynching legislation, whereas I was simply frank enough to write you very sincerely regarding my position and expressing some of the thoughts I was considering while reaching a decision.

Marshall, not yet twenty-seven years old, kept up the pressure:

> I do not challenge your position on the Costigan-Wagner bill as being opposed to it but rather on the ground of your statement: "let me say frankly that I have had a great difficulty in coming to a decision on this

Carl Murphy, the publisher of the *Afro-American*, used his newspaper to protest lynchings, to support civil rights, and to publicize and document Thurgood Marshall's career. *Courtesy of* Afro-American *Newspaper Archives and Research Center.*

Clarence M. Mitchell Jr., as a young reporter for the *Afro-American*, wrote extensively about the Armwood lynching and Marshall's early law practice. *Courtesy of Clarence and Juanita Mitchell family.*

bill." My letter was an attempt to give you the facts which to my mind remove the "difficulties" expressed in your former letter.

When a bill of this character is proposed, we as your constituents expect you as our representative to back it whole-heartedly or have a good and substantial reason for not doing so.[32]

On April 13, 1935, Marshall again wrote to Senator Tydings, urging him to remain in Washington, DC, to vote on the Costigan-Wagner Bill, rather than join a congressional investigation committee trip to the Virgin Islands:

Perhaps a Senator of one of the states not affected by any lynching stigma could leave at this time, but it is difficult to see how a Senator from Maryland, with its record of lynching atrocities, would not be on the floor when the Costigan-Wagner bill is voted upon. [33]

Ultimately, Southern senators filibustered and defeated all proposed federal antilynching legislation. The Maryland state legislature's actions on antilynching legislation mirrored those of the US Congress. Several bills similar to those proposed to Governor Ritchie by Marshall and his colleagues were introduced over the years, only to suffer the same fate as Costigan-Wagner.

In the months following the meeting in the governor's office, Thurgood Marshall and Clarence Mitchell, who had attended the same high school and college and had competed on the same debating team, assisted each other in their respective endeavors. For three years, Marshall kept making news, and, with the support and encouragement of *Afro-American* publisher Carl Murphy, Mitchell reported it all. Marshall and Mitchell would later work side by side at the national NAACP, with Marshall as its chief lawyer and Mitchell as its chief lobbyist.

Chapter 2

The Baltimore
Grocers' Grandson

"There were two big grocery stores in Baltimore, and each of them was owned by one of my grandfathers. If they had any business acumen, or the children had had any, they would have been very wealthy people," stated Thurgood Marshall in a 1977 interview.[1]

THE FAMILY BUSINESS

Thorney Good Marshall's obituary appeared in the *Afro-American* in January 1915, while his grandson and namesake was in the first grade at School 103 in Old West Baltimore, a row-house section of the city to the northwest of downtown. The obituary read:

> Baltimore businessmen will mourn the death of that intrepid old grocer, T. G. Marshall, who was perhaps the most prosperous in his line of business, in the city. In his life he exemplified the spirit of "the gospel of work" and could be seen every morning at his post of duty, together with his children, who are his most valuable assets. The "Marshall family" is a shining example of what "push, energy, and unity" can do for the colored man.[2]

Both grandfather and grandson were originally named "Thoroughgood," and both chose to change their names. Young Thoroughgood had recently returned from New York to his birthplace, Baltimore, with his parents and his older brother William Aubrey, whom everyone called by his middle name. The brothers would grow up surrounded by strong and supportive family members and a clear sense of identity. Both sets of grandparents were Baltimore grocers.

The T. G. Marshall Store, the largest black-owned grocery store in the city, stood on the southeast corner of Dolphin and Division Streets and was a source of pride to Baltimore's black business community. Thorney Good, a pillar of his community, advertised extensively in the *Afro-American* newspaper, local business directories, and souvenir booklets. In these advertisements, he described his store as "the largest and most progressive colored grocery in Baltimore."[3] His best-selling products were meat, bread, potatoes, milk, flour, sugar, and cooking oil.[4] Thorney Good Marshall prided himself on the store's efficient delivery service. "Drop us a card or phone call and your order will be promptly attended to," his advertisements proclaimed.

Thorney and his wife, Annie Marshall, purchased the property at 535 Dolphin Street after selling a smaller store on Somerset Street in South Baltimore.[5] The new building became the Marshall family's urban homestead.[6] The grocery store occupied most of the first floor of the three-story corner building with large plate-glass windows. The narrow building, only twenty feet wide, was more than seventy feet deep, with a side-street entrance that led to living quarters on the second and third floors. Thurgood Marshall's grandparents, aunts, and uncles worked in the store and lived above it.

Thorney Good Marshall was a handsome, self-made man. Born in New Church, Virginia, he saw military service in the American West as one of the US Army's celebrated Buffalo Soldiers. In 1879, he married Annie E. Robinson of Baltimore and settled in her hometown. They raised four sons—William (Thurgood's father), Cyrus W., Thomas Roye, and Thoroughgood[7]—and daughters Mary, Margaret, and Anne.[8] Thorney Good Marshall was tall, had a commanding presence, and spoke with a powerful voice. He enjoyed regaling the family with stories about his exploits as a young soldier "out West."

Anne married Sandy Burns.[9] Mary never married. She and Margaret spent most of their working years wearing the store's striped aprons. Their brothers Thomas Roye and Thoroughgood also spent many years working at the store. After serving in World War I, Cyrus became a high school mathematics teacher yet remained close at hand. Only William, Thurgood's father, set out on his own path.

This 1898 photograph shows Thurgood Marshall's grandparents, aunts, and uncles. Front (from left): Cyrus, Annie, Margaret, Thorney Good, Thomas Roye, Annie. Rear (from left): William, Mary, Thoroughgood. *Courtesy of Norma Anderson.*

A handsome man, grandfather Thorney Good Marshall served as a "Buffalo Soldier" in Texas and later became a Baltimore grocer. *Courtesy of Cyrus Marshall family.*

Thorney Good Marshall was a trustee of Sharp Street Memorial United Methodist Church. Also vocal and active in community affairs, he was remembered for starting a movement to raise money for the first American flag to fly over a black school in Baltimore.[10] Upon his death, the *Afro-American* commented that "he was very successful in business and his career in trade should inspire those who believe that racial enterprises merit support of the thousands of colored people here."[11]

Annie Marshall—the Marshall family's matriarch, who seldom left the Dolphin Street building—was industrious, very frugal, and an early recycler. She plaited rugs from odd strips of cloth and saved all combustible materials, such as paper, peach pits, and fruit baskets, to use as fuel in the winter. She read extensively and solved crossword puzzles daily. Annie earned notoriety for resisting a utility company's efforts to install a pole in front of the Dolphin Street store. After trying to persuade the city to reject the idea, she placed a rocking chair over the yellow mark at the planned location of the pole and sat down whenever the work crew appeared. After a couple of days of Annie's applying this early sit-in tactic, the utility company gave up and never installed the pole.[12]

Thorney's death at age sixty-five was a great shock to the family because he had appeared to be in good health. He died on a Sunday, after returning from church and having dinner, from a massive heart attack. Annie, along with her sons and daughters, continued to run the Marshall grocery store for seventeen years after Thorney's death. A photograph of a handsome, young Thorney Good Marshall was added to the store's advertisements. The family sold the store in 1930, when Thurgood Marshall was in his first year of law school.[13]

THE OLIVE BRANCH

Thurgood Marshall's maternal grandfather, Isaiah Olive Branch Williams, was also a Baltimore grocer. He died fourteen years before Thurgood's birth, but Thurgood learned much about him from his family. Isaiah Williams was born a free black in rural Maryland before the Civil War and served on Union vessels during the conflict. After the war, he sailed on Navy ships patrolling the Pacific coast of South America.[14] After

Amount of Goods Sold During The Year 1913
—AT—

T. G. MARSHALL'S

535½ DOLPHIN STREET   BALTIMORE, MD.

$1,000.00 For Vegetables and Fruit
   250.00 For Poultry
 1,012.35 For Butter and Eggs
   115.12 For Wooden, agate and glass-
   395.58 For Cakes   {ware
    59.75 For Paper, twine and trays
   111.28 For Candy
    54.27 For Notions
    77.87 For Tobacco

15600 Loaves of Bread
  177 Barrels of Flour
   60 Barrels of Sugar
 3370 Gallons of Oil
  563 Pounds of Tea and Coffee
  150 Bushels of Potatoes
  730 Gallons of Milk
23576 Pounds of Meat

We wish to thank our many customers for their patronage during the
year 1913 and also to assure them that
we will do all in our power to have
them continue.

T. G. MARSHALL—GROCERY
Dolphin and Division streets

This photograph of Thorney
Good Marshall in front of his
store appeared in the souvenir
booklet for a black business
convention held in Baltimore,
one month after Thurgood
Marshall was born in 1908.
*Courtesy of Afro-American
Newspaper Archives and
Research Center and Cyrus
Marshall family.*

his discharge from the Navy, Isaiah settled in Baltimore and married a Baltimore schoolteacher named Mary Fosset.

The family moved to 63 Orchard Street and opened a grocery store there. Williams then leased and later purchased a second store building on Denmead Street (now 20th Street), just north of the Baltimore City boundary.[15] They operated the Denmead Market in a high-income, white neighborhood, where poorer blacks lived in nearby alley housing. Thurgood repeated family lore about his grandfather's generosity. He said, "The door was left open to the basement of his home and his store, and the poor Negroes that lived in back had access to go down there and get wood, coal, and vegetables and stuff. And he would tell them, 'Now, don't take more than you need.' Nobody ever did."[16]

Grandmother Annie Marshall ran the grocery store for fifteen years after her husband died. *Courtesy of Cyrus Marshall family.*

"My grandmother was a very strong person. I would talk with her for hours on end, and her life went all the way back to the early days of the Negro, right after Reconstruction, Her husband knew all the prominent Negroes in those days. I would just listen to her for hours on end, and I think she had a great influence." Thurgood Marshall

In 1888, Baltimore City annexed the neighborhood where the Denmead Market was located in an expansion that more than tripled the size of the city. While operating both stores, Williams bought a home on Biddle Street in Baltimore's prestigious Bolton Hill neighborhood.[17]

Williams became active in Republican Party politics and pressed for public education for black children. He led Baltimore's black community in mass meetings that successfully demanded the criminal prosecution of a Baltimore City police officer for "The Cake Walk Homicide." The officer, who shot and killed a man after responding to complaints about the noise at a cakewalk party at which dance couples competed for a cake prize, was convicted of manslaughter.[18] Williams was also comfortable using the courts. In 1892, he sued for damages and obtained a favorable jury decision after a stable behind his house was damaged during the construction of a railroad tunnel.[19]

Isaiah and Mary Williams had six children, to whom they gave creative names. They named one daughter Denmeadia Marketa, after their grocery store on Denmead Street. Their older son, Avon Nyanza; and another daughter, Avonia Delicia; were both named after William Shakespeare's birthplace, Stratford-upon-Avon. Thurgood Marshall's mother, Norma Arica, was named after Vincenzo Bellini's 1831 opera, *Norma,* which Isaiah had seen in the port city of Arica in Chile. Isaiah and Mary named their younger son, Fearless Mentor; and their youngest daughter, Ravine Silestria; after a place in Bulgaria.

Isaiah Williams and his family operated Denmead Market until his death at the age of fifty-seven in 1894.[20] A year later, Mary Williams sold the store to Charles J. Bonaparte, a prominent, white Republican leader and a relative of France's Napoleon Bonaparte.[21]

SUPPORTIVE PARENTS

William Canfield Marshall, the oldest son of Thorney Good Marshall and Annie Marshall, chose not to work at the family grocery store. Instead, he worked as a waiter in hotels, in restaurants, and on railroad dining cars. He married Norma, the sister of Fearless Williams, and they soon had a son, William Aubrey, in September 1905. Their second son, Thoroughgood, was born on July 2, 1908. After Thoroughood's birth, the family relocated to Harlem in New York City and moved in with Norma's sister, "Medi," and her husband, Clarence "Boots" Dodson. The men worked on the New York Central Railroad while the women took care of the two little boys.[22]

Five years later, with Thoroughgood—or Thurgood, as he would soon be known—about to begin school, the family returned to Baltimore and moved in with Norma's brother Fearless Williams at 1634 Division Street. William Marshall, Thurgood's father, was rather enigmatic; some regarded him as distant, while others found him quite personable. Although he had limited formal education, he was well-read, interested in politics, and kept abreast of current events. He had a loud voice and alternated between being talkative and taciturn.

William Marshall would not tolerate racist remarks from whites and instilled the same attitude in his sons. William Marshall told his sons to respond immediately and directly to racist epithets. He would rail against "the white man," but many of his closest friends, including the neighborhood precinct police captain, were white. He liked to play with words and reformulate common racial slurs. He often gave the backhanded compliment, "That's mighty black of you." He referred to a nonconformist as "the white man in the woodpile." According to Charles Burns, "Thurgood's father's complexion was so fair that many white people would question him. He would always tell them that his mother was white and his father black. He got a bang out of that."[23] Thurgood adored his father, and, as an adult, emulated his father's use of pointed racial humor.

Until Thurgood was in college, William Marshall worked as a waiter in Baltimore hotels, in country clubs, and on railroad dining cars. Sometimes he was unemployed. Some of his jobs were seasonal. He occasionally became ill, and sometimes he would just quit. In later years, Thurgood claimed that his father would quit a job "at the drop of a hat." Because money was usually tight, William Marshall's family lived with his wife's relatives until Thurgood was in high school.

While Thurgood was in college, William Marshall obtained the two best jobs of his life. For three years he was the head waiter at the Maryland Club, an exclusive businessman's lunch club in Baltimore. Afterward, he became the head steward at the Gibson Island Club. Situated off the western shore of Chesapeake Bay approximately twenty-five miles south of Baltimore City, Gibson Island was a private retreat for several of the wealthiest and most prestigious families in Maryland. According to Charles Burns, who worked there several summers, "At Gibson Island it wasn't just how much money you had, it was the color of your blood. It was a strictly blue-blood resort. All the people you read about in the papers

Thurgood Marshall was born July 2, 1908, in Baltimore, Maryland. The birth certificate recorded the name "Thoroughgood." In 1946, "Thoroughgood" was crossed out and "Thurgood" substituted. *Courtesy of Maryland State Archives and Thurgood Marshall family.*

RETURN OF A BIRTH. A39924

To the Office of Registrar of Vital Statistics, Board of Health, Baltimore City.

No. of Child of Mother, (state whether 1st, 2d, 3d, &c.) Second

1. Name of Child, (Thoroughgood) Marshall

2. Sex, (state whether male or female) male

3. Race or color, (if not of the White Race) colored

4. Date of Birth July 2nd

5. Place of Birth, (Street and number) 543 McMechen St.

6. Full name of Mother, Norma Arica Marshall

7. Mother's Maiden Name, Norma Arica Williams

8. Mother's Birthplace, Baltimore City

9. Full name of Father, William Canfield Marshall

10. Father's Occupation, Waiter

11. Father's Birthplace, Baltimore City

Name of Medical Attendant, or other person who makes this Return, Mrs. Mn. Brown

Address, 563 Dolphin St.

Remarks, 1 9 0 8 0 0 0 4 2 0 3

RECEIVED FOR RECORD
AUG -11 1908
JAS. BOSLEY M.D.
COM'R OF HEALTH

were members there. It was a country club, based on yachting. There were many summer homes on the island, a golf club, and tennis courts. It was a playground for the very, very rich."[24]

William Marshall, as the steward of the clubhouse, supervised the entire staff. "He was in charge. He had one boss that was the man who ran the whole operation."[25] To Burns, this meant that William Marshall "had a white man's job." Burns explained that "the cooks, waiters, busboys, and porters worked for him."[26]

William Marshall's position as chief steward carried another perk. As Burns explained, "He had his chauffeur drive him to see his mama every week. He couldn't drive, but the whole time he was at Gibson Island, he had a chauffeur and a station wagon from his job."

As a boss, William Marshall was at the same time ornery and affable, stern and softhearted. Thurgood adored his father and confirmed the man's contradictions, saying, "He was one of the most delightful people you would want to run across, who considered himself as a firm, tough customer. The nicest guy that ever lived. In his later days, he became a country club steward. One of his famous jobs was to fire a guy at night and go pick him up and rehire him the next day."[27]

The country club resort was open only from late spring until early fall. During periods of unemployment, William Marshall went to the courthouse in Baltimore and watched civil and criminal trials. At home, he and his sons frequently discussed politics, race relations, and news events. William and Thurgood put their loud voices to good use during these discussions, which often became vigorous debates. Aubrey would sometimes grow quiet as the intensity of the exchanges between William and Thurgood grew. Discussions about specific topics would go on for several days, with Thurgood using the breaks to refine arguments and to assemble information supporting his positions.

In later years, Marshall would credit his father with making him an advocate and these discussions at home with stimulating his interest in competitive debating and confronting injustice. Marshall said of his father, "He did it by teaching me to argue, by challenging my logic on every point, by making me prove every statement. He never told me to be a lawyer, but he turned me into one."[28]

Burns agreed, saying, "I really believe that Thurgood's career got started because of his father's feelings about the injustices that we all faced. I think his father had a tremendous influence on that part."[29]

William Marshall was also somewhat contrary. According to William H. Murphy,[30] a neighbor who, as a teenager, delivered the *Afro-American* newspaper to the Marshall home, William Marshall would sometimes go out of his way to act contrary to his wife's more refined demeanor. Fully aware of his wife's disapproval, he would sit on the front marble steps of their home in his undershirt "just to get on Norma's nerves."[31] Throughout his life, William Marshall also drank heavily, but he could hold his liquor and was seldom visibly drunk. Quite a bit of William's loud voice, contrariness, sharp tongue, disputatious nature, and heavy drinking rubbed off on his son Thurgood.

Norma Marshall was the antithesis of her husband's unpolished character. She was dignified, articulate, and well-groomed. She had a smooth, brown complexion, high cheekbones, vibrant eyes, and a ready smile. She pulled her hair back in an attractive bun, and she was always impeccably dressed.[32]

Norma wanted to become a teacher like her mother. Soon after graduating from high school, she enrolled in the normal school for teachers. Before finishing, she met William Marshall, and they got married. Norma had her first child, William Aubrey, and stayed home to care for her son. Less than three years later, a second son arrived. Thoroughgood Marshall was born on July 2, 1908, in a small apartment at 543 McMechen Street, near the 1700 block of Pennsylvania Avenue, where twenty-five years later, he would supervise a picket line and represent his first client.

People who knew Norma Marshall were impressed by her intelligence and grace. She played the piano and was an avid reader and bridge player. Norma was active in several women's social clubs, some of which raised money for the local branch of the NAACP. After Thurgood began school, she completed her teacher's training and became a substitute kindergarten instructor. During the summers, she worked as a playground director.[33] However, one's ability to obtain a new full-time teaching position in Baltimore depended on political connections, so Thurgood was in college before Norma secured a full-time teaching position for herself.[34]

Norma Marshall loved children, and children loved her. "His mother was a very beautiful woman with chiseled features and a soft brown color, with dead straight hair. Norma was a very fine person," said Nellie Buchanan, who taught Latin for nearly fifty years and had Thurgood as a high school student.[35] Charles Burns agreed, saying, "Aunt Norma was

William Marshall, Thurgood's father, worked as the head steward at a country club. He expressed strong opinions about political and social issues. *Courtesy of Thurgood Marshall family.*

Norma Williams Marshall, Thurgood's mother, worked as a kindergarten teacher. She was determined that her two sons obtain college degrees and become professionals. *Courtesy of Thurgood Marshall family.*

just a sweet, beautiful lady who really loved young people. That was a part of her being. She really loved young folks."[36] Betty Phillips of the *Afro-American* called Norma "a woman of never-flagging enthusiasm and energy." Another friend said of Norma that "she radiated sunshine and had more bounce than anyone else around her."[37] Much of Norma's energy, enthusiasm, and optimism rubbed off on her younger son.

Although Norma Marshall never taught in her sons' schools, she and William paid close attention to Aubrey's and Thurgood's homework and grades. Most of their sons' teachers lived in the neighborhood and kept a watchful eye over the boys. The family discussed school matters at home, and both Norma and William attended school-related events unless William was out of town on railroad business. Norma and William expected their sons to succeed. "It was taken for granted that we had to make something of ourselves. Not much was said about it; it was just in the atmosphere of the home," Marshall remembered.[38]

Norma's love for her sons was boundless, and she boasted about Aubrey and Thurgood to anyone who would listen. She proudly described Thurgood as "a hard worker, diligent student, fearless and adventuresome, a champion of the little fellow."[39] Norma provided her sons with constant approval, encouragement, and support. "Norma Marshall was a very caring mother. She went to all lengths to see to it that they were educated, that they got a good education," said Juliet Carter, Charlie Burns's sister.[40] "I can see her now, sitting in the yard, talking about her two boys," Carter recalled. "I am proud of my two boys. Both are fighters. One is fighting for equal rights, and the other is fighting TB disease," said Norma Marshall in 1977.[41] Carter recalled one evening on which both Aubrey and Thurgood were to receive awards in different locations. Because Norma Marshall could not attend both awards ceremonies at the same time, she skipped them both to avoid showing favoritism.

Thurgood remained impressed with his mother's energy and fortitude, recalling that "my father was the noisiest and loudest, but my mother was by far the strongest."[42]

BROTHER AUBREY

William A. Marshall—called by his middle name, Aubrey—was born on September 15, 1905, at 1127 Argyle Avenue, where the young family briefly lived, about three blocks from the Marshall family store. For almost three years, he was the only grandson and nephew to a large array of aunts and uncles. Aubrey was a bright, industrious child, and his grandmother, Annie Marshall, was his favorite relative. He began school in New York and returned to Baltimore when he was in the third grade.

Thurgood and Aubrey attended the same schools but did not socialize or play together, and they were never close. Friends and family noticed that they had very different personalities and all but ignored each other. Thurgood was gregarious and talkative, while Aubrey was more reserved, although he did display an interest in girls earlier than did Thurgood. Both brothers held after-school jobs from an early age. Aubrey worked at the family store; Thurgood found jobs at other stores. Aubrey tended to be neat in appearance; Thurgood paid little attention to his attire and was often unkempt. Aubrey was sickly as a child; Thurgood was seldom ill. Aubrey was thin, with angular features; Thurgood was less so. Aubrey looked more like the relatives in his father's family; Thurgood resembled his mother's family. According to Charles Burns, "Aubrey was not assertive in nature like the father and Thurgood." Most people found Thurgood to be the more handsome of the two brothers. Carrie Jackson recalled, "Thurgood and Aubrey were sort of different. Aubrey was more social minded than Thurgood. I think Aubrey was more impressed with Aubrey than Thurgood was impressed with Thurgood. I don't think Thurgood was as impressed with himself."

Aubrey worked at the family grocery store. Thurgood visited, but never worked or stayed at the store. In fact, as Thurgood recalled about the one night he was supposed to stay at 535 Dolphin Street, "I only spent one night. I cried and raised so much hell that my grandfather made them take me back up the street about three o'clock in the morning. I guess I was about three or four."[43] As Thurgood became older, grandmother Annie Marshall became an important influence in his life. Thurgood said, "My grandmother . . . was a very strong person. I would talk to her for hours on end, and her life went all the way back to the early days of the Negro, right

William Aubrey Marshall, two and a half years older than Thurgood, attended Lincoln University and Howard University Medical School. *Courtesy of William A. Marshall Jr.*

Dr. William Aubrey Marshall specialized in treating respiratory illnesses. *Courtesy of William A. Marshall Jr.*

after Reconstruction, and her husband knew all of the prominent Negroes in those days. I would just listen to her for hours on end, and I think she had a great influence on me."[44]

In school, Aubrey was more studious than Thurgood and got better grades. Aubrey read books for enjoyment, whereas Thurgood's reading was utilitarian and goal oriented. In school, Aubrey liked science, chemistry, and foreign languages. Thurgood preferred civics and modern history and very much disliked studying foreign languages. Thurgood was obviously bright, but he studied just hard enough to get good grades. Teachers, schoolmates, and neighbors who knew both brothers expected that Aubrey would become the more successful of the two.

AUNTS AND UNCLES

There was never a time while growing up when Thurgood Marshall felt disconnected from his family. He remained regularly in touch with several intelligent and attentive relatives. Both grandmothers and ten aunts and uncles lived in the neighborhood. His father had three brothers and three sisters, all of whom remained in Old West Baltimore. His mother's brother and three of her sisters also lived in the neighborhood. Only Denmeadia lived in New York. When Marshall was about ten years old, Uncle Avon moved his family to Knoxville, Tennessee.[45]

Soon after Thurgood's birth, William Marshall moved his family to New York City, seeking better employment. They joined Denmeadia (Aunt Medi) and her husband, "Boots," in their Harlem apartment. Boots helped William obtain employment on the New York Central Railroad. When Thurgood was six years old, the Marshalls returned to Baltimore so that Norma could care for her ailing mother, Mary E. Williams, who lived with Norma's brother, Fearless, at 1632 Division Street in Old West Baltimore.

Fearless Williams—Thurgood's "Uncle Fee"—had worked for the Baltimore & Ohio Railroad (known as the B&O) since 1906, when he began as a floor porter. Fearless was later assigned to the office of a B&O vice president. Then in 1916, he became a porter in the office of Daniel Willard, the president of the B&O Railroad. Eventually, Fearless became Willard's personal assistant, a position in which he set up meetings, greeted

From age one to six, Thurgood and his family lived in New York City with his mother's sister Denmeadia Dodson and her husband. *Courtesy of Thurgood Marshall family.*

Young Thurgood at about age three. *Courtesy of Thurgood Marshall family.*

guests, took messages, and assisted in Willard's office. This job earned Fearless Williams substantial prestige in the black community and enabled him to obtain railroad jobs for relatives and friends. Fearless also arranged for much of the railroad's sleeping car and dining car linens to be washed at his brother-in-law's laundry; as a result, that laundry became one of the largest black-owned businesses in Baltimore.[46]

Fearless Williams was an active and influential leader in Old West Baltimore. He was a founder of the city's largest black savings and loan association, the president of a real estate company, and a trustee of the city's principal black hospital.[47] An active lay leader in the Catholic Church, he fought racial discrimination in the local parishes. For example, just as Thurgood was about to graduate from high school, the *Afro-American* reported, "Fearless M. Williams, 1632 Division Street, one of the leading Catholic laymen of the city, advised today against compliance with the order of St. Gregory's Catholic Church, Gilmore and Baker Streets, excluding colored worshippers."[48] On two occasions, Fearless Williams ran for office in the local Republican Party organization.[49] He also wrote letters to the editors of newspapers.[50]

With William Marshall often away on railroad trips for four to five days at a time, Uncle Fee, who had no children of his own, became a major figure in Thurgood's life. Charlotte Shervington, who lived two houses away from Fearless Williams, recalled, "Thurgood was very close to that part of his family. Whenever I thought of Thurgood, I thought of his uncle. We called him Uncle Fee." Thurgood particularly enjoyed Sunday drives to the Eastern Shore of Maryland in Uncle Fee's large automobile. Fearless's household also included Thurgood's maternal grandmother, Mary Williams, who replaced Aunt Medi as Thurgood's "second mother."

Thurgood also maintained close relationships with his father's relatives. These included his paternal grandmother, Annie Marshall, and his Uncle Cyrus, the mathematics teacher who entertained him with war stories—he had served in the US Army and had fought in Europe during World War I. Uncle Thoroughgood, the first member of the Marshall family to work for the railroad, also held his ground in a family of storytellers. Finally, Thurgood's uncle Thomas Roye, and his aunts Margaret and Mary were always to be found around the family grocery store.[51]

Although Thurgood had many relatives within a few blocks of home, he had few cousins. Only one of the aunts and one of the uncles had

When Thurgood was six years old, he and his family returned to Baltimore and moved in with his mother's brother, Fearless Williams, shown here at work as the personal assistant to the President of B&O Railroad. *Courtesy of B&O Railroad Museum.*

children in town. Thurgood's closest cousin was his Aunt Annie's son, Charles Thoroughgood Burns, who was seven years younger than Thurgood and who eventually changed his own middle name to "Thurgood." The other cousins were substantially younger. Marshall, as a child, hardly knew his cousin Avon N. Williams Jr., who lived in Tennessee, where he became a prominent political leader and civil rights lawyer.[52]

The Marshall and Williams families were assertive and independent people who all worked very hard. Thurgood and Aubrey both held after-school jobs from the age of seven. Both also worked full-time jobs during the summers. While Aubrey worked at the family grocery store, Thurgood found employment with J. Henry Hale, who operated a grocery store on Division Street, close to Uncle Fee's house. Hale and Fearless were close friends, and Marshall befriended Hale's son, Sammy. In addition to regular grocery fare, Hale's store carried an extensive selection of coffees and teas from around the world. Young Thurgood did not mind helping around the store, but his favorite task was pulling his red wagon through the neighborhood while making deliveries for Mr. Hale.

A loud voice, assertiveness, respect for education, an extraordinary capacity for work, and an intolerance for racial prejudice were traits that Thurgood Marshall inherited from his parents and both their families.

THE NEIGHBORHOOD

When Thurgood and his family returned to Old West Baltimore, the neighborhood was in transition. Back when the Civil War ended, Baltimore's black population lived scattered throughout the city, with most blacks residing in small alley houses behind the main residential streets. Over the next three decades, two main concentrations of African Americans developed—one in South Baltimore and another just northwest of downtown. At the turn of the century, blacks began to move further northwest into areas occupied mostly by German immigrants. In 1901, the German-American School became the Colored High School. A decade later, the area had the largest black population in Baltimore.

When Marshall was born in 1908, Old West Baltimore was still fairly integrated, with white and black families living in close proximity.

Baltimore had the fourth-largest urban black population of any US city, after Washington, New York, and New Orleans. In the 1910 census, the black population of 84,779 people was 18 percent of the city's population but occupied less than 10 percent of the city's residential units and even less of the city's acreage.[53]

As the black community grew block by block, some whites began to demand that political leaders take action to control the "Negro invasion." Between 1911 and 1914, while Marshall was living in New York, the Baltimore City Council passed a series of ordinances to hem in the black population. The laws attempted to make it a crime for a black person to move into a block with a majority of white residents, and vice versa. Several American cities copied the Baltimore ordinances until 1917, when the US Supreme Court held that the use of criminal statutes to enforce racial segregation was unconstitutional. White communities and real estate companies then began to use racially restrictive covenants in deeds and other devices to deny housing to blacks in most Baltimore neighborhoods.

Marshall's childhood neighborhood, Old West Baltimore, occupied approximately sixty city blocks, with five main streets running north to south for twelve blocks. Blacks and whites interacted with each other on a daily basis. The section of Division Street where the Marshall's family lived with Fearless Williams was racially mixed. One block to the east, Druid Hill Avenue—with its large, three-storied residences boasting elaborate interior woodwork and white marble steps—was becoming the most prestigious residential street in black Baltimore. Streetcars rumbled down Druid Hill Avenue, and there were grocery stores, tailor shops, beauty parlors, barbershops, pharmacies, and doctors' offices on almost every corner. McCulloch Street, one block to the east, was residential and predominantly white. Madison Street, one more block to the east, remained exclusively white.

Pennsylvania Avenue, the street just west of Division Street, was the main commercial boulevard, with stores, movie houses, nightclubs, restaurants, taverns, professional offices, and pawn shops. Whites owned most of the businesses, but most of the patrons were black. West of Pennsylvania Avenue, the residential lines between black and white were blurred. Blacks tended to occupy the alley houses and side streets, while whites lived on the wider streets. The shifting boundaries led to tensions between the races. The northern limit of Old West Baltimore remained at North Avenue.

One month before Thurgood Marshall was born, Baltimore's black business leaders proudly hosted the ninth annual national convention of Booker T. Washington's National Negro Business League. The convention's souvenir book contained photographs of black-owned businesses, with one photograph showing Thorney Good Marshall standing proudly in front of his grocery store at Division and Dolphin.[54] As Thurgood Marshall began school, the *Coleman Directory*, a black business directory for Old West Baltimore, listed twenty-seven physicians, ten lawyers, eleven licensed pharmacists, eight dentists, sixteen caterers, twenty-two undertakers, and seventeen "tonsorial artists," or barbers.[55]

In the streets of Old West Baltimore, black children and white children played together and formed friendships. Sometimes, the youths formed cliques based on color lines and fought each other. Although young Thurgood had both black and white playmates, he sometimes became involved in the tussles between black public school children and white youngsters, mostly Italians attending a nearby Catholic school. The altercations became so frequent that Immaculate Conception Catholic School decided to dismiss its students half an hour ahead of the black public school to reduce the fights. Years after Marshall became a lawyer, a former student at Immaculate Conception, also a lawyer, showed Marshall a scar from a rock Marshall had thrown at him as a youngster. Even so, Thurgood was not much of a street fighter. He would fight when he felt that he had to, but he would more often avoid the fights and go home. "Aubrey was the tough one. He did all the fighting," mother Norma recalled.[56]

Whatever tensions existed among the neighborhood children always quickly faded after a heavy snowstorm. The hill that ran down Division Street from Mosher Street, near Uncle Fee's house, was a great sledding slope enjoyed by children of all races. Sadly, rigid racial segregation continued in churches, restaurants, movie theaters, and schools.

THE PERFECT ELEMENTARY SCHOOL

Henry Highland Garnett School 103 (or School 103 for short) was named for a famed abolitionist and orator and was generally regarded as the best elementary school for blacks in Baltimore's racially segregated school

Marshall was a top student in Henry Highland Garnett School 103, considered to be the best elementary school for black children in Baltimore City. Most of the eighth-grade students listed to the right continued to be Marshall's classmates through high school. *Courtesy of Afro-American* Newspaper Archives and *Research Center and the Baltimore City Archives.*

Henry Highland Garnett School 103

Wm. H. Lee, Principal

James Carr	Ethel Rusk
Edna Brown	Anita Short
Earl Campbell	Roberta Scott
Dorothy Dow	Consuella Smith
Carrie Dorsey	Bertha Tilghman
Charlotte Harris	George Thomas
Catherine Hill	Julia Woodhouse
Montstella Jones	Charlotte Watson
Dorothy Jones	Rosa Hance
Laura Jones	Jean Alexander
Marjorie Lynch	Edna Watty
Thurg'd Marshall	Gertrude Bennett
Dorothy Newby	V. Bowman
Mary Mendezes	Lillian Hall
Thelma Press	Bessie Lake
Thos. Peninston	Margaret Loudon

system. The "Division Street School," as it was most often called, was located just two blocks south of Uncle Fee's house and two blocks north of the Marshall grocery store. The impressive, two-story brick building with six classrooms on each floor was designed to let plenty of natural light into the classrooms. Because the school did not have a recreation area, school officials closed the street in front of the building to vehicular traffic during the day, and thus the street became a playground.

The African American community was proud of School 103. The school had a reputation for solid instruction, and many of the pupils came from homes where parents valued education. More children of black professionals attended School 103 than any other elementary school in Baltimore. School 103 had twenty teachers—seventeen women and three men, including Principal William Lee. The teachers were African Americans and lived in the neighborhood. The school tended to produce intelligent, confident children who went on to high school.

According to Carrie Jackson, "School 103 was quite a school with fine families. I went to Division Street School from the fourth grade straight on through. Thurgood was in my class. I don't remember too many boys in my class—just Thurgood, James Carr, and the Mack boy. We all, including Thurgood, stayed in the same classes."[57]

Thurgood Marshall attended School 103 from the first through the eighth grade and was always grouped with the best students. A dozen young people were his classmates from elementary school through high school. Because the group was mostly girls, it was sometimes called "the sissy class." Marshall's classmate Carrie Jackson remembered that "there was with our group a pervasive expectation of success. Scholarship was a natural because our parents expected us to do well in school. There was no such thing as 'I might fail geography.' You were expected to pass. Parents saw to it that you studied. Parents knew what teachers had given you. There was no such thing as no homework."[58]

Among the first signs of Thurgood's strong independent streak was his decision to change his name. He grew tired of writing out "Thoroughgood," so in the second grade, he announced that his name was "Thurgood." His family and friends began using the name, and, although no official name change was made, school officials and others eventually cooperated. The first official action to change Marshall's first name did not occur until 1948, when Thurgood was forty years old. For unknown reasons,

William Marshall had the state vital records office draw a line through "Thoroughgood" on Marshall's birth certificate and write in "Thurgood." The legal effect of this action remains unclear.[59]

Thurgood's best friend from grade school through high school was a physician's son, Jimmy Carr. Thurgood was well liked by most of his classmates. They regarded him as intelligent, inquisitive, and entertaining; his argumentative streak amused many of his peers. "Thurgood had a good disposition and got along with his classmates. He was not a bore. He just accepted his inquisitiveness. We're not critical at that stage. He was friendly," said Charlotte Watson Shervington, another one of Marshall's classmates.[60]

"Thurgood was thin, with ivory-colored skin, beautiful black hair. He was not impressed with his looks, but I guess you could call him a pretty nice looking chap," recalled classmate Carrie Jackson. "Thurgood was restless, inquisitive, and a bit untidy. He would drive his mother crazy. The boys wore shirts inside their pants. Thurgood's shirt was always coming out. His mother was the epitome of neatness. She would be so disgusted with him, I guess until we reached the eighth grade. Thurgood didn't care about his personal appearance. He wasn't dirty, just sloppy," Jackson remembered.

Shervington agreed that Marshall was a good student. She recalled, "Thurgood was a person full of fun, quite positive, and very, very smart. Teachers would give tests, and according to results of the test we were reseated in the classroom. Thurgood was always in the first, second, or third seat in the first row. I was always around the back of the second row or the upper part of the third. So that was how consistent his academic abilities always have been." Carrie Jackson also remembered that the seating arrangement was based on test grades, with the best students sitting in front of the class. She competed with Thurgood for top honors in English and arithmetic.[61]

In Baltimore's public schools, the most gifted students were often accelerated through elementary school, and Marshall was no exception. Carrie Jackson recalled, "If you were a good student, you were allowed to skip a grade. That particular class, almost the entire class, skipped the upper half of the seventh and part of the eighth grade. That made us get into high school a year earlier than we should have." In June 1921, thirty-three girls and five boys, including Marshall, graduated from School 103 and moved on to high school.[62]

Chapter 3

Marshall's High School Years

Attached to Thurgood Marshall's admissions application to Lincoln University was a personal statement—his handwritten summary of his high school years.

Since the day I entered high school, I've always tried to take advantage of every opportunity.

While in my first year, I twice made the highest average in the class. It was in the first year that I started my debating career. I worked hard and, as a reward, I was made captain of the varsity team, which debated in Wilmington, Delaware.

In the second year, my studies were so heavy that I gave up debating. During the term I made a final average in Mathematics, which was 95%.

My third year was the hardest of all. Nevertheless, I started debating again and was re-elected captain of the debating team. Many times during the term, I gave short talks before the student body on certain requirements of school life and also talks on the activities of the student council of which I was a representative. While in this year I was elected a member of the class treasury committee.

In the fourth year, I studied hard to keep my average above 85% in order to become an honor graduate. I was again elected captain of the first debating team of the school. I was also elected one of the spokesmen for the Toussaint L'Overture Library Club. I was also made chairman of the scholarship committee of the school. At the end of the term, I graduated as an honor student.[1]

The history of Marshall's high school began in 1867, when Baltimore mayor John Lee Chapman signed an ordinance establishing schools for

African American children.[2] In 1892, the city government established a high school for colored youngsters. Though the school initially offered only a manual training program, which taught boys construction and industrial trades and taught girls sewing and other homemaking skills, four years later the school added an academic curriculum.[3] White teachers taught the classes, which were held in downtown buildings.

The new school became known as the Colored High School, and in 1901 it acquired black administrators and teachers and moved into the former German-American School building at Pennsylvania Avenue and Dolphin Street in Old West Baltimore.[4] This building, only nine years old, was originally an elementary school, and it did not have a cafeteria, auditorium, or gymnasium. It stood next door to the Northwest Police Station and one block from the Marshall grocery store, from which the school bought its supplies for home economics classes. Since the school building had no large meeting rooms, school gatherings were held in nearby churches and theaters on Pennsylvania Avenue.[5]

The Colored High School became severely overcrowded because Baltimore City had only one black high school and because the school had to accommodate black students who came from surrounding counties that had no high schools for African Americans.[6] To accommodate the pupils, the Colored High School ran on shifts, with one group of students attending from 8:30 a.m. to 1:00 p.m. and a second group attending from 1:15 p.m. to 4:45 p.m. Students shared desks in sixteen classrooms, with bookshelves in the hallways serving as the school library.[7]

A NEW SCHOOL TAKES SHAPE

Faced with chronic overcrowding and inadequate facilities, blacks in Baltimore began to demand more and better-equipped schools. The *Afro-American* ran articles, editorials, and cartoons about the problems of overcrowding at black schools. "With nearly one-third of the 13,000 colored children in the public schools of the city crowded out of buildings and compelled to attend half-time classes, the problem of finding more room for a growing population is becoming acute," the newspaper reported.[8]

Efforts to improve education for African Americans in the city were in

In 1921, as Marshall entered high school, his parents finally acquired their own home and the family moved to Druid Hill Avenue, the most fashionable street in the neighborhood. *Courtesy of Maryland Historical Trust.*

Marshall's friends Juanita Jackson and Anita Short lived in the neighborhood and attended the same schools as Marshall. *Courtesy of the Clarence and Juanita Mitchell family.*

full swing as Thurgood Marshall completed the eighth grade and prepared to enter high school. Junior high schools did not exist as separate entities in Baltimore at that time. In March 1921, black and white leaders convened and discussed the need for better educational facilities. A month later, a meeting of five hundred people at the Bethel African Methodist Episcopal Church led to heightened demands for the construction of a new Colored High School. The keynote speaker was attorney W. Ashbie Hawkins, Baltimore's leading civil rights lawyer.

Baltimore City was enjoying an era of prosperity. Weapons production for World War I had given way to a growing demand for consumer goods like washing machines, refrigerators, radios, and automobiles. The city's economy boomed as Baltimore companies produced steel, leather, glass, rubber, and textiles. The Baltimore & Ohio Railroad had its headquarters and train-maintenance facilities in Baltimore. Tax revenue funded construction of new streets, bridges, swimming pools, and schools.

The city planners put a new black high school into their improvement plans. The Colored High School's alumni association—led by Gough McDaniels, who would later teach and mentor Thurgood Marshall—was adamant that the new building include a gymnasium, an auditorium, a cafeteria, a school library, and an infirmary. As Marshall entered the Colored High School in September 1921, city officials had just selected a location for the new building.

HIGH SCHOOL STUDENT

Thurgood Marshall's class would be the last to graduate while the old Colored High School building was still in use. Marshall brought his signature ink-stained pockets, loose shirttails, handsome face, loud voice, and penchant for argument to high school. Scoring well on the entrance exams given at the beginning of ninth grade, Marshall was again grouped with the most promising students.

The Colored High School boasted an impressive faculty of sixty-eight members, many of whom had graduated from prestigious Northern colleges such as Wellesley, Columbia, Smith, Amherst, and Brown. Several teachers had master's degrees. The school's principal, Mason A. Hawkins,

The extremely overcrowded Colored High School that Marshall attended had no auditorium, gymnasium, cafeteria, or library. *Courtesy of the Baltimore City Archives.*

..THE..

GROUND BREAKING

OF THE

NEW COLORED JUNIOR-SENIOR

HIGH SCHOOL

Corners
CALHOUN, BAKER and CAREY STREETS

MONDAY, APRIL 30TH, 1923

3:00 o'clock P. M.

WILL BE CONDUCTED UNDER THE
MANAGEMENT OF A COMMITTEE
OF CITIZENS

Marshall could only watch the new high school being built, realizing that his class would be the last one in the old Colored High School building. *Courtesy of Afro-American Newspaper Archives and Research Center.*

Addresses will be made by the Mayor of the City and others, representing the Public Improvement Commission, The Board of School Commissioners, The Board of Superintendents, The Citizens in General, The High School, and the Alumni Association.

MUSIC WILL BE FURNISHED BY A. JACK THOMAS BAND AND A CHORUS OF 400 HIGH SCHOOL PUPILS

Ministers of the City are Requested to Notify
Their Congregations of this Meeting

had obtained a bachelor's degree from Harvard, a master's degree from Columbia, and a doctorate from the University of Pennsylvania. The vice principal, Carrington L. Davis, had been a Harvard College classmate of President Franklin D. Roosevelt.[9] Employment options for educated blacks outside the teaching profession were limited, and the academic credentials of black high school teachers in Baltimore City often exceeded those of their white counterparts.

The teachers struggled to provide quality education in the very crowded and inadequate building. Several of the teachers were quite demanding of the students. Marshall quickly adjusted to having several teachers in different classrooms and began to thrive in the competitive atmosphere. In four years, he was never late for school and missed only one day of classes. He earned mostly good grades, doing especially well in history and mathematics. Marshall got an A in the geometry class taught by Fannie Barbour (who insisted that students solve solid geometry problems in ink), and he also got an A in his uncle Cyrus Marshall's algebra class. Although he did not usually enjoy studying foreign languages, Marshall (along with several other young men) signed up for a Latin class because it was taught by an attractive new teacher named Nellie Buchanan, and he enjoyed the class and did well in it. Science teacher Perry D. G. Pennington urged Marshall to attend Pennington's alma mater, Lincoln University, and to consider joining Pennington's fraternity, Alpha Phi Alpha.

As Essie Hughes, Marshall's classmate from the ninth grade through high school, remembered, "The particular group that I was in and Thurgood was in, we were advanced and we had to take all subjects. We weren't allowed to eliminate any of the subjects. We got the college preparatory to the extent that many of the students in the class of '25 were able to go into Smith College and into Wellesley. Miss Fannie Barbour had us taking college entrance examinations whether we were going to college or not. We just had to take it."[10]

Thurgood's cousin, Cyrus Marshall Jr., agreed, saying, "I am not just saying that because my father worked there, but because I believe that we had in those days a group of dedicated teachers who knew everybody, knew all the children just about. That extra knowledge and concern was to our benefit."[11]

MARSHALL FINDS A MENTOR

History teacher Gough Decatur McDaniels became Marshall's favorite teacher and his first important mentor outside his family. Daniels was more than an outstanding history teacher and debate coach in school. An intellectual, an artist, a civil rights leader, and an activist, he was a quintessential Renaissance man. He had attended Brown University, graduated in 1910, and won the college's most valuable student award, the Gaston Medal for oratory.[12]

McDaniels began teaching in 1911 at Coppin Normal School and later joined the faculty at his alma mater, the Colored High School. McDaniels was an early leader of the Baltimore branch of the NAACP. When the black community fought against housing segregation ordinances in 1913, McDaniels helped organize grassroots community opposition. As the president of the high school's alumni association and as head of the Baltimore Colored Teachers' Association, McDaniels spearheaded efforts to get a new high school built for black students.[13] From the time McDaniels graduated with honors from Brown University and returned to Baltimore, he was a constant presence and force in the leadership of the city's black community. His students noticed his constant engagement in important community causes. Marshall's classmate Essie Hughes reminisced, "Mr. McDaniels, our history professor, also was very active in the NAACP. Gough McDaniels was the type of person who was willing to confront any type of discrimination. For a number of years, he imbued us with this spirit of black peoplehood, way back in those days."[14]

McDaniels was also active in the leadership of Alpha Phi Alpha fraternity, was president of the Colored Municipal Employees' Association, and served as head of the Baltimore Colored Teachers' Association. McDaniels, a World War I veteran, was also recognized as an impresario and a serious participant in the arts. He wrote poems, songs, and plays, and organized a theatrical club.[15] When Baltimore City opened its first swimming pool for the city's black residents in 1921, McDaniels became the pool supervisor.[16]

Thurgood Marshall and Gough McDaniels immediately bonded. Marshall admired McDaniels's breadth of knowledge and his many interests and involvements. Marshall sought to impress this Renaissance man and got As in the two history courses he took from McDaniels. The teacher saw promise in this young man who exhibited such a passion for argument.

MARSHALL LEADS CLASS DISCUSSIONS

In McDaniels's history classes, students gave reports on current events. As Essie Hughes recalled,

> I first noticed Thurgood Marshall because he was outstanding when it came to discussing things. We had a history teacher by the name of Gough McDaniels. Once a week, every Monday, we had to give a current history report. Well, of course we read the papers. Some read and digested it and some just read it. Thurgood always chewed and digested his news, and he'd get up there and Mr. McDaniels would always have to say, "All right, Thurgood, your time is up." He would not only exceed the time, but he had read many other sources. You see, we were reading the *Baltimore Sun* and the *Baltimore American*. Thurgood, no doubt, was reading *Time* magazine and something else.

Marshall often went beyond simply preparing and giving his weekly presentation; he would also frequently insist on returning to a point he had talked about during the previous week's report. According to Essie Hughes,

> When we would have little debates . . . Mr. McDaniels would say, "Now we are going to discuss the Teapot Dome issue." . . . We would read headlines ten or twelve minutes before we got into his class. [But] Thurgood would wait and listen. His timing was psychologically impeccable. Just as we thought that we had put everything over in a big way and Mr. McDaniels was giving us [a score of] 90 or 85, Thurgood would come up and say, "Now wait a minute, there's something else." It would come right at the time just when we thought that we had made the score. "But, have you considered this?" he would say.[17]

Classmate Charlotte Shervington concurred: "Thurgood was a marvelous student. He could outtalk and out-argue anybody. But he did not have an empty head. He was well prepared for anything of which he spoke."[18]

Marshall's habit of returning to a topic and rearguing certain points had begun with heated discussions at home with his father and would carry over into his professional career. Although Marshall challenged other people's arguments, his remarks rarely came across as offensive. McDaniels encouraged Marshall's passion for argument and reinforced the youth's healthy sense of skepticism.

Thurgood Marshall liked to hear his Uncle Cy tell stories about his service in World War I. *Courtesy of Cyrus Marshall family.*

Cyrus Marshall remained an advisor to Thurgood for many years. *Courtesy of Cyrus Marshall family.*

Cyrus Marshall taught Thurgood and generations of students mathematics at the Colored High School, later named Frederick Douglass High School. *Courtesy of Cyrus Marshall family.*

The litigator inside Marshall began to manifest in very tangible ways when he was in high school. "Thurgood never approached any situation without first being thoroughly prepared, and that began with his classes in school," Charlotte Shervington remarked. Marshall's classmates accepted his speeches with good humor and respect because they knew his arguments were backed by solid research.

Carrie Jackson recalled that Marshall was so well prepared and meticulous in high school that he often challenged assertions made by his teachers in their lessons. Looking back on her school days with Marshall, Jackson said,

> He was very argumentative and curious, an old doubting Tom. You would have to prove it to him, especially in our history class or economics. We had a bit of economics under Mack Fitzgerald, and Thurgood didn't agree with some things. He would get that queer look on his face, and you would know that Thurgood wasn't believing it or wasn't understanding it. You had to go back over it entirely.
>
> When Thurgood would question he had definitely done his homework. He was not a showoff just shooting off his mouth. He was knowledgeable. He liked to understand and he liked to be able to report what he believed. I don't think the teachers resented this. It might have been a form of flattery for teachers to have a pupil say, "I don't agree with that," or "I don't understand that," or "Are you sure that this is so?" I think it's a form of flattery. I don't think it was showish. I know it wasn't for Thurgood."[19]

DEBATER AND LEADER

When Marshall entered high school, competitive debating, which had become a national sensation among colleges, was spreading to the high school level all over the country. Gough McDaniels, himself an acclaimed orator, decided that Baltimore's Colored High School should join the movement.

Debating competition between American colleges had begun slowly in the late-nineteenth century. Then, two debates between Harvard and Yale in 1922 provided the spark that ignited an explosion of interest in intercollegiate debate competitions. Nearly three thousand people attended the Harvard-Yale debates, which were reported in major newspapers around

Gough McDaniels was Marshall's high school teacher, debate coach, and mentor. *Courtesy of Afro-American Newspaper Archives and Research Center.*

65

CERTIFICATE OF RECOMMEN[DATION]

...pted by Association of Colleges for Negro Youth.

This is to certify that .... THURGOOD MARSHALL ....
(Give Name in Full)

of .... 1838 Druid Hill Avenue ....
(Number and Street)   (City)

*was } graduated from the *Frederick Douglass* High School of *Baltimore, Md.*
was not }   (Name)   (Location)

*graduated } on *January 31* 19*25*, has completed the work shown in detail below, and is hereby
leaving }

officially recommended for admission without examination to the ....
(College or Department)

of .... LINCOLN UNIVERSITY ....
(University or College)

Date of Birth ....19........ Entere this Shool *September 13* 1921. He is in the Second Third of his class. *First*

He took the .... Psychological Test .... 19........, and received the score of ....

Date *July 16* 1925 .... *Mason H. Hawkins* .... Principal

STUDIES	Yrs. of Crs. When Taken (I II III IV)	No. of Weeks Pursued	No. of Periods per Week	Grade	STUDIES	Yr. of Crs. When Taken (I II III IV)	No. of Weeks Pursued	No. of Periods per Week	Grade
ENGLISH—First Year	21-22	40	5	90	PHYSICS				
Second Year	22-23	"	"	85	Laboratory	22-24	40	5	90
Third Year	23-24	"	"	93	CHEMISTRY				
Fourth Year	24-25	20	"	70	Laboratory				
History of Literature					BOTANY				
GREEK—First Year					Laboratory	22-23	40	5	78
Second Year					ZOOLOGY				
Third Year					Laboratory				
LATIN—First Year	21-22	40	5	91	PHYSIOGRAPHY				
Second Year	22-23	"	4	86	GEOGRAPHY				
Third Year	23-24	"	"	85	INTRODUCT'RY SCIENCE				
Fourth Year	24-25	20	"	82	Laboratory				
FRENCH—First Year	22-23	40	"	72					
Second Year	23-24	"	"	79	AGRICULTURE				
Third Year	24-25	20	"	80	COMMERCIAL BRANCHES				
Fourth Year					"				
GERMAN—First Year					"				
Second Year					"				
Third Year					"				
Fourth Year					"				
SPANISH—First Year					DOMESTIC ART				
Second Year					DOMESTIC SCIENCE				
Third Year					MECHANICAL DRAWING	21-23	60	2	85
Fourth Year					FREE HAND DRAWING	21-23	80	2	76
HISTORY—Ancient	21-22	40	4	92	INDUSTRIAL TRAINING				
Medieval and Modern	23-24	40	4	92	MANUAL TRAINING				
English	24-25	20	4	91	MUSIC				
United States					NORMAL TRAINING				
Civics					PUBLIC SPEAKING				
ALGEBRA—Elementary	21-22	40	5	91	Other Subjects				
Advanced	24	20	5	90	Bench work	21-22	40	2	80
GEOMETRY—Plane	22-23	40	5	93	Machine Practice	23	20	2	85
Solid	23-24	20	5	93	Printing	22	20	2	90
TRIGONOMETRY	24-25	20	5	88	Wood turning	23	20	2	80
					Physical Training	21-23	60	2	85

Passing Grade in School *65%* Grade required for Recommendation to College *75%* Length of Recitation Period *45*
Mark (L) any subjects occupying double periods.   Specify by (PG) any subjects taken subsequent to graduation
*Cross out lines not applicable.

Please fill out the blank completely, using typewriter if convenient.
DO NOT FAIL TO STATE THE COLLEGE OR DEPARTMENT OF THE UNIVERSITY THE APPLICANT WISHES TO ENTER

Marshall's high school record reveals an intelligent young person who got high grades in most subjects. *Courtesy of Lincoln University, Hughes Library Archives.*

the nation. Other colleges joined in. The next year, Princeton debated Yale and Michigan competed against Wisconsin. A year later, Pennsylvania debated Cornell and Stanford debated the University of California. Intercollegiate debating spread, and its popularity grew to rival that of athletics, with debating being promoted by some as the middle season between football and baseball.

By the middle of the 1920s, college debating leagues had been established, and many colleges and universities had debating clubs. The spread of debating down to the high school level was natural, and competitive high school debating was in full swing when McDaniels began organizing his program a year or two before Marshall arrived at the Colored High School.

McDaniels invited Thurgood Marshall to join the debate team while Marshall was still in the ninth grade. Marshall performed so well and demonstrated such leadership that by the end of the year, he had become the team captain. Marshall's debate team included Anita Short, who had been Marshall's classmate and friend in elementary school.

The debate team competed against black high schools in Maryland, Delaware, and the District of Columbia. Occasionally, they faced a team from a teacher's college or the freshman team from a four-year college. Prohibition and the Tea Pot Dome scandal provided the most common debate topics. Practicing lawyers often served as the debate judges, and school singers and musicians typically performed during intermissions between the speeches. Because the Colored High School lacked an auditorium, most local debates were held either in churches or at the Douglass Theater on Pennsylvania Avenue, one block away from the high school.

Debating was a challenging and demanding intellectual activity that required careful research and preparation. McDaniels required his debate team members to read scores of articles and books on government, history, and economics. Debaters were taught to handle their knowledge with poise and readiness. Groping for words or committing grammatical errors was unacceptable. McDaniels expected rebuttals to be responsive, logical, convincing, and entertaining. Criteria on which McDaniels evaluated his debaters included voice quality, strength of delivery, enunciation, word selection, and mastery of subject matter. Marshall enjoyed every aspect of debating, even the semiformal attire. Although he normally paid little attention to his clothing, he enjoyed dressing up for the debates.

One of Marshall's best friends during his years at the Colored High School was Calvin Roach. They shared a love of debating, and the two young men constantly tested their persuasive skills against each other. "Thurgood and Calvin were so thick because they used to debate a lot between each other," Carrie Jackson said. "Calvin was very intelligent, and they would get into heated discussions." Marshall often walked home from debate practices with his classmate from School 103, Anita Short, whom he nicknamed "Bowlegs."[20]

Marshall continued debating during the eleventh and twelfth grades, and was the team captain each year. In the classroom and as the debate coach, Gough McDaniels introduced Marshall to the art of disciplined advocacy based on research. Marshall and his classmates also observed that McDaniels was an activist and opinion leader beyond the classroom. By his personal example during Marshall's high school years (and later during Marshall's first three years as a lawyer), McDaniels helped shape Marshall's priorities.[21]

Although it consumed much of his time, debating was not Marshall's only extracurricular activity. A leader among his peers, he served on the student council, on the school's committee that interviewed applicants for college scholarships, and as an officer of one of the school's literary clubs.

While in high school, Marshall grew to be six feet two inches tall. Thin and lanky, he walked with a loping gait that earned him the nickname "Legs." As Carrie Jackson remembered, "He was a very attractive-looking fellow in high school. But, I don't think it mattered to him." Nellie Buchanan, who was Marshall's Latin teacher, recalled, "I began teaching at Douglass [Frederick Douglass High School, as the Colored High School became known in later years] in 1923. Thurgood was one of the boys. He wasn't particularly interested in girls, and his clothing was sloppy. But, he was a good student. When it came time for debates, he was really there. He debated on the team all the years he was here. That showed you his inclination to use his power of speech and reasoning."[22]

Marshall was popular, but he did not spend much idle time with any particular group because he had so many extracurricular activities and after-school jobs. "There always seemed to have been some sort of employment, little odd jobs. There was never a lull in Thurgood's activity, whether it was school or work," said Carrie Jackson about her classmate.

THE WORLD BEYOND SCHOOL

Marshall attended high school at the beginning of the "Roaring Twenties," a decade defined by flashy clothing, flappers, jazz music, Prohibition, speakeasies, and colorful gangsters like Al Capone. The newspapers and radio were filled with the exploits of Lou Gehrig, Babe Ruth, and Charles Lindbergh. Yet Marshall, unlike his more outgoing classmate, the future entertainer Cab Calloway, preferred the safety and security of his family and neighborhood. Marshall enjoyed watching sports but was not athletic and never played on a team. He seldom read anything for pleasure, except western comic books. He read serious material only when he needed to prepare for a debate or a history presentation.

His mother remembered a happy, disputatious youngster, saying, "It was the easiest thing in the world for him to make friends with people, and he could argue and talk like a professional. As a youngster he liked animals, was friendly with everybody in the street, and liked to read western stories and listen to them on the radio. . . . If he saw a stray cat or dog, he was ready to take it home."[23] At one time, his pets included a cat named Kitty, a dog called Mike, and a white rat with pink ears he called Willie. He taught them to tolerate each other and eventually succeeded in getting them to eat together out of the same plate.

Marshall's concern for the downtrodden extended to people. Norma Marshall recalled that young Thurgood would bring home hungry playmates: "Come to my house. Mommy will give you some food and a place to sleep. Our home got to be known as the 'Friendly Inn.'"[24]

On January 21, 1923, Marshall was confirmed at St. Katherine of Alexandria Episcopal Church, which worshipped using the formal "sung mass." The church registry recorded his original name, "Thoroughgood Marshall."[25] Later, Norma Marshall and her son switched their affiliation to the less formal St. James Episcopal Church, the only Episcopal church in Baltimore with a black priest. Its rector, George F. Bragg, became Marshall's occasional spiritual adviser. Marshall attended Sunday church services and participated in church youth activities.

During Marshall's first year in high school, the family moved out of Uncle Fee's house and purchased a three-story row house three blocks away, at 1838 Druid Hill Avenue. The mortgage payments added to

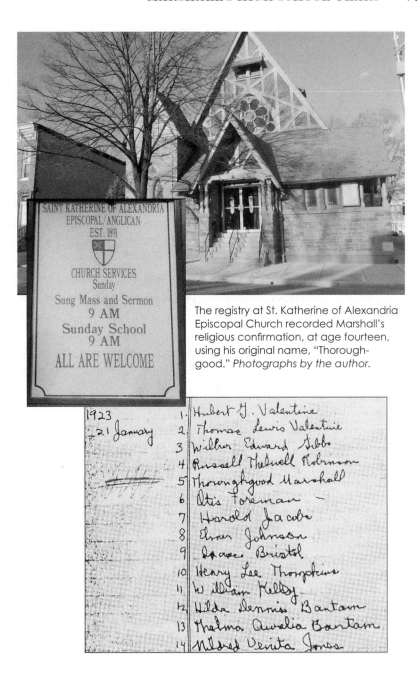

The registry at St. Katherine of Alexandria Episcopal Church recorded Marshall's religious confirmation, at age fourteen, using his original name, "Thoroughgood." *Photographs by the author.*

the financial pressures on the family. The following year, Aubrey went to college at Lincoln University, incurring additional costs. As William Marshall struggled to pay the mortgage, Norma assumed responsibility for the college education payments. Aubrey was often threatened with expulsion because of money owed to Lincoln.

No longer living down the block from Henry Hale's store, Thurgood found a job as a delivery boy for Schoen and Company, a high-end women's clothing store on Charles Street in downtown Baltimore. Morton S. Schoen, the manager of the family-owned business, trusted Thurgood and had him ride the streetcars to deliver hats and other clothing to customers' homes and offices. Marshall's job at Schoen and Company served as Marshall's first foray beyond Old West Baltimore. Although Marshall rarely encountered trouble while making his rounds, he once got into a scuffle while riding a streetcar after a middle-aged man insulted him with a racial slur. Following his father's instructions to fight anyone who called him a "nigger," Marshall attacked the man. Marshall was arrested and taken to a police station. Mr. Schoen quickly came to the police station and, when told what had started the fracas, managed to extricate Marshall without any formal criminal charges or further complications. In later years, Marshall often mentioned Schoen's reaction as evidence of the decency of most white people.

FINISHING HIGH SCHOOL

When Marshall was in high school, the black press and community followed the construction of the new colored high school with great anticipation. The building under construction would occupy three-fourths of a city block. It would include a cafeteria accommodating seven hundred students at one sitting, large science laboratories, a home economics section with multiple kitchens, a music room, a health suite, a separate industrial arts structure, and a sixteen-hundred-seat auditorium.[26] Many Baltimoreans were excited that the building would be the first black high school in the nation to have an indoor swimming pool. Much pomp and circumstance accompanied the groundbreaking ceremony. Workers began to raise the new structure as Marshall was finishing the tenth grade in the old building.[27]

Charles Street runs through the center of Baltimore from South to North. Everything to the left is in West Baltimore. Everything to the right is in East Baltimore. Marshall's high school job was in the next block to the north. *Courtesy of Maryland Historical Trust.*

Marshall, as a teenager, delivered hats for the Schoen & Co. clothing store on Charles Street in downtown Baltimore. *Courtesy of Maryland Historical Society.*

Marshall became a leader of his high school debate team and served on the student council. He graduated with honors at age sixteen. *Courtesy of Thurgood Marshall family.*

A few months later, the Baltimore City Board of School Commissioners named the high school in honor of Frederick Douglass, who had escaped from slavery in Maryland and become a renowned statesman.[28] All of Marshall's schools were named for freedom fighters. Marshall's elementary school was named after the famous abolitionist and orator, Henry Highland Garnett. His college was named in honor of the president who signed the Emancipation Proclamation, Abraham Lincoln, and his law school bore the name of the first head of the post–Civil War Freedman's Bureau, Oliver Otis Howard.

Marshall could only watch as the new school building went up, aware that he would never attend classes there. Realizing that he needed to start raising money for college, Marshall took extra courses and completed his high school graduation requirements a semester early, in February 1925. He then left school and went to work full-time. With Marshall gone, Anita Short, Frances Male, and Lena Hodges became the school's first all-female debating team.[29]

On June 24, 1925, Marshall attended his high school graduation ceremony at Baltimore's Lyric Theatre, which would not allow black performers on its stage until twenty years later. Because the 345 graduates were the largest graduating class in the school's history, there was no time for a formal commencement speech. Instead, Baltimore Mayor Howard Jackson simply presented the diplomas as each student's name was called.[30] The school then held a "Formal Commencement Reception" for the graduates later that evening at the New Albert Hall on Pennsylvania Avenue.

In his last two semesters, Marshall had obtained his best grades in high school, making him one of only fourteen students—and one of just three young men—to graduate with honors.[31] Young women comprised the vast majority of the graduating honors students, and his friend from School 103 and debate teammate, Anita Short, was the class salutatorian.[32] Essie Hughes believed that "Thurgood was serious but not to the extent that he was a bookworm. He could easily have been valedictorian, if he wanted to. He wasn't a bookworm in that respect. To be valedictorian, one had to balance in all of the subjects. But I think Thurgood didn't want to be worried with all the subjects."[33]

Marshall's personal statement on his application to Lincoln University confirmed his pragmatic and utilitarian approach to school work. He wrote, "I studied hard to keep my average above 85% in order to become an honor graduate." Thurgood's cousin Cyrus Marshall Jr. also threw light on Thurgood's pragmatic work style, explaining that "Thurgood was not really a plodder. If there were nothing to do, he wouldn't do anything. But if it was something important to do, he would stay on the task until the job was done. He didn't believe in making a mountain out of a molehill."[34]

When Marshall applied to Lincoln University, he identified on the application form his intended life's work as "Lawyer." His cousin Juliet recalled, "My mother always said that as little boys, Aubrey and Thurgood seemed to know what they wanted to do."[35] Her brother, Charles Burns, agreed, saying, "My mother said Thurgood always wanted to be a lawyer and Aubrey always wanted to be a doctor, and they played at that." To Burns, the end result was preordained: "I think everyone that knew Thurgood knew he was an intelligent guy, a very smart fellow. You knew that he was obsessed with being a lawyer and he was assertive. I don't think anyone thought he wouldn't be successful."[36]

Chapter 4

Lincoln University

Before Thurgood Marshall submitted his application to Lincoln University, there was some doubt as to whether the family could finance Thurgood's college education. His brother Aubrey was about to enter his senior year at Lincoln University, and most of Aubrey's tuition and fees for his junior year remained as yet unpaid. Fearful that Lincoln might reject Thurgood's application for financial reasons, Norma asked Reverend W. W Walker, a Lincoln University alumnus who lived a few doors away to intercede.

Reverend Walker's letter to the acting university president began by putting in a good word for the Marshall family and then moved on to explaining their financial circumstances. Reverend Walker wrote, "The head of the family has had a long siege of illness lasting for more than a year. That necessitated their making an arrangement with Prof. Grimm to finish paying Aubrey's bill at Lincoln this summer. Mr. Marshall is well again, and on the job. And, of course, will meet this obligation. The mother is very anxious about the entrance of Thurgood into Lincoln, fearing the faculty will be influenced against him because of what she owes."[1]

As Thurgood was about to mail his application to Lincoln University, the family still owed the university $335.50 out of the total $372.00 charge for Aubrey's tuition, room, board, laundry, books, and other fees.[2] Lincoln's registrar reminded Norma Marshall of Lincoln's "strict policy that no student could be graduated unless his bill was completely paid up." Expressing doubt that the family could pay for both Aubrey and Thurgood's education, the registrar wrote that "it would be a pity for a younger son to endanger the graduation of the older son." The university official suggested that it might be "advisable for the younger boy to remain out of school and earn money for a year."[3]

That was unacceptable to Norma Marshall. She pressed the university to admit Thurgood. She wrote to the registrar, saying,

> Reverend Walker also advised me to ask you if Thurgood's name could be placed on the list of boys applying for work at school. Aubrey has been able to procure work each year at school, and I would certainly appreciate it if you would place his name on the lists. My boys both have always worked after school and are both at work this summer to secure their tuition for next term.
>
> I am at present working as director in one of our City Playgrounds, and as soon as my regular work begins the 1st of July, I will pay up Aubrey's bill for last winter. This work continues through the summer, and I promise to pay up back money in full before he comes back to school in the fall.[4]

The Lincoln registrar responded to Norma Marshall's plea by suggesting a different approach: "I write frankly about the situation, appreciating a mother's interest in the progress and welfare of her boys. Possibly, you can pay Aubrey's bill early in the summer, and then the way will be clear for considering Thurgood's case further."[5]

Norma Marshall accepted the registrar's proposal and paid Aubrey's bill during the summer. Thurgood's application was then accepted, and he was given a campus job. However, that would not be the end of the Marshall family's financial difficulties at Lincoln.

THE "BLACK PRINCETON"

Thurgood Marshall's application for admission to Lincoln required information about his family, academic record, and ambitions. One answer on the application blank was not answered correctly. In response to the question, "What church do you attend?" Marshall wrote "Madison Avenue Presbyterian Church," the largest black Presbyterian church in Baltimore. However, that answer was not true. Thurgood, along with his mother and his brother, was an Episcopalian and attended St. Katherine of Alexandria Episcopal Church, where he had been confirmed three years earlier. His father's side of the family were longtime members of Sharp Street

Methodist Church. Uncle Fee was a Catholic. There were no Presbyterians in Marshall's family. Yet, Presbyterians had founded Lincoln University, and, at the time Marshall applied for admission, seven of the school's nine tenured professors were ordained Presbyterian ministers.

Lincoln University, founded in 1854 by a Presbyterian minister and his Quaker wife, was originally named Ashmun Institute and, after Abraham Lincoln's assassination, was renamed for the president.[6] Its charter called for "the scientific, classical, and theological education of colored youth of the male sex." Lincoln became the first degree-granting college for African Americans in the United States. Most of the all-white, male faculty were Presbyterian ministers. With three hundred students in southeastern Pennsylvania, the school was revered by many blacks as the "Black Princeton," and its faculty included several Princeton graduates. Lincoln attracted talented black male students from the eastern and upper-southern United States and from West Africa. Although the curriculum stressed the classics and foreign languages, the school also had a strong premedical program. More than half of Lincoln's graduates went on to professional graduate schools. Lincoln later claimed that, after its first one hundred years, its alumni included 20 percent of the nation's black physicians, the presidents of more than thirty-five colleges and universities, and hundreds of church leaders.

The university sat in a beautiful, pastoral setting, surrounded by open fields and woods four miles outside of Oxford, Pennsylvania. In 1925, Lincoln University was in a period of transition. The board of trustees was having difficulty finding a new president.[7] The facilities were showing their age, and old classrooms needed repair, although a new science building for the popular premedical program was almost complete. The dormitories had spartan rooms, and there were only communal showers in a separate bathhouse.

So many graduates of Frederick Douglass High School (the former Colored High School) went on to Lincoln University that teachers spoke of a "Lincoln pipeline" running from Baltimore to the college in southeastern Pennsylvania. In September 1925, seven young Baltimoreans, including Thurgood Marshall, passed through the pipeline. Marshall went from a black high school with mostly female teachers to an all-male college with an all-white male faculty.

Marshall attended Lincoln University, the nation's oldest historically black college, founded by Presbyterian ministers in southeastern Pennsylvania between Philadelphia and Baltimore. Marshall's application correctly stated that he planned to be a lawyer and incorrectly stated that he attended a Presbyterian church. *Courtesy of Lincoln University, Hughes Library Archives.*

Marshall made this transition smoothly. His roommate at Cresson Hall, James H. Murphy, belonged to the Baltimore family that owned and published the *Afro-American* newspaper. Marshall's solid high school education paid off at Lincoln, and he earned good grades during his first year, without much effort. He spent more afternoons playing pinochle than studying.

Marshall worked in the bakery on campus, where each evening he and a fellow student baked bread. They then placed the bread in a cupboard to be served two days later. Marshall believed that the school intentionally served day-old bread to reduce food consumption. The students found the cafeteria food filling but entirely unappetizing. The campus job paid 20 percent of Marshall's tuition and fees.[8]

The most disturbing reality faced by Marshall and his seventy-four freshman classmates was the well-entrenched tradition of upperclassmen hazing freshmen. New arrivals were expected to wear blue beanie caps and short pants with socks held up by garters. Upperclassmen often stopped random freshmen and quizzed them about the school's history and the names of buildings on campus. Freshmen could not enter through the front doors of most campus buildings. They had to arrive at football games fifteen minutes early and sit together in a designated area of the stands. The hazing often turned violent and included forced haircuts and beatings. Lincoln students liked to douse each other with buckets of water. Everyone was fair game, from a student walking under an open window to a student fast asleep in bed. In later years, Thurgood Marshall bragged that at Lincoln, he learned to "throw water around a corner." Sophomores, collectively calling themselves "the Gods" or "Zeus," were the most aggressive at hazing the freshmen "Dogs." Not all freshmen enjoyed playing the role of victims, however; some would resist, resulting in fights—or "pushing knuckles," in campus slang.

The faculty tried to prevent hazing with the same zeal that upperclassmen tormented freshmen. Periodically, the school suspended students caught hazing. Occasionally, they permanently expelled serious offenders. Hazing usually subsided after "the rabble" (Lincoln slang for the student body) gathered around an annual campus bonfire a few nights before the traditional Thanksgiving Day football game against Lincoln's archrival, Howard University. Marshall experienced only modest hazing because he was over six feet tall, because he had several "homeboys" from Baltimore who looked out for him and each other, and because his debating skills quickly earned the respect of his fellow students.

Oratory played a major role at Lincoln. The school prided itself in training eloquent public speakers and expected "Lincoln men" to be comfortable addressing large audiences. Several of the faculty members had been successful preachers. Many of the students planned to be ministers of various religious denominations. During the year, several powerful speakers came to campus. In his freshman year, each student was required to take a course in public speaking and then deliver a speech to his classmates in the Mary Dod Brown Memorial Chapel as a final exam. The school sponsored several student oratory contests during the year. At the annual graduation exercises, awards were given to students who had distinguished themselves as orators.

Competitive debating showcased the pinnacle of the Lincoln oratory tradition. Each year, the faculty selected three debate teams. Freshman and sophomore teams competed against each other and against freshman and sophomore teams at other colleges. The varsity debate team represented Lincoln at major intercollegiate competitions. Many students competed for a limited number of spots on the teams. The selection process for the varsity debate team began in October, with a preliminary round of debates in the school's Mary Dod Memorial Chapel. During the preliminary round, the faculty judges reduced the field to twelve competitors. Final debates and selection of the three-member varsity team occurred in November or December. Each debater had to compete each year—a student who was selected for the varsity team one year was not guaranteed a position on the team the following year.

When the school newspaper published the debate-team rosters for the 1925–1926 academic year, Thurgood Marshall became the first freshman to win a spot on Lincoln's varsity debate team.[9] One of his teammates was sophomore Richard Hill, another alumnus of the Gough McDaniels debate program at Baltimore's Frederick Douglass High School. An editorial in the campus newspaper explained the importance of Lincoln's debate program: "Lincoln is now going through a period of expansion. Any publicity which can be given the intellectual achievement of the institution will surely be beneficial during this period. In debating, the University has a potential source of publicity which should be developed. It is the boast of the institution that it trains Negroes who can hold their own in any intellectual endeavor."[10]

Lincoln's varsity debate team competed against teams from other black universities such as Morgan College in Baltimore, Howard University in Washington, DC, and Virginia Union University in Richmond. Before the competitions, the Lincoln debate team spent weeks in preparation. Once a debate topic was announced, the first task was research. Materials about the topic were assembled, and the team members began to read widely to obtain a deep understanding of the matter. The main question and related issues were analyzed. Often, the team members would begin to specialize, with each man seeking to become an expert on some of the issues. With an understanding of the issues, debaters would then turn to planning the team's arguments and its responses to arguments that opposing teams might make. Finally, the team would hold practice sessions, focusing on voice control and oratory delivery, until each team member was confident he could perform in competition before an audience. Just as he did in high school, Marshall enjoyed all aspects of debating: the research, the group discussions, the practice arguments, the travel, and the competitions. During his high school years, he had become comfortable with the black-tie attire worn during competitions. He was proud that the faculty believed he possessed the intellect and the strong oratorical skills needed to represent the school.

The Lincoln faculty was uneven in terms of teaching quality, with some very good teachers and a few approaching senility. The faculty and their families lived in a housing complex across from the campus but had very limited contact with students outside the classrooms. The faculty, which doubled as the administration, took a laissez-faire attitude toward most nonacademic and nonfinancial student matters. Upperclassmen made and enforced the norms of campus life, with the exception of the occasional disciplinary measures the faculty took in response to student hazing.

Marshall's academic performance during his first year at Lincoln was slightly above average. Mathematics remained a strong area for him. Foreign languages continued to be a weak spot, as they had been in high school. He got an A in Edwin Reinke's required course on the Bible, but he continued to prefer current events and modern history to subjects relating to antiquity. He never failed a course but did get one D and five Cs during his time at Lincoln.[11]

Marshall's favorite faculty member, sociology professor Dr. Robert M. Labaree, was also the university librarian and faculty adviser to the debate team. Labaree, born in Persia to missionary parents, had attended Marietta College in Ohio and Princeton Theological Seminary. Following two five-year pastorates in Pennsylvania and a decade of missionary work in Persia, he joined Lincoln's faculty in 1917. Like Gough McDaniels, Marshall's high school debate coach, Labaree saw special promise in Marshall and became his mentor. Labaree encouraged Marshall's natural skepticism and helped Marshall hone his research skills, introducing him to new publications in the process. Marshall was not the only student upon whom Labaree had a dramatic impact. Marshall's classmate, the poet Langston Hughes, called Labaree his favorite professor at Lincoln.[12] Clarence Mitchell, who entered Lincoln two years after Marshall, described Labaree as "the man who really got me interested in things like sociology, anthropology, comparative religion, and things of that sort."[13]

In 1927, Marshall and his roommate, Baltimorean James W. Murphy, took these photographs of each other in front of their dormitory, Cresson Hall. *Courtesy of William W. Murphy.*

Marshall's favorite professors at Lincoln were Robert Labaree (left), who coached the debate team, and Walter Livingston (right), who taught mathematics. *Courtesy of Lincoln University, Hughes Library Archives.*

By his second semester, Marshall had settled comfortably into the macho environment of Lincoln. Marshall began to develop a more serious interest in the opposite sex, and he began to pay some attention to his own grooming. He cultivated a thin mustache and became a lifelong chain smoker. Lincoln students tended to spend weekends away from the campus, with Philadelphia being the most common destination and pursuing young women being the most common objective. A train from Philadelphia stopped at the station in Oxford, four miles from the campus. A few students had cars, but hitchhiking was safe and very common at that time. Marshall also occasionally went to Baltimore or to Atlantic City, the home of his close friend and classmate Monroe Dowling. Back at the dorm, Marshall became quite a raconteur, entertaining residents with yarns about his weekend exploits. In later years, Marshall would refer to these sessions as "mostly sitting round, telling lies." Classmates remembered Marshall as "an animated beanpole; a boisterous, gregarious, argumentative type who usually dominated every bull session."[14]

Although the dormitory discussions and debate topics often touched on racial and political matters, Marshall showed no special interest in civil rights while in college, and he certainly gave no indication that it would become his life's work. He participated in a brief protest against the segregated seating practices at the Oxford Theater (located in the town of Oxford), where black customers were required to sit in the balcony. On one occasion, Marshall and six other Lincoln students took seats in the orchestra level, which was reserved for whites, and refused to leave when asked to do so by the usher and manager. Although the students were permitted to remain for the completion of the film, the theater continued its discriminatory seating policy for several more years.

As a freshman at Lincoln University, Marshall rarely spent time with his brother Aubrey, who was in his senior year and preparing to attend medical school at Howard University. For Thurgood, the end of examinations in June 1926 meant going back to work to earn money for his sophomore year.

THE DINING CAR WAITER

The Baltimore & Ohio Railroad, headquartered in Baltimore and known as the B&O, traveled from Washington, DC, to points north and west. The B&O was very proud of its upscale dining car service. Thurgood Marshall began working as a dining car waiter on the B&O on June 11, 1926, the week after his examinations ended at Lincoln. His employee card listed his date of birth as June 11, 1905, exactly twenty-one years before his first day at work.[15] The information was inaccurate. Marshall was born on July 2, 1908, and he was not quite 18 years old. His height and mature appearance may have helped him pass for twenty-one, but more importantly, his uncle Fearless Williams was the personal assistant to the president of the railroad and was thus in a position to pull a few strings for Thurgood.

Unlike sleeping car porters, who worked for the Pullman Company of Chicago, the dining car staff were B&O employees. A crew usually consisted of a steward, three or four waiters, and three cooks. On B&O trains, the cooks and waiters were black; the steward, who functioned as the crew's foreperson and kept track of the money and supplies, was always white.

The galley, or kitchen, took up about one-third of the dining car and was quite cramped. In addition to facilities for food storage and preparation, the galley had storage units for pots, pans, china, glasses, and cutlery. All meals were prepared on board by the head chef and his assistants, using fresh meats, vegetables, and fruits. The remaining two-thirds of the dining car was the dining room. The tables on most B&O dining cars were arranged with a row of four-person tables on one side of the center aisle and a row of two-person tables on the other side. As passengers arrived, they were seated as determined by the steward, who usually filled tables entirely, without leaving any empty chairs. As a result, individuals and couples often ate at tables with strangers.

The job of the waiter was extremely demanding. He provided advice about the menu to help guests make their selections. The passengers filled out their own meal card, using a pencil and a pad provided at each table. The waiter then verified the order and delivered it to the galley. Delivery of drinks and food required skill, agility, and stamina. In the summer, the galley often became steaming hot. With meat roasting, bread and pies baking, and vegetables grilling, the temperature often exceeded one hundred degrees Fahrenheit. Working from the tight and hot galley, the dining car waiter had to bring heavy trays down the center aisle of a moving and swaying car and serve the meals to customers smoothly. The waiter was expected to remain pleasant and neat, in a white uniform with a bow tie. At the end of the meal, the waiter returned to the customer the order blank on which the steward had written the amount owed. The customer gave the money to the waiter, who delivered it to the steward, minus the tip. After the customers at a table left, the waiter cleared the table and reset it with linens, silverware, and glasses.

Railroad waiters had to be patient and thick skinned. They were expected to endure and ignore rude and often racist remarks from customers. The railroad's dining car workers had not yet been unionized when Marshall worked for the B&O. Marshall worked mainly on trains traveling from Washington, DC, through Baltimore and western Maryland on their way to the Midwest. A second route he traveled began in Washington and went through Baltimore and Philadelphia to New York. Crews typically worked twelve to fourteen hours a day and would be on duty several days at a time, working on one train on the outbound leg of the trip and switching to a different train for the return trip. The waiters often spent nights sleeping in corners of the train or in cheap hotels during stopovers. Marshall's salary was fifty-five dollars per month, with no overtime pay. The railroad expected the waiters to supplement their salaries with tips from customers.[16]

During the summer after his freshman year at Lincoln University, Marshall worked on the B&O Railroad until September 18, 1926, three days before school resumed.

THE SOPHOMORE-YEAR "JINKS"

September 1926 found Norma Marshall in a situation similar to the one she had been in a year earlier. The family owed money to Lincoln University for the previous year, and Norma was scrambling to make arrangements for her son Thurgood to return to college. In a letter to the registrar, she acknowledged that she owed $108.50 from the previous year and explained that her husband had been ill and that that she had barely been able to pay Aubrey's bill so that he could graduate. She promised to pay the outstanding balance from Thurgood's first year "as soon as I receive my first school check" and promised to make future required payments without delay. She assured the college that "Thurgood is working and will have his first-semester money on entering school."[17]

Thurgood saved enough money from his summer job to begin the fall term. As a sophomore, he now had the privilege of hazing freshmen, which he did with vigor. However, the hazing that got him in trouble was an incident in which he was minimally involved.

In September 1926, Professor Walter L. Wright, the interim president of the university, issued a directive banning hazing for the remainder of the school year. Although the sophomores toned down the hazing, they did not stop completely. Three weeks after Dr. Wright issued his directive, a group of sophomores summoned several freshmen to room 23 of Cresson Hall "for a conference." One of the sophomores produced a hair clipper and, as each freshman sat in a designated chair, the student with the clipper cut a cross in the freshman's hair as Marshall and other sophomores looked on. Suddenly, someone knocked on the door. Those in the room responded, "Piss and slide under!" which was Lincoln slang granting permission to enter. To the students' disbelief and chagrin, in stepped Professor Wright. He calmly expressed his disappointment with the situation and then recorded the names of the twenty-two sophomores in the room, including Thurgood Marshall and his roommate, James Murphy.

155. Druid Hill Ave.
Feb. 18-1926.

Prof. Yumm:

Dear Sir.
          My first
payment will be on the
8th of March when I receive
my check. I had thought
of sending Mr Marshalls
check which he was to have
received Tuesday. But
because he has been at
home for the past two
weeks sick with the Grippe

His substitute received
half of his salary. He
went back to work to
day. The teachers are
paid by the 8th of each
month. I will send my
check on that date and
the balance to make up
a $150 on the 16th when
Mr Marshall is paid.
By June I will have
paid Aubrey's complet
bill. And Thurgood's
for this second semester

Norma Marshall constantly pleaded
with university officials for time to pay
her sons' tuitions and school fees.
*Courtesy of Afro-American Newspaper
Archives and Lincoln University, Hughes
Library Archives.*

1838 Druid Hill Av.
July 16-1927

Prof. McDowell;
          Registrar of Lincoln University.
          Enclosed find check
for $100 on Thurgood Marshalls
bill, I will send balance just
as soon as possible.
          Very truly yours.
          Mrs W. C. Marshall.

Bal 214.09

Two days later, a posted notice announced that the twenty-two students were suspended and had to leave the campus by that weekend. Marshall was suspended for a week. Murphy and a few others were sent home for two weeks. One student was excluded for the remainder of the semester. Murphy's connection to the *Afro-American* newspaper did not spare him from public embarrassment. The newspaper reported the incident, listing each student's name, hometown, and length of suspension.[18] Marshall's classmate, the poet Langston Hughes, who had not been in the dorm room, assisted the sophomores in drafting an admission of "collective guilt," which Thurgood Marshall and other disciplined students signed. The sophomores were permitted to return to school, and freshman hazing ended for that year.[19]

Upon his return to Lincoln, Marshall faced his next challenge—pledging Alpha Phi Alpha, the nation's oldest African American fraternity. Marshall's high school teachers Gough and Pennington had assumed that Marshall would become an "Alpha," especially since Aubrey had joined. However, Marshall was undecided because his best friend at Lincoln, Monroe Dowling, planned to join the rival fraternity Omega Psi Phi. Fraternity pledging lasted longer and was more violent than freshman hazing, but Marshall endured it and joined Alpha Phi Alpha.

Debating again became Marshall's priority, and he competed on both the sophomore and varsity teams.[20] Marshall also began to be known for his fiery speeches at football pep rallies. Support for the varsity debate team was augmented by the addition of Charles R. Boothby to the Lincoln faculty. A recent graduate of the nationally recognized debating program at Bates College in Maine, Boothby was recruited to Lincoln as "a specialist in dramatics and debating."[21] As Labaree continued to advise the team and chair the faculty committee on debating, Boothby became the varsity team's coach and began to use his contacts to expand the reach of Lincoln's debating program by arranging competitions with white colleges. Up until that time, there had never been a debate between a black college and a white college.

During Marshall's sophomore year, Lincoln's varsity debate team made history when it participated in the first interracial college debate. On December 16, 1926, Lincoln University and a team from England's Oxford University met at Bethel A.M.E. (African Methodist Episcopal) Church in Baltimore and debated Prohibition. The topic was "Resolved, That This House Opposes Any Change in the Eighteenth Amendment." Although Thurgood

trained with the team and traveled to Baltimore, he did not actively participate in the debate. Boothby and Labaree, the faculty advisers, believed that
having just one Baltimorean, Richard Hill, on stage was enough to please the
hometown crowd. The Englishmen were entertaining and witty but tended to
go off on tangents unrelated to the debate topic. The Lincoln students were
less humorous but were well prepared and adhered closely to the subject.
The consensus of the 1,800 persons in attendance was that the Lincoln team
won. Black newspapers in New York, Philadelphia, and Pittsburgh[22] hailed
the event as "the first interracial international debate."[23]

Marshall joined the Alpha Phi Alpha fraternity. Marshall is on the second row, sec-
ond from the right. His roommate James Murphy is on the second row, far left. Front
row, left to right: Andrew Jenkins, Mark Parks, Leroy Morris, Daniel Thomas, Macon
Berryman. Second row: James Murphy, Joseph Meadohgh, Wendell Hughes,
Thomas Cross, Thurgood Marshall, Thomas Morse. Third row: Howard Jason, Thomas
Webster, William Thompson. *Courtesy of Thurgood Marshall family.*

Thurgood Marshall did participate in the next Lincoln debate, which
was of even greater historical significance. On February 26, 1927, Lincoln
University and Penn State University faced off in the first debate ever
between a black American college and a white American college. This
debate predated by nearly a decade the much-publicized interracial debates
by the team from Wiley College of Texas in the 1930s. More than nine
hundred people witnessed the Lincoln–Penn State debate at Union Baptist
Church in Philadelphia.

The topic was again about Prohibition: "Resolved, That the Volstead
Act Should be Modified to Permit the Manufacture and Sale of Light

Wines and Beer." The Lincoln team consisted of Richard Hurst Hill, R. Esdras Turner, and Thurgood Marshall. They argued in the affirmative that the Prohibition law was too stringent and had brought about class privilege. After prolonged deliberation, the judges voted two to one in favor of Penn State.[24]

The debate received much attention from the press.[25] "Penn State . . . has been the first institution to stretch its hands across the color line and ask for a debate with a sister college of color. At the present time we cannot think of a better way to banish snobbery and Ku Klux fallacies from college halls," declared the *Afro-American* in an editorial. The press also noted sophomore Marshall's oratorical performance, with the *Philadelphia Tribune* commenting that "with possibly a little more experience, Thurgood should stand preeminently above most of the debaters of color in collegiate competitions in the country."

During his sophomore year, Marshall studied more than he had during his first year, improved his grades, and earned sophomore academic honors.[26] Marshall's loud and boisterous demeanor led the student newspaper to dub him "The Quietest" in his class. Despite his outgoing personality, he did not belong to a particular clique.

After his sophomore year ended, Marshall took three weeks off before returning to his job as a railroad dining car waiter. His salary remained fifty-five dollars per month, plus tips.

JUNIOR YEAR: THE HIGH AND LOW POINTS

In September 1927, for the third year in a row, Norma Marshall had to write Lincoln University pleading for additional time to pay the overdue bill from her son's previous year. She stated that she had not worked during the summer and that payment would have to "wait until my first school check." She promised, "I will send you $100 on October 6. $114 balance due November 6, Thurgood will bring with him money for first semester this year." Norma explained that she was no longer just a substitute teacher[27] and added, "I assure you that there will be no more delay in my payment of bills, since I was made a regular teacher this past June and can depend on my salary every month."[28]

Marshall's junior year proved eventful. As he made the debate team for the third time, the student newspaper printed a long article, entitled "Introducing Our Debate Prestige," that boasted of Lincoln's past successes and gave the ambitious debate schedule for the year, which included two debates in New York City and a debate at prestigious Harvard University.

On December 12, 1927, Marshall debated at New York's City College. Two days later, he participated in a highly publicized debate against the National Students' Union of England, which represented the University of London, the University of Reading, and the University of Edinburgh. The Lincoln and English teams met at Mother African Methodist Episcopal Church in Harlem on the question "Resolved, That the Attitude of The Anglo-Saxon Race Toward The Colored Races Under Its Control Is Unethical and Prejudicial To Progress."

The New York and New Jersey Lincoln alumni associations sponsored and advertised the New York debates in newspapers and mailings.[29] Three thousand people paid one dollar each to attend. Lincoln, represented by Thurgood Marshall, Malcolm Dade, and Richard Hill of Baltimore, argued in the affirmative. They condemned British imperialism and argued that no group of Anglo-Saxons would at any time treat a "colored group" the same way as it would treat its own race. Marshall declared that "the history of the Anglo-Saxon races has been one of imperialistic oppression for the sake of business advantages." The English debaters responded that even though the majority of Britons did not favor their nation's imperialism, native races in most British colonies would not have reached their present state of development without British assistance. Both teams received thunderous ovations from the large audience, and no winner was announced.[30]

Later in his junior year, Marshall participated in his most trying and personally difficult debate. Lincoln agreed to debate the Liberal Club of Harvard University on the controversial topic "Resolved: That Further Intermixing of Races in the United States Is Desirable." The announcement of the upcoming debate drew the attention of the local Ku Klux Klan chapter, which demanded that the debate be canceled or the topic be changed. As the debate approached, the Klan's threats increased, and rocks were thrown through the window of the Liberal Club's building.[31]

Despite the threats, the two teams met at the Tremont Temple in Boston, before an audience of more than two thousand. The event was arranged as a fundraiser for Lincoln's endowment fund and grossed over

$1,000.[32] Matters became really intense when the organizers assigned Lincoln the negative argument and Marshall's team would have to argue that "intermixing of races" was undesirable. Thurgood Marshall spoke first and focused his eighteen-minute opening argument on interracial marriage. He argued that interracial marriage produced children that were neither black nor white and who were then excluded from both races. He criticized "intermixing" as detrimental to families and society.[33] Marshall's teammate Richard Hill observed that interracial marriage was illegal in twenty-eight states. He pointed out that a colored man with "a small percentage of white, Indian and Negro blood" was, under state law, a white man in Oklahoma, an Indian in Michigan, and a Negro in Florida.[34]

Following the debate, Marshall and Hill attended a celebratory dinner and spent the night in a Harvard dormitory. According to Marshall's teammate Hill, "The fact that Marshall and I stayed in Klavery Hall, one of the dormitories, was in part the cause of the trouble." Hill added that "we were handsomely treated by the students of Harvard University."[35]

Besides raising money for the endowment fund, the debate yet again raised the profile of Lincoln, which the *Harvard Crimson* referred to as "the pioneer Negro college." However, the arguments that Marshall felt compelled to make on the debate stage were so much in conflict with his personal beliefs that, in later years, Marshall seldom mentioned his debate at Harvard University.

The Harvard debate had barely passed before Marshall's junior year grew even more dramatic. A week after the Harvard event, Marshall, Monroe Dowling, and three other Lincoln students went to Baltimore for the weekend. As they had done on many previous occasions, the students hitchhiked back to Oxford, Pennsylvania. A northbound truck stopped and picked them up. Unfortunately, the truck broke down in the small town of Rising Sun in Cecil County, Maryland, a few miles south of the Pennsylvania border. As a garage mechanic repaired the truck, the local sheriff came by and told the students that "you niggers had better be out of town before sundown." The truck was repaired, but, as it pulled away, Marshall was a few yards behind. He ran to catch up and hopped aboard the moving vehicle. As he jumped onto the truck, the tailgate came down and injured one of his testicles. After reaching Lincoln in excruciating pain, he was taken to Baltimore for medical treatment. Despite their best efforts, his doctors were unable to save the testicle. Marshall thus acquired a new nickname "One Ball."

Ku Klux Warned Lincoln Men To Change Subject

CAMBRIDGE, MASS.—Bricks, to which were attacked Ku Klux Klan notes were hurled thru the windows of the Harvard University Liberal Club, which debated last Thursday with a team from Lincoln, Pa. University on the subject "Resolved That Further Intermixing of the Races is Desirable." NO DECISION WAS GIVEN.

Ku Kluxers were riled because of the subject of the debate and sent word to the club forbidding the discussion. The club paid no attention to the warnings and the bricks were thrown.

Richard Hurst Hill and Thurgood Marshall, both Baltimore men represented Lincoln. Harvard club debaters were Harem Hubbard and William Fairbanks.

LINCOLN, PA. (By Wire)—No one was injured in the Ku Klux outbreak at Harvard, Richard H. Hill told the Afro Wednesday morning.

"The fact that Marshall and I stayed in Klaverly Hall, one of the dormitories was in part the cause of the trouble," he said.

Mr. Hill added "We were handsomely treated by the students of Harvard University.

MARSHALL   HILL

Marshall personally disagreed with the arguments he made against interracial relationships in the debate against Harvard. *Courtesy of Afro-American Newspaper Archives and Research Center.*

BIG INTERNATIONAL DEBATE

WEDNESDAY EVENING, DECEMBER 14, 1927
8:30 o'Clock

At NEW MOTHER ZION A. M. E. CHURCH
140-6 West 137th St., the Rev. J. W. Brown, Pastor

Between

National Students' Union of England
(white)

REPRESENTING UNIVERSITY OF LONDON, UNIVERSITY OF
____ AND UNIVERSITY OF EDINBURGH.

and

____versity of Chester Co., Pa.
(colored)

___hat the Attitude of the Anglo-Saxon Race To-
__es Under Its Control Is Unethical and Prejudi-

___ces of New York and New Jersey Lincoln
__ Alumni Associations.

___ on Sale at New Mother Zion A. M. E. Church,
___ Amsterdam News and New York News.

___people heard Marshall strongly condemn
___e debate against the team from Eng-
___ican *Newspaper Archives and Research*

Marshall remained out of school for the remainder of the semester. All records at Lincoln record him as having withdrawn on account of illness. Yet the recovery must have been quite fast, because two weeks after the accident, Marshall went back to his old job as a dining car waiter. Marshall's employee card at the B&O headquarters showed that he began work that year on April 3, 1928, and continued until August 31, 1928.[36] Correspondence between his mother and Lincoln officials suggests that the real reason Marshall stayed out of school for the semester was due to his continuing financial problems. The Marshall family owed Lincoln most of the fees for the first semester of his junior year. Norma Marshall haggled with the school over how much she had to pay for the fragment of the second semester that Thurgood had completed before his injury.[37] Thurgood continued working as a dining car waiter for the remainder of the semester and through the summer of 1928.

SENIOR YEAR: BACK ON TRACK

Marshall returned to Lincoln in September 1928, a semester behind his entering class. Having established himself as a formidable debater affectionately known as "The Wrathful Marshall," he rejoined the varsity debate team. Yet he had to go through the annual selection process like everyone else. This time, the students who made the varsity debate team along with Marshall included Marshall's best friend, Monroe Dowling from Atlantic City, and another friend, Clarence Mitchell from Baltimore.[38]

In November 1928, Lincoln again debated a team from Oxford University at Baltimore's Bethel A.M.E Church. The topic was a familiar one: "Resolved, That Prohibition Is the Most Effective Means of Controlling the Liquor Traffic." This time, the Baltimorean on the team was Thurgood Marshall, a fact prominently noted by the *Afro-American*'s headline, "Baltimore Boy in Team Which Will Lock Horns with English Lads."[39] However, only 250 people attended because the organizers charged fifty cents for admission; the first debate between Lincoln and Oxford had been free. The audience voted in favor of Lincoln.[40] For the first time, a black college's debate was reported in Baltimore's largest newspaper, the *Sun*. The headline read, "Negro Debaters Win over Oxford."[41]

The absence of black faculty members at Lincoln had been a recurring matter of discussion and controversy among the alumni, national black leaders, and the press.[42] The controversy erupted once again in the spring of 1929. In a survey of the student body, two-thirds of the students, including Marshall, favored keeping the faculty white. The survey led to a firestorm of criticism from some organizations, especially the NAACP.[43] Some students explained that they feared black professors would display favoritism toward students who were members of their own fraternities, whereas white professors would be free of such bias. Marshall initially sided with the majority, who opposed integrating the faculty, until Langston Hughes and Professor Labaree persuaded him otherwise. The university's administration insisted that the students did not speak for the university and that the issue of integrating the faculty "has never come before the college faculty or the board of trustees. When and if it did, the administration would express itself."[44] The next year, Lincoln hired its first black faculty member.

Upon completing the school year, Marshall returned to his job on the B&O as a dining car waiter, still earning the same salary.

MARSHALL'S LAST SEMESTER AT LINCOLN

As September 1929 approached, Marshall still needed several credits to graduate. Once again, before the semester began, Norma Marshall had to write the usual letters to Lincoln University to get a payment extension.[45] That fall, however, Marshall would not be returning to school as a bachelor. He had met and fallen in love with Vivian Burey, a beautiful University of Pennsylvania student, whose parents, Christopher and Maude Burey, operated a successful catering business in Philadelphia and in Riverton, New Jersey. "Thurgood was the funniest looking man. When I met him, he was six foot one and weighed 141 pounds—nothing but skin and bones," Vivian recalled.[46]

They decided to get married, but realized that both sets of parents wanted them to wait at least until they had obtained their college degrees. "First we decided to get married five years after I graduated, then three, then one, and we finally did just before I started my last semester."[47]

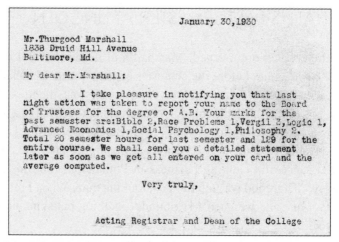

Marshall did well in courses he liked, such as mathematics and the required Bible courses. He received his lowest grades in foreign languages. *Courtesy of Lincoln University, Hughes Library Archives.*

January 30, 1930

Mr. Thurgood Marshall
1838 Druid Hill Avenue
Baltimore, Md.

My dear Mr. Marshall:

    I take pleasure in notifying you that last night action was taken to report your name to the Board of Trustees for the degree of A.B. Your marks for the past semester are: Bible 2, Race Problems 1, Vergil 2, Logic 1, Advanced Economics 1, Social Psychology 1, Philosophy 2. Total 20 semester hours for last semester and 129 for the entire course. We shall send you a detailed statement later as soon as we get all entered on your card and the average computed.

        Very truly,

        Acting Registrar and Dean of the College

In his last semester, Marshall raised his grade point average enough to graduate cum laude, after the Board of Trustees waived one missing credit hour. *Courtesy of Lincoln University, Hughes Library Archives.*

Vivian's sister, Irene, had eloped and gotten married a few months earlier in one of the "wedding chapels" in Cecil County, Maryland. Fearing another elopement, the parents consented to the marriage, announced the engagement, and arranged a large wedding.[48] Vivian and Thurgood were married on September 4, 1929, at the Cherry Memorial Baptist Church in Philadelphia, with Marshall's roommate from Baltimore, James Murphy, as his best man. Thurgood was twenty-one years old, and "Buster," as Vivian was called by family and friends, was eighteen. The newlyweds moved into a small apartment near the Lincoln campus.[49]

Marshall's weekend jaunts were over, and he did not rejoin the debate team. He instead focused on completing his academic requirements to earn a degree. He took a very heavy course load, registering for courses on race problems, the Bible, logic, advanced economics, social psychology, philosophy, and the works of Virgil for a staggering total of twenty credit hours. Without the distractions of debating or weekend trips, he earned mostly As and Bs and significantly raised his grade point average. He finished the semester 1 credit shy of the 130 credits required to graduate. In late January 1930, the board of trustees of the university voted to waive the last credit and allow Marshall to graduate.[50]

As he had done with his high school graduation, Marshall would have to leave school in January and return in June for the graduation ceremony. The newlyweds remained in the area, with Buster working as a secretary and Thurgood working as a bellhop and a waiter, including a short stint in the catering business operated by his in-laws at the Riverton Yacht Club on the Delaware River. During the winter following the completion of his academic work at Lincoln, Thurgood was involved in a second automobile accident. While hitchhiking from Lincoln back to Baltimore following a snow storm, he was picked up by a motorist. The automobile hit an ice patch and went out of control, throwing Marshall and the driver out of the vehicle. The driver's head hit a rock, killing him instantly. Marshall was thrown into a pile of hay and sustained only a minor injury to his back.[51]

The 1930 Lincoln University commencement ceremony was held in Livingston Hall. Of the sixty-two graduates, sixteen graduated with honors, five graduated magna cum laude, and eleven graduated cum laude. Both of Thurgood Marshall's parents were present as he graduated cum laude. The graduation ceremony began with an invocation by Reverend W. W.

Before his last semester at Lincoln, Marshall married Vivian "Buster" Burey, a junior at the University of Pennsylvania, whose parents were caterers. *Courtesy of Afro-American Newspaper Archives and Research Center.*

To Wed Philly Belle

THOROGOOD MARSHALL

Son of Mr. and Mrs. William Marshall, of 1836 Druid Hill avenue, to wed Miss Vivian Burey, formerly of Philadelphia.

Walker, Marshall's neighbor, who, five years earlier, had written to Lincoln's acting president urging the university to admit Marshall, even though his older brother's school fees were overdue.[52] At the ceremony, sophomore Clarence M. Mitchell Jr. received an award for excellence in debating.[53] A telegram was then read from Owen J. Roberts, a trustee of Lincoln who had just become an associate justice of the US Supreme Court. Then Marshall and his fellow graduates sat in stunned silence as the main commencement speaker, Dr. Joseph Holley, the president of Albany Normal and Agricultural College in Georgia, proclaimed, "Thank God for slavery." He described a recent trip to Africa he had taken (under the auspices of the Presbyterian Mission Board), during which he had seen scantily clad native men and women loading goods on ships. Holley told the commencement audience, "But for slavery, I, too, would be naked, uploading European ships in West Africa."[54]

After graduation, Thurgood and Buster moved into his parent's house in Baltimore, where Buster redecorated Thurgood's third-floor bedroom. Marshall left Lincoln University with an education that would serve him well. He had acquired a strong command of language, having studied American literature, Shakespeare, Latin, French, Greek, Plato, the Bible, Virgil, Cicero, and Milton. His understanding of the human condition had been broadened by courses in sociology, psychology, social psychology, ethnology, and ethics. He had prepared for a career of advocacy with courses on public speaking, rhetoric, and logic. He had been a competitive debater for eight years.[55]

Chapter 5

Educating a Social Engineer

"**C**harlie saw the big picture. He taught us all to be social engineers,"[1] said Thurgood Marshall about Charles Houston, the dean of the law school where Marshall had thrived. "While in the Law School, I served as student assistant librarian for two years, was a member of the Court of Peers for one year and Chief Justice of the Court of Peers during the last year," Marshall recalled.[2]

Thurgood Marshall did not apply to the University of Maryland School of Law in Baltimore because he knew that none of the programs offered by his state's largest university admitted African Americans.[3] He instead applied and was admitted to the law school at Howard University in Washington, DC. Because he could not afford to live in Washington, for the next three years, Marshall commuted from Baltimore six days a week. After getting up at 5:00 a.m., he walked a mile to the B&O station on Mount Royal Avenue. When he arrived in Washington, he walked a few blocks from Union Station to the law school, where classes began at 8:00 am. Fortunately for Marshall, the law school was not located on the main campus of Howard University, which was much further from Union Station.

THE CAPSTONE

Marshall attended Howard at a time of major transformation at the historically black school. Howard University, founded in 1869, called itself "the capstone of Negro education." Howard's law school had produced more than 70 percent of the black lawyers in the United States. Yet when Marshall entered the law school, it lacked accreditation from the American Bar Association (ABA) and the Association of American

Law Schools (AALS). In 1926, Mordecai Wyatt Johnson became the first African American president of Howard and announced that one of his top priorities would be to upgrade the law school and get it fully accredited.

Johnson wanted the law school to provide better training for black lawyers. His desire to improve the school stemmed in part from a conversation with Supreme Court Justice Louis Brandeis, who had told Johnson that the justices on the Supreme Court could tell when a brief had been prepared by a black lawyer. Brandeis said that black lawyers all too often brought before the Court cases with records that were too incomplete and briefs that were too deficient to permit even sympathetic justices to take the case seriously. Johnson reported that Brandeis had told him that the men of that tribunal had "longed for someone to so present the cases in the Negro's behalf that decisions might be rendered in harmony with right and justice so clearly and forcefully pleaded that the end would be inevitable."[4] According to Oliver Hill, Marshall's classmate at Howard, "Mordecai Johnson had determined to make Howard a first-class law school to train Negroes to carry cases to the Supreme Court with records that the Court could handle."[5]

Howard University had to make many changes to earn accreditation. The ABA and AALS only accredited schools with full-time day programs, but Howard offered only a part-time evening program. Johnson's proposal to convert Howard Law to a day program met immediate resistance from the law school's faculty and students. Most faculty members were judges and practicing lawyers during the day. Many of the students held day jobs and had families to support. Johnson's inability to persuade the faculty initially stalled his efforts. However, when Dean Fenton Booth resigned in 1929, Johnson took advantage of the vacancy to replace Booth with a more progressive dean who shared his vision for the law school. Johnson appointed Charles Hamilton Houston as head of the law school. Even though Houston had full administrative responsibility for the school, he took the title of "vice dean."

Houston was born in Washington, DC, in 1895. He attended Amherst College, graduating in 1915 as the valedictorian of his class. After serving in France as an officer in the US Army during World War I, Houston returned to the United States in 1919 and entered Harvard Law School. He became an editor of the *Harvard Law Review* and graduated cum laude. A year later he obtained from Harvard an advanced law degree. He then traveled and studied in Europe before joining his father's law firm in Washington,

DC. In 1924, he began teaching at the Howard University School of Law, where his father also served on the faculty. Professor Houston quickly earned a reputation for being a rigorous law teacher who challenged his students. Although Houston claimed that he enjoyed failing poorly performing students, most of the students found him approachable and fair.

Houston became very active in the National Bar Association, the organization of black lawyers from around the country. He began to give special attention to assembling data about the status of blacks in the legal profession. His surveys documented the scarcity of black lawyers, especially in the South. In 1928, Houston found that there were 1,230 black lawyers in the United States, the equivalent of 1 black lawyer for every 9,677 African Americans, compared to 1 white lawyer for every 695 whites. Southern states, in particular, faced an alarming shortage of black attorneys. In some parts of the South, the ratio of black citizens to black lawyers was as great as 200,000 to 1. He found that many American jurisdictions did not allow black lawyers to practice in their courts. Houston's research also revealed that many black clients were reluctant to hire black lawyers because they feared that they would not have influence in a judicial system dominated by whites.[6]

In June 1929, the board of trustees of Howard University, upon the recommendation of President Mordecai Johnson, appointed Charles Houston to lead the law school.[7] Houston agreed with Johnson on the need for dramatic change at the law school. In addition to a day program, accreditation required a full-time law faculty and a more comprehensive law library. In 1930, as Houston began to phase out the evening program, six part-time white professors resigned. They were replaced with full-time law professors, most of whom were black.[8] Houston boasted about the credentials of the September 1930 entering class, which included Lincoln graduate Thurgood Marshall.[9]

HOWARD BECOMES ACCREDITED

As Marshall and his classmates entered law school, they were aware that the school was in transition and that the reforms that had been adopted were becoming controversial within the university and among the alumni. The black press devoted much space to the unfolding drama surrounding the changes. But Houston pressed on with the support of Mordecai Johnson, whose determination to bring change to Howard almost cost him his position as university president. Some university trustees, faculty members, and alumni wanted to remove both Johnson and Houston. A committee of the trustees recommended that the law school dean be "a man of mature age and experience [who is] equipped for the profession of law teaching and who is willing to devote his entire time to the administration of the school." The trustees believed that Houston lacked these qualities, but Johnson persisted and continued to stand firmly behind Houston.[10]

Houston set about changing Howard's approach to legal education, including raising admissions standards.[11] He discouraged students from having outside employment during the school year. As the schedule and grading became more difficult, students were asked to leave due to poor grades or irregular attendance. The school's enrollment dropped dramatically from 1929 to 1933.

Houston sought to expand his students' experiences and contacts by taking them on field trips to courthouses, law firms, jails, mental institutions, prosecutors' offices, and government offices. Marshall's classmate Oliver Hill explained that "Charlie was giving us an opportunity to get some experience and ideas about what was happening and about things that we would not have had an opportunity to know anything about. Most of those visits were done on Saturday."[12]

Houston also invited famous and successful lawyers to address the students. Guest speakers included renowned attorney Clarence Darrow; Samuel Leibowitz, the main defense lawyer in the Scottsboro case; attorney Arthur Garfield Hayes; Harvard Law School dean Roscoe Pound; Erwin Griswold; William H. Lewis, the nation's first black federal prosecutor;[13] and Edward H. Morris, the railroad attorney from Chicago who was reputed to be the nation's wealthiest black lawyer.[14]

One year after Marshall began law school, Houston and Johnson's hard work came to fruition. The American Bar Association announced that the Howard University School of Law had met the ABA's accreditation requirements. Will Shafroth, a Denver attorney, had conducted a two-day inspection of the law school for the ABA and filed a favorable report.[15] The law school had introduced a three-year, full-time day program; had hired four full-time instructors; and had assembled a law library of more than 7,500 volumes. The school now required admitted students to

Marshall's law school dean and mentor, Charles Houston, was a national leader among African American lawyers. *Courtesy of Scurlock Studio Records, Archives Center, National Museum of American History, Behring Center, Smithsonian Institution.*

Charles Houston (left) brought famous lawyers like Clarence Darrow (center) to speak at Howard Law School while Marshall was a student. Howard President Mordecai Johnson is on the right. *Courtesy of Scurlock Studio Records, Archives Center, National Museum of American History, Behring Center, Smithsonian Institution.*

have completed at least two years of college before enrolling. The ABA accepted Shafroth's findings, and the ABA's Council on Legal Education and Admissions to the Bar approved Howard Law for accreditation by unanimous vote.[16] In December 1931, the Howard University School of Law became a member of the other law-school-accrediting body, the Association of American Law Schools.

Houston had also changed the racial composition of the faculty to seven black professors and five white professors.[17] He repeatedly rejected offers by President Johnson to promote him to the official rank and title of dean; he did this to make the point that his salary and all the faculty salaries were too low to merit that title.[18]

MARSHALL SHINES AT HOWARD

Marshall's class was the first group to complete Howard University School of Law's full-time day program. The class had a high attrition rate. Some students left due to financial pressures. Others found the course work too demanding. Several were asked to leave because of low grades. Marshall's class, initially totaling thirty-nine students, shrank to just eight students in the three years he was at Howard.

Marshall thrived amid the ongoing controversy and transformation. William Hastie, who taught legal research and later became the first black federal judge in the United States, was very impressed with Marshall and gave him the best grade in his class. He later claimed that Marshall was the best first-year law student he had ever taught. Hastie said of Marshall, "He was extremely keen and alert in analyzing problems. He and his partner prepared a brief at the end of the year that was better than many briefs I have seen by practicing lawyers."[19] Marshall also excelled in the first-year moot-court competition.[20] Marshall finished his first year of law school with the highest grade point average in the class. At the university's 1931 graduation ceremony, following Marshall's first year at Howard, he was given the Callaghan Prize for obtaining the highest grade in Legal Bibliography.[21] Marshall attributed his academic success to hard work: "I got through simply by overwhelming the job. I was at it 20 hours a day, seven days a week."[22]

Marshall's academic achievement did not go unnoticed. The law school had one paid student position, that of assistant librarian. The position was reserved for the highest-achieving student in the school. After his first year in law school, Marshall became the assistant librarian. The job paid half of Marshall's $142 tuition and fees but required him to remain at the school until 6:00 p.m. Classes at the law school ended at 11:30 a.m., so before beginning his shift at the library, Marshall had his main meal of the day at a nearby restaurant, which was run by the followers of a charismatic religious leader. As classmate Oliver W. Hill remembered, "Every day after classes ended at 11:30, Thurgood and I would go down to Father Divine's restaurant on Ninth Street. You said, 'Peace, it is wonderful,' and you would get a good lunch for twenty-five cents or a deluxe meal for thirty-five cents. I was a quarter man, and sometimes Thurgood was a thirty-five-cent man."[23] After lunch, Marshall would head back to the law school library, where he would study during most of the time he was on duty.[24] He would seldom get back to Baltimore before 9:00 p.m.

Professor William H. Hastie gave Marshall the highest grade in the course on legal research and his chance to work on an actual case. *Courtesy of Scurlock Studio Records, Archives Center, National Museum of American History, Behring Center, Smithsonian Institution.*

James A. Cobb, a judge on the District of Columbia Municipal Court, taught Marshall constitutional law. *Courtesy of Afro-American Newspaper Archives and Research Center.*

In his second and third years, Marshall continued to perform well at Howard University, remaining the top student in his class. He got an A in the course on evidence taught by Houston and won the competition in the moot-court course taught by Nathan Cayton, a judge on the Washington, DC, Municipal Court. Marshall also got an A in Walter W. Cook's course on conflict of laws and an A in Theodore Cogswell's course on wills and estate administration. Marshall earned a B in the course on constitutional law taught by Judge James Adlai Cobb, who had been on the law school faculty since 1916.[25] Marshall also got Bs in the course on municipal corporations taught by Leon Andrew Ransom and the course on insurance taught by the dean's father, William Houston. In his third year, Marshall researched and drafted, for Alfred J. Buscheck's course on corporations, an impressive paper titled "The Fairness of the Reorganization Plan in Industrial Corporations." The paper was about large non-railroad companies that faced financial distress.

In his three years at Howard, Marshall received grades below a B in only two courses, a C+ in a course on common-law pleading and a D in a course on legal history. Both of these courses were taught by George E. C. Hayes, a lawyer who argued *Brown v. Board of Education* with Marshall two decades later.[26]

Marshall's fellow students admired and respected him. He was elected associate justice and then chief justice of the Court of Peers, the student honor judiciary. Marshall and his classmates became embroiled in a conflict over the election of class officers. One slate of candidates, all members of Marshall's own Alpha Phi Alpha fraternity, claimed victory. Another group of students, who were not Alpha Phi Alpha members, challenged the election results and supported a different slate of candidates as the legitimate winners. The class was evenly divided, with two factions of twelve members each and two sets of class officers. Both Marshall and Oliver Hill claimed to be the class representative to the student council. The controversy even spilled over into the press.[27]

A pragmatic truce developed. Hill recalled, "I helped organize and became the leader of the Coalition of non-Alphas. Thurgood was the leader for the Alphas. So, anything Thurgood and I could agree on happened. If we didn't agree, it didn't happen. This situation continued throughout our law school career."[28]

HOWARD LAW CLASS SPLIT IN FACTIONS

WASHINGTON. — Struggling for class leadership, the 22 members of the second year at the Howard University law school have split into two equally divided factions each with its own set of officers, each claiming to be the real representatives.

The double election followed several class meetings which ended in unusual disorder, one being halted by a member of the faculty. As the rival groups have not been able to effect any compromise, a movement is on foot to have the relative rights of the two parties adjudicated in the moot court.

The 16 officers representing the class of 22 are: president, Leslie Perry, Lorenzo Henderson; vice president, William T. Alexander, Marcellus Harris; secretary, Anthony Pierce, Otho Branson; treasurer; Hayden Johnson, Edward Saunders.

Parliamentarian, Armond Scott, Jr., H. Reginald Mitchell; student council, Oliver W. Hill, Thurgood Marshall; publicity, Edward B. Muse, Charles Young; sergeant-at-arms, Perry Ferguson, L. N. Reaves.

Marshall (rear right) worked as the Assistant Law Librarian. Oliver Hill, his best friend in law school, is in the rear left. *Courtesy of Scurlock Studio Records, Archives Center, National Museum of American History, Behring Center, Smithsonian Institution.*

Marshall and Hill led competing factions of law students in a split that was never resolved, producing two complete sets of class officers. *Courtesy of Afro-American Newspaper Archives and Research Center.*

Marshall and Hill, who had become friends during the first year of law school, often agreed on student government matters. Hill later described Marshall as having "the fine quality of being reasonable with others in the resolution of problems."[29] But one lasting result of this stalemate was that the Howard Law class of 1933 never took the set of class pictures that traditionally appear on the walls of the law school.

THE HOME FRONT

Back in Baltimore, Marshall's home at 1838 Druid Hill Avenue had become quite crowded. Marshall, his wife, and his parents were already living there when Aubrey moved in with his wife, Sadie (whom he had married during medical school), and her mother, Helen Prince. Aubrey's son, William Aubrey Marshall Jr., was born soon after. Marshall's grueling schedule left him with little time or energy to do much at home other than study and sleep; sleeping probably offered him some respite from the tension at home. Aubrey spent two years as a low-paid intern at Provident Hospital and then tried to build a private medical practice, even as his persistent cough developed into tuberculosis. Norma Marshall and Sadie were both schoolteachers, but the two never became close and barely tolerated each other. Helen assumed final authority on matters relating to Aubrey Jr. Thurgood's wife, Vivian, worked odd jobs, mostly in stores, but could not find steady work. There were simply too many people living under one roof and sharing one bathroom. William Marshall, on the other hand, was enjoying the best summer job of his life, as the steward at the posh Gibson Island resort on the western shore of Chesapeake Bay. Thurgood stayed focused on his schoolwork.

GIBSON ISLAND

During the summers of his law school years, Thurgood again worked as a waiter, but in a more comfortable and pleasant setting than the railroad dining cars. His father hired him to work at Gibson Island, a private country club resort serving "old money" families. The working conditions, hours,

After Thurgood returned to Baltimore, the family home at 1838 Druid Hill Avenue became quite crowded, housing Thurgood and his wife, Thurgood's mother and father, Thurgood's brother and his wife, his brother's mother-in-law, and his brother's infant son. *Courtesy of Thurgood Marshall family, William A. Marshall Jr., and Maryland Historical Trust.*

and pay were much better than those at the railroad job, and the clientele was more pleasant and predictable than the railroad dining car customers.

Gibson Island was connected by a gated causeway to the Western Shore of Chesapeake Bay. In addition to approximately one hundred summer and year-round homes on large lots, there was a golf course, tennis courts, a swimming pool, and facilities for yachts. The Gibson Island Clubhouse, which had opened in 1924, had imposing pillars and a majestic porch with a colorful awning. It was the center of activity on the island. Marshall and the other waiters served drinks on the lawn of the clubhouse and meals in the dining room. The mint julep was the most popular summer beverage at the club, the arms of the New England–style lawn chairs having been modified to provide a wide, flat surface for the drink.

Thursday and Saturday nights were special. The Thursday-night lobster buffet was a highlight, as was the Saturday-night dance, to which the men wore black ties and the women brought fans. The hostess, Mrs. Bidwell, enforced the codes of dress and decorum for the children and the adults. The famous Rivers Chambers Orchestra often provided the music.

Albert Fox, the manager of the clubhouse and William Marshall's supervisor, knew that young Thurgood was a law student, and Fox was very supportive of Thurgood. Albert's wife, Ethel Fox, was also fond of Marshall, whom she described as having "the sunniest, most wonderful disposition."[30] During hours off from his duties as a waiter, Marshall made extra money doing odd chores around the Fox home and babysitting their daughter, Jean. According to Jean, "Mother did not like being in the sun and did not like pushing the baby carriage. So, they would have Thurgood Marshall take me for rides around the neighborhood."[31] Marshall and Albert Fox remained friends, communicated with each other, and periodically met for many years. However, Fox could never convince Marshall to call him "Albert."

Marshall was also popular with his coworkers. At the end of the work day, Marshall often verbally entertained the maids, cooks, gardeners, and other "help" as they gathered on the steps of the monument to Gibson Island's founder, Judge W. Stuart Symington, to await the bus back to Baltimore.

Each summer while in law school, Marshall worked as a waiter at the Gibson Island Club, where his father was the chief steward. *Courtesy of Maryland Historical Trust.*

Albert Fox (left), the manager of the Gibson Island Club, and his wife liked Marshall and allowed him to earn extra money babysitting their infant daughter, Jean (above). *Courtesy of Jean F. Crunkleton.*

Marshall fondly remembered the four summers he spent at Gibson Island, working around bankers, admirals, generals, business owners, ambassadors, railroad officials, builders, judges, and legislators.[32] It must have been a valuable learning experience.

THE GEORGE CRAWFORD CASE

In Marshall's second year at Howard, Houston began to notice the bright young man from Baltimore. Professor William Hastie had given Marshall the highest grade in the class on legal research, and Marshall's work as assistant librarian also caught Houston's attention. According to Oliver Hill, "Charlie saw Thurgood in the library every afternoon, and Thurgood became his protégé."[33] Marshall's first research assignment for a real case was not for Houston, however, but for Professor William Hastie. The case involved an African American, Thomas Hocutt, who sought admission to the University of North Carolina's School of Pharmacy. The case floundered on a procedural technicality but gave Marshall his first exposure to litigation.[34] Three years later, Marshall would resume the fight against racial discrimination committed by state universities.

The first case on which Marshall worked with Charles Houston would have a lasting impact on their relationship and was a turning point in Marshall's life. The George Crawford case marked the beginning of Thurgood Marshall's work in criminal law. In January 1933, as Marshall began his final semester at Howard, a black man from Virginia named George Crawford was arrested in Boston, Massachussetts, and was charged with murdering two white women in Loudon County, Virginia. The NAACP became convinced of Crawford's innocence after an alibi witness placed him in Boston at the time of the murders and other information suggested that the real culprit was the victims' own brother. To the NAACP, Crawford's case bore a striking resemblance to the ongoing "Scottsboro Boys" case. Two years earlier, nine black youths had been convicted of raping two young white girls on a freight train near Scottsboro, Alabama. When eight of them were sentenced to death, the so-called Scottsboro Boys became a national cause célèbre, and their lawyers were provided by the International Labor Defense (ILD).

The NAACP feared that if Crawford were extradited from Massachusetts to Virginia, he would be lynched. In addition, the NAACP strongly doubted that Crawford could receive a fair trial in Leesburg because blacks had never served on juries in Loudon County. The NAACP decided to fight Crawford's extradition from Massachusetts to Virginia and enlisted Charles Houston's help.

Houston turned to the assistant librarian and asked Marshall to perform research and determine whether a federal judge could use a writ of habeas corpus to block Crawford's extradition. Using the research skills that had won him praise from his professors, Marshall prepared a lengthy memorandum titled "Suggestive Memorandum on Possibility of Habeas Corpus Grounded on Violation of Due Process."[35] Houston was impressed by Marshall's research and relied on the memorandum as the case progressed.

NAACP executive secretary Walter White invited Houston to travel to New York to meet with him. From New York, they would then go to Boston to discuss the case with NAACP lawyer R. Butler Wilson. Houston asked Edward P. Lovett, then an associate attorney in Houston's father's law firm, to accompany him to New York. Houston then decided to bring along the third-year law student who had done the legal research—Thurgood Marshall. This would be the first of three road trips that Marshall would take with Houston in the 1920s, each of which would strengthen the bond between the two men. In New York, Marshall so impressed Walter White that the NAACP's press releases about the Crawford case erroneously listed Marshall as one of Crawford's lawyers, even though Marshall was still a law student.

On April 24, 1933, Butler Wilson sent the good news that White and Houston wanted to hear. Federal judge John Lowell had issued an order that blocked Crawford's extradition to Virginia. Lowell held that the grand jury that indicted Crawford in Virginia had been unconstitutionally selected because blacks had been excluded. According to Lowell, because any conviction on that Virginia indictment would ultimately be reversed, sending Crawford back to Virginia served no legitimate purpose.

Lowell's decision was a judicial lightning bolt. The NAACP issued press releases announcing the Crawford victory as a "smashing victory over the South's lily-white jury system."[36] According to the NAACP, the extradition of blacks to the South to face all-white juries and potential lynchings recalled the days of fugitive slave laws, when Southern slave owners would send bounty hunters to the North to capture and return escaped slaves. Judge Lowell's decision, if left standing, meant that federal judges in the North could block the return of black defendants to hostile environments. At this point, Marshall felt that even as a law student, he was already making history.[37]

White Southerners were appalled by Judge Lowell's intervention, calling it an unparalleled assault on state sovereignty. A congressman from Virginia initiated impeachment proceedings against Judge Lowell. Lawyers and legal scholars joined both sides of the debate. Even some scholars sympathetic to civil rights believed that Judge Lowell had over-reached and that the proper remedy was to challenge any conviction first in the state appeals courts and then before the US Supreme Court.

The euphoria of Judge Lowell's supporters was short-lived. Six weeks later, the US Court of Appeals for the First Circuit reversed Judge Lowell's decision.[38] The impeachment proceedings against Judge Lowell were then aborted by his sudden death. In October, the US Supreme Court dealt the final blow to the case by refusing to review the First Circuit's decision.

Virginia police took Crawford to Leesburg, Virginia, to stand trial. After debating whether a well-connected white lawyer should be recruited to help defend Crawford, Walter White and Charles Houston decided the time had come for black lawyers to handle a serious criminal case in the South without the help of white lawyers. Houston was joined on the defense team by Howard Law School professor Leon Andrew Ransom and by two recent Howard graduates, Edward Lovett and J. Byron Hopkins. Marshall would have liked to participate in the Crawford trial, but he was too busy in Baltimore. During the trial in Leesberg, Marshall was in Baltimore supervising a boycott and picketing of white-owned businesses that refused to hire blacks.

Certain Marshall biographers repeat the mistaken belief that Marshall, as a law student, assisted the defense team during the trial in Leesburg, Virginia. The source of this false impression is a paragraph in an autobiography by Walter White. White described "a lanky, brash, young senior law student who was always present. I used to wonder at his assertiveness in challenging positions by Charlie Houston and the other lawyers. But I soon learned of his great value to the cases in doing everything he asked, from research on obscure legal opinions to foraging for coffee and sandwiches."[39]

White's timing was a year off. The Crawford trial occurred in December

1933, six months after Marshall graduated from law school. During the trial, Marshall was in Baltimore, occupied each day with the Buy Where You Can Work campaign, and did not get to Leesburg. Apparently, Marshall's research and assistance in preparing for the federal-court extradition proceedings in Boston months earlier in Massachusetts had made a strong impression on White.

Before the trial in December 1933, Houston learned that Crawford had lied about his alibi and that he had been involved in the crime. When confronted, Crawford changed his story and told Houston that he had only intended to steal from the women. He blamed his accomplice for the shooting. Houston tried without success to get the Virginia trial judge to dismiss the indictment on the grounds that the grand jury selection process had excluded Negroes. The defense team then relied on cross-examining the prosecution's witnesses and challenging the prosecution's arguments. Concerned about suborning perjury, Houston did not call the defendant or any other defense witnesses to testify. Crawford was convicted of double murder. When the judge sentenced Crawford to life imprisonment and did not impose the death penalty, the NAACP celebrated that Crawford's life had been spared. With Crawford's consent, Houston did not appeal, fearing that a new trial would reopen the death penalty threat.[40]

Marshall followed the developments after the trial, as the ILD and the American Communist Party criticized Houston for not allowing Crawford or his alibi witnesses to testify.[41] This would not be the last time that the ILD would criticize Houston or Marshall.

THE ROAD TRIP TO NEW ORLEANS

In June 1933, Marshall was the only law student to be graduated cum laude from Howard University Law School. The commencement ceremony was held outside on a sweltering one-hundred-degree day.[42] Two weeks later, he took Maryland's difficult bar examination, which at the time had a passage rate of less than 50 percent. Marshall then returned to his summer job at Gibson Island while awaiting the bar exam results.

At the end of the summer, while still anxious about whether he had passed the bar examination, Marshall accepted Houston's invitation to accompany him on a trip to the Deep South. Houston's main objective was to document and photograph the stark differences between black and white schools. This was Marshall's second road trip with Houston and the one that impacted him the most. As they traveled by car through several states down to New Orleans, the two men talked. Staying overnight with Houston's friends along the way and eating mostly fruit as they traveled in Houston's car, they spent many hours building the foundation of a relationship that would last until Houston's death in 1950.

Marshall's first journey to the Deep South left him with lasting memories of the region's grinding poverty and the miserable conditions in the black schools. Many of these schools had dirt floors, lacked electricity and plumbing, and had leaky roofs. Even the "worst" school for white children that Marshall saw was not as decrepit as the "best" school for black children. Marshall was appalled at the misery he witnessed, and he long remembered giving an orange to a small boy who did not know that the fruit had to be peeled before being eaten.

As they traveled together, "Dean" and "Marshall" became "Charlie" and "Thurgood." The two men had very different personalities, but they shared important traits—intellectual brilliance, a strong work ethic, a good sense of timing, and an appreciation for thorough research and fact-finding. During this trip, Houston elaborated on his often-repeated conviction that unless black lawyers were "social engineers," they were "parasites." A year later, when Houston was facing some student unrest at the law school, Marshall offered to return to his alma mater and help calm things down. "If you need me to give anybody hell just let me know,"[43] he wrote to Houston.

Soon after returning to Baltimore, Marshall learned that he had passed the Maryland bar examination. On October 11, 1933, he traveled to Annapolis, where he took an oath and signed the "test book" that all new Maryland lawyers sign. He was now Thurgood Marshall, attorney at law.[44] An official certificate for Marshall to hang on his office wall arrived two weeks later.

Chapter 6

A New Lawyer Joins
the Brotherhood

"I have had quite a job getting offices here and have been refused almost every place because of being colored. However, Al Hughes and McGuinn located a place downtown and I went to see the man with them and he is going to rent four rooms together and I will have one of them with the use of the waiting room and the girl. So, if everything turns out all right I will open up about the first of the month," Marshall wrote to Houston in October 1933. He also observed that "it certainly feels funny not being in school and being able to sleep in the mornings."[1]

Marshall set up shop in early November, and the *Afro-American* announced that the young lawyer's practice was now open for business.[2] The article also claimed that Marshall "had one of the highest averages ever attained in the bar association examination." In truth, Marshall had scored slightly above the minimum passing score on the examination, which had less than a 50 percent passing rate overall.

Marshall was the 60th black person to be admitted to the Maryland bar, but only 33 of his predecessors remained active, out of a total of more than 2,700 lawyers in the state.[3] With an average of less than two new black lawyers admitted to the Maryland bar each year, each black lawyer who signed the "test book" at the Maryland Court of Appeals in Annapolis received publicity in the *Afro-American*. Marshall had joined a special brotherhood of black Baltimore lawyers who had been fighting for civil rights for decades.

When Marshall became a lawyer on October 11, 1933, he signed the "Test Book" that all new Maryland lawyers sign. Marshall's signature is the seventh from the top. *Courtesy of Maryland Court of Appeals and Thurgood Marshall family.*

BALTIMORE'S BLACK LAWYERS

One of Charles Houston's first projects as dean of Howard University Law School had been to travel around the country and assess the quantity and quality of black lawyers practicing in the United States. Between November 1927 and January 1928, Houston visited Boston, New York, Philadelphia, Chicago, Toledo, Cleveland, Gary, and Baltimore. In each city, he met with and inquired about the black lawyers practicing there. He acquired additional information by way of mailed questionnaires.

Houston's preliminary report, sent to Dean Roscoe Pound of Harvard Law School, was quite uncomplimentary about most black lawyers around the country, particularly those lawyers who exclusively served black clients. Houston observed that "in general, they tend to regard the profession as a trade for exploitation, and I find a lack of response to civic and racial matters which do not touch their own personal interests." Yet, Houston's nationwide study of African American lawyers recognized that black lawyers in Baltimore had a tradition of activism unlike any other group of lawyers he had seen. He wrote:

> The marked exception to this statement is found in Baltimore. . . . The reason for this exception is probably found in the fact of their attitude towards the profession. Without exception, these men consider the lawyer as a defender of rights and an officer of the court for the protection of the community. There has never been a case of discrimination or oppression brought to the attention of these men that they have not acted on with or without fee. As a result, they have no equal as a class in sober self-respect, quiet confidence, and sense of duty.[4]

Two decades later, another black lawyer, Azzie B. Koger, in a pamphlet about the history of Maryland's black lawyers, would share similarly positive observations. He wrote, "The Negro has come to regard the Negro lawyer as the champion of his rights before the courts and looks constantly to the Negro lawyer to lead, as a sort of legal Moses, to the land of freedom and promise. . . . The Negro lawyer accepts this challenge and very seriously regards the responsibility of leadership in this field. . . . He has proved [his] ideals about temporal values. The Negro lawyer has sought to bring members of our group a fuller view of a finer and richer life."[5]

Marshall was joining a formidable brotherhood with a rich heritage that included Marshall's most compelling role models: Everett Waring, Harry Sythe Cummings, W. Ashbie Hawkins, and Warner T. McGuinn. They had already defined the main priorities of what would be Marshall's civil rights agenda—protecting the franchise, resisting segregation in transportation, pursuing open housing, and fighting for education. They had also demonstrated that the most effective tool in pursuing a civil rights agenda was the Fourteenth Amendment to the US Constitution, which states, "No state shall make or enforce any law which shall abridge the privileges or immunities of citizens of the United States; nor shall any state deprive any person of life, liberty, or property, without due process of law; nor deny to any person within its jurisdiction the equal protection of the laws."

MARYLAND'S FIRST BLACK LAWYER

After the Civil War and the passage of the Fourteenth Amendment with its equal protection clause, a Maryland statute limited the practice of law to white males.[6] In 1877, Charles S. Taylor, a black attorney from Massachusetts, applied for admission to the Maryland bar with the assistance of US Attorney Archibald Stirling Jr. Taylor was admitted to practice before the federal courts in Maryland, but the state courts denied his application, and he appealed to Maryland's highest court. The Maryland Court of Appeals ruled against Taylor, stating that permission to practice law was not a citizenship right protected by the Fourteenth Amendment and that the states had not transferred their right to regulate the practice of law to the federal government.[7] Taylor returned to Massachusetts.

Black Baltimoreans, led by Reverend Harvey Johnson, the pastor of Union Baptist Church, formed the Brotherhood of Liberty in 1884 to fight for the right to serve on juries, the right to practice law, and other rights. They hired a white attorney, Alexander Hobbs, to again challenge the exclusion of blacks from law practice. Charles R. Wilson, another member of the Massachusetts bar who was at the time teaching school in Maryland, applied to practice before the trial court in Baltimore City, then called the Supreme Bench of Baltimore City. On March 19, 1885, the five Baltimore judges ruled that race alone could not prevent Wilson's admission to the bar. Even though Maryland's appeals court had not changed its ruling in the Taylor case, the trial judges surmised that, if presented with the matter, the Court of Appeals would reverse its 1877 ruling in light of an intervening US Supreme Court decision that confirmed the right of blacks to serve on juries.[8] When Wilson was found not qualified for reasons not related to his race, Reverend Johnson traveled to Washington, DC, and recruited a young attorney, Everett James Waring, to relocate to Baltimore. On October 10, 1885, the Supreme Bench of Baltimore City granted the motion of Assistant State's Attorney Edgar H. Gans, admitting Everett Waring as the first African American member of the Maryland bar.[9] The next year, Waring was joined at the bar by Joseph S. Davis, a law graduate of Howard University.[10] A year later, John Prentiss Poe, who had been engaged by the legislature to draft a codification of Maryland statutes, removed the word *white* from the statute governing admission to the Maryland bar.

Everett Waring, born in Springfield, Ohio, on May 22, 1859, was from a prominent black family that included many professionals. According to one account, Waring's family had produced "twenty-five teachers, two preachers, two lawyers, one doctor, an elocutionist, and an artist, beside businessmen, farmers, and contractors."[11] One writer claimed that "no family has contributed more to the general advancement of the colored race."[12]

After editing a newspaper, Everett Waring attended law school at Howard University in Washington, DC, while working for the federal government. After being admitted to the Maryland bar in 1885, Waring immediately joined the fight for civil rights, and his first case was based on the equal protection clause. He challenged the legality of Maryland's "bastardy" law that allowed white women to seek financial support for children born out of wedlock but did not provide black women the same right. Waring represented a black woman against "a colored man who had betrayed her under the promise of marriage." The defendant moved to dismiss the case. The announcement that Waring would appear in court to argue against the dismissal "attracted an unusual throng." Lawyers, ministers, and other citizens packed the courtroom for the first argument in a Maryland court by a black lawyer. As one observer reported, "The courtroom was crowded with spectators, both colored and white, among whom were some of the most prominent lawyers of the city of Baltimore. When Mr. Waring concluded, remarks of congratulations were audible from his brother members of the bar, as to his knowledge of law and the able manner in which he conducted the case."[13]

Everett J. Waring, Maryland's first African American lawyer, was the first black lawyer to argue a case before the US Supreme Court. He challenged unfair treatment of black people by law enforcement officials and courts. *Courtesy of Louise Dorcas.*

Waring put on an impressive show as he argued that the discriminatory law deprived his client of the equal protection of laws. The Supreme Bench, "though expressing regret," dismissed the case and upheld the Maryland law.[14] But the black citizens of Maryland knew that Maryland's black lawyers had begun their journey. A report stated, "The memorable test of the 'Bastardy' Act before the full bench of the Supreme Court of Baltimore City, conducted by a colored lawyer and the first of his race that ever appeared at that bar, will never be forgotten by the colored citizens who were present and who had labored and hoped and look for the opening of the Maryland bar to colored lawyers."[15]

Waring's challenge to the "bastardy" law was the first of many occasions on which African American lawyers in Maryland would challenge state practices on the grounds that the state was denying to its black citizens the equal protection of the law. The inequity of the bastardy law was soon corrected when the word *white* was deleted in the same low-profile codification process that had corrected the lawyer-qualifications statute.

THE NAVASSA ISLAND CASE

Everett Waring also became the first African American attorney to argue a case before the US Supreme Court. The case involved criminal prosecutions of men who had been contract workers on the small island of Navassa, located between Jamaica and Haiti. The US government had since 1857 claimed ownership of the island, which held large deposits of guano—seabird excrement that was much valued as a fertilizer. In 1890, black laborers in Baltimore were recruited by a phosphate company to go to Navassa Island to mine the guano. The company promised them decent working conditions and good wages in a "tropical paradise." The recruiters were aided in their efforts by the fact that many black workers in Baltimore had recently lost their jobs to immigrants from Europe. Between 1870 and 1890, blacks in Baltimore had been forced out of several occupations that they had dominated for decades, particularly ship caulking, brick making, oyster processing, and stevedoring.[16]

Upon arrival on the island of Navassa, the black workers encountered horrendous working conditions, economic exploitation, and slave-like treatment, including imprisonment and beatings. Because the company charged exorbitant prices for food, medical care, bedding, and other necessities, the workers inevitably ended up owing money to the company and were not permitted to leave the island while in debt.

Following particularly cruel treatment of a group of workers by a new manager, the workers revolted. The 11 white supervisors had guns but were no match for 148 workers armed with sticks, machetes, and rocks. In the melee, six of the managers of the Navassa Phosphate Company were killed. Several of the workers were arrested, brought to Baltimore, paraded through the streets in chains to the jail, and charged with murder.[17]

The matter received extensive local and national attention, with sentiment running from condemnation of "the massacre" to sympathy for the exploited defendants. In the black community, there were door-to-door solicitations of funds for the workers' defense. Local leaders, led by Reverend Harvey Johnson and the Brotherhood of Liberty, hired Everett Waring to represent the defendants. John S. Davis and Archibald Stirling joined the defense team.[18]

The trials, divided according to the victims, lasted from November 1889 to February 1890. The defendants gave vivid testimony as to the hardships and brutality they had endured on the island. Three of the men were convicted of murder, fourteen were convicted of manslaughter, and twenty-three were convicted of rioting. The three found guilty of murder were sentenced to death by hanging. Waring appealed, challenging the jurisdiction of the United States over offenses committed on the Caribbean island. John Davis and three white lawyers—John Henry Keene Jr., Archibald Stirling, and J. Edward Stirling—joined the brief, the first brief to be filed in the US Supreme Court by a black lawyer.

Waring's argument before the US Supreme Court was even more dramatically reported than his first appearance in state court on the bastardy law. The *New York Age* proclaimed that "the race made a grand step forward on Wednesday Last. On that day, E. J. Waring Esq, the young and brainy lawyer of Baltimore, made an argument before the United States Supreme Court."[19] A second *New York Age* article further drove home the historical significance:

> On Wednesday of last week, one of the most impressive and significant events in the jurisprudential history of the Republic transpired at Washington . . . when Messers. E. J. Waring, J. Edward Sterling, and J. S. Davis appeared before the Federal Supreme Court as counsel for the defendants in the case of the Navassa rioters. . . .
>
> In 1856 the case of Dred Scott . . . was argued before the Supreme Court by learned counsel, members of the Caucasian race; and in rendering the opinion of the Court, Chief Justice Roger B. Taney laid down as sound law and practice that the Negro has no rights that a white man is bound to respect.
>
> Mark the change. Thirty-four years after the rendering of this monstrous decision . . . Negroes appear before the same Court, full-fledged

lawyers and counselors at law, residents of the erstwhile slave state of Maryland, and argue a question of federal jurisdiction.

The appearance of these Afro-American lawyers before the Supreme Court . . . is an event of National moment and significance, which we cannot permit to pass without notice.[20]

The US Supreme Court affirmed the lower court's decision and established federal jurisdiction over offshore possessions of the United States. Waring and others then persuaded President Benjamin Harrison to commute the death sentences to life in prison.[21] In his statement commuting the sentences, President Harrison stated that the workers had been placed in an aggravated situation and treated like slaves. He also observed that there had been no federal government official on the island to whom the workers could complain.[22]

Waring also bought lawsuits challenging racial discrimination. He sued the owners of the *Mason L. Weams*, a Chesapeake Bay steamer, for attempting to force Reverend Robert McGuinn to eat at a dining room table reserved for blacks. The federal judge, finding that the facilities were "separate but equal," dismissed the lawsuit.[23]

Waring made additional history and received criticism in the black community for agreeing to defend six white men who were prosecuted for assaulting a young black woman. Waring thought that neither white lawyers nor black lawyers should choose their clients on the basis of race.[24] Thurgood Marshall agreed—four decades later, the first significant case that he tried in court was in defense of a white lawyer facing disbarment.[25]

HARRY SYTHE CUMMINGS

Harry Sythe Cummings, the third black lawyer in Maryland, was admitted to the Maryland bar in 1889. After graduating from Lincoln University in 1886, he attended the University of Maryland School of Law and was one of two African Americans to graduate from the University of Maryland before the school shut its doors to blacks. The school remained segregated for almost fifty years until 1935, when Thurgood Marshall brought the lawsuit that desegregated the school and admitted Donald Gaines Murray.[26] The other black University of Maryland graduate was Charles Johnson, who practiced law until his death in 1896.

Harry Sythe Cummings, elected to the Baltimore City Council in 1890, successfully fought attempts to disenfranchise African American voters and seconded the nomination of President Theodore Roosevelt at the 1908 Republican Convention in Chicago. *Courtesy of Louise Dorcas.*

Cummings, a gifted orator,[27] became the first black person to hold elected office in Baltimore,[28] serving on the Baltimore City Council from 1890 to 1892, from 1897 to 1899, and from 1907 to 1919. He became a national leader among black Republicans. At the 1904 National Republican Convention in Chicago, Cummings, at age 38, delivered one of the speeches seconding the nomination of Theodore Roosevelt for president.[29] When a group of Maryland legislators attempted to disenfranchise black voters, Cummings helped lead the opposition.

Cummings considered his most significant contributions to be in education. He authored the ordinance that added kindergarten classes to Baltimore's public schools. He convinced Mayor Ferdinand C. Latrobe and his fellow council members to establish a high school program for black youngsters.[30]

Although initially called the Manual Training School, its mission included training black school teachers. In 1925, Thurgood Marshall graduated from the high school that had developed from Cummings's initiative. Cummings also took advantage of a councilman's prerogative and awarded a scholarship to the first black student to attend the Maryland Institute Art and Design School.[31] Because Baltimore City appropriated funds annually for the college, each member of the city council could select one scholarship recipient. In later years, black students appointed by other council members were denied admission to the college, leading to one of the first attempts in the nation to use litigation to desegregate an educational institution.

Cummings was a voice of resistance when the forces of segregation began passing laws to segregate residential areas of the city. He fought against repeated attempts to disenfranchise black voters and to deny insurance to black homeowners. He argued for the hiring of black teachers and the inclusion of blacks on juries. Cummings lived at 507 Mosher Street, around the corner from where Marshall lived. Cummings served in the city council and remained an influential leader until his death in 1921 at the age of 51. Upon his death, for the first time, the flag over City Hall flew at half-staff in honor of a black man.

W. ASHBIE HAWKINS

William Ashbie Hawkins, another resident of Marshall's neighborhood and Maryland's eleventh black lawyer, became Thurgood Marshall's personal hero.[32] Before turning to the law as a career, Hawkins had been an educator and writer. He was the principal of the largest black school in Baltimore County and president of the state organization of African American school teachers.[33]

In 1889, Hawkins enrolled at the University of Maryland School of Law, riding a horse-drawn trolley between Towson and Baltimore each day to attend classes. John L. Dozier was the other black student at the law school. Elements of the faculty and student body decided that they did not want students of color to attend the institution and petitioned the university leadership to remove them. After one year of attending class, Hawkins and Dozier were expelled from the law school, which remained all white until Marshall's successful case in 1935 on behalf of Donald Gaines Murray.

W. Ashbie Hawkins, expelled from the University of Maryland Law School as it re-segregated in 1891, finished at Howard University and became the first lawyer for the Baltimore NAACP and fought racial discrimination on multiple fronts. Marshall frequently called Hawkins his personal hero. *Courtesy of Louise Dorcas.*

Hawkins completed his legal education at Howard University, became a lawyer in 1893, and immediately became an aggressive opponent of racial segregation and discrimination as legal counsel for the newly formed Baltimore branch of the NAACP. He helped black Republican candidates get into state primary elections, won victories against Jim Crow transportation practices and laws, and argued court cases that overturned several versions of the infamous residential segregation ordinances. He took his battles not just to the courts but also to regulatory bodies such as the state Public Service Commission.

W. Ashbie Hawkins argued more cases before the highest court of

Maryland than any other black lawyer of his time.[34] In an ironic twist of fate, he was cocounsel in one case with John Prentiss Poe, the dean of the University of Maryland School of Law, who had pressed for Hawkins's expulsion from law school six years earlier.[35]

Hawkins authored pamphlets, magazine articles, and letters to the editor. As a lawyer, writer, publisher, and political organizer, Hawkins participated in almost every significant Maryland civil rights matter in the first quarter of the twentieth century. In 1920, concluding that the Republican Party was not adequately rewarding black voters for their loyal support, Hawkins ran as an Independent Republican candidate for the US Senate. He ran a noisy but ultimately doomed campaign that began to cause black voters to reevaluate their ironclad allegiance to "the party of Lincoln."

Protecting black voting rights and voter education became cornerstones of Hawkins's legacy. Hawkins, who was still practicing law when Marshall joined the bar, died in 1941.

WARNER T. McGUINN

Warner T. McGuinn, the sixth black lawyer admitted to the bar in Maryland, graduated from Yale University Law School in 1887, moved to Baltimore in 1890, and became an influential lawyer and political leader.

McGuinn was educated in public schools in Richmond and Baltimore before earning his bachelor's degree in 1884 at Lincoln University. During the summers, he checked hats at the famed Casino in Newport, Rhode Island. Blessed with a nearly perfect memory, supposedly "he could look at 400 men, take their hats, note their faces and the contour of their heads and give each his right hat without making an error."[36]

McGuinn entered Yale University School of Law in 1887. As president of the Kent Law Club, one of his duties was to greet campus visitors coming to address the club. McGuinn met the famed writer Samuel Clemens, better known as Mark Twain, at the New Haven railroad station and escorted him to the dean's house. He later introduced Twain at the public meeting. Twain took a liking to McGuinn and asked the dean about him. Upon learning that McGuinn was working his way through school, Twain offered to pay McGuinn's fees. The dean explained to McGuinn that

Warner T. McGuinn, a distinguished lawyer and political leader, championed the rights of blacks and women. When Marshall became a lawyer, McGuinn shared with him office space, furniture, clients, and knowledge. *Courtesy of Roberta Polk.*

Twain and the dean agreed that they would "like to see what [he] could do if [he] were unhampered."[37] Twain paid McGuinn's fees, freeing McGuinn to spend his last year at Yale without a part-time job. At his graduation, McGuinn received the Townsend Prize for Oration in a contest judged by the chief justice of the US Supreme Court, a US senator, and the president of the New York Central Railroad. McGuinn and Twain remained friends until Twain's death.

From 1890 to 1896, McGuinn served as a commissioner of liquor licenses in Baltimore. McGuinn tried his first case of importance in October 1891. Assisted by Harry Cummings, he won a jury verdict of $500 for a client who had lost three fingers while using a chain saw.[38]

In 1918, he began several terms as an elected member of the Baltimore

City Council. McGuinn was well respected in Baltimore and was an early civil rights pioneer. He served on the Baltimore City Council from 1919 to 1923 and from 1927 to 1931. He was also counsel for the *Afro-American* newspaper and helped organize the Baltimore branch of the NAACP. In 1933, McGuinn was in the twilight of his career as a distinguished lawyer, politician, and political organizer.

PROTECTING THE RIGHT TO VOTE

With the end of Reconstruction and the election of segregationist Democrats, many Southern states adopted measures to disenfranchise black voters. Several states changed their constitutions to prevent blacks from voting, while others employed legislative measures such as poll taxes and literacy tests. These restrictive measures often included a grandfather clause, under which a person did not have to comply with the new voting measures if he or his grandfather could have voted before the Civil War.[39]

Both statutes and constitutional amendments aimed at disenfranchising blacks were attempted in Maryland. However, these efforts proved less successful in Maryland than in other states for three main reasons. First, the state's Republican Party relied heavily upon black voters and fought to preserve suffrage for blacks. Secondly, Maryland contained a growing white population of first- and second-generation European immigrants who feared losing the right to vote because they were not protected by the grandfather clauses. Finally, black leaders, especially the few black lawyers in Maryland, fought against the franchise restrictions before they could become firmly established.

In 1901, the Maryland legislature began to change election laws to make it difficult for black voters to identify the Republican candidates on ballots. Blacks constituted half of the Republicans in Maryland.[40] The elections statute was amended to prohibit the use of party emblems and logos on voting ballots and required that candidates' names be listed in alphabetical order. Lawyers and other black leaders responded by organizing classes in black precincts to teach illiterate voters to recognize the word *Republican*. In 1904, the Maryland legislature modified the election laws to remove all party names from the ballot. This time, lawyers and other black leaders responded by organizing classes to teach voters to recognize the individual names of candidates.

The Maryland Democrats then tried to disenfranchise black voters through state constitutional amendments. Between 1904 and 1911, three separate amendments—named after their respective authors, Poe, Strauss, and Digges—were presented to the voters, and each was rejected.

In May 1910, the leading black lawyers in Baltimore, including Harry Cummings (front center), W. Ashbie Hawkins(second row center), and Warner T. McGuinn (third row, second from right), visited Reverend Harvey Johnson, the pastor of Union Baptist Church, who brought the lawsuit that gave blacks the right to practice law in Maryland. *Courtesy of Louise Dorcas.*

John Prentice Poe, dean of the University of Maryland School of Law, drafted the first amendment in 1905. The amendment would have restricted the right to vote to male citizens who qualified in one of four categories. Three of the categories imposed restrictive requirements, and one of the categories was a grandfather clause granting the right to vote to male descendants of a person who had been entitled to vote as of January 1, 1869. Since the Fifteenth Amendment to the US Constitution, which guaranteed all male citizens the right to vote, had not been passed until 1870, the measure would have effectively disenfranchised blacks. The measure was rejected in 1905, partly due to solid opposition from black voters and white immigrants.

The second proposed amendment was drafted in 1908, the year of Marshall's birth. In an effort to reduce opposition from immigrants, Maryland attorney general Isaac Loeb Strauss drafted an amendment that would have added a special exception for certain foreign-born citizens or male descendants of citizens naturalized after 1869. Despite this attempt to split the two biggest blocks opposed to disenfranchisement, blacks and immigrants, voters rejected the Strauss Amendment in 1909.

The third proposed amendment was sponsored in 1911 by Walter M. Digges, a member of the Maryland House of Delegates. The amendment expressly guaranteed voting privileges for all of the state's white citizens of legal age and residency but required all others to hold property valued at least $500. The provision was defeated by blacks and white Republicans.

In addition to mobilizing local opposition to each of these disenfranchisement attempts, Harry Cummings enlisted the support of the national black leader Booker T. Washington and of the Catholic Church.[41] Cummings was joined in these efforts by other black lawyers such as W. Ashbie Hawkins, Cornelius Fitzgerald, and William McCard. McGuinn joined the fight to protect the voting rights of blacks and also supported early efforts to extend the franchise to women.

Thurgood Marshall began law practice in a law office headed by Warner T. McGuinn. As Marshall's career unfolded, he never lost sight of the primacy of the franchise, as identified by his predecessors, Cummings, McGuinn, and Hawkins. Soon after Marshall arrived at the NAACP headquarters in 1936, he began working on voting rights cases. His second argument before the US Supreme Court challenged the Texas Democratic Party's all-white primary election and established the right of black voters to participate in political-party primary elections.[42]

THE FIGHT FOR EQUAL HOUSING

Baltimore's black citizens confronted severe restrictions regarding where they could obtain housing. At the beginning of the Civil War, Baltimore had the largest free black population of any city in the United States. That population was scattered throughout the city but was largely relegated to alley housing, except in one concentrated area near the harbor in east Baltimore and another one near the railroads in south Baltimore. As the city grew, an even larger black community grew around "Old West Baltimore," to the immediate northwest of downtown. Blacks expanded into areas occupied mainly by first- and second-generation European immigrants. By the time that Marshall was born, many whites had become alarmed by the growth of the black population and had begun to pressure their political leaders to do something about "the Negro invasion."

In 1911, the Baltimore City Council began passing ordinances making it a crime for blacks to move into white neighborhoods. George W. West, a white council member, pushed through the first such law when George W. F. McMechen, a black lawyer, moved his family into a house on McCulloch Street, which was still an all-white street. McMechen, the first person to graduate from the newly renamed Morgan College (formerly Centenary Biblical Institute), was an alumnus of Yale University Law School. The West Law made it a crime for a black person to move to a majority-white block, and vice versa. Harry Cummings resisted passage of the West Law in the City Council. Attorneys W. Ashbie Hawkins and Warner T. McGuinn successfully challenged in court two versions of the ordinance on technical, nonconstitutional grounds.[43] The state appellate court ultimately upheld a third version of the law in 1913.[44]

The following year, lawmakers amended the ordinance to prohibit the establishment of black churches and other social institutions for blacks in majority-white blocks. Hawkins and McGuinn challenged this third ordinance on the grounds that it violated the Fourteenth Amendment's equal protection clause. When the trial court ruled against them, Hawkins and McGuinn immediately appealed. But the Maryland Court of Appeals delayed issuing a ruling because the US Supreme Court had agreed to hear *Buchanan v. Warley*,[45] a Louisville, Kentucky, case challenging a similar law that made it a criminal offense for blacks to move into a white neighborhood. Hawkins filed in the Supreme Court an amicus curiae brief on behalf of the NAACP. In *Buchanan*, the Supreme Court ruled that it was unconstitutional to use criminal laws to enforce racial segregation in housing, rendering the Baltimore ordinances moot.

After *Buchanan v. Warley*, those seeking to exclude blacks from neighborhoods turned to other tactics. Real estate agencies refused to show blacks houses in white neighborhoods. Violence was sometimes used. Owners placed racially restrictive covenants in property deeds. As Marshall grew up in Baltimore, much of the city was off limits to African Americans because courts enforced, through injunction, covenants that excluded "Negroes and persons of Negro extraction."[46]

Marshall saw firsthand the harmful effects that housing discrimination had on black populations. During the late 1910s through the 1930s, the black population of Baltimore grew dramatically, with families arriving mainly from rural Maryland. Many migrants came for the jobs created during World War I and for the attractions of urban life during the Roaring Twenties. Despite rapid growth in numbers, by 1930, Baltimore's black population did not occupy a significantly greater portion of the city's area than it had in 1915. Overcrowding, already a serious problem, became significantly worse during this period and led to a dramatic increase in the incidence of communicable diseases.[47]

Fighting housing discrimination became another agenda item that Marshall carried with him to New York from Baltimore. In 1948, Marshall argued *Shelly v. Kraemer*, in which the US Supreme Court held that the Fourteenth Amendment prohibits courts from enforcing racially restrictive covenants in property deeds.[48]

FIGHTING DISCRIMINATION ON PUBLIC TRANSPORTATION

Laws requiring racial discrimination in public transportation became a matter of particular concern to Maryland's early black lawyers because they saw these laws as steps backward.[49] Although racial discrimination existed, there were no laws in Maryland requiring segregation on trains, steamboats, or street cars. In 1904, four years before Marshall was born, things began to change. The Maryland General Assembly passed its first Jim Crow law and required racial segregation on passenger trains. The law imposed steep fines on rail companies, their employees, and customers who did not comply. Additional Jim Crow laws were passed in 1908. One new law required steamship companies to provide separate toilet and sleeping quarters for black and white passengers. Another statute required railroads to provide separate cars—not just separate compartments—for the two races.[50] A third statute required segregation on all electric streetcars, except those in Baltimore City.

Black Marylanders, led by religious leaders and lawyers, rallied against these new laws with boycotts, petitions, and speeches. Hawkins and McGuinn lobbied the legislature to repeal the laws, and other black lawyers such as Cornelius Fitzgerald and William McCard organized community boycotts.

Black lawyers repeatedly assembled evidence that separate public accommodations for blacks were always of inferior quality to those for whites. Hawkins filed complaints with the Maryland Public Service Commission, citing substandard dining and sleeping accommodations for blacks on railroads and steamboats.[51] He also filed complaints with the federal Interstate Commerce Commission.[52] Hawkins defended a passenger on the Washington, Baltimore & Annapolis Electric Railroad who had refused to sit in an area designated for colored passengers.[53] These cases did not end the racial segregation, but they did lead to improvements in conditions for black travelers.

Fighting racial discrimination against travelers became a third agenda item that Marshall took up from the black Maryland lawyers who came before him. Like Hawkins, Marshall would work to dismantle public transportation segregation laws, and, ultimately, he would argue before the US Supreme Court two major cases involving transportation discrimination. Almost a decade before the famous Rosa Parks incident in Alabama, a black woman named Irene Morgan, who was traveling on a bus between Virginia and Maryland, was arrested when the bus stopped at a station in Virginia and she refused to relinquish her seat to a white person who had just boarded, as required by Virginia law. Accepting Marshall's argument based on federal statutes regulating interstate commerce, the US Supreme Court held that segregating travelers on buses traveling between states interfered with the free flow of interstate commerce.[54]

Marshall also argued before the Supreme Court a case involving discrimination in a privately owned restaurant attached to a bus station. In *Boynton v. Virginia*, a Howard University student traveling home for Christmas refused to stay in the colored section of a restaurant at the Richmond, Virginia, bus terminal. The Supreme Court reversed the defendant's trespass conviction and outlawed racial segregation in any facility that is "an integral part" of interstate transportation, including waiting rooms and station restaurants.[55] W. Ashbie Hawkins would have been proud of the Baltimore lawyer he had inspired.

SECURING EDUCATION FOR YOUNG PEOPLE

Thurgood Marshall's most celebrated legal victory, the 1954 Supreme Court decision in *Brown v. Board of Education*, declared public school segregation unconstitutional. But the struggle that culminated in the Court's landmark decision in *Brown* actually began much earlier. In 1897, W. Ashbie Hawkins filed what may have been the first school desegregation lawsuit in the nation. The Maryland Institute Art and Design School, which at the time placed primary emphasis on mechanical drawing, was a private institution. In exchange for an annual appropriation from the Baltimore City government, each member of the city council could award one scholarship to the school. When the college refused to admit a black student designated by a black council member, Hawkins sued, again relying on the equal protection clause of the Fourteenth Amendment. Hawkins lost the case, but principles he advanced about the Fourteenth Amendment's applicability to private institutions that receive government funds would later become law.[56]

The quest for equality in educational opportunity that his predecessors had started would occupy much of Marshall's career as a lawyer. Before challenging segregated public education directly, Marshall fought some very important preliminary battles. In 1936, he filed the first of many lawsuits that challenged the discriminatory practices under which black public school teachers were paid lower salaries than white teachers with comparable credentials and experience.

Even on the issue of teacher pay, Warner T. McGuinn and W. Ashbie

Hawkins had set the stage a decade earlier. In 1925, McGuinn and Hawkins brought a lawsuit challenging unequal teacher pay in the Baltimore City schools. Their lawsuit was dismissed, but it brought attention to the disparities and prompted Baltimore City officials to equalize the salaries of the city's black and white schoolteachers. Teacher pay discrimination in the twenty-three Maryland counties outside of Baltimore City and throughout the South became the first item on Marshall's agenda when he relocated to New York in 1936.[57] Marshall's efforts to bring about equal educational opportunity would continue up to and beyond *Brown v. Board of Education.*

BLACK LAWYERS AS LEADERS

In addition to handling legal matters and civil rights work, black lawyers in Baltimore were also community leaders. Almost every one of the black lawyers who welcomed Marshall to the Baltimore bar held multiple leadership positions. Black lawyers served on the boards of organizations, advised community groups, served as trustees and stewards of churches, coordinated charitable drives, led fraternal organizations, and were active in politics. Cummings and McGuin became national leaders among black Republicans. W. Ashbie Hawkins was the supreme chancellor of the Knights of Pythias, a national fraternal organization, and his law partner, George W. F. McMechen, was the national president of the Improved Benevolent and Protective Order of Elks of the World. Waring and Cummings had also been prominent Elks.

STARTING OUT DURING THE GREAT DEPRESSION

Thurgood Marshall joined the brotherhood of black lawyers in the early years of the Great Depression. Four years earlier, on October 24, 1929—known as Black Thursday—thirteen million shares were traded on the New York Stock Exchange as prices dropped more than they had ever done before in a single day. A general economic turn down was beginning just as Marshall entered law school in 1930. The Depression, which had deepened through his three years at Howard University, had taken a firm hold of the nation by the time Marshall began to set up his law practice.

Baltimore mayor Howard Jackson (left) and Maryland governor Albert Ritchie (right) were states' rights Democrats who opposed and delayed implementing in Maryland President Roosevelt's New Deal programs. *Courtesy of Maryland State Archives.*

Depression bread lines in Baltimore in 1931. *Courtesy of Afro-American Newspaper Archives and Research Center.*

Baltimore was hit particularly hard by the Great Depression, and the city's recovery was slowed by politics. In the 1920s, economic growth in Baltimore had been aided by low wages and low unionization. Baltimore officials publicized Baltimore's compliant workers as they sought to encourage new businesses to open in the city and existing businesses to relocate there. But the Great Depression dramatically slowed down Baltimore's industries. By 1930, street-corner apple sellers were a frequent sight downtown. By 1931, thousands of Baltimoreans obtained their only meal of the day on bread lines, as one out of every eight Baltimore workers was unemployed.

Maryland and Baltimore were governed by chief executives who were reluctant to step in and lend a hand. Maryland's governor, Albert Ritchie, and Baltimore's mayor, Howard Jackson, preferred to rely on private volunteerism, instead of direct government assistance, to address the problems of the unemployed. But soon private agencies were overwhelmed by the number of people who lacked a job and needed help.

Both the governor and the mayor lacked enthusiasm for Roosevelt's New Deal programs. Ritchie, who had lost the 1932 Democratic presidential primary to Roosevelt, did not like the growth of the federal government he was witnessing and openly opposed the National Recovery Act. Howard M. Jackson, who took office as Baltimore's mayor in 1931, shared Ritchie's belief that citizens' problems should be dealt with through private resources and not through governmental intervention. Both men were suspicious of federal programs—particularly if there was any requirement for local matching funds—and moved very slowly in applying for and receiving federal New Deal relief.

Consequently, the state and the city received far less than their fare shares from the National Recovery Administration, the Civil Works Administration, the Public Works Administration, the Civilian Conservation Corps, and the Works Progress Administration. Maryland and Baltimore received very few loans to individual homeowners from the Home Owners' Loan Corporation.

Maryland did not create its Department of Public Welfare until after Ritchie left office in 1935. The failure of the New Deal to reach more Marylanders prolonged and intensified individual suffering. Only states in the Deep South provided less direct assistance to their unemployed citizens than did Maryland.

1838 Druid Hill Avenue
Baltimore Maryland
October 19, 1933.

Dear Dean:

One of the lawyers over here named Bob McGuinn,
a nephew of old man McGuinn,has a case which will necessiate
the use of a writ of Habeas Corpus. He called me this
evening and asked me about the Crawford case. We made
several copies of the material while working on the case
and I thought you might have some of those copies. If not,
could you send me your copy and I will take care of it.
I as yet do not know the facts in the case but he says the
Crawford case will help.

It certainly feels funny not being in school and
being able to sleep in the mornings. I was admitted to the
Court of Appeals last week and will be admitted to the Supreme
Bench of Baltimore City the first Saturday in November. I
have had quite a job getting offices here and have been refused
almost every place because of being colored. However, Al
Hughes and McGuinn located a place down town and I went to
see the man with them and he is going to rent four rooms
together and I will have one of them with the use of the
waiting room and the girl. So, if everything turns out
all right I will open up about the first of the month.

Too bad the Crawford case was lost. Who will
defend him in Va.? Every one over here right now is talking about the lynching last night. Something will come out
of it for two reasons. One is that one State Trooper is
still unconscious and the other is that Judge Duer is a
Republican and Ritchie is a Democrat; Ritchie has placed
the blame on Duer and he will in turn tell something about
Ritchie.

See you soon

Thurgood

Marshall described to his law school dean, Charles Houston, the start of his law practice. *Courtesy of Thurgood Marshall Papers, Manuscript Division, Library of Congress, Washington, DC.*

Thoroughout the South and in Maryland, blacks bore the heaviest burden of the Depression. Until the 1920s, when Marshall went to high school, the black population in Baltimore had remained less than 10 percent of the total population. But during the decade between 1920 and 1930, the black population of the city rose dramatically faster than the white population. By 1930, African Americans comprised almost 20 percent of the city's population.

They came seeking jobs, but their employment situation remained tenuous. All but a handful of blacks were casual laborers or domestic servants. Blacks were systematically excluded from public employment. There were no black librarians, police officers, firefighters, or health inspectors. Schoolteachers were the only black, professional public employees.

During the Depression, many blacks who had obtained jobs during World War I and its aftermath became unemployed, as white business owners laid off black employees. As unemployment grew in Baltimore, black employees were displaced by whites even in menial occupations that had for decades been almost exclusively held by blacks, including jobs as domestic servants. By 1931, the black unemployment rate in Baltimore was double that of whites. A lawyer, particularly a black lawyer, starting a law practice in Baltimore in October 1933 faced formidable challenges.[58]

Black Baltimoreans had difficulty obtaining relief from private or governmental sources. Black workers were systematically excluded from relief programs, and, when relief rolls were cut, black families were usually the first to be removed. In 1934, the city finally opened an office of the Baltimore Emergency Relief Commission at Druid Avenue and Lafayette Avenue, five blocks from Thurgood Marshall's house. Even then, there were persistent charges that the agency was unfair in its treatment of blacks.[59]

Although the official national policy was against racial discrimination in the recovery program, these programs were administered by state and local officials, and there was widespread discrimination. Other interest groups such as labor unions, businesses, and farmers were far better organized than blacks to apply pressure to the Roosevelt administration and the New Deal administrators.

Of the four major New Deal programs, only the Public Works Administration (PWA) was fairly administered. The Agricultural Adjustment Administration actually reduced the number of blacks working in agriculture by a third. The Civilian Conservation Corps (CCC) was highly discriminatory. The National Recovery Administration was downright hostile to blacks. The PWA, however, under Harold Ickes, tried to be equitable. The second most successful program in reaching blacks in all Maryland was probably the CCC camps. There were ultimately thirty CCC camps in Maryland. All of them were racially segregated, and Maryland never did fill its CCC quota.[60]

THE PHOENIX BUILDING

Marshall agreed to share a suite of offices with two black lawyers—Warner T. McGuinn, known as the "dean" of black lawyers, and William Alfred Carroll Hughes Jr., one of the most recently admitted black lawyers and the son of a prominent Methodist bishop. After graduating from Lincoln University and Boston College Law School, Hughes was admitted to the Maryland bar in 1931. The next black lawyer to be admitted would be Thurgood Marshall.

McGuinn, Hughes, and Marshall leased the sixth floor of the Phoenix Building at 4 East Redwood Street in downtown Baltimore. No black lawyer had previously rented office space below Fayette Street in Baltimore's central business district. The major cluster of black lawyers was located four blocks north at 14 East Pleasant Street, a building purchased in 1914 by a group of black lawyers and renamed the Banneker Building. It has been continuously occupied by black lawyers ever since.[61]

Marshall and his officemates were able to move into the Phoenix Building because it was owned by Adolph Ginsberg, one of the few white commercial landlords in the city who was willing to rent office space to blacks.[62] Ginsberg purchased the Phoenix Building in 1925. Marshall and his two colleagues rented a suite of four large, mahogany-clad offices on the top floor of the building. The Phoenix Building also housed a printers' union, an advertising company, a publishing company, Ginsberg's real estate office, and a small restaurant.[63]

Next to the Phoenix Building towered a gigantic monument to failure, the Baltimore Trust Company Building. Right before the stock market crash of 1929, Baltimore Trust Company had completed its ornate office building, which was the tallest in the South and fashioned in the extravagant Art Deco style of Manhattan skyscrapers. The Baltimore Trust Company never reopened following President Roosevelt's March 1933 bank holiday. The twenty-seven-story building stood almost entirely vacant in October 1933 and remained mostly vacant until 1940. The dormant skyscraper next to the Phoenix Building stood as a reminder to young Marshall that failure was very possible since he was opening his law business during the most prolonged financial downturn in American history.

PHONES { OFFICE: CALVERT 6246
Residence: LAfayette 3675

THURGOOD MARSHALL
ATTORNEY & COUNSELLOR AT LAW

601 - 604 PHOENIX BUILDING

4 E. Redwood Street

BALTIMORE   MARYLAND

Marshall and two other lawyers rented the top (sixth) floor of the Phoenix Building, next to the vacant twenty-six floors of the bankrupt Baltimore Trust Company. *Courtesy of Baltimore Museum of Industry.*

Chapter 7

Buy Where You Can Work

Before the picketing was started, the girls in the Opportunity Makers Club asked me what should be done and what they could do and could not do. I told them first of all it would be necessary to get the police regulations. I went down to Commissioner Gaither and laid out the entire plan before him; told him the purpose of the picketing; told him when it was supposed to be held, when it was to start. He wanted to know what stores were in the movement. I told him. He wanted to know who the owner of the store was and what precinct it was in. I told him all of those facts, and he told me it would be perfectly all right.[1]

This was Marshall's testimony about his meeting on the fourth floor of Baltimore Police Headquarters, at which he told Police Commissioner Charles D. Gaither about plans to picket three stores on Pennsylvania Avenue that refused to hire black salespeople.

Gaither, an ex–brigadier general in the Maryland National Guard, had been Baltimore's chief of police for over a decade. He assured Marshall that the planned protests would not pose a problem. Even at this early stage in his career, the young lawyer recognized that diplomacy and respect went a long way when dealing with powerful people. His preference for direct negotiations with government and law enforcement officials would also become a hallmark of his career.

SHOPPING WHILE BLACK

The Buy Where You Can Work campaign captivated Baltimore's black community in December 1933, two months after Marshall became a lawyer.[2] As the mild Baltimore fall turned into a frigid winter, Marshall embarked upon his first community-organizing campaign. Baltimore's weather was nothing new to the young attorney; he had been born and raised in a city known for its hot and humid summers and often brutal winters.

The corner of Lafayette and Argyle Avenues was at the heart of Old West Baltimore. The steeple of Bethel A.M.E. Church can be seen in the background. Blacks and whites lived in this ethnically diverse neighborhood that included many first- and second-generation European immigrants. *Courtesy of Maryland Historical Trust.*

Retail shopping was often a humiliating experience for blacks in Baltimore. African Americans met with contempt when they tried to shop for clothing downtown. Many of the smaller shops barred blacks completely, and the big department stores would not allow them to try on garments. A black customer who wanted to purchase shoes would draw the outline of his or her foot on a brown paper bag and present it to the clerk, who would determine the shoe size. Receipts issued to black customers were marked "final sale," which meant that the merchandise could not be returned to the store.

An area of the city where African Americans could shop with some measure of dignity was Pennsylvania Avenue. "The Avenue," as it was affectionately called, was the business, commercial, and entertainment district of Old West Baltimore. At its center was the Douglass Theater, later named the Royal Theater. It was one of the great concert venues on the East Coast, rivaling the legendary Apollo Theater in Harlem. Many of the nation's most successful black entertainers—including Dinah Washington, Billy Eckstein, Nat King Cole, and Billie Holliday—regularly dazzled Pennsylvania Avenue audiences.

Despite the Avenue's bright lights and mesmerizing nightlife, the fabled thoroughfare was not immune to the dark scourge of racial discrimination. Although African Americans could shop on Pennsylvania Avenue for clothes and food without being treated like lepers, they could not work as sales clerks in many of the stores where they spent their money. Black Baltimoreans decided to take a stand against this discriminatory practice by organizing a boycott.

"JUST A LONG-LEGGED DREAMER WITH LOTS OF GALL"

Like Marshall, Kiowa Costonie was a man of contrasts. As *Afro-American* journalist Ralph Matthews described him, Costonie was idealistic but practical; he could sway an audience but was easily deceived. He gave sound marital advice but could not keep his own marriage together.[3] He claimed to hate charlatans but profited from selling "blessed handkerchiefs." To Matthews, Costonie was "just a long-legged dreamer with lots of gall."[4] A colorful character through and through, Costonie was the activist who launched the Buy Where You Can Work campaign.

Kiowa Costonie, originally from Utah, was orphaned before the age of four. He had escaped from several abusive foster homes and been on his own since his teens. In his early twenties, he made it to vaudeville, where he adopted the stage name "Tony Green." He then began to make a name for himself as a charismatic faith healer. A suave, handsome, and well-dressed man who sometimes wore a turban, Costonie delivered lectures to all-female crowds about how best to preserve a marriage. Costonie came to Baltimore from Washington, DC, where he had married a beautiful young socialite.[5] They divorced four years later.[6]

Like many other religious leaders, Costonie sought to improve the economic and social status of his followers. In October 1933, following a brief voter-registration campaign, he spearheaded Baltimore's Buy Where You Can Work campaign. Costonie initially approached two women's organizations in Old West Baltimore for help. Vivian Marshall, Thurgood's wife, was the president of the Opportunity Makers Club, a group of educated young women that sought to assist its members in finding employment and starting small businesses. Elvira Bond, the wife of legendary divorce lawyer Roy S. Bond, headed the Housewives' League, a group of older women who sought to promote their husbands' professions and businesses.[7]

In cooperation with these two groups and a few other leaders such as Lillie Jackson, Costonie lobbied two of Baltimore's largest grocery store chains—American Sanitary Company (ASCO) and the Great Atlantic and Pacific Tea Company (A&P)—to hire black employees or face a boycott by black customers. He told the companies' managers that sixty thousand people would begin a boycott of stores that had mostly black customers but refused to hire black sales clerks. ASCO almost immediately agreed to hire twenty-two black men. After three days of boycotting and picketing, A&P gave in to Costonie's demands and hired nine full-time and twelve part-time black clerks.[8]

Activists had already used the Buy Where You Can Work concept in the 1920s and 1930s in Chicago, Detroit, Cleveland, Toledo, New York, and Washington, DC, with varying degrees of success. After the relatively easy victory he enjoyed in negotiating with ASCO and A&P to give jobs to colored workers, Costonie decided to bring the campaign to Old West Baltimore's main commercial strip, Pennsylvania Avenue.[9] Businesses there, which were locally owned and not part of national chains, resisted.

In November 1933, Marshall began to keep a tin box containing index cards bearing the names of his clients. Costonie became Marshall's first documented client, as Marshall placed into the file box a card with the words "Kiowa Costonie Personal Attorney" and Costonie's telephone number.

From that point on, Marshall played a prominent role in the Buy Where You Can Work effort. He joined the citizens' committee that Costonie formed to support the campaign, attended organizing meetings, and provided legal advice. He threatened to sue a merchant for $50,000 for allegedly defaming Costonie. When demonstrations replaced negotiations, Marshall handled the arrangements with police and then personally supervised the picketing. Marshall's wife, Vivian, and her Opportunity Makers Club furnished many of the picketers. The boycott became a real family affair, with Marshall's father periodically dropping by to check on the picket line.

THE CITY-WIDE YOUNG PEOPLE'S FORUM

Costonie recruited a third group to participate in the Buy Where You Can Work campaign. For three years, the City-Wide Young People's Forum (CWYPF, known informally as "the Forum") had been educating and motivating Baltimore's black community under the leadership of Lillie Mae Carroll Jackson and her daughters, Virginia and Juanita.

Lillie Mae Carroll was born in Baltimore on May 25, 1889, to a family that traced its roots back to Charles Carroll of Carrollton, one of the signers of the Declaration of Independence.[10] Her father, Charles Henry Carroll, was an educator; and his wife, Amanda Bowen Carroll, ran a boarding house in Baltimore. Lillie Mae met her husband, Keiffer Jackson, when he was a guest at her mother's boarding house. Jackson, a Methodist evangelist, was touring the United States, showing religious movies. The couple married in 1910, and they traveled across the country together. During their travels, they had three daughters and a son. Eventually, the family returned to Baltimore and settled on Druid Hill Avenue, a few blocks from Thurgood Marshall's family.[11] Lillie Jackson then joined the almost moribund Baltimore branch of the NAACP.

The couple resolved to provide their children with a quality education. All the children, and especially Virginia and Juanita, excelled in school. After college in Pennsylvania, Juanita and Virginia returned to Baltimore and established the City-Wide Young People's Forum. The Forum was an instant success. On Friday evenings from October through April, the Forum drew crowds of thousands to local black churches to hear speakers from around the country.

Beginning in 1931, Marshall and his wife regularly attended the Friday night programs of the City Young People's Forum at which speakers addressed political, social, and religious issues. In February 1936, Marshall addressed the Forum about the nationally famous Scottsboro case. *Courtesy of* Afro-American *Newspaper Archives and Research Center and Clarence and Juanita Mitchell family.*

JANUARY 3, 1936—"The Thesis of Municipal Government"—Mr. George Sellmayer, President City Council; Bethel A. M. E. Church, Druid Hill Avenue and Lanvale St.

JAN. 10th—"Can Ethiopia Win?"—Rev. Paul Schilling; Enon Baptist Church, Park Avenue near Dolphin St.; Rev. A. J. Payne, pastor.

JAN. 17th—"What is Man's Worst Enemy?"—Dr. George Crabbe, President Anti-Saloon League; Fountain Baptist Church, E. Madison St., near Gay, Rev. Mr. White, pastor.

JAN. 24th—"Is the Negro Too Religious?"—Dr. Selby V. McCasland, Professor of Religion at Goucher College; John Wesley M. E. Church Sharp and Montgomery Sts., Rev. W. H. Dean, pastor.

JAN. 31st—"How I Escaped from the Georgia Chain-Gang"—Angelo Herndon, Cosmopolitan Community Church, Madison and Lafayette Avenues; Rev. Frederick Douglas, pastor.

FEBRUARY 7th—"The Scottsboro Case"—Attorney Thurgood Marshall, Counsel for the Baltimore Branch of the N. A. A. C. P.; Clarence M. Mitchell of the Afro-American; Bethel A. M. E. Church.

FEB. 14th—"The Police Department of Our City"—Secretary George Brennan of the Police Department; Sharp St. M. E Church, Dolphin and Etting Sts., Rev. R. F. Coates. pastor.

FEB. 21st—"Interracial Youth Conference"—St. Mark's Lutheran Church, 22nd and St. Paul Streets.

FEB. 28th—"Does the Church Have Youth Appeal?"—Dr. Ross W. Sanderson, Executive Secretary, Baltimore Federation of Churches and William B. Dorsey, Vice President City-Wide Young People's Forum; Whatcoat M. E. Church; Rev. T. J. Tildou ,pastor.

MARCH 6th—"Ethiopia Fights for Justice"—John W. Shaw, Consul General of Ethiopia, New York City; Bethel A. M. E. Church.

The list of speakers included progressive leaders and intellectuals such as author Zora Neale Hurston; poet Sterling Brown; congressman Oscar De Priest; future congressman Adam Clayton Powell; and NAACP leaders Walter White, Mary White Ovington, and W. E. B. DuBois. These distinguished guests discussed race relations, the Great Depression, African American literature and music, criminal justice, religion, and politics. Occasionally, there were debates between speakers who held opposing views. Thurgood and Vivian Marshall regularly attended the Forum's Friday-evening events, beginning when he was in law school and continuing until they moved to New York at the end of 1936.

While the Forum presented several artistic and musical programs, it focused mainly on political and social issues. The Euel Lee murder case had erupted the same month as the Forum's founding, and the lynching of Matthew Williams on the Eastern Shore occurred just two months later. The harsh reality of racist violence called for activism in the black community. As early as 1932, while Marshall was still in law school, the Forum lobbied for the repeal of Jim Crow laws that had been enacted around the time Marshall was born. These laws required racial segregation on trains and steamboats. In 1933, the Forum added to its mission statement a new objective, "To open up avenues and create opportunities of employment for efficient, qualified young people."[12]

Costonie contacted the leaders of the Forum and the leader of the Opportunity Makers Club, Vivian Marshall. He asked that each group help him implement the Buy Where You Can Work campaign. Since the objectives of the campaign coincided with the Forum's new mission, the Forum agreed to support Costonie's boycott of businesses that refused to employ blacks and suspended its regularly scheduled Friday-evening program so that members could join the picket line.[13]

THEY TAKE TO THE STREETS

After the initial quick successes with the two grocery store chains, the Buy Where You Can Work campaign's primary targets became the Tommy Tucker variety store and two women's clothing shops, all located on the 1700 block of Pennsylvania Avenue. Unlike the grocery chains, these stores were locally owned. Costonie, Lillie Mae Jackson, and Elvira Bond negotiated with the owners in the hope that they would agree to hire some black clerks as the city's grocery store chains had done. The negotiations failed when the store owners, Aaron and Robert Samuelson, refused to yield. Costonie's flamboyant style had not made a favorable impression on the Samuelsons, who argued that blacks were free to open their own businesses but should not dictate how whites ran theirs.

Marshall's first client, Kiowa Costonie, led the Buy Where You Can Work campaign to boycott stores that refused to hire black sales employees. *Courtesy of* Afro-American *Newspaper Archives and Research Center.*

Marshall (second from right) negotiated with the police and personally supervised the boycott demonstrations. *Courtesy of Afro-American Newspaper Archives and Research Center.*

On the morning of Friday, December 8, 1933, the picketing began on the 1700 block of Pennsylvania Avenue, according to the plan that Marshall had presented to the police chief. Marshall stood watch at the picket lines, kept in touch with the supervising police officers, and made sure the picketers followed the rules. Marshall was, as he would later testify, "in charge" and present "practically all the time."[14]

The Buy Where You Can Work campaign picketed the stores in four three-hour shifts between 9:00 a.m. and 9:00 p.m. for twelve days. The picketers organized themselves on Pitcher Street, around the corner from the 1700 block of Pennsylvania Avenue. They obtained signs at that corner and, when not on the picket line, huddled together in cars to keep warm during some very cold early-winter days. The picketers followed Marshall's picketing protocols. They did not impede the store entrances or talk to prospective customers, and they kept moving.

The first few days, the demonstration proceeded smoothly and effectively. Marshall's meeting with the police commissioner had paved the way so effectively that one police officer was disciplined by his superiors for being "discourteous" to the picketers.[15] However, Marshall was surprised when the police officers insisted that each demonstrator walk a route that covered the entire block between Laurens Street to Wilson Street, even though they were targeting only three of the ten or eleven stores on the block. Nonetheless, Marshall firmly insisted that anyone who did not follow the instructions had to leave the picket line.[16]

After the first few days, conditions at the demonstration began to deteriorate. Counterdemonstrators supporting the store owners appeared, and the police officers had to keep them away from the picketers. One man was arrested and accused of intimidating store customers. Norma Marshall was jostled by a counterdemonstrator and was followed home in a threatening manner.[17] The signs that Marshall had approved demanded some black employment, but a group of older demonstrators showed up with unauthorized picket signs that demanded the stores hire only black employees.[18] Marshall suspected that these interlopers had been sent by a leftist group. At a meeting of the Opportunity Makers Club and other supporters of the picketing, Marshall, speaking on behalf of Costonie, had to dispel rumors that downtown white merchants were planning a wholesale firing of black employees in retaliation for the demonstrations.[19]

MR. SAMUELSON GOES TO COURT

The picketing led to a dramatic drop in sales at all the businesses on the block.[20] On December 20, the picketing came to an abrupt halt. Aaron Samuelson and other merchants on the 1700 block of Pennsylvania Avenue went to court, and Chief Judge Samuel K. Dennis issued a temporary injunction against the picketing. Police Commissioner Gaither announced that he interpreted the injunction as requiring the arrest of any person carrying out any type of boycott activities directed at the stores on the 1700 block of Pennsylvania Avenue. The injunction ended the picketing and effectively ended the campaign, even though Walter White came down from New York and urged the picketers to continue.[21]

Five months later, the trial for a permanent injunction began. Marshall's officemates, Warner T. McGuinn and William A. C. Hughes, represented the picketers in court.[22] During the hearing, the merchants attempted to portray the picketers as raucous and disorderly. They complained that picketers had blocked customers attempting to enter their stores. They even alleged that some of the demonstrators were drinking whiskey while they picketed.

Taking the stand as a witness, Marshall gave formal and respectful responses to questions from McGuinn. Marshall testified that he was present throughout the picketing and that the demonstrators were quite orderly.

"Now, were any of these pickets stationed in any of the entrances of these stores?" McGuinn asked Marshall.

"Not one. They had strict orders not to stop: if they stopped they had to get off the avenue. That is what they were told when they went out there," Marshall said.

"They kept moving?" McGuinn asked.

"Yes sir," Marshall replied.

"During the time that you observed this entire picketing did you observe any of the picketers, authorized picketers pull anybody from the stores?" McGuinn asked.

"No, never," Marshall said.

"Did you see any of the authorized pickets attempt to discuss or argue with people—prospective customers entering any of the stores?" McGuinn questioned Marshall.

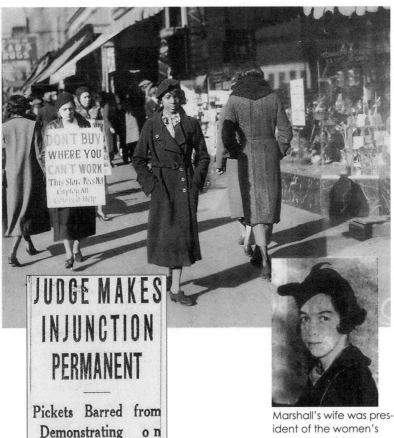

JUDGE MAKES INJUNCTION PERMANENT

Pickets Barred from Demonstrating on Pennsylvania Ave.

SAYS GAITHER WAS MISLED

Should Have Jailed All Marchers.

Marshall's wife was president of the women's group that did most of the picketing and dramatically reduced sales at the targeted stores. *Courtesy of* Afro-American *Newspaper Archives and Research Center.*

A judge issued an injunction against the picketing and surmised that Marshall had misled the police commissioner as to the purpose of the picketing. *Courtesy of* Afro-American *Newspaper Archives and Research Center.*

"No, they did not. That is the reason I was up there—because they were told not to say anything to anybody, if they talked they had to stop and go home," Marshall replied.

"During that period did you observe any arguments between the picketers and any of the customers or anybody else on the streets?" McGuinn asked.

"No, sir," Marshall replied.

Marshall described his meeting with the police commissioner and the picket-line rules they had agreed upon. Marshall testified that he had personally supervised the picketing and enforced those rules. There was no stopping, no talking, and no making threats. Marshall and other defense witnesses testified that the merchants had hired counterdemonstrators who tried to disrupt the picketing. Both sides testified as to the economic effectiveness of the demonstrations, with the merchants claiming that their sales had dropped by 60 percent during the picketing.[23]

In rendering a decision to make the injunction permanent, Judge Albert S. J. Owens gave no consequential weight to Marshall's testimony. He said that he believed that the picketers had been loud and threatening, had intimidated and accosted customers, and had improperly interfered with the plaintiffs' businesses. As to Marshall's conversation with the police commissioner, Judge Owens seemed unable to accept that this young lawyer had obtained the police commissioner's approval in good-faith negotiations. Owens surmised that the police commissioner must have been misled. "There is some testimony that they consulted General Gaither, the Police Commissioner, and he informed them that they were within their legal rights and sent policemen to protect them," Owens stated in his hearing summary. "I am sure that the movement was never properly explained to General Gaither and he came to the conclusion that it was a labor dispute, which, of course, it was not, and if he had known the facts he would have caused the arrest of every one of the marchers on the charge of disorderly conduct, if not upon more serious charges."[24]

Judge Owens issued a permanent injunction against any further Buy Where You Can Work demonstrations in the 1700 block of Pennsylvania Avenue and scolded the leaders of the campaign, describing their actions as improper and most likely criminal.[25] After a frenzied fundraising effort led by Lillie Jackson, the campaign raised enough money to appeal. McGuinn and Hughes handled the appeal before Maryland's highest court, which affirmed Judge Owens's order.[26]

ON THE OFFENSE AT LAST

The short-lived Buy Where You Can Work campaign changed the mind-set of black Baltimore. The *Afro-American* recognized the campaign's clout and suggested that if such activism could deprive two boycotted stores of 60 percent of their business in a few days, surely African Americans in Baltimore could win more jobs in stores if they organized again.[27]

The Buy Where You Can Work campaign became a milestone and a turning point in political activism for Baltimore's black community. For the first time, the community undertook a proactive protest. Until then, the community had always reacted from a defensive posture to events that affected it, such as the attempts to disenfranchise black voters in the early 1900s, the restrictive housing ordinances, and incidents of police brutality. The Buy Where You Can Work campaign was different. This time, the black community struck first, and Thurgood Marshall led the charge. Marshall's cousin Charles Burns believed that the campaign had a lasting effect on Marshall. Burns said, "Thurgood walked that line from early in the morning to dark. I think that's when he really got charged up in the area of civil rights. That's the first time I knew where he got physically or actively involved."[28]

Despite his passion for just causes, Marshall could not financially sustain such time-consuming activism. He had not earned a penny for the long hours he spent working on the boycott campaign. Thurgood Marshall needed to turn his attention to starting a profitable law practice.

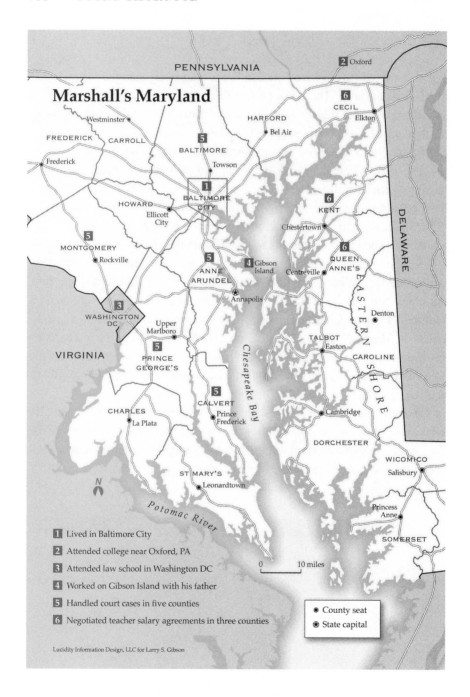

Marshall's Maryland

PENNSYLVANIA

2 Oxford

6 CECIL

Elkton

Westminster

HARFORD

Bel Air

FREDERICK   CARROLL

5 BALTIMORE

Frederick

Towson

1 BALTIMORE CITY

DELAWARE

HOWARD

6 KENT

Ellicott City

Chestertown

5 MONTGOMERY

Rockville

5 ANNE ARUNDEL

4 Gibson Island

6 QUEEN ANNE'S

Centreville

Annapolis

3 WASHINGTON DC

Upper Marlboro

Denton

VIRGINIA

PRINCE GEORGE'S

TALBOT

Easton

CAROLINE

E A S T E R N   S H O R E

Chesapeake Bay

5 CALVERT

Prince Frederick

Cambridge

CHARLES

La Plata

DORCHESTER

WICOMICO

Salisbury

N

ST MARY'S

Leonardtown

Potomac River

Princess Anne

SOMERSET

1 Lived in Baltimore City

2 Attended college near Oxford, PA

3 Attended law school in Washington DC

0   10 miles

4 Worked on Gibson Island with his father

5 Handled court cases in five counties

6 Negotiated teacher salary agreements in three counties

● County seat

✳ State capital

Lucidity Information Design, LLC for Larry S. Gibson

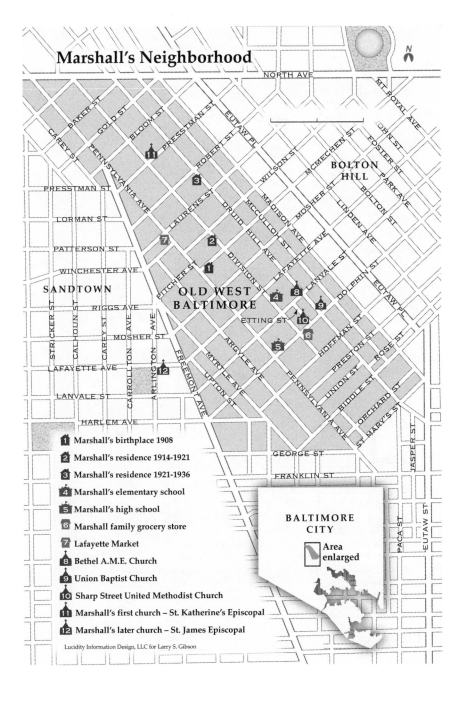

Marshall's Neighborhood

1 Marshall's birthplace 1908
2 Marshall's residence 1914-1921
3 Marshall's residence 1921-1936
4 Marshall's elementary school
5 Marshall's high school
6 Marshall family grocery store
7 Lafayette Market
8 Bethel A.M.E. Church
9 Union Baptist Church
10 Sharp Street United Methodist Church
11 Marshall's first church – St. Katherine's Episcopal
12 Marshall's later church – St. James Episcopal

Lucidity Information Design, LLC for Larry S. Gibson

Marshall's Baltimore

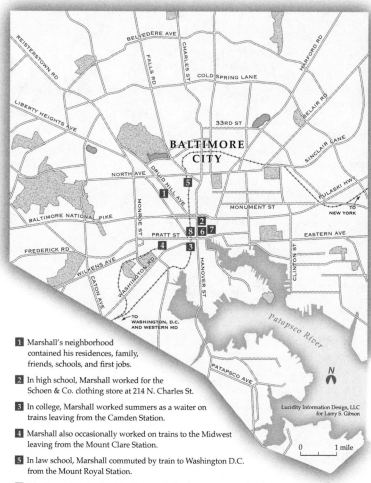

Lucidity Information Design, LLC
for Larry S. Gibson

0   1 mile

1 Marshall's neighborhood
   contained his residences, family,
   friends, schools, and first jobs.

2 In high school, Marshall worked for the
   Schoen & Co. clothing store at 214 N. Charles St.

3 In college, Marshall worked summers as a waiter on
   trains leaving from the Camden Station.

4 Marshall also occasionally worked on trains to the Midwest
   leaving from the Mount Clare Station.

5 In law school, Marshall commuted by train to Washington D.C.
   from the Mount Royal Station.

6 After becoming a lawyer, Marshall established his law office in the Phoenix Building at
   4 E. Redwood St.

7 Beginning in 1933, Marshall represented clients at the Baltimore City Courthouse.

8 In 1935, Marshall sued the University of Maryland Law School, forcing it to admit black students.

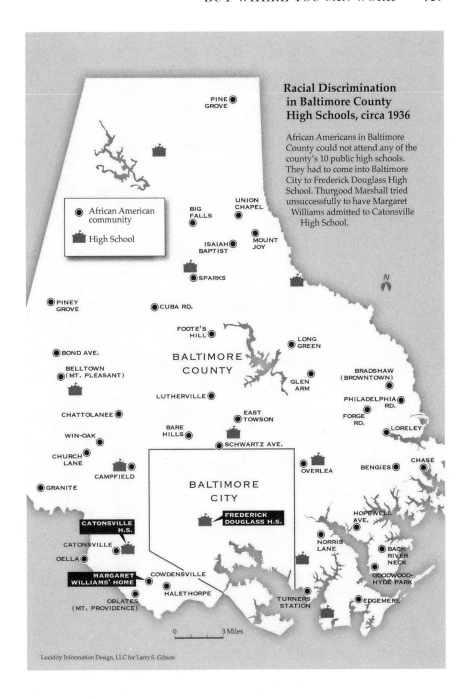

Racial Discrimination in Baltimore County High Schools, circa 1936

African Americans in Baltimore County could not attend any of the county's 10 public high schools. They had to come into Baltimore City to Frederick Douglass High School. Thurgood Marshall tried unsuccessfully to have Margaret Williams admitted to Catonsville High School.

● African American community

🏫 High School

PINE GROVE

UNION CHAPEL

BIG FALLS

MOUNT JOY

ISAIAH BAPTIST

SPARKS

PINEY GROVE

CUBA RD.

FOOTE'S HILL

LONG GREEN

BALTIMORE COUNTY

BOND AVE.

BELLTOWN (MT. PLEASANT)

GLEN ARM

BRADSHAW (BROWNTOWN)

PHILADELPHIA RD.

LUTHERVILLE

FORGE RD.

CHATTOLANEE

EAST TOWSON

LORELEY

WIN-OAK

BARE HILLS

CHURCH LANE

SCHWARTZ AVE.

CAMPFIELD

CHASE

GRANITE

BALTIMORE CITY

OVERLEA

BENGIES

FREDERICK DOUGLASS H.S.

HOPEWELL AVE.

CATONSVILLE H.S.

CATONSVILLE

NORRIS LANE

BACK RIVER NECK

OELLA

MARGARET WILLIAMS' HOME

COWDENSVILLE

GOODWOOD-HYDE PARK

HALETHORPE

OBLATES (MT. PROVIDENCE)

TURNERS STATION

EDGEMERE

N

0   3 Miles

Lucidity Information Design, LLC for Larry S. Gibson

Chapter 8

Black and White
and Red All Over

"**M**r. Ades is on trial for incidents that occurred while he was concerned with the defense of Negro litigants, which means that colored people should automatically be on his side," Thurgood Marshall was quoted as saying in the *Afro-American* on February 3, 1934. Marshall's thoughts on Ades appeared in the newspaper's column "The Inquiring Reporter" in response to the question, "Do you believe that our leaders should become actively interested in the fight to disbar Bernard Ades?"[1] Three months earlier, Marshall's high school mentor and debate coach, Gough McDaniels, had made a similar appeal for the black community to support Bernard Ades "for the great work that Ades has done." McDaniels condemned the exclusion of Ades from a meeting held at a black church to protest the lynching of George Armwood."[2]

Bernard Ades was the irrepressible lawyer for the Maryland chapter of the International Labor Defense (ILD), the legal arm of the American Communist Party. The ILD provided defense counsel in several of the high-profile, racially charged court cases of the time. In Maryland, Ades represented Euel Lee, who was accused of killing four members of a white family near Ocean City, Maryland, in October 1931.

Ades, while representing Lee, had succeeded in establishing some new legal rights for black Marylanders. After an initial refusal of the local court to change the venue of the trial from the lower Eastern Shore, Ades convinced the Maryland Court of Appeals that Lee could not get a fair trial on the Eastern Shore. Realizing that any conviction on the Eastern

171

Shore would be overturned by Maryland's highest court, the Circuit Court of Somerset County sent the case for trial in Towson, the county seat of Baltimore County. In Towson, Lee was convicted by a jury and sentenced to hang.[3] Ades again went to the Court of Appeals, complaining that the Baltimore County trial judge, Frank Duncan, had violated Lee's right to a fair trial by excluding blacks from the jury. Judge Duncan admitted that, although blacks were on the court's list of eligible jurors, during his twenty-three years on the bench, he had selected for jury service only white men. The Court of Appeals reversed Lee's convictions and ordered that he be given a new trial by a jury for which blacks were eligible.[4]

Unfortunately for Lee, the new trial resulted in another conviction and death sentence. Ades again appealed, on the grounds that, although the jury pool had included three blacks, the prosecutors had used their three peremptory challenges to exclude all the blacks from the jury.[5] This time, however, the appellate court refused to reverse Lee's conviction and death sentence. Lee was hanged in the Maryland Penitentiary, ten days after George Armwood was lynched and less than a month after Thurgood Marshall became a lawyer.[6]

Ades was not just irrepressible, he was also dogged in defense of his clients and a very able attorney. However, Ades's conduct and statements offended many lawyers and judges, particularly when he called Lee's conviction and death sentence a "legal lynching."[7] William Caldwell Coleman, a federal judge from the Eastern Shore of Maryland, decided to teach Ades a lesson.

A FEDERAL JUDGE ATTACKS

During a proceeding on behalf of Euel Lee, Coleman summarily suspended Ades from practicing law before the federal court in Maryland and appointed two distinguished members of the bar to prosecute and permanently disbar him.[8] Judge Coleman called Ades's motivations into question and accused Ades of injecting himself into the Lee case and other cases not to assist the accused but to exploit their unfortunate situations to further the cause of the ILD and the Communist Party. Ades was also accused of intimidating and threatening a witness for the prosecution in the Lee case, an elderly black woman named Martha Miller. Perhaps the most disturbing charge against Ades was that he had persuaded Euel Lee to sign a document that purported to give Ades custody of Lee's body after he was executed. Coleman charged that Ades had not informed Lee that he planned to take the body to Harlem for a rally and incite the black community to action by casting Lee as a martyr.

The petition filed by the court-appointed prosecutors also charged Ades with meddling in two other capital cases, one on the state's Eastern Shore and the other in southern Maryland. He was accused of attempting to insert himself into the matter of George Davis, who was charged with rape in Kent County. By all accounts, Davis was satisfied with the work of the defense lawyer assigned to him, and he rejected Ades.[9] Ades also allegedly tried to press his way into the case of a man named Page Jupiter, who was accused of murder in July 1933 in Charles County. Finally, Ades was accused of publishing false statements in the press, ravaging the state for racist treatment of blacks in the justice system.[10]

Thurgood Marshall joined the Ades defense team, believing that "colored people should automatically be on his side."[11] Marshall's principles, and not his need for money, propelled him into this next battle, which came right after the time-consuming Buy Where You Can Work campaign. Like his adventure with Kiowa Costonie, Marshall's work in defense of Ades would offer no relief to Marshall's desolate bank account; he worked pro bono. The Ades case would thrust Marshall into the public eye, a place where he would thrive for many years. But, of most immediate importance to Marshall, he would again be working with Charles Houston.

SCOTTSBORO

Observers were surprised when Ades sought legal representation from Charles Houston, in light of the very public disagreements that had occurred between the ILD and the NAACP over the role of black lawyers in some high-profile cases. "The selection of Mr. Houston came as a surprise, because Mr. Houston is one of the chief attorneys for the NAACP, and the feeling between this organization and the ILD has not been the best since the Scottsboro case disagreement," noted the *Afro-American*.[12]

By early 1934, the Scottsboro Boys saga had dominated the black press for almost three years and was still going strong. In the 1930s, as the Great Depression gnawed at America, thousands of people hopped on freight trains and traveled across the country in search of a better life. In March 1931, nine black youths hopped on one of those freight trains at various locations along the Southern Railroad line. They, too, yearned for the elusive American dream of abundance, so on that day, they cast their lot with others headed from Chattanooga to Memphis, Tennessee. Haywood Patterson, 18; Eugene Williams, 13; and brothers Roy and Andy Wright, ages 12 and 19, respectively; wanted to find work hauling logs on the Missouri River. The other five youths—Clarence Norris, 19; Ozzie Powell, 16; Charlie Weems, 19; Willie Roberson, 17; and Olen Montgomery, 17— from different parts of Georgia did not know each other.

There were not just black youths on board the train. There were white riders, too, creating an integrated gang of hobos all looking for brighter days. Yet, back home where they hailed from, chances are they would have never been in such close proximity to each other for any length of time.

Tensions between the blacks and the whites soon turned into violence. A fight was sparked when one of the white boys allegedly stepped on Haywood Patterson's hand. As the train traveled, the black youths and the white youths slung insults, stones, and fists back and forth, with the whites getting the worst of it and the black boys tossing several of the white boys from the slow-moving train near Stephenson, Alabama.

The white youths who had been ejected from the train made their way back to Stephenson and reported the fight to the stationmaster, telling him they wanted to press charges. The incident was reported to the Jackson County sheriff, Matt Wann, who called one of his deputies who lived near the train's next scheduled stop in the town of Paint Rock, Alabama. The deputy, Charlie Latham, was instructed to deputize as many white men as he needed to "capture every Negro on the train."

Latham soon rounded up about fifty men armed with shotguns. They stormed the train and arrested nine black youths at gunpoint and charged them originally with assault and attempted murder of the whites they had thrown from the train in Stephenson. Also, to the surprise of the deputized Paint Rock mob, there were two young white women dressed as males hoboing aboard the freight train. At that point, the fate of the nine black youths hauled in for fighting turned onto a decidedly more perilous path. The two white females, Ruby Bates and Victoria Price, both from Huntsville, Alabama, accused several of the black youths of raping them, a capital offense in the South from Alabama to Maryland.

The nine youths, who had been hauled twenty miles from Paint Rock to the town of Scottsboro, Alabama, were held in a two-story jailhouse. Word quickly spread through Scottsboro that two white women had been raped by a gang of black men, and a lynch mob of hundreds soon formed in front of the jailhouse in search of swift, vigilante justice.

On March 26, 1931, the youths were taken by armed guard from Scottsboro to Gadsden, Alabama, for "safekeeping." By March 31, 1931, the so-called Scottsboro Boys were indicted by an all-white Jackson County grand jury, and they were arraigned later that day.

From the time they were jailed in Scottsboro until their arraignment, these mostly illiterate young men had not consulted with an attorney, family members, or each other. On April 6, 1931, two of the Scottsboro Boys, Charlie Weems and Clarence Norris, were sentenced to death. Within a couple of days, all of the youths—except for the youngest, Roy Wright— were handed death sentences.

News of the Scottsboro Boys case roared across black America like wildfire, and over the next several years, the different phases and machina- tions of the controversial case dominated the headlines of the black press. At an early stage of the Scottsboro matter, it appeared that NAACP lawyers would represent the Scottsboro defendants. Soon, however, the NAACP found itself in competition with the ILD to represent the Scottsboro Boys. The NAACP charged the ILD with exploiting the case to further the Communist Party's cause, while the ILD argued that the NAACP was too conservative and accommodating in its advocacy. Ultimately, all of the defendants chose to accept the legal counsel supplied by the ILD. In response to accusations that they were intending to martyr the defendants, the ILD recruited nationally prominent attorneys—first, constitutional lawyer Walter Pollak, who had successfully argued the first appeal before the Supreme Court; and then Samuel Leibowitz, one of the nation's most highly regarded criminal defense lawyers, who represented the Scottsboro Boys during the subsequent retrials.[13]

Providing the lawyers in the most publicized racial case the century had seen thus far remained a source of pride for the Communists and a source of irritation for black lawyers and the NAACP. The case proceeded through several trials and appeals, and by early 1934, the Scottsboro defendants were in the middle of a series of new trials ordered by the US Supreme Court.[14]

As the Scottsboro cases proceeded, the NAACP, Charles Houston, other black lawyers, and the black press remained ambivalent about how to react to the ILD's efforts in defense of the Scottsboro Boys.[15] Notwithstanding the clashes between the NAACP and the ILD at the national level, there was substantial cooperation between the two groups in Baltimore. As the *Afro-American* reported, "By unanimous vote of its executive committee, the Baltimore branch of the National Association for the Advancement of Colored People instructed its attorney, W. A. C. Hughes, Jr., to render what assistance possible in the fights being made by the International Labor Defense to equalize white and colored teachers' salaries, to repeal the Jim Crow law and to pass an Equal Rights measure."[16]

The George Crawford case, in which Thurgood Marshall had become involved while still in law school, provided an opening for Charles Houston and other black lawyers to take on a high-profile criminal case in the South. Houston recognized the potential and seized it. "The men feel if Crawford could be defended by all Negro counsel it would mark a turning point in the legal history of the Negro in this country," Houston wrote in a letter to Walter White, the secretary of the NAACP, on October 17, 1933.[17] The ILD would later criticize Houston's defense efforts and charge that Crawford, who received a life sentence instead of the death penalty, had been "sold out." In light of this friction between the two organizations, Houston and Marshall were not surprised when the ILD failed to show gratitude for their defense of Ades.

COUNSEL OF RECORD

When Ades asked Houston for assistance, Houston was defending George Crawford in Leesburg, Virginia. Houston agreed to help Ades as soon as he finished the Crawford case.[18] In the meantime, Houston asked his former student, Thurgood Marshall, to begin working on the Ades matter. He suggested that Marshall become admitted to practice before the US District Court in Maryland, on which Judge Coleman sat.

The ILD and the American Civil Liberties Union (ACLU) made sure the Ades case received national attention.[19] With much of the local and national legal community watching, twenty-three-year-old Thurgood Marshall went to work. He got admitted to the federal bar, as Houston had suggested, and began to serve as a liaison between the Ades defense team, the judge, and the prosecuting lawyers. "Motion filed in due form. Not necessary to file memorandum of authorities. Clerk could not set date for hearing. I went to see Judge Coleman and had a short conference with him," wrote Marshall to Houston on January 8, 1934.[20]

Marshall quickly learned the ropes under Houston's guidance. At one point, he had to obtain access to the transcripts of the court proceeding at which Judge Coleman had originally suspended Ades. Believing that the judge had the transcripts on file in his chambers, Marshall asked Houston for help, writing, "There are transcripts of both the habeas corpus proceedings. If you send me a letter to Judge Samuel K. Dennis asking him to allow us to use them I think they will help out. . . . I do not know whether or not he will let us have them, but he might do so. He is Chief Judge of the Supreme Bench of Baltimore City."[21]

However, Houston decided that it was time for him to step back. He seized on this opportunity to encourage Marshall to build his own relationship with Chief Judge Dennis. "You do not have to wait on me," Houston replied to Marshall. "As counsel of record, make your own contacts with Judge Dennis and go right ahead. This is better for you, because it gives you an opportunity to become acquainted with the Baltimore judges."[22]

Marshall followed Houston's advice and embraced his role as counsel of record. He convinced the lead opposing counsel, Craig McLanahan, who was an experienced attorney, a brigadier general in the Maryland National Guard, and a future judge on the Supreme Bench of Baltimore City, to obtain the transcripts Marshall needed. "McLanahan will get the transcripts for both the Euel Lee mandamus case and the George Davis habeas corpus case," Marshall reported to Houston. "He will let us have them within a week. He will also let us have a list of the newspaper articles he intends to rely upon within a week."[23] Marshall was learning that developing a working relationship with opposing counsel reduced tension and helped the case move along smoothly. Such relationships became a trademark of Marshall's career.

One week later, on February 20, Marshall provided Houston with an outline of the discussions he'd had with the prosecuting attorney:

I was just talking to McLanahan, and the result of the conversation is as follows:

    1. They will press all of the charges set out in the rule to show cause.

    2. He will let us have the transcript by Thursday.

    3. Will send itemized statement as to newspaper articles tomorrow. The main contention will be around the same matter as in the State Bar Association, to wit: the Page Jupiter case.

    4. He is going to get statements from Judge Stein, who heard the Page Jupiter case, and Judge Frank, who heard the Euel Lee and George Davis cases, and Judge Bailey from Eastern Shore.

    5. He asked me whether it would be agreeable to have these statements in lieu of their presence in the trial. I told him that I understood your position in the matter was that you wanted the Eastern Shore gentlemen present.[24]

As Marshall learned to use diplomacy to deal with the prosecution, he was pestered with suggestions from his client, Ades, who had his own views about how to best prepare the defense.[25] Always wanting to "push the envelope," Ades kept suggesting motions and strategies that both Marshall and Houston thought would be counterproductive.

Even as Marshall grew more empowered in his role, neither he nor Houston were lulled into complacency by the cordial relationship they had developed with the prosecution. Judge William Coleman was known to be tough on lawyers, particularly black lawyers. In 1928, he had suspended George Pendleton, a prominent black attorney in Baltimore, for filing a claim that Coleman thought had been inadequately investigated.[26]

At one point during the Ades proceedings, Judge Coleman engaged in a cat-and-mouse game with Houston in an apparent attempt to lure the attorney into contempt of court. The defense team wanted to see the court reporter's original notes of the hearing at which Judge Coleman had suspended Ades. They wanted to verify everything that had been said at that proceeding because they believed that Coleman had no valid basis for suspending Ades. Houston suspected that the official transcripts submitted by the court reporter were not complete. Under the headline, "Ades Papers Were Tampered With, Says Houston," the *Afro American* reported the dispute:

Charles H. Houston, one of the attorneys for Bernard Ades, filed in United States District Court, a petition charging that the original records

Charles Houston (left) and Marshall (right) represented Bernard Ades (center), a white attorney who faced disbarment in federal court. *Courtesy of Afro-American Newspaper Archives and Research Center.*

ADES' LAWYERS PRESENTED HERE

Admission to the local jurisdiction of the Federal Court was granted for the defense counsels of Bernard Ades by Judge W. Calvin Chesnut at the opening of the court session Thursday.

Thurgood Marshall, James G. Tyson, Leon A. Ransom, and Edward P. Lovette were those presented by Josiah F. Henry, Jr.

All of them with the exception of Mr. Marshall are natives of Washington, D.C. Dean Charles H. Houston, of the Howard University Law School, will also be associated with the case, but is at present in Chicago, Ill. Mr. Ades faces disbarment proceedings instigated by Judge William C. Coleman.

in the case had been tampered with and changed. . . . As the AFRO went to press, Mr. Houston, after making an attempt to force Judge Coleman to make available documents which would prove his charge, was preparing to ask the Court of Appeals now sitting here to reverse the entire proceedings. Judge Coleman held that certain documents in the case were private. Houston will also point out the illegality of Judge Coleman's sitting as judge in a case which he himself initiated. A hot court tilt is in progress as this is written.[27]

Houston's actual motion and argument were more oblique and respectful than the press report indicated. Nevertheless, Marshall watched as Judge Coleman repeatedly tried to lure Houston into explicitly accusing court officials of impropriety. Houston remained measured but very persistent in his remarks and insisted that he had a right to see the court reporter's original notes.[28] Judge Coleman pretended not to understand Houston's point. Houston repeated his position clearly while avoiding the judge's traps. He got the inspection he requested and was not held in contempt. The verbal sparring between Houston and Judge Coleman provided a valuable learning experience for Marshall. Marshall learned that a lawyer could prove his point and have his request granted by the judge as long as he acted firmly. "Lose your head, and lose your case," Houston would often tell Marshall.

Aware that Houston and Marshall wanted Coleman to recuse himself from the case, Judge Coleman told Marshall that if he pressed for the recusal, Coleman would have Marshall arrested for contempt of court. Just in case, Marshall borrowed bail money from *Afro-American* publisher Carl Murphy, which Marshall then kept in his pocket during appearances before Coleman.

JUDGE SOPER INTERVENES

Houston and Marshall resolved to get the case away from Judge Coleman, who wished to act as judge, jury, and executioner. With few places to turn, Houston and Marshall went to see Morris A. Soper, a sympathetic, liberal judge on the US Court of Appeals for the Fourth Circuit, who had served with Coleman as a US District Court judge before his appointment to the appellate court. Houston and Marshall wanted Soper to take the case away from Coleman and preside over it himself. Soper was reluctant at first. He said that the procedural rules did not allow an appellate judge to displace a lower-court judge. Fortunately, for reasons never expressed, Soper changed his mind and took over the case.[29] Despite this positive development, Houston still doubted that they would succeed and referred to the upcoming trial before Soper as Ades's "funeral."[30]

With Soper as the new judge, preparation for the Ades trial consumed practically all of Thurgood Marshall's time and attention. Back at Howard University, where Houston was still the "vice dean" of the law school, his involvement with a Communist lawyer raised questions within the administration. Houston responded to an inquiry from Howard University president Mordecai Johnson concerning his work on the Ades case with an explanation of why defending Ades was important to the struggle for civil rights. "I respect him," Houston wrote, "and stand by him when he is being persecuted in his professional status for his efforts on behalf of full Negro citizenship and equal protection of the law." Houston also pointed out that Marshall was doing most of the work on the Ades case.[31]

The trial before Judge Soper began in February 1934 and continued for a week, with Houston and Marshall taking turns examining witnesses. This was Marshall's professional debut and his first significant trial as a lawyer. A virtual "Who's Who" of black Baltimore came out to show their support for the defense of Bernard Ades. Every day, the courtroom audience included prominent lawyers, clergymen, and community leaders. Marshall's father also attended.[32]

During the five-day trial, Houston and Marshall struggled to keep the evidence and arguments focused on Ades's alleged misconduct rather than on his Communist sympathies. They argued that Ades had done what a lawyer must do to protect clients in hostile environments. They portrayed Ades as an idealistic lawyer for unpopular clients who needed aggressive and courageous advocacy. At the trial, Ades rejected the opportunity to retract his most incendiary statement about the Maryland justice system— his labeling of the Euel Lee case as a "legal lynching." Ades testified, "While I realize that I might aid my case by changing my statement, I cannot do it. In criticizing the officials of the court, I had a sense of my duty as a member of the bar and an officer of the court, but, as a citizen, I also had a right to an opinion and to express it."[33]

Large Crowd in Court During Ades's Trial

Clergymen and Lawyers and Laity Display Keen Interest in Proceedings

The courtroom was crowded at all four sessions of the disbarment trial of Bernard Ades in the United States District Court, Wednesday and Thursday.

A large delegation of clergymen appeared at the afternoon session Thursday following a meeting of the Interdenominational Ministerial Alliance. The ministers displayed keen interest in the proceedings. Among those seen throughout the courtroom were the Reverends Ernest Lyon, J. T. Colbert, C. H. Matthews, W. H. Young, A. J. Payne, George A. Crawley B. G. Dawson, C. C. Ferguson, D. E. Rice.

Among the attorneys were F. Everett Lane, W. A. C. Hughes, Jr., George W. F. McMechen, Linwood Koger, A. B. Koger, Gregory Hawkins, George Pendleton, Peter Woodbury and C. C. Fitzgerald.

Others seen in the courtroom were:

Dr. and Mrs. Howard Young, Dr. and Mrs. Edward Wheatley, Mr. and Mrs. Robert Young, Dr. and Mrs. Joseph Thomas, Dr. Louise Young.

Mrs. Fannie Howard, Josiah Diggs, Willard W. Allen, Robert Coleman, Mrs. Ruth Shipley, Mrs. W A. C. Hughes, Jr., Dr. and Mrs. H. S. McCard, Mrs. Addie Fowler; Mrs. Grace McCard, William Marshall, Dr. and Mrs. Albert Blumberg, white, of Johns Hopkins and Mr. Ades's brother.

ADES PAINTED AS IDEALIST AS TRIAL CLOSES

Mr. Houston Urges Reprimand of All Officials for Acts.

'ATTACK ON REDS HALTED BY JUDGE

Motives of Organization Not His Concern.

BALTIMORE—

A two-and-a-half-hour argument, in which Bernard Ades was painted as an idealist and a reformer ahead of his time, by Charles H. Houston, chief defense counsel, brought to a dramatic close the disbarment proceedings against the former, in the United States District Court, Monday.

Judge Morris Soper reserved his decision as the hands of the clock

Judge Morris Soper presided at the federal hearing, at which Marshall and Houston argued that Ades was a well-intended, forceful advocate for unpopular clients. *Courtesy of Afro-American Newspaper Archives and Research Center.*

BERNARD ADES IS REPRIMANDED BY COURT

Judge Soper Lifts Suspension, Gives Attorney Warning.

ONLY TWO OF 8 CHARGES PROVED

Service in Getting Colored Jurors, Noted.

BALTIMORE.—After two weeks' consideration, during which time the disbarment case against Bernard Ades was held under advisement by Judge Morris Soper, the jurist rendered a decision Monday morning reprimanding the attorney and lifting his suspension, which has been in force since October, 1933.

Brought Eight Charges

Eight charges were filed against Mr. Ades, and prosecuted vigorously by J. Craig McLanahan and Eli Frank, Jr., appointed by the bar association. Only two of the charges were regarded by Judge Soper as having been sustained.

Mr. Ades and his counsel, Charles H. Houston of Howard University, and Thurgood Marshall, local attorney, were summoned to the bench, where Judge Soper read the reprimand. The legal opinion, contained in a forty-page document, was filed for publication but was not read.

Not Disbarred

BERNARD ADES, militant I.L.D. attorney, whose disbarment trial ended with a public reprimand by Judge Morris Soper in the U.S. District Court Monday. At the conclusion of the trial Mr. Ades refused to make a statement other than to say that he would read all his statements "over twice" in future.

Judge Soper did not disbar Ades, but instead issued a reprimand, the mildest form of discipline. *Courtesy of Afro-American Newspaper Archives and Research Center and Maryland State Archives.*

Believing that he and Ades had agreed on his closing point, Houston conceded to Judge Soper that some of Ades's conduct might merit a mild reprimand but certainly did not justify Ades's disbarment or suspension from the practice of law.

Soper did not immediately announce his decision, and Houston and Marshall anxiously awaited the judge's ruling for two weeks. "Every time the telephone rings or I see the mailman, I have a sinking feeling in my stomach because I am afraid that it is word from Judge Soper that Ades is going bye-bye. Please wire me as soon as the decision is handed down," Houston wrote to Marshall.[34]

Their concerns were unfounded. On March 19, 1934, Judge Soper released his decision. He found Ades not guilty of most of the charges and imposed only a reprimand. According to Soper, Ades had done only two things worthy of disciplinary action, publicly accusing the Maryland judiciary of conducting a "legal lynching" and improperly encouraging Lee to will his body to Ades.[35] Soper lifted Judge Coleman's suspension, and Ades was permitted to resume practicing before the federal court.[36] Houston immediately praised his former student. "In noting credit for Ades decision major portion of credit due to Thurgood Marshall of Baltimore Bar who prepared case and had full charge of defense," wrote Houston in a telegram to the *Afro-American* the day after Soper's decision.[37]

AN UNGRATEFUL CLIENT

Soon after the Soper ruling, Ades spoke about Houston and Marshall in anything but glowing terms. Ades claimed that Houston had essentially "sold him out" when he advised Judge Soper to reprimand him for his actions in the Lee case and in some of his statements to the press.[38] Houston, on the other hand, maintained that Ades knew he was going to recommend the reprimand to Soper and that Ades had agreed to the concession offered by Houston.[39]

Ades criticized Houston in the press. "Bernard Ades has informed Dr. Charles H. Houston of the Howard Law School that he disapproves of the Washington attorney's defense of Ades in Baltimore courts, on charges of unprofessional conduct," the *Afro-American* reported. "Dr. Houston represented Mr. Ades before the U.S. district court for Maryland, when the Communist attorney received a reprimand, upon the suggestion of Dr. Houston."[40] So, not only did Houston and Marshall not get paid, but they were publicly criticized for their hard work.

Two weeks after Judge Soper's ruling, the ILD issued a scathing press release condemning everyone involved in the Ades matter, from the state prosecutors to Judge Coleman and even Judge Soper.[41] Ades's defense team was not spared either. Ignoring the fact that Ades had asked Houston to defend him in court, the ILD reiterated its criminal justice platform and criticized the NAACP. Ades joined the ILD in condemning Houston for suggesting to Judge Soper that Ades be reprimanded.[42]

Houston responded with an angry letter of his own, accusing the ILD of misrepresenting what had occurred at the trial before Soper.[43] Houston maintained that Ades had known about and had approved of, in advance, Houston's comments to Judge Soper conceding that a reprimand might be appropriate. Houston denounced the ILD for lacking the basic professional courtesy to consult with him before releasing the statement. He then demanded a list of everyone to whom the ILD had sent its statement so that he could write to them and set the record straight. Houston threatened that, if the ILD did not provide the list within a week, he would release his own statement to the press. The ILD did not respond, and the dispute became even more public.

"IS HE CRAZY?"

The Bernard Ades story was far from over. Certain Maryland judges and lawyers were determined to muzzle Bernard Ades. A few short weeks after Houston and Marshall saved Ades from federal disbarment, the Bar Association of Baltimore City came after the Communist attorney in state court. "Renew Ades Ouster," was the banner headline in the *Afro-American*. "A renewal of the attempt to punish Bernard Ades, militant I.L.D. attorney who figured in the Euel Lee Case, was made that week when charges were filed against him with the grievance committee of the bar association of Baltimore city, Wednesday."[44]

The Bar Association of Baltimore City, which consisted of only white attorneys, had seized upon one of the guilty findings in the Ades case before Judge Soper. Ades's custody of Lee's body became the subject of their new offensive. Soper's other guilty finding about Ades's verbal attacks on the Maryland bar and bench was also cited in the Bar Association's petition.

Ades, audacious and bombastic as ever, lashed out at the Baltimore City Bar Association in the black press. "Pot Can't Call Kettle Black, Ades Tells Bar," read the *Afro-American* headline. Ades denied the right of the Baltimore Bar Association to try him on charges of professional misconduct, because the association did not represent all of the lawyers in Baltimore.[45] In a letter to George R. Veazy, chairman of the bar grievance committee, Mr. Ades challenged the right of the association to try him "because of the apparent prejudice which permeates the official policies of the Association."[46]

Even more audaciously, Ades now reached out to Houston and asked him to represent him in the new matter brought by the Baltimore City Bar. For Houston to once again defend Ades, while Ades was publicly criticizing him, was a bridge too far. Houston wrote to Ades and sent a carbon copy to Marshall. Houston explained that he would not represent Ades in his state disciplinary proceedings unless Ades issued a written statement attesting to his complete satisfaction with the defense provided by Houston and Marshall in federal court.[47] Ades responded with a long letter in which he insisted that Houston had acted contrary to their agreed-upon strategy when he suggested that Judge Soper reprimand him. Ades stated that he would not proclaim his complete satisfaction with Houston's and Marshall's work, and that for the time being, he would represent himself in the state disciplinary proceedings.[48]

When the *Afro-American* published the letter that Ades sent to Houston, Marshall sent a note to Houston to alert him. Marshall expressed his reaction to Ades's conduct with three words, "Is he crazy?"[49]

ADES AND THE MONUMENTAL CITY BAR ASSOCIATION

Ades later approached the all-black Monumental City Bar Association, seeking a letter to bolster his defense in the state disciplinary case. Having argued that the Bar Association of Baltimore City had no authority to prosecute charges against him because it excluded blacks and women, Ades sought a statement from the Monumental City Bar Association affirming that its members wished to join the Bar Association of Baltimore City.

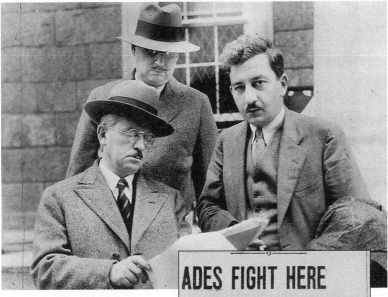

After Ades publicly criticized the efforts of Houston and Marshall on his behalf, they refused to represent him in state court. Other lawyers defended Ades and he was convicted and suspended from law practice. *Courtesy of* Afro-American *Newspaper Archives and Research Center.*

ADES FIGHT HERE BECOMES NATIONAL

The fight to disbar Bernard Ades, Euel Lee defense attorney, took on a national aspect this week when it was announced that a number of national bodies have entered the case.

Taking the position that the right to defend prisoners without cost was at stake in the proceedings in the Federal Court here presided over by Judge William C. Coleman, representatives of the American Civil Liberties Union, the International Juridical Association, the International Labor Defense, the N.A.A.C.P., the National Committee for the Defense of Political Prisoners, and the Socialist Lawyers' Association sent a telegram to Mr. Ades on Tuesday that they would back the fight.

At a hearing last week, Dean Charles H. Houston, chief defense counsel for Ades, charged that documents in the case had been tampered with. The question has also been raised as to the propriety of the case being tried before Judge Coleman.

To the surprise of many of its members, Monumental City Bar Association president U. Grant Tyler rejected Ades's request. Without consulting the membership, Tyler told Ades that black lawyers did not want to join the Bar Association of Baltimore City. Immediately, several black attorneys expressed sharp disagreement with Tyler. In spite of Ades's lack of gratitude for his services in the federal court, Marshall expressed his disagreement with the bar association president. "I disagree with Mr. Tyler on the matter of admission to the white bar association. I feel that the time has come when Negroes should demand any right they have a chance to get. Having defended Mr. Ades, it is quite natural that my views are still in accord with his in that regard," Marshall explained to the *Afro-American.*[50]

STATE COURT HEARING

When the state court hearing finally began in December 1934, Joseph P. Brodsky and Joseph Kuntz, two white ILD attorneys from New York, who had worked on the Scottsboro case, represented Ades. Most of the admitted evidence was the same as that presented at the hearing before Judge Soper. This time, however, the result was different. Nine judges of the Supreme Bench of Baltimore City suspended Ades from practicing law for three months.[51]

Later in 1934, Bernard Ades ran as the Communist Party's candidate for governor of Maryland. He received eighty votes.

Houston and Marshall were proud that they had been more successful at defending Ades than were his white, Communist lawyers. As the rivalry between black lawyers and the ILD continued, Houston believed that the Crawford and Ades cases had publicly demonstrated that black attorneys could stand their ground and impact court decisions. Houston felt that his work to train effective black lawyers was coming to fruition in his young protégé. Years later, Janet Ades, the daughter of Bernard Ades, would report that, whenever her father discussed the unsuccessful attempt to disbar him in federal court, he invariably referred to the future justice of the US Supreme Court as "young Thurgood."[52]

Chapter 9

The Civil Cases

Working on Bill Taylor's case. Carl Murphy is interested in it. We have demanded a hearing before the civil service commission. Dr. Cook is a Negro Hater—openly opposed to equalization of teachers salaries, etc.— have a chance in this case to expose some of his underhand[ed] activities—he is crying that this is the first time in fifty years that he has been brought up in a hearing. Although Bill will most likely be thrown out, I can nevertheless do a little exposing. Do you think NAACP would be interested? Bill has very little money. Only makes about $90 a month. The entire matter will eventually get to Republican Governor who would like to get something on Democrat Cook—might help to put skids under Cook. 12:00 O'clock—tired as hell—see you later.

Marshall wrote this letter, found among the NAACP papers deposited at the Library of Congress, in July 1935 to Charles Houston. At the time, he was trying to build a civil law practice in the middle of the Great Depression, and he also had an ongoing interest in political machinations. Marshall was writing about a black man named William Taylor who was the registrar of the Bowie Normal School, and Cook was the state superintendent of schools. As the letter suggests, Marshall was working very hard in mid-1935. The landmark school desegregation case at the University of Maryland Law School, to which Marshall had devoted many days with minimal financial reward, still demanded his attention. The Bill Taylor matter promised more work with little pay. So, while handling important civil rights cases, Marshall tried to turn his attention to building a profitable law practice. Over the course of three years, Marshall handled more than seventy-five civil matters unrelated to civil rights. He learned from each experience but barely made enough in fees to cover his expenses.

MARSHALL STRUGGLES THROUGH HIS FIRST CIVIL CASES

Marshall took on his first civil case in November 1933, just as he was setting up his practice at the Phoenix Building in downtown Baltimore. Marshall thought *Howard v. Gaither and Fairfield Western Maryland*

Marshall represented clients before seven of the eleven judges of the Supreme Bench of Baltimore City in the courthouse now named for Marshall's friend and colleague Clarence Mitchell. *Courtesy of Maryland Historical Society and Maryland State Archives.*

Dairy Inc.[1] would be a sure winner. Marshall's client, McKinley Howard, was driving through Anne Arundel County with a passenger when Gaither, driving another car, had stopped in the middle of the road, turned off his lights, and started a conversation with the driver of a milk truck headed in the opposite direction. The lights on the milk truck were also off. Howard's car slammed into the back of Gaither's vehicle. Marshall filed separate lawsuits for personal injuries sustained by Howard and his passenger. Marshall was confident he would win. He figured that no reasonable judge or jury would expect a motorist driving at night to anticipate two vehicles standing in the middle of the road with no lights on. Marshall, working on a contingency basis, would be entitled to one-third of any money judgment or settlement won by the plaintiff.[2]

The young lawyer's anticipation of an easy payday proved mistaken. The local dairy company was well established and popular. The rookie lawyer faced seasoned counsel from the formidable and well-respected law firm of Marbury, Gosnell, and Williams.[3] The case went to a jury trial before Samuel K. Dennis, chief judge of the Supreme Bench of Baltimore. The judge's emphasis in his jury instructions on Maryland's contributory negligence law doomed the plaintiff's case. Judge Dennis told the jury members that if they believed that the plaintiff was even slightly to blame for the accident, they would have to find for the defendants, even if the defendant was more at fault for causing the accident.[4] The jury of twelve men found for the defendant.

Marshall soon took up another civil case. He represented a pedestrian who was struck by a taxi while crossing Calhoun Street in West Baltimore. Marshall sued the taxi driver and the owner of the cab company for the plaintiff, who sought $2,500 in damages. Marshall again found himself before Chief Judge Dennis. This time, Marshall and his client agreed to settle the case for a small sum, with the defendant paying the court costs.[5]

In Marshall's third civil case, he represented a mother whose young son had been hit by a car while he was crossing the street.[6] The defendant alleged that the boy had darted out into traffic and that there was no way she could have stopped her car in time. This case was Marshall's third consecutive appearance before Chief Judge Samuel K. Dennis. The defendant hired the firm of Marbury, Gosnell, and Williams, Marshall's opponents from the dairy-truck case, and this traffic-accident case would prove to be as frustrating as that one. Judge Dennis again issued a strong contributory-negligence instruction to the jury. This time, he added comments that virtually assured victory for the defendant. Judge Dennis told the jurors that it was highly probable that the young boy had darted into traffic and was at least partially responsible for the accident. The deck was once again stacked against young Marshall, and the jury found for the defendant.

There were two other noteworthy "dud" cases in Marshall's early career. *Haley v. Rainer*, another car-accident case in which Marshall represented the plaintiff, was dismissed by a judge before it went to trial.[7] *Clark v. Kellert*, a damages case, was also dismissed.[8] A few years later, the court found that the plaintiff in *Clark* had made a procedural error and ordered the plaintiff to pay costs.

Thus, Marshall's first civil cases resulted in two clear losses, a technical draw, two incompletes, and little money.

MARSHALL REPRESENTS PROMINENT BLACK BUSINESSES

Despite his struggles, Marshall did acquire a few paying business clients, often with the assistance of his uncle Fearless Williams. One such client was the Ideal Building & Loan Association, the largest black-owned lending institution in Baltimore. Marshall's uncle Fearless sat on Ideal's board of directors, also acting as the board secretary. Marshall became the company's legal counsel. He aided loan settlements, filed deeds, prepared mortgage documents, and signed mortgage releases.

Marshall represented two other important black businesses. Although his senior officemate, Warner T. McGuinn, continued to be the main attorney for the *Afro-American*, the newspaper's treasurer, John Murphy, arranged for Marshall to handle some of the newspaper's legal matters. In one case, Marshall successfully defended the newspaper in a dispute about several pieces of printing equipment and supplies.[9] In another case, Marshall filed suit for Murphy after Murphy was involved in a car accident while driving a company car. The suit claimed damages of $500.[10] The jury found in favor of Murphy and awarded him $277.21, which represented a substantial recovery in 1936.

Marshall created index cards for each of his clients. *Courtesy of Thurgood Marshall Papers, Manuscript Division, Library of Congress, Washington, DC.*

Marshall also served as counsel for a large, black-owned laundry business. Uncle Fearless's brother-in-law, T. Wallis Lansey, owned the Druid Laundry, which cleaned and pressed large quantities of linens for the B&O Railroad's sleeping and dining cars.

In March 1936, Marshall took the case of *Orville Penn v. The Progressive Grand Ancient United Supreme Host of Israel of the U.S.A.*, the latter party to the case being a fraternal order.[11] A past presiding officer of Progressive alleged that the current presiding officer and the recording secretary had conspired to withdraw $400 from the organization's bank account for their own personal use. Marshall, representing two of the defendants in the case, filed an answer stating that only $14.85 had been in the account. The judge granted Marshall's motion to dismiss the case.

THE DIVORCE CASES

Marshall also earned a steady stream of small fees from uncontested divorce cases. In Maryland, uncontested divorces filed on the grounds of abandonment followed a specific, routine process, which Marshall quickly mastered. Maryland law required a hearing before an examiner, which was a court official ranked below a judge. The spouse seeking the divorce had to appear before the examiner with a witness. Both the spouse seeking the divorce and the witness had to testify that the spouses had resided apart for at least three years and that there was no hope of reconciliation. Unless the defendant took part in the proceedings, the party seeking the divorce posted notice of the pending divorce in the local newspapers.

Marshall's first divorce case was *Wilbur G. Matthews v. Addie J. Matthews*.[12] Marshall represented the wife, having been referred by his friend, prominent Baltimore divorce attorney Josiah Henry. Henry represented the husband. Veteran black lawyers often assisted young lawyers by sending them the opposing party in a divorce case. The husband, who worked as a chauffeur, claimed he had been married for twenty-five years when his wife abandoned him. The husband testified that despite "doing his best" to please his wife, she left him for no apparent reason. The court granted the divorce.

Marshall filed two divorce cases on a single day in March 1934. *Marion*

Lawyer Is Named as Guardian for Insane War Vet

Action Makes Mother Eligible for His $900 Bonus.

EX-SOLDIER IS NOW IN STATE HOSPITAL

Procedure Necessary in Similar Cases.

An order appointing Thurgood Marshall, attorney, as guardian for James Griffin, 40, insane World War veteran, so that his mother, Mrs. Mary Dorsey of 535 Wilson Street, may obtain his adjusted service bonus was signed in the circuit court by Judge Charles Stein, Wednesday.

The action reulted from a petition filed by Mrs. Dorsey, last week requesting that a competent person be named supervisor over her son's estate. According to the document, Griffin is a patient at the Crownsville State Hospital.

Marshall's diverse law practice included matters referred to him by judges. *Courtesy of Afro-American Newspaper Archives and Research Center.*

Wife of Robert P. McGuinn Gains Legal Freedom

A decree of absolute divorce was granted to Mrs. Willie Mae McGuinn, wife of Robert P. McGuinn, executive secretary of the Governor's Higher Education Commission, by Judge Supplee of the circuit court, this week.

Mrs. McGuinn, who is the former Miss Willie Mae Thomas, charged that her husband deserted her in 1932. She asked for the custody of two children by her husband and alimony of $50 a month. Both of her requests were granted by the court.

The secretary of the commission entered a plea for divorce first, on the grounds of desertion,

In seven of his ten divorce cases, Marshall represented the wife, including the wife of a good friend and fellow lawyer. *Courtesy of Afro-American Newspaper Archives and Research Center.*

Boone Arnold v. Benjamin Arnold was an uncontested divorce in which Marshall represented the wife.[13] The complaint stated that the husband had abandoned the wife and that the current whereabouts of the husband were unknown. In the second case, Marshall represented a wife who claimed that her husband had left her a little more than eighteen months after they were married.[14] The decree was not officially issued until 1946, twelve years later, when Marshall had been in New York for almost a decade. The plaintiff explained that she did not completely carry through with the divorce because she had a hope, however small, that she and her husband would reconcile.

In January 1935, an odd twist of fate put Marshall in the awkward position of representing the wife of Robert McGuinn, a friend and fellow lawyer. McGuinn filed for divorce, alleging that his wife had abandoned him and that he had done nothing to precipitate her leaving. Marshall, however, filed a cross-complaint arguing that McGuinn had abandoned his wife. Compared to Marshall's other divorce cases, the McGuinn divorce became complicated. The case pitted Marshall against his friend and involved negotiations over custody and child support. When the court granted the divorce, Marshall's client won child support and custody of the couple's children.[15] Marshall and McGuinn then resumed their friendship.

Marshall handled a total of ten divorce cases in Maryland. He represented the wife in such cases seven times.[16]

THE BILL OF PARTICULARS

Marshall also had a civil case that hit close to home when he represented his brother Dr. Aubrey Marshall in yet another auto-accident matter.[17] Aubrey Marshall had rear-ended another driver, causing bodily injury and damage to the car. The victim sued Aubrey for $2,500 in damages. Thurgood Marshall employed a defense tactic that he would use on a regular basis. He filed a bill of particulars, a formal request to obtain more detailed information about the plaintiff's claims and accusations. The bill of particulars is an effective defense device because it requires the plaintiff to list the specific harm he or she has suffered, beyond the simple boilerplate statements required by the common law. Use of the bill of particulars also provided Marshall additional time to prepare his defense strategy while putting pressure on the plaintiff to respond or otherwise lose his cause of action. Marshall's tactic worked. The plaintiff abandoned his claim, and the court ruled in favor of Aubrey Marshall.

Judge Eugene O'Dunne, who ruled in Marshall's favor on several bills of particulars, would play a major role in Marshall's early career.[18]

THE BRIDGE TO MARSHALL'S CIVIL RIGHTS CASES

The Bill Taylor case was an important bridge from Marshall's conventional civil practice to his groundbreaking civil rights work. William Taylor grew up in Baltimore and was an outstanding athlete. After his football and basketball careers ended, he became a coach at Morgan College in Baltimore and at Marshall's alma mater, Lincoln University. He also coached at Sam Houston College in Texas before taking a position at Bowie Normal School in Prince George's County, Maryland.

Bowie Normal School hired him to be an athletic coach and to serve as the school's registrar. Yet, Taylor could not work as the registrar because, apparently not wanting Taylor actually to function as the registrar, the college never gave him a key to the room where the student records were kept.

Albert S. Cook, the Maryland state superintendent of schools, suspended Taylor indefinitely as Bowie's registrar, accusing him of "inefficiency and incompetency." Taylor protested that since he had never been allowed to perform his duties, he could not possibly be found inefficient or incompetent. Taylor asked Marshall to represent him. Marshall promptly appealed Taylor's suspension to the state civil service commissioner. He argued that the superintendent's criticism of Taylor was so vague that it violated the relevant personnel regulations and made it impossible for Taylor to defend himself against the accusation.[19]

Marshall wrote to the national headquarters of the NAACP to see if the organization would support the case.[20] Marshall described Dr. Cook as "a Negro Hater—openly opposed to equalization of teachers' salaries." Marshall also told the NAACP that he would use the case to expose all of Dr. Cook's wrongdoings. Cook vehemently protested that this was the first time in fifty years that he was called to a hearing. Marshall also explained

Bowie Registrar Wins F i g h t to Keep Position

Bill Taylor Is Sent Back by Civil Service Head After Ouster.

ORDER, EFFECTIVE AT ONCE, SENT TO COOK

"Never Had a Chance," Commissioner Says.

BALTIMORE — Following a hearing before Col. Harry C. Jones, white, state civil service commissioner, William (Bill) Taylor, ousted registrar of Bowie Normal School, was ordered reinstated on Monday.

The order was effective at once, according to Colonel Jones, and a copy of it was sent to Dr. Albert S Cook, white, state superintendent of education.

Mr. Taylor was dismissed from the position when Dr. Cook and Leonidas S. James, principal of the school, charged that he was incompetent and inefficient.

Records Locked Up

At the hearing Mr. Taylor, who was represented by Thurgood Marshall, attorney, charged that he had never been given an opportunity to demonstrate his skill as a registrar in that the principal of the school had prevented his having access to records.

Most of these records were kept under lock and key, Mr. Taylor said, and he was never given the combination to the school safe in addition to his not being able to see the records that were locked up.

The commissioner held that Mr. Taylor had been employed on other duties, as the hearing revealed, to the extent that it was impossible for him to perform the duties of registrar.

Marshall protected the job of a college administrator in a case that the NAACP had turned down. *Courtesy of Afro-American Newspaper Archives and Research Center.*

that the *Afro-American* was already conducting an investigation and that, although the case faced possible dismissal, it would "nevertheless do a little exposing." Marshall believed that he could exploit state politics to his advantage, especially since "a Republican Governor [would] like to get something on [the] Democrat, Cook." Less than a year earlier, Republican Harry Nice had beaten the long-term Democratic governor, Albert Ritchie.

Marshall felt confident that Taylor's matter would be the type of case the NAACP would embrace. However, the civil rights organization and Charles Hamilton Houston did not share Marshall's perspective. Houston wrote to the executive secretary of the NAACP, Walter White, that the NAACP should not get involved because the conflict was between "a Negro principal and one of his teachers."[21] Houston wrote a similar letter to Marshall on the same day.[22] White agreed with Houston and refused to bring the NAACP into the case.

Marshall did not see the Taylor matter simply as a conflict between a black teacher and a black principal; he saw it as a conflict between Taylor and a racist, white state school superintendent. Marshall stuck to his guns, even though he knew that he would have to work for free and had only a slight chance of saving Taylor's job.[23]

Despite rejection by the NAACP, Marshall persevered and won the case in August 1935. The state commission overseeing the Taylor matter ordered the school to reinstate Taylor as registrar.[24] Marshall had won a case that he believed fit within the NAACP's national campaign of fighting discrimination in schools.[25]

MARSHALL'S OTHER MATTERS

Marshall handled a number of other civil matters during his three years as a lawyer in Maryland, including personal injury claims, product liability cases, workers' compensation cases, and claims against insurance companies. He drafted wills, served as the executor of estates, drafted contracts, worked on zoning matters, obtained liquor licenses for some clients, and opposed liquor licenses on behalf of other clients. Exhibiting confidence in Marshall's character and competence, Judge Stein appointed Marshall the legal guardian of a mentally disabled veteran.

Although Marshall's foray into private practice had a rough beginning, he quickly became an effective lawyer. Between 1933 and 1936, Marshall participated in about seventy-five civil matters. Given his growing expertise at handling civil cases, Marshall could have gone on to a successful and lucrative career in private practice. Instead, he decided to focus on other cases.

Chapter 10

The Criminal Cases

By June 1935, Marshall had been a lawyer for less than two years. As he struggled to build his civil law practice, he also took on some criminal cases, some of which were referred to him by the NAACP. On June 7, he reported to NAACP assistant secretary Roy Wilkins on one such case:

> Pursuant to your letter of June 3rd, I looked into the case of James Poindexter. I visited him at the Death House and on the same day (Tuesday) went to the Circuit Court for Montgomery County at Rockville, to inspect the docket entries there. On Wednesday, I had a conference with Judges Woodward and Willard at Frederick, Maryland. They are the same Judges who tried William Carter, which case I also investigated, so they knew what I was there for. They talked very freely and frankly. On Thursday, I got permission from the Governor to see the parole folder on the case and inspected that in his office. . . . A report on this case is enclosed.[1]

"GUILTY AS HELL"

James Poindexter was one of two black men charged with the brutal rape of a white teenage girl and the beating of a white teenage boy in Montgomery County, Maryland. The newspapers described the other defendant, William Harold, as a severely retarded "imbecile" who could not fully grasp the seriousness of his crime.[2]

After being convicted and sentenced to hang, Poindexter wrote a letter to the NAACP from Maryland's death row asking that the organization "send one of your lawyers to investigate my case and see if I can get a fair trial."[3] The defendants were scheduled to be hanged in a few days when Roy Wilkins, Walter White's assistant at the NAACP's national office, asked Marshall to investigate.[4]

Baltimore was connected by an extensive electric streetcar system. This is the corner of Dolphin Street and Madison Avenue in Old West Baltimore. The Marshall family grocery store (right) was three blocks away. *Courtesy of Maryland Historical Trust.*

Marshall promptly went to work. Over the course of five days, he met with the condemned man, inspected the records at the Montgomery County Circuit Court in Rockville, interviewed two of the three judges who had presided over the case, and looked over the case file in the governor's office in Baltimore. He then prepared a detailed report to the NAACP in which he concluded that, based on his investigation, Poindexter was "guilty as Hell" of the crimes of which he had been convicted. Marshall described the facts of the case in great detail. The state had significant and substantial evidence against Poindexter and Harold. A physician who examined the girl less than an hour after the rape testified she had been a virgin before the attack occurred and that she had contracted syphilis as a result of the rape. Marshall determined that both Poindexter and Harold had been treated for syphilis during prior incarcerations. The girl also gave an accurate description of the attackers that led police to the room where Poindexter and Harold stayed. Officers discovered in the room a pocket torn from the pants of the teenage boy.[5]

Marshall had already met with Governor Albert Ritchie following the Armwood lynching in 1933. Having established a relationship with Ritchie, he felt comfortable returning to the governor's office to review the file. Marshall reported that there were only two items inside the folder that could help the defendants. First, the governor had received correspondence asking him to commute Harold's sentence to life in prison because of his mental retardation. "I joined in [the plea to commute the sentence] a month ago and joined in a letter sent by the Bar Association for that purpose," Marshall added. In addition, the father of the victimized girl had asked for clemency for both men. Marshall recommended that the NAACP not intervene on behalf of Poindexter:

> In view of the present policy of the N.A.A.C.P. I do not think that there is anything the Association should do on this case, for the following reasons:
> a. There is no question of his guilt.
> b. Because of the mentality of the other man, voiced by psychiatrists, it is evident that Poindexter was the instigator.
> c. There is no constitutional question involved so far as the record goes.
> d. The question of his insisting on a jury trial does not appear in the record. Rather, there is a record that the election for a jury trial was withdrawn.[6]

Beginning to develop his lifelong opposition to the death penalty, Marshall informed Wilkins that "I am contemplating writing the Governor and urging clemency on the basis of the letter from the girl's father, not because of the trial or the record, but on the basis that the death penalty seems to be for Negroes alone."[7]

The NAACP followed Marshall's recommendation to stay out of the Poindexter case. "My idea is that we ought not to have anything further to do with the case,"[8] wrote Roy Wilkins to Marshall. Less than a month later, Poindexter and Harold were hanged. Marshall was invited to witness the execution, but he declined to attend.

Less than a month after the Poindexter matter, the NAACP sought his advice on other matters. Marshall's attention to details, his political savvy, and the important relationships he had developed with powerful people had made him the NAACP's "go-to" man in Maryland. The prompt, efficient, and thorough assessment of potential clients and cases quickly became Marshall's trademark. His cautious approach to the Poindexter case was due in part to his experience with an earlier death penalty case that had also ended grimly.

THE BLACK DILLINGERS

On the hot, muggy night of July 22, 1934, the infamous bank robber John Dillinger died in a blaze of gunfire outside Chicago's Biograph Theater. But prior to his death, Dillinger's legendary exploits had inspired three young black men who had wreaked havoc in the Washington, DC, area earlier that same year. Thurgood Marshall agreed to represent one of these men.

Donald Parker, 24; Gordon Dent, 30; and James A. Gross, 25; all three of whom were black Washingtonians, went on a brief crime spree, robbing people in Prince George's County and the nation's capital. After a holdup at a gas station in northeast Washington, DC, the trio fled the scene, but a Prince George's County constable stopped them and attempted to arrest them. Parker, Dent, and Gross overwhelmed the constable; took his gun, badge, blackjack, and police car; and then brazenly used the police car to commit other crimes. The local press sensationalized these crimes and dubbed the trio "The Black Dillingers."[9]

The Black Dillingers then went one step too far. They fatally shot John Geary, the operator of a gasoline station and barbecue stand, during a robbery in Prince George's County. According to the *Washington Post*, Geary's last words were, "That fellow didn't give me a break at all. He walked in and shot and didn't even give me a chance to put up my hands."[10] Although physicians originally thought that Geary would survive, he died a few days later from a gunshot wound to the chest that had punctured his right lung.[11]

Geary's death put the Black Dillingers on a path that led to the gallows. The prosecutor in Upper Marlboro, the Prince George's County seat, promptly added murder to the list of charges against the defendants, who had been arrested in Washington, DC. Given the crime and four eyewitnesses—Geary's seventy-year-old father, the local sheriff's son, and two waitresses who saw the shooting—the state had a strong case against the trio and little reason to offer a plea bargain.

In custody, the three men confessed. Gross admitted to being the shooter but claimed the shooting was accidental. Gross stated, "I told [Geary] to halt . . . but he kept coming toward me, looking me right in the eyes. I told him to stop, but he didn't. Then I squeezed the trigger and the gun went off accidentally."[12] Each of the Black Dillingers received $9.08 from the robbery.

Marshall agreed to represent Gross at the request of a friend who knew the defendant's mother. Had Marshall been a more seasoned lawyer, he might not have accepted such a serious case so far from Baltimore in Upper Marlboro, located in tobacco country in southern Maryland. Marshall, who had been practicing law for only six months, was perhaps intrigued by the sensational case or may also have been motivated by a desire he shared with Charles Houston to expand the recognition of black lawyers. This was the first time that a black lawyer had handled a serious case in Prince George's County. Regardless of his reasons for coming to Gross's defense, Marshall probably knew that his client faced dismal odds.

Marshall advised Gross to plead guilty to the charges in hopes of receiving mercy from the judges. The lawyers of the other Black Dillingers told their clients to do the same. In most Maryland counties, two or three judges usually presided over a case where a defendant could face the death penalty. Circuit judges Joseph C. Mattingly and William Loker were not moved by the guilty pleas or Gross's explanations. They sentenced Gross, Dent, and Parker to be hanged.[13]

The governor signed the death warrant for the execution of Marshall's client, James Gross. *Courtesy of Maryland State Archives.*

Last Hope Fades for Pair Convicted in Holdup-Murder

Governor, Who Gave 60-Day Reprieves, Signs Death Warrants.

THIRD MEMBER OF GANG SERVING LIFE

Warrant Also Signed for Convicted Rapist.

ANNAPOLIS, Md.—Final hope for two Washington bandits once saved from the Maryland gallows faded, Wednesday, when Governor Harry W. Nice signed the death warrants for Gordon Dent and James A. Gross.

Dent and Gross, together with Donald Parker, also of Washington, were convicted in the Prince Georges County Circuit Court last July, and were sentenced to death for the murder of John T. Geary, Jr., white barbecue stand proprietor, during one of a series of holdups on the night of May 22, 1934.

Gross, one of the so-called "Black Dillingers," was hanged in the Maryland Penitentiary. Marshall became a firm opponent of the death penalty. *Courtesy of Afro-American Newspaper Archives and Research Center.*

Although Marshall asked the governor to commute Gross's sentence to life, the plea was not successful. Gross and Dent were executed on Good Friday, April 19, 1935.[14] Governor Ritchie's statement justified the executions because Gross was the shooter and Dent had dragged the wounded Geary into a room and forced him to open the cash register. The third member of the gang, Parker, was ultimately spared the death penalty. In his last week in office, Maryland governor Albert Ritchie commuted Parker's sentence to life imprisonment. Ritchie believed that Parker should receive a lesser punishment because, although Parker had driven the getaway car, he had not gone into the store and had not participated in the actual killing. Parker had also been the first of the three defendants to cooperate with the police investigators.[15]

WILLIAM CARTER

On Halloween night 1934, a young, white playground instructor in the western Maryland town of Frederick was sexually assaulted while walking home. She was brutally beaten and her jaw was broken. Police arrested a sixteen-year-old black youth named John Mahammit and charged him with assault with intent to rape, a capital offense in Maryland. Police took Mahammit to the Baltimore City Jail for "safekeeping." Law enforcement officials were wise to remove Mahammit from Frederick to the Baltimore City Jail. Barely a year had passed since George Armwood's horrific lynching on the Eastern Shore. Two local newspapers, the *Frederick Daily News* and the *Frederick Post*, devoted extensive coverage to the arrest. The newspapers reported that the police felt certain they had the right person, but were continuing their investigation to "strengthen any weak links in the state's case against Mahammit."[16]

In less than a week, the police learned that they had arrested the wrong person. The female victim, who had originally identified Mahammit as her assailant, changed her mind and insisted that Mahammit was not the person who attacked her. The police then arrested a different person, William Carter, and charged him with the crime. Within two days of his arrest, Carter reportedly confessed that he had attacked the young woman. Carter initially claimed that Mahammit had also participated in the assault, but several days later, Carter recanted that statement and admitted that he had acted alone. Police returned Mahammit from Baltimore to the Frederick jail.[17]

The Frederick grand jury reconvened and formally charged Carter with the crime. The indictment included twelve charges against Carter and none against Mahammit. The victim totally exonerated John Mahammit, and he was released from custody.[18]

Soon after Mahammit's release, reports began to circulate that the Frederick police had beaten a confession out of Carter. The rapid arrests of Mahammit and Carter, reports of a forced confession, and the rounding up of other black suspects led the Baltimore branch of the NAACP to become concerned about the case. The Baltimore NAACP sought Marshall's help.

Marshall traveled to Frederick, about sixty miles northwest of Baltimore City, to investigate the matter. He met with the prosecutor and the local circuit court judge, who invited Marshall to represent Carter. Marshall returned to Baltimore and interviewed Carter, who was being held in the Baltimore City Jail. Marshall decided that Carter was being treated fairly and that he would not become Carter's defense attorney.

Three judges presided over the case, as was customary in criminal cases when the death penalty was applicable. Racial tensions in Frederick were so high that, out of fear for Carter's safety, the judges did not give advance public notice of the trial date. However, the court notified Marshall, who returned to Frederick to observe Carter's trial. In the one-day trial, the prosecution called thirteen witnesses and the defense rested after only twelve minutes, nine of which were used for Carter's confession on the stand. The circuit court judges, Hammond Urner, Arthur D. Willard, and Charles W. Woodard, immediately pronounced Carter guilty of assault with intent to rape, a capital offense. Surprisingly, the judges did not impose the death sentence but instead sentenced Carter to life in prison.[19]

Marshall told journalists from the *Afro-American* and local reporters that in his opinion, Carter had been given a fair trial. Marshall also submitted a report to the NAACP, stating his belief that Carter was probably guilty and had not been "railroaded" by the state. Marshall explained that although the judges invited him to participate in the case, he had declined to do so because Carter's counsel was "able and contentious."[20] To Houston, Marshall was more to the point. "The case in Frederick was a flop and merely the result of over anxiety on the part of people up there. He is guilty as the devil and [has] been sentenced to life."[21] Marshall also sent copies of his NAACP report to Chief Judge Urner, who had presided over the case, and to the *Afro-American*, which published Marshall's assessment.[22] In a concluding memorandum to the NAACP headquarters in New York, Marshall complained that "I lost time and money running up there [to Frederick] three days. . . . All total, I think the only thing gained is the possibility of establishing a branch of the NAACP there."[23] In fact, he had gained much more in credibility, contacts, geographical reach, and experience. He had also seen how a case of mistaken identity could have led to the prosecution of and grave injustice against an innocent man, John Mahammit.

With the Black Dillingers case fresh in his memory, Marshall decided to pick his battles with greater care. The objectivity and candor he displayed while observing Carter's trial strengthened his credibility with judges in Maryland and helped him in future cases. The original certainty of the police that Mahammit was the perpetrator also furthered Marshall's developing opposition to the death penalty.

MARSHALL WINS FIVE CAPITAL CASES

Following the Gross case, Marshall put together an impressive string of victories in lower-profile capital cases during 1935 and 1936. In August 1935, Everett A. Ball was charged with the stabbing death of his cousin, Hillary Ball. He was indicted for murder. With Marshall as his lawyer, he pleaded not guilty. Marshall tried the case before Judge Owens in Baltimore, who found the defendant not guilty on all charges.[24] In November 1935, George Clark was charged with raping his wife. Again, Marshall tried the case before Judge Owens, and again he won an acquittal for his client.[25] In January 1936, James Dudley was charged with rape. At his first trial, Dudley was represented by Warner T. McGuinn. The jury could not reach a unanimous verdict, resulting in a mistrial. At the retrial a month later, Marshall represented Dudley. In a bench trial, Judge Stein found the defendant not guilty.[26] In each of these cases, Marshall successfully poked holes in the prosecution's evidence.

Marshall was on a roll. In his next capital case, Marshall made headlines when he charged that police officers had coerced a teenage boy into confessing to murder.[27] Seventeen-year-old Virtis Lucas stood accused of the fatal Christmas Day shooting of Hyman Brilliant, a white accountant and sole provider for his large family.[28] Shortly after his arrest, Lucas was hospitalized, and rumors spread that police had beaten a confession out of him. Lucas's mother asked the local NAACP to take over the case. Marshall, acting on behalf of the Baltimore NAACP branch, agreed to defend Lucas. The *Afro-American* covered the case closely.[29]

Baltimore NAACP Takes Up Case of Shooting Suspect

Boy Held in Connection with Death of White Man Given Lawyer.

CHILD IN HOSPITAL AFTER QUESTIONING

Expert Will Not Say Pistol Was Used.

The Baltimore branch of the NAACP, Thursday, took over the case of Virtis Lucas, 16-year-old suspect, who is being held in connection with the fatal shooting of Hyman Brilliant, white, on Christmas morning, in the Northeastern police district.

[Editor's Note—Lucas is listed on police dockets as 15. When the case began, his mother said that he was 14 and at present, however, she states that he is 15.]

Action by the branch followed on the heels of an executive meeting on Wednesday. According to Mrs. Lillie M. Jackson, president of the organization in the city, many requests that the branch investigate the case had come to her since the boy's arrest.

Thurgood Marshall, one of the branch's legal staff, was asked to take the case by the boy's mother, Mrs. Lula Hawley. Mrs. Hawley

Marshall represented clients in the Northwestern District Police Magistrate's Court in this building "under the clock" that was located next door to Marshall's former high school. *Courtesy of Baltimore City Archives.*

As Marshall improved with each criminal case, this young man, originally charged with murder, spent only a few weeks in jail. *Courtesy of* Afro-American *Newspaper Archives and Research Center.*

When Marshall interviewed his client, Lucas admitted that he had stolen a gun from an apartment in the house where he lived and had fired it while in an alley. Lucas insisted that he had shot the gun into the air three times. Lucas denied that he heard a scream after he shot. Lucas told Marshall that the police had interrogated him all night and that he had eventually signed a statement given to him by the police, but that he had not been given a chance to read the statement he had signed.

Marshall represented Lucas at the coroner's investigation into the death of Hyman Brilliant. Nine people testified. A physician testified that Brilliant was brought to the hospital unconscious and in poor condition and that Brilliant died shortly thereafter, without ever regaining consciousness. The doctor further testified that he thought he saw powder marks on Brilliant's suit coat, an indication that Brilliant was shot at close range. The taxi driver who transported Brilliant to the hospital did not see the incident or hear gunshots but testified that Brilliant "just told me he was shot by some nigger three times." Five friends and acquaintances of Lucas also testified that Lucas had come over to a friend's house with a handgun and said that he intended to shoot his gun in celebration of Christmas. Four of the friends testified that Lucas returned to his friend's house and said that when he fired the gun, he had heard someone screaming after the third shot. The final witness called was Virtis Lucas, whom Marshall advised not to testify.[30]

Marshall had his work cut out for him. He attacked two apparent inconsistencies in the evidence. First, the police acknowledged that Lucas was at least 150 feet away from the shooting victim when he fired his weapon. Yet the coroner testified that he observed powder burns on the victim's suit coat, indicating that the victim was shot at close range. A ballistics expert stated that the gun found at Lucas's house did not appear to have been fired. Marshall's defense strategy received even greater support a few days later when police interrogated two new suspects.

However, Marshall still had a problem because one of the witnesses claimed that Lucas admitted to hearing a scream after his third shot. To further complicate matters, the ballistics expert reversed his earlier opinion and concluded that the gun found at Lucas's house could have fired the fatal shot.[31]

The grand jury charged Lucas with murder, burglary, and several lesser charges.[32] These serious charges did not deter Marshall. He met with the prosecutors and convinced them that their case was weak. Prior to trial, the prosecutors dropped the murder charge and pursued only the manslaughter charge.[33]

At trial, Marshall put on a strong defense. He presented evidence that Lucas had been coerced into signing a confession that he was not allowed to read. Marshall also showed that the police tip that led to Lucas's arrest was from a woman who told police about Lucas only after a friend of hers had been arrested in connection with the case. In his cross-examinations, Marshall questioned the motives of the state's witnesses. Finally, Marshall placed Lucas on the stand. Lucas admitted to firing the gun but denied hearing a scream or observing other signs that he may have shot someone.

Lucas was found guilty of manslaughter.[34] Marshall arranged a plea deal for the burglary charge, which was reduced to larceny. Marshall had created so much doubt as to what really happened that Lucas was sentenced to only six months' imprisonment. Furthermore, he was given credit for time served. Marshall had succeeded in reducing a potential death sentence to a three-month prison sentence, an impressive showing for the up-and-coming lawyer.[35]

Marshall's final Maryland capital case took place in October 1936, exactly three years after he had passed the bar. Linwood Dorsey was charged with assault with intent to murder. With Marshall as his attorney, Dorsey pled not guilty and went to trial. Judge Bond found Dorsey not guilty of the capital charge of assault with intent to murder. Although the judge found Dorsey guilty of the simple assault charge, Dorsey served only one day in jail, a testament to Marshall's growing skill as a criminal defense lawyer.[36]

BASTARDY, NUMBERS, AND CHELTENHAM

Marshall represented at least three men in "bastardy" cases, a now-obsolete forerunner of a child-support action. Bastardy involved a criminal proceeding against a man accused of fathering a child out of wedlock. A conviction for bastardy resulted in the court ordering the defendant to pay a specified amount of money each month to the mother until the child reached fourteen years of age. In Marshall's first bastardy case, his client pled guilty and was ordered to pay two dollars a month in child support.[37] A few months later, Marshall represented another defendant who pled guilty and was ordered to pay ten dollars a month in child support.[38] Marshall then represented a man who pled not guilty and was acquitted.[39]

Four Accused Cheltenham Boys Freed

N.A.A.C.P. Attorney Acts to Prevent Rape Charge.

INVESTIGATION EXONERATES THEM

Matron's Story Still Shrouded in Mystery

UPPER MARLBORO, Md.—The four inmates of Cheltenham Reformatory who were held in connection with an alleged attack on Mrs. Eva Smith, white, dining room matron, were released, Monday, according to reports from the office of State's Attorney Alan Bowie, Tuesday.

The four youths are Hugh Davis, 20, of 630 S Street, northwest, Washington; Raymond Smith, 18, of 1236 W. Lafayette Avenue; Lawrence Huey, 16, of 615 W. Lanvale Street, and Ernest Patton, 17, of 608 Cumberland Street, Baltimore.

NAACP Causes Release

The release of the boys was brought about by Thurgood Marshall, attorney for the Baltimore Branch of the NAACP, who conducted an investigation here, Friday, on the request of Mrs. Lillie Jackson, president of the Baltimore unit.

The attorney interviewed the accused boys, police officials and Hal T. Kearns, white, superintendent of Cheltenham School of Reformation, during his probe of the arrests. During a conference with the State's Attorney, Mr. Marshall was promised that the

Boys Held in Maryland "Scottsboro" Case

Three of the four youths from the House of Reformation at Cheltenham, who wer locked up last week at Upper Marlboro and questioned concerning an alleged attemp to attack a white matron at the institution. The woman's living quarters wer searched as soon as she screamed but no one was found on the floor of the mai building where the attack is supposed to have occurred. The boys are Hugh Davi D.C., Lawrence Huey, Raymond Smith and Ernest Patton, all of Baltimore.

Based on his investigation, Marshall obtained the release of four youths falsely accused of raping a reform school matron. *Courtesy of Afro-American Newspaper Archives and Research Center.*

Marshall also participated in several minor criminal cases involving such things as assault and illegal gambling. Most of these cases were heard before magistrates "under the clock" atop the cupola of the Northwest Police Station, next door to the building where Marshall had attended high school. In his one "numbers" case that reached the circuit court, Marshall's female client faced ten counts for running a numbers racket out of her home. In those days, most states did not have state-run lotteries, and many criminals set up illicit numbers games in many American cities. Marshall had his client plead guilty to two minor offenses, and she paid a fine and court costs amounting to seventy-two dollars.[40]

Marshall also handled cases involving juveniles. The most serious case involved four youths at the state boy's reform school in Cheltenham, Maryland. In February 1936, Marshall took over a case that the *Afro-American* briefly called "Maryland's Scottsboro Case." Four black youths at the House of Reformation at Cheltenham in Prince George's County were accused of assaulting a white woman who worked at the reform school. They were transferred to the jail for adults. The NAACP learned about the matter and asked Marshall to investigate.[41]

Marshall immediately undertook his signature, detailed investigation. He determined that the woman's story could not be true. The assailants could not have fled the scene without the woman's screams alerting the guards on duty. Marshall learned that each boy had a credible alibi that was supported by at least one witness. Marshall went directly to Alan Bowie, the state's attorney in Prince George's County, who was the same prosecutor Marshall had encountered in two other cases. Using the information that he had assembled and the credibility that he had established with Bowie, Marshall convinced Bowie that the young men were innocent. Soon thereafter, the accused youths were released, further solidifying Marshall's reputation as a lawyer.[42]

Chapter 11

The Murder of Kater Stevens

"**I** have been brought into the Kater Stevens case over in Bladensburg and am happy to be in it," Marshall wrote to Walter White of the NAACP on September 10, 1934. "Sooner or later, we will have these people awake here in Maryland. They had a rumor down in that county that a Negro lawyer could not try a case there. However, I tried a murder case down there in July and the people seemed satisfied. Now this case will open their eyes further."[1]

Marshall had not really "tried" the murder case in Prince George's County. He had represented one of the so-called Black Dillingers, and his client had pleaded guilty. Perhaps "the people" did seem "satisfied," but Marshall's client received a death sentence. Although Marshall brashly expressed hopes of getting "these people awake," it was Marshall whose eyes were about to be awakened by the Stevens case. No other case during Marshall's early career taught him more about being an effective lawyer. Although Marshall was eager to use the Stevens case to raise awareness about the unfair treatment of African Americans in the judicial system, the case threw him a few curveballs that taught him many valuable lessons.

A TRAFFIC ACCIDENT GOES BADLY

On the night of July 22, 1934, Kater Stevens[2] was driving through Prince George's County with his wife, Mildred Stevens, on their way home to P Street in northwest Washington, DC. Stevens, a thirty-one-year-old black laborer, hit a car driven by a white woman. Following the minor accident, a police officer arrested Stevens for "reckless driving and intoxication" and took him before a nearby justice of the peace. The magistrate ordered Stevens held without bond and instructed Stevens's wife to go home without him. Mildred Stevens would never again see her husband alive.[3]

Charles Flory, a local police officer, proceeded to drive Stevens to the county jail. Flory would later claim that Stevens bolted from the car when they stopped at a traffic light and that while chasing after Stevens, Flory tripped over a pile of wood and accidentally shot Stevens in the back.

Witnesses painted a very different picture. Edward Smallwood was two cars behind the Stevens car. He reported that a young white boy walked up to the left side of the Stevens car and punched someone inside. Smallwood said, "A colored man, who I afterwards learned was Kater Stevens, got out of the car on the right side, came around to the left side of the car and engaged in a fight with the white boy, knocking him to the ground." According to Smallwood, Flory chased Stevens into an alley and fired three shots. As Stevens walked back out of the alley, Flory raised his pistol and fired one more shot. Smallwood said that he got out of his car and ran up to find Stevens lying with his head to the road. For Smallwood, it was clear that the officer had "shot [Stevens] down in cold blood."[4]

Seeking justice, Mildred Stevens retained Belford V. Lawson Jr., a Washington, DC, attorney who had graduated from Howard Law School one year before Thurgood Marshall. Lawson, who had been a college football player and an economics professor prior to law school, also had cofounded the New Negro Alliance, which had organized the Buy Where You Can Work campaign in Washington, DC.

Lawson went to work on the case. He wrote to Prince George's County state's attorney Alan Bowie, demanding an immediate investigation into Flory's "outrageous and unlawful action" that caused Stevens's death.[5] Lawson obtained an affidavit from Smallwood recounting the events on that fateful evening. To raise awareness and money, Lawson helped organize a meeting at the First Baptist Church in Bladensburg, and he solicited aid from a group called the Federation of Colored Women's Clubs.

After Prince George's County officials refused to perform an autopsy on Kater Stevens, Lawson arranged for Dr. Robert Jason of the Howard University School of Medicine to perform an autopsy instead. Jason, who had performed nearly three hundred autopsies,[6] concluded that the bullet's trajectory made Flory's account implausible. The bullet that killed Stevens had traveled on a downward route,[7] which seemed to contradict Flory's account that the gun went off while he was falling down.[8] Furthermore, Stevens had not been shot in the back, as Flory claimed. "Gunshot wound involving the chest and abdomen. . . . Death was due to the hemorrhage from the structures torn or perforated by the missile," concluded Dr. Jason in his report.[9] He opined that Stevens had slowly bled to death over two hours.[10]

Stevens's death appeared to be another all-too-familiar incident of police brutality. The only unanswered question was whether the justice system would hold the Bladensburg police officer accountable. Upper Marlboro, the Prince George's County seat, is in the southern part of the county. The landscape was similar to that of Virginia and the Carolinas, and its countless tobacco fields served as reminders of the thriving slave economy that had existed there less than a century earlier. The county's black residents had seen little change in racial attitudes. An evenhanded government investigation of Flory was hardly to be expected. When the coroner's inquest into the death of Kater Stevens exonerated Flory, the black community was disappointed but not surprised.

"Citizens Want Bailiff Held as Man's Slayer," was the *Afro-American* headline of August 18, 1934:

Aroused by the fatal shooting of Kater Stevens, 942 P Street, north-west, Washington, D.C., of which Charles Flo[r]y, white, town bailiff, is accused, an enraged citizenry of Prince George's County met at the First Baptist Church here, Tuesday night, and outlined a plan for protesting what has been termed a whitewashing of the case. Stevens was shot here several weeks ago in an alleged attempt to escape, after having been ordered jailed on a charge of traffic violation. A week after his death, the justice of the peace called an inquest which was branded as a "farce" when the judge allegedly refused to allow attorneys for the family of the deceased to cross-examine or question any of the witnesses. . . . Mr. Lawson, who represented the family of the deceased at the inquest, out-lined the incident surrounding the murder, termed it a "legal lynching," and urged all organizations and churches of the county, as well as indi-viduals, "to speak out unstintingly and emphatically against this mas-sacre of an American citizen."[11]

MARSHALL BECOMES INVOLVED

Lawson sought help from the NAACP national office and its Washington, DC, and Baltimore branches.[12] Walter White wrote to Maryland governor Albert C. Ritchie: "We wish to request investigation by the Maryland authorities of the circumstances of the killing of Kater Stevens, a colored man, resident of the District of Columbia, who was killed on July 22, 1934, near the District of Columbia line, at Bladensburg, Maryland, by Officer Charles Flory."[13] White sent a similar letter to Maryland Attorney General W. Preston Lane Jr.[14]

Walter White of the NAACP asked Thurgood Marshall to look into the matter. A few days later, Marshall placed a new index card in his client file box, listing Mildred Stevens as the client and the subject matter simply as "Murder."[15]

Marshall had become increasingly aware of the importance of relationships and political realities. A pragmatist at heart, the young attorney tended to size up matters according to his own quick assessment of the personalities involved. He began with an unfairly negative opinion of the local prosecutor, Alan Bowie. Marshall described Bowie as "a typical county prosecutor" and declared that "we cannot put any faith in either him or his promises."[16]

Expecting a lack of cooperation from Bowie, Marshall decided to try to sidestep him and turned again to Governor Ritchie. He hoped that Ritchie would order Maryland's attorney general to pursue a criminal case against Flory. Meanwhile, Marshall began drafting a wrongful death suit to be filed on behalf of Mrs. Stevens.

Marshall sought the advice of Judge Eugene O'Dunne of the Supreme Bench of Baltimore City.[17] Marshall had heard that that while O'Dunne was still practicing law, he had once persuaded a Maryland attorney general to take a police brutality case out of the hands of the local prosecutor. Marshall informed White that he was eager to test this new approach in the Stevens case: "There is one more angle of this case which I am working on which just occurred to me yesterday. That is, there seems to be a possibility of instituting a prosecution without the aid of the State's Attorney. I have an appointment with Judge O'Dunne tomorrow morning to talk it over because I understand he did so a long time ago, before he was placed on the bench."[18]

Belford V. Lawson, a young Washington lawyer, and Marshall represented the widow of a motorist who was killed by a police officer following a minor traffic accident. *Courtesy of Afro-American Newspaper Archives and Research Center and Thurgood Marshall Papers, Manuscript Division, Library of Congress, Washington, DC.*

Marshall had been cultivating a relationship with O'Dunne. A month earlier, O'Dunne had entertained in his courtroom Marshall and sixty other black lawyers who were attending the annual convention of the National

Bar Association. Marshall had appeared on some civil matters before O'Dunne, an independent, somewhat eccentric, and unpredictable judge who would soon preside over the most important civil case of Marshall's early career. Marshall found O'Dunne approachable and willing to offer advice, although in this case, O'Dunne's advice was not what Marshall wanted to hear. The judge told Marshall that in the Stevens matter, his only option was to work with Bowie, the local prosecutor.[19]

Despite his pessimism, Marshall decided to try to persuade Bowie to seek an indictment against Flory. He quickly concluded that operating under the umbrella of the NAACP would help and that Bowie would be more likely to take action if he saw the case attracting national attention. Marshall explained his strategy to Lawson, writing, "I suggest that we get Walter's consent to apply to Bowie as representatives of the NAACP, then we should write Bowie and place him in the middle. Let me know immediately what your reaction is to this plan. Perhaps it will be wise to write Judge Mattingly as well."[20] Marshall characterized Judge Mattingly, the local circuit judge, as "wealthy, independent and not contaminated with that county atmosphere."[21] Walter White agreed and authorized Marshall and Lawson to bring the case on behalf of the NAACP, making the Kater Stevens matter Marshall's first NAACP case.[22]

White urged Marshall to continue to pursue Governor Ritchie, pointing out that Ritchie "ought at this particular time [to] be exceedingly sensitive and more willing to cooperate, with the election in the offering. I think if I were you, I would get over to him not only that Negroes are watching him in this case and are deeply stirred by it, but also that they are far from satisfied with his handling of the Eastern Shore lynching of Armwood."[23]

Marshall sent Ritchie a letter requesting a meeting.[24] Governor Ritchie's response to Marshall was just as Judge O'Dunne had predicted. Ritchie replied, "In this State, prosecutions and the investigation of crime are entirely in the hands of the local judicial authorities in Baltimore City and in the various counties in the State. There is nothing more that I could do at the present time, unless Mr. Bowie requests the assistance of the Attorney General. If he wants that, it will gladly be granted."

Ritchie deferred to Bowie, just as O'Dunne had predicted. Marshall's attempt to engage Ritchie was not altogether fruitless, however. In his letter, the governor promised to get in touch with Bowie to better ascertain the prosecutor's intentions and then write back to Marshall.[25]

Marshall decided to continue engaging Ritchie about the Stevens case. He wrote back, citing a provision of the Maryland Constitution that authorizes the governor to order Maryland's attorney general to step in and take over as prosecutor if the local state's attorney refuses to cooperate.[26] Marshall, a rookie attorney, had the audacity to give Maryland's governor a lesson on the constitution of the very state he governed.

Marshall went even further. He complained to Ritchie that, despite numerous attempts to persuade Bowie to launch an official investigation into the Stevens slaying, Bowie was still dragging his feet. Marshall then mentioned the subject of his first meeting with the governor, writing that "the outrageous and unjustifiable conduct of this police officer, Charles Flory, at the present time is just as great a disgrace to the law enforcement agencies of the State as [was] the Armwood lynching. We cannot escape being reminded of the truly unsatisfactory conclusion of that case and its so-called 'investigation.'"[27]

Marshall also wrote directly to Bowie, explicitly requesting that Bowie bring Flory before a grand jury.[28]

THE CRIMINAL CASE

On September 24, 1934, Bowie finally replied with news that Marshall wanted to hear. Bowie had placed the case on his grand jury docket for the October term of the Prince George's County Circuit Court. Marshall's aggressive lobbying of Ritchie and Bowie was finally paying off.

Marshall wrote two letters to follow up on Bowie's commitment. First, he sent a much more gentle letter to Governor Ritchie, stating, "I appreciate what interest you have exhibited in this matter and it seems that for the present we will leave the case entirely in Mr. Bowie's hands."[29] Then, he wrote to White, letting him know that he had "let up the pressure" on Ritchie but would pursue the governor's assistance in the future, if needed. More dramatically, Marshall told White about a bold political offer that he had made to Bowie, who was up for re-election. He wrote, "I have succeeded in placing Bowie in the middle. . . . He is running for re-election and needs some Negro votes. I made him a proposition that if he succeeded in having Flory indicted and tried, I would arrange with the Democratic

PHONES { OFFICE: CALVERT ~~6245~~
Residence: LAfayette 3675

6246

THURGOOD MARSHALL
ATTORNEY & COUNSELLOR AT LAW
601 - 604 PHOENIX BUILDING
4 E. Redwood Street
Baltimore, Maryland

September 26, 1934

Mr. Walter White, Secretary,
N. A. A. C. P.,
69 5th Avenue,
New York, N.Y.

Dear Walter:

Enclosed please find a copy of the declaration in
the Stevens case. I think it will stand up. The case will
not be heard before April, the first Civil Jury Term in the
county.

I have succeeded in placing Bowie "in the middle."
Wrote him a letter last week demanding that he present the
case and had a conference with him. He is running for re-
election and needs some Negro votes. I made him a proposition that if he succeeded in having Flory indicted and tried
I would arrange with the Democratic committee to be sent to
Prince George County and campaign for him. As a result of
this proposition he called Lawson and me and sent me the
letter, copy of which is enclosed.

Up to date everything is going fine and I have let
up on Governor Ritchie for the time being, but reserving the
right to open the matter up if anything bad turns up.

Sincerely,

Thurgood Marshall.

P.S. I forgot to tell you before that our good-friend
Senator Goldsborough (supporter of Judge Parker) was defeated
in the primary.

TM:lw
Encl:- 2

Marshall struck a political deal with the prosecutor to get the police officer indicted for killing Kater Stevens. *Courtesy of Afro-American Newspaper Archives and Research Center and Thurgood Marshall Papers, Manuscript Division, Library of Congress, Washington, DC.*

Stevens Killing Goes To Grand Jury

BALTIMORE, Md., Oct. —State's Attorney Alan Bowie of Prince George's County informed Attorneys Thurgood Marshall of this city and Belford V. Lawson of Washington, D. C., that the case of the Kater Stevens slaying will be submitted to the Grand Jury at the October Term of the court

Stevens, a Washington, D. C. mo-.orist, was slain July 22 by Charles Floy, a police officer at Bladensburg, Md., who declared that Stevens refused to halt when hailed. Evidence pointed to the fact that Stevens was killed at close range but a prejudiced coroner's jury exonerated the white policeman. The District of Columbia branch of the National Association for the Advancement of Colored People and the national office are backing the prosecution of Floy.
— NEGRO COUNCILMAN —

committee to be sent to Prince George's County and campaign for him."[30] This would not be the last time that Marshall would cut a political deal to his advantage.

Marshall kept Clarence Mitchell of the *Afro-American* and Roy Wilkins of the NAACP apprised of the developments. Marshall also began to discuss the cases with Charles Houston, who had in the summer of 1934 taken a leave of absence from Howard University to serve as special counsel to the NAACP. The *Afro-American* and the NAACP did what they could to keep the case in the public spotlight. After Bowie promised to convene a grand jury, the NAACP announced the news in its weekly national press release, giving a special nod to Marshall, Lawson, and Bowie.

Amid these tumultuous events, Thurgood Marshall was about to celebrate his one-year anniversary as a practicing lawyer. Either Marshall's initial assessment of Bowie was premature, or he had managed to make Bowie an offer too tempting to refuse. Regardless of the reasons for Bowie's about-face, Marshall was developing as a strategist, with an expanding reservoir of political confidence.

Marshall then offered to assist Bowie in the case. He sent Bowie a research memorandum explaining the law governing justifiable homicide. The memorandum concluded that a police officer could not justifiably use deadly force to recapture a person who had been arrested for a misdemeanor. "We intend using this law in the civil case against Charles Flory but I thought it might be of some assistance to you. If there is anything further that either Mr. Lawson or myself can do you have but to call on us,"[31] Marshall wrote to Bowie.

In mid-October, a grand jury in Prince George's County indicted Charles Flory for manslaughter. Lawson wrote to White and Marshall to tell them the exciting news.[32] Apparently, the good news had spread quickly through the grapevine. The day Lawson learned of the indictment, the black community in Prince George's County was already applauding the victory. "People in Prince George's County are tickled to death. You & I are really big Niggers out there. Folks have been calling up all day,"[33] Lawson announced to Marshall.

The indictment was a step in the right direction, but it was not a conviction. Marshall kept a watchful eye on Bowie. "I understand Charles Flory has been indicted for manslaughter. Will you be so kind as to advise me of the date of this trial? I would like very much to be present at that time and if it is agreeable with you and Judge Mattingly, Mr. Lawson and I would like very much to participate in the trial,"[34] he wrote to Bowie.

Marshall traveled to Upper Marlboro, met with Bowie, and reported back to White with the confidence of a seasoned trial lawyer.

> Yesterday I went down to Prince George['s] County to check on the Flory case. Bowie informed me that the case was to come up in a week or two. I insisted that we be given notice of the time of trial which he gladly consented to do. However, he does not deem it wise to allow us to participate in the trial for two reasons: first, we are officially retained by the widow of the deceased, second because a recent decision of the Court of Appeals seems to discourage such procedure. I am undecided as to whether to attempt to force him or not.[35]

Marshall did not remove himself entirely from the criminal prosecution. On the day the Flory manslaughter case was set for trial, Marshall prevented a catastrophe that threatened to destroy all of his and Lawson's good work. Smallwood, the key witness who purportedly saw Flory shoot Armwood "in cold blood," failed to appear in court. Marshall saved the day by convincing Bowie to delay the start of the trial. In a letter to White, Marshall left no doubt that he blamed Lawson for the Smallwood fiasco: "Between you and me, the next time I am going to handle those witnesses myself. Bowie is not to blame for the mixup and I think I know who fell down on the job."[36]

Before the start of the new criminal trial, Flory's defense attorney in the civil case, who was also Bowie's unsuccessful opponent in the state's attorney election, filed a demurrer challenging the legal basis of Mildred Stevens's civil lawsuit.[37] Marshall was busy in Baltimore managing the early stages of an important case against the University of Maryland, in which Lawson expected to participate. Lawson handled the communications with Flory's attorney, and another scheduling snafu occurred. The original hearing date for the defense demurrer was postponed. Marshall, who was to argue against the demurrer, did not learn of the rescheduling until he had traveled the sixty miles from Baltimore to Upper Marlboro for the hearing. Marshall was clearly displeased, and he let his cocounsel know. "I went to Upper Marlboro as per your instructions. I found the court opening its April term, calling the docket and etc., and there was no possibility of reaching our case, nor had it been set down for hearing. I cannot be running down there for the fun of it. I trust you will be able to get expenses for these trips," Marshall complained to Lawson.[38]

The Kater Stevens case was the first matter that Marshall handled with the national staff of the NAACP, shown here is their New York offices: Roy Wilkins (assistant secretary), Mary White Ovington (treasurer), William Pickens (field secretary), and Walter White (secretary). *Courtesy of* Afro-American *News-paper Archives and Research Center.*

As the working relationship between Lawson and Marshall deteriorated, the relationship between Marshall and Bowie improved. Marshall's patient persistence with the local prosecutor he had originally dismissed as narrow-minded paid off. The Flory manslaughter trial finally began on May 6, 1935, ten months after Stevens had been killed. Although Marshall and Lawson did not examine witnesses or make arguments, Bowie permitted both of them to join him at the prosecution's trial table. Bowie presented the jury with the evidence that Marshall had prepared and organized for him. He called eyewitnesses who testified that Flory had chased Stevens up an alley and fired shots at him. Smallwood testified that Flory shot Stevens while the latter was coming toward him. Dr. Jason testified that Stevens had been shot through the chest, with the bullet taking a downward course. In his closing argument, Bowie argued legal points from Marshall's memorandum of law and asked the jury to find Flory guilty of manslaughter.[39]

A black lawyer actively assisting in the prosecution of a white police officer in southern Maryland was unheard of in 1935. The first black assistant prosecutor in Maryland was not hired until 1954, when George Rosedom became an assistant state's attorney in Baltimore City.[40] A subsequent NAACP press release highlighted the participation of Marshall and Lawson in the Flory case.

While Flory's criminal trial benefited Marshall's reputation, the young lawyer was disappointed by the outcome. After just two hours of deliberations, the jury of eleven white men and one black man returned a verdict of "not guilty."

THE CIVIL CASE

Marshall was not pleased, but he did not linger over the defeat. He still had the civil wrongful death case pending. Marshall's report to Charles Houston, now in New York working as NAACP special counsel, was pragmatic. He wrote, "After the verdict in the criminal case, it seems that we must push the civil case. Although I cannot see what immediate good will come of a judgment in our favor or as to collecting it, nevertheless, it will worry [Flory] and help the people some."[41]

Marshall informed Lawson that they had beaten the demurrer and that the civil case would move forward to trial. Marshall also pressed Lawson for money, but he probably could have used more tact. "I am now due expenses for three trips to Upper Marlboro, not to mention the loss of three days. See what you can do on this as soon as possible,"[42] Marshall urged Lawson. The struggling Baltimore attorney was not satisfied with Lawson's curt response: "Enclosed is my check in the sum of $5.00 on account of services rendered in the Kater Stevens case. This is all we have on hand at this time."[43]

Marshall expressed his displeasure to Charles Houston, who had taken a leave of absence from Howard University to work full-time for the NAACP in New York.

Only a small part of my expenses has been paid, which has not been enough to even pay for gasoline despite several trips, for example, three trips to Upper Marlboro to argue the demurrer. I have been informed that a substantial amount has been taken in. . . . Lawson has done nothing except to handle the money. He has done no research, took no part in drafting the pleadings, and wasn't even present on the argument of the demurrer. At the criminal trial, all he did was collect witnesses and be a witness himself. The brief filed for the State's Attorney was drawn up by me. From past experience I would like to escape being further associated with our dear friend. Therefore, I would like very much to demand an accounting of money received and expenses, with an idea of being able to withdraw from the case without prejudice on our part.[44]

Marshall's complaints about Lawson's shortcomings were overstated. Lawson had not collected additional funds, and Lawson had actually done a substantial amount of work. Lawson was the first counsel of record. He had obtained the autopsy and had met with the witnesses. Lawson had also originally focused public attention on the shooting of Stevens. He had helped fan the flames of discontent in the black communities in Prince George's County, Washington, DC, and Baltimore. Once Marshall became involved, Lawson did take on a secondary role. Marshall, under financial pressures unrelated to this case, failed to acknowledge his colleague's valuable contributions to the case and felt cheated.

Walter White informed Lawson of Marshall's complaint. Lawson was not pleased and told White that Marshall "should have taken this matter up with me in the first instance" and that Marshall had misrepresented the facts. Two days later, Lawson sent a terse letter to his fellow Howard Law graduate. He wrote, "I suppose you know that the above case is set for trial tomorrow, October 16th. I have just a few minutes ago been advised."[45]

Marshall had not been aware of the trial date. The next morning, he rushed to Upper Marlboro. On October 16, 1935, Marshall and Lawson tried the case of *Mildred Stevens v. Charles Flory* in the Circuit Court of Prince George's County. As in the criminal case, a key witness failed to appear. This time the missing witness was the pathologist, Dr. Jason. Without Dr. Jason's testimony, the civil case against Flory would almost certainly fail because Stevens's legal team needed to prove the cause of death.

Marshall explained to Houston how he saved the day with some quick thinking and artful deception:

> We approached the Bench at the close of our three witnesses with the idea of either getting a stipulation or taking a non-suit. Counsel for the defendant was aware of the fact that Jason's testimony was very damaging and would prove not only the cause of death, but also that Stevens was not shot in flight. We told him that we expected Jason in about an hour, and that unless he stipulated, we would ask permission of the Court to put him on when he arrived. After a little time, counsel for the defendant was willing to stipulate that Kater Stevens died from gun shot wounds and that he would excuse proof of death. That was his bad move and our good fortune.[46]

In fact, Marshall did not expect Dr. Jason to arrive. Marshall had bluffed the opposing counsel into admitting a key fact that filled a potentially devastating gap in Marshall's evidence. It was not the only occasion when Marshall's pragmatism worked at the expense of the truth.

With that looming disaster averted, the trial proceeded. The jury, composed of eleven white men and one black man, deliberated for three hours and returned a verdict of $1,200 for Mrs. Stevens.

LESSONS LEARNED

Marshall felt triumphant about the final result of the Kater Stevens matter and summed up his thoughts in a report to Houston, writing, "The fact of a county jury rendering a verdict for the plaintiff who was a resident of Washington, D.C., and whose husband was also a resident of D.C. is, in my mind, a step forward. The amount of the verdict was far beyond our fondest hopes. And although it is our belief that the defendant is judgment proof, it is nevertheless a moral victory by having him tied up in litigation for eighteen months in addition to criminal prosecution although he was acquitted."[47]

Marshall's persistent search for the silver lining in otherwise unfavorable outcomes became one of his trademarks. It is unknown whether Marshall was aware of the parallel between the Kater Stevens case and the 1875 case of the Cake Walk Homicide, in which his grandfather Isaiah Williams had rallied the black community and obtained a manslaughter conviction of a police officer who had killed a man at a noisy neighborhood party.[48]

The Stevens case lasted for more than a year, from July 1934 to October 1935. During this time, Marshall continued to learn about politics, media manipulation, witness management, dealing with other lawyers, and the economics of law practice. His confidence grew, and he learned that, even in areas with a deep Southern culture, he could still convince judges, prosecutors, and juries to do the right thing. Marshall cemented his relationship with the national NAACP staff. Marshall was also developing as a strategic thinker, increasingly sensitive to the importance of politics and personal relationships in achieving results, even though his assessments of people were not always correct. Marshall had begun with an unfairly negative opinion of local prosecutor Alan Bowie, and he had permanently damaged his relationship with Belford Lawson. As a consequence, Marshall and Houston purposely excluded Lawson from the University of Maryland School of Law case.

Chapter 12

The First Step on
the Road to *Brown*

Thurgood Marshall wrote to Charles Hamilton Houston as they were about to undertake the landmark case *Murray v. Pearson*, the first major school desegregation victory in the nation. It was a case that historians now regard as the first step on the road to *Brown v. Board of Education*.

> Thanks so much for the check. I believe we are getting started on the case and have a good applicant. He is Donald G. Murray, age 21, grandson of former Bishop Gaines (deceased). He is a graduate of Amherst, 1934. We filled in the application, had a Photostat made, and sent it in with the two dollar investigation fee required. His grandmother, widow of Bishop Gaines, has consented to have her name joined as a taxpayer. I have the law practically worked out along with the law in Maryland as to mandamus. Am now working on the petition.[1]

Marshall believed that Murray's Amherst degree, his prominent family,[2] and his calm and pleasant disposition made him an ideal plaintiff. Marshall also had some thoughts as to which judge would be best for the case. He wrote, "If you are going to take an active part in the trial I suggest we bring it before Judge O'Dunne, otherwise I suggest Judge Frank."[3] Marshall had developed positive relationships with the independent, nonconformist Eugene O'Dunne and the liberal judge Eli Frank. From O'Dunne's comments to the National Bar Association in 1934, Marshall knew that O'Dunne thought highly of Charles Houston.

By 1935, Houston and the national office of the NAACP were ready to resume efforts to challenge taxpayer-supported facilities that operated under Jim Crow rules. The plan was to use money from the American Fund for Public Service, called the Garland Fund, to bring lawsuits to force the Southern states that insisted on segregated facilities to make them equal. The expectation was that equalization would often be too expensive and would lead to desegregation. Maryland seemed like a good place to start.

"THE NEGRO PROBLEM"

African Americans had very limited opportunities for higher education in Maryland in 1935. The most advanced level of education Maryland provided its black citizens was a two-year degree from Princess Anne Academy on the Eastern Shore and two-year teaching degrees from Coppin Normal School in West Baltimore and Bowie Normal School in Prince George's County. When Marshall was in his last year of law school, the Baltimore branch of the NAACP began to emerge from inactivity and announced that it would challenge the exclusion of blacks from the state's main institution of higher education, the University of Maryland.[4] "Local N.A.A.C.P. to Start Fight on Color Bar in State Supported Institution," the *Afro-American* proclaimed.[5]

A month later, the *Afro-American* reported what appeared to be the first steps of the challenge. "Two Apply At Md. U." was the headline, with the subheading, "Mitchell and Seaborne File Applications." The article reported that Clarence Mitchell had applied to obtain a master's degree from the graduate school and that Harold A. Seaborne, also a graduate of Lincoln, had sought admission to the law school.[6] In truth, neither Mitchell nor Seaborne had yet applied to the university,[7] although they would eventually do so.[8]

The *Afro-American* articles caught the attention of the university's administration. "There are enclosed two clippings from the *Afro-American*, a Baltimore newspaper published by colored people," wrote Willard M. Hillegeist, registrar of the University of Maryland, to President Raymond A. Pearson in early March 1933.[9] "Seaborne has not filed his application, although he has been mailed a blank."[10] Harold Seaborne would later report that, when he went to the law school, to his surprise, he was escorted into the dean's office. Dean Roger Howell handed him an application and asked why he wished to apply to a school that had been racially segregated since 1891. Seaborne could not remember how he responded.[11]

Before Hillegeist—known affectionately to his colleagues as "Hille"—wrote to Pearson to inform him of the *Afro-American* story, the university president had already begun to prepare. He had sent a series of letters to other Southern college presidents for insight into how they were dealing with "the Negro problem."

Advice and information were flowing in. Julian A. Burruss, president of Virginia Polytechnic Institute in Blacksburg, observed that Section 140 of the Virginia Constitution explicitly stated, "Mixed schools prohibited—white and colored children shall not be taught in the same school."[12] The presidents of the University of North Carolina at Chapel Hill, the University of Tennessee,[13] and the University of Florida sent similar responses. Pearson forwarded all of these letters to the attorney general of Maryland, William Preston Lane Jr.[14] The correspondence revealed a key difference between Maryland and the Southern states with laws that mandated racially segregated education. In Maryland, segregated schools were a matter of practice and not required by law.

In anticipation of the NAACP's announced initiative, Pearson helped push new legislation through the 1933 session of the Maryland General Assembly. The legislation began to create a scholarship fund that would help blacks attend educational institutions outside Maryland if they wished to pursue a course of study that was offered at the University of Maryland but not at Princess Anne Academy.

THE APPLICATIONS BEGIN

What had been a provocative threat in the pages of the *Afro-American* in January 1933 became a reality for Pearson and his university on July 12, 1933; that was the date when Harold Arthur Seaborne applied to the University of Maryland School of Law.

Hillegeist's response to Howell, the law school dean, was emphatic.[15]

The "nigger" [Harold Arthur Seaborne] has applied for admission. Please formulate a reply for me that is "Bernard Ades" proof. Do you suggest that I talk to the President before I send the official reply to the applicant? There is enclosed a copy of the latest legislative enactment on negro education in Maryland.[16]

Note that Bernard Ades was the communist lawyer whom Thurgood Marshall had represented a year earlier.

Dean Howell, who was at his summer home in New England, sent Hillegeist an equally panicked response:

I have your letter of the 13th with respect to a negro applicant for admission to the Law School. I have sent Mrs. Anderson a letter to be written you, as a matter of formal record, but thought I'd also drop you a line direct, so as to give my ideas informally and off the record. I'm afraid it wouldn't be possible to formulate a reply that would be "Bernard Ades proof," as his organization is undoubtedly going to make a test case of the matter. The only thing that would keep him quiet would be to admit the man: this would probably make him drop dead, but unfortunately is out of the question, of course.[17]

The university president, the dean of the law school, and an assistant attorney general then collaborated in drafting a response to the applications of Seaborne and any other African Americans who sought to attend the University of Maryland. On July 26, 1933, President Pearson sent a rejection letter to Seaborne:

I am in receipt of your application of July 12th for admission to the School of Law of the University of Maryland. Under the general laws of this State, the University maintains the Princess Anne Academy as a separate institution of higher learning for the education of Negroes. In order to insure equality of opportunity for all citizens of this State, the 1933 Legislature passed Chapter 234, creating partial scholarships at Morgan College or institutions outside of the State for Negro students who may desire to take professional courses or other work not given at the Princess Anne Academy. Should you desire to make application for such scholarship, notify me, and I shall see that such application is duly filed. Under the circumstances, I am herewith returning postal money order of $2.00 forwarded to the University as payment of record investigation fee.

President Pearson's letter failed to inform Seaborne that no money had yet been appropriated for the out-of-state scholarships and no administrative process had been set up to process scholarship applications.[18]

Over the next several months, six more black Marylanders sought admission to the University of Maryland School of Law, some prompted by the NAACP and others acting on their own.[19] Each applicant received the same rejection letter as had been sent to Seaborne, with the same misleading reference to a scholarship for an out-of-state school.

MURRAY APPLIES

Charles Houston agreed with Marshall that the Amherst graduate with the impeccable credentials would be a strong plaintiff against the University of Maryland. The Murray case would be the second NAACP lawsuit aimed at desegregating a state professional school. In 1933, Thomas R. Hocutt, a student at the North Carolina College for Negroes, was denied admission to the University of North Carolina's School of Pharmacy. With the assistance of another Houston protégé, Howard University law professor William Hastie, Hocutt had sued to gain admission. (Marshall, as an assistant librarian at Howard Law School, had assembled some materials for Hastie.) Unfortunately, the judge dismissed the case when Hocutt's undergraduate college failed to forward his transcript and records to the University of North Carolina.

Marshall orchestrated Murray's application process. Donald Gaines Murray applied to the University of Maryland School of Law on January 24, 1935.[20] President Pearson sent his standard rejection letter and returned the money order for the application fee. He suggested that Murray apply to the Howard University School of Law in Washington, DC:

> May I bring to your attention the exceptional facilities open to you for the study of law in Howard University in Washington. This institution is supported largely, if not entirely, by the Federal Government. It has one of the best plants in the country. Its School of Law is rated as Class "A." It is fully approved by the American Bar Association and it is a member of the Association of American Law Schools. I understand the cost of attending the Howard University School of Law is only about

THURGOOD MARSHALL
ATTORNEY AT LAW
604 PHOENIX BUILDING
4 E. REDWOOD ST.
BALTIMORE, MD. ·

January 25, 1935

Charles H. Houston, Esq.,
420 Fifth Street, N.W.,
Washington, D.C.

Dear Charlie:

Thanks so much for the check. I
believe we are getting started on the case
and have a good applicant. He is Donald G.
Murray, age 21, grandson of former Bishop
Gaines (deceased). He is a graduate of
Amherst, 1934. We filed in the application,
had a photostat made and sent it in with
the two dollar investigation fee required.
His grandmother, widow of Bishop Gaines has
consented to have her name joined as a tax
payer.

I have the law practically worked
out along with the law in Maryland as to
mandamus. Am now working on the petition.
If you are going to take an active part in
the trial I suggest we bring it before Judge
O'Dunne, otherwise I suggest Judge Frank.

Will let you know anything new.

Sincerely,

Thurgood Marshall.

Marshall selected Donald Murray (center) as the plaintiff to challenge the racial discriminatory admission policy of the University of Maryland School of Law. *Courtesy of Afro-American Newspaper Archives and Research Center and Thurgood Marshall Papers, Manuscript Division, Library of Congress, Washington, DC.*

$135.00 per year, plus a nominal matriculation fee when first entering and a nominal diploma fee on graduation. This is considerably less than is paid by students in the School of Law in the University of Maryland. Their payments in the Day School are approximately $203 per year and in the Night School, $153 per year, plus somewhat larger charges than Howard University for investigation, matriculation, and diploma.[21]

After reviewing Pearson's letter, Marshall drafted a letter on Murray's behalf to the University of Maryland's Board of Regents:

> On January 24, 1935, pursuant to and in accordance with the rules and regulations set out in "The Catalogue and Announcement of the School of Law" (1934), I made application to be admitted as a student in the University of Maryland Law School September - 1935 and forwarded the prescribed two dollars ($2.00) by a P.O. money order for investigation fee. By letter dated February 9, 1935, the officials of the University refused to consider the application and returned the application and money order. I am a citizen of the State of Maryland and fully qualified to become a student of the University of Maryland Law School. No other State institution affords a legal education.
>
> The arbitrary actions of the officials of the University of Maryland in returning my application [were] unjust and unreasonable and contrary to the Constitution of the United States and the Constitution and laws of this state.[22]

Marshall's request that the regents review Murray's application within a reasonable time received no response.

MURRAY SUES

On April 20, 1935, Murray sued the University of Maryland in the Baltimore City Court, complaining that the law school had arbitrarily rejected his application. Hillegeist informed Pearson when the Baltimore sheriff attempted to serve the school's president with papers connected to the Murray case.[23] On April 24, Pearson fired off a letter to the attorney general, Herbert R. O'Connor, mentioning the fund the legislature had created for out-of-state scholarships. He wrote, "We thought when the law (Chapter 234) was passed by the Legislature two years ago, the question of admitting a Negro to the University of Maryland at College Park or in Baltimore had been settled."[24]

In addition to Charles Houston and Thurgood Marshall, the court pleading listed William I. Gosnell as plaintiff's counsel. His name was added to the legal papers as a small concession to Marshall's fraternity, Alpha Phi Alpha, which had offered to join forces with the NAACP to sue the University of Maryland for not admitting black students. In October 1934, the Washington-based attorney Belford V. Lawson informed the NAACP's Baltimore branch that Alpha Phi Alpha had appropriated some money for the case and was ready to organize a finance committee, a research committee, and a legal committee. The fraternity's enthusiasm to join the suit received a cool reception from Marshall and Houston. "What about the University of Maryland case? B. V. Lawson has been writing me and seems to think that the fraternity is going to try the case along with the local branches of the N.A.A.C.P. I am up a tree as to what is going to be done," Marshall wrote to Houston.[25]

Marshall's reluctance to work with Lawson arose from his dissatisfaction with how they had worked together on the Kater Stevens case in Prince George's County. Marshall's belief that Lawson had withheld money from him and had not carried his share of the workload resulted in a rift between the two fraternity brothers that never healed. Houston and Marshall decided to move forward without Alpha Phi Alpha but to include on the record as cocounsel the fraternity's Baltimore lawyer, William Gosnell, who would play no active role in the case. Houston suggested to the fraternity that the fraternity's war chest would best be spent fighting segregation in other states.[26] At the fraternity's national convention some years later, Marshall had to address the concerns raised by Lawson about how Alpha Phi Alpha had been excluded from the case.

An internal memorandum prepared by Marshall outlined his ambitious plan to put on trial the "separate but equal" educational facilities and their inferior conditions, not just at the graduate level but also at virtually all schools reserved for African Americans throughout the state. Nevertheless, the original complaint drafted by Marshall stated that Murray had been arbitrarily excluded from the university and purposely did not mention Murray's race. Marshall, suspecting that his complaint could be more easily dismissed if the pleading relied on Murray's race, wanted the university to be the first party to mention race.

Marshall's strategy worked. An assistant attorney general filed a response stating that Murray was not eligible for admission because the

University of Maryland was an institution for white students and because Maryland provided "separate but equal" education for black students at Princess Anne Academy and through scholarships to out-of-state institutions. The university's answer claimed that to admit Murray would cause white parents to withdraw their children from the university. Marshall was elated. He wrote, "The entire question of Negro education in the state is now open. We can now put in evidence all the inequalities."[27] Marshall would later use the Murray case as a cornerstone to dismantle Jim Crow educational practices in Maryland and throughout the country.

Marshall immediately demanded access to the minutes of the university's Board of Regents to determine what, if anything, they had said about Murray's application:

> On behalf of Donald G. Murray, 1522 McCulloh Street, we hereby make demand upon you to instruct your Secretary to permit us to inspect the minutes of the Board of Regents of the University of Maryland for the years 1920 to date. This morning we visited the offices of the Board of Regents and requested the right to inspect the minutes of said Board. We were told that this could not be done without instructions from you. We had been previously informed that you had given instructions prohibiting the inspection of the minutes by the public. The actions of your agents, servants, and employees acting under your instructions are directly contrary to and in violation of Acts of Maryland 1916, Ch. 372, Sec. 4. . . . We, therefore, request you to permit us to exercise our rights under the Laws of this State. However, if you continue to deny us this right aforementioned to inspect the minutes of the said Board of Regents we shall be forced to avail ourselves of the remedies provided by law.[28]

Marshall sent a similar letter to George M. Shriver, chairman of the Board of Regents.[29]

Pearson responded, "The minutes of the Board are available at reasonable times for your inspection as the law requires. I regret you did not make the request of me personally instead of taking the matter up with a clerk in the office." Pearson also informed Marshall that he "would endeavor to be present"[30] when Marshall came to inspect the minutes.

After examining the Board of Regents's minutes and finding nothing of significant value, Marshall met with the University of Maryland counsel, Assistant Attorney General Charles T. LeViness III. Marshall shared with

Houston his initial impressions, writing, "Been in touch with LeViness III. He will handle the case. Service O.K. Does not need any copies of the bill. Will answer on Monday. Says he is working on the case now. Very agreeable."[31]

Marshall stayed in constant contact with Houston during the early phases of the lawsuit and also kept Carl Murphy, the *Afro-American* newspaper's influential publisher, apprised of events as they developed. The newspaper rallied Baltimore's African American community behind Murray's cause and the new NAACP strategy of using litigation to combat racial segregation.

At Houston's suggestion, Marshall began to assemble evidence documenting the conditions in Maryland's "separate but equal" education facilities. He travelled to Princess Anne Academy and several counties, photographing the interiors and exteriors of black schools and white schools. Marshall reported his travels to Houston:

> Made a full day yesterday. . . . Went down the Delaware side. Stopped in Havre de Grace and caught the colored and white schools there. The colored school is a dump and is in the shadow of Senator Tyding's house. Spoke to the Senior Class of the High School. A Lincoln Man is Principal and told me to say whatever I wanted to and I did. Took inside pictures of labs and classrooms at Princess Anne. Had to do it in a hurry while Kiah was out. Got away before he returned. . . . Also took pictures of Salisbury Elementary [white].[32]

In response to the university's answer to the initial complaint, Marshall filed in court a document called a replication that outlined in great detail the disparities between black and white schools in the state. Marshall focused in particular on the inadequacy of the Princess Anne Academy, a poorly equipped two-year school with no baccalaureate or professional degree programs. Marshall used statistics to demonstrate that the black schools and the white schools were anything but equal.[33]

In his replication, Marshall solidified his legal position:

> Donald Murray admits that he is a Negro. He denies that the State of Maryland provides adequate, or satisfactory or equal educational facilities or opportunities to Negroes of the State, or that the State maintains

separate institutions of learning for Negroes except in the elementary, high school, normal and agricultural departments or levels. He denies that any of said separate institutions are adequate, or satisfactory or equal, but avers that severally and collectively that [all] are inadequate, unsatisfactory and inferior to similar institutions for the education of white persons provided and maintained by the State of Maryland, in violation of the 14th Amendment to the Constitution of the United States.[34]

The following month, Assistant Attorney General LeViness made a trip to Princess Anne Academy at Pearson's urging. He discovered that Charles Houston had been there just days earlier, again with a camera. In a report to President Pearson, LeViness wrote:

Pursuant to our conversation in reference to the Princess Anne Academy, I visited this institution on June 2nd and 3rd and found that Dr. Houston had been there and had made a thorough inspection of the school and had questioned a number of the officials and students. I also found that numerous pictures had been made, both of the exterior and interior of the Academy. In one place they had made pictures of a series of double decker beds, in rather poor condition, which they asserted was a dormitory, but which I was informed was only used for visiting football players. Other pictures taken on the interior were of the assembly hall, the library and the laboratory.

LeViness added a rather dubious explanation for his decision not to take pictures, writing, "After looking over the Academy, I decided against taking any pictures for our purpose. In my opinion the Academy is in excellent physical condition both inside and outside and entirely adequate for the purpose it is designed to serve."[35]

THE RIGHT JUDGE

On June 3, 1935, Marshall sent Houston a telegram that read simply, "Case before O'Dunne June Eighteenth -Thurgood."[36] LeViness sought a postponement.[37] Yet the judge was ready to proceed without delay. "Case in for eighteenth. O'Dunne says must be tried before twenty fifth otherwise goes over until September. Will force for next week," Marshall said in another telegram to Houston.[38]

Judge O'Dunne was one of the most colorful characters to have sat on the Baltimore City bench. Born Eugene Dunne, of Anglo-Irish descent, he had changed his name to Eugene Viscount O'Dunne. He did this after his father, Edmund Dunne, a prominent lawyer and later chief justice of the Arizona Territory, received the title of viscount from the pope for establishing the Catholic settlement of San Antonio, Florida. After graduating from Princeton University and the University of Maryland School of Law, Eugene O'Dunne worked as a surveyor in Colombia, South America, where he was held hostage by guerrillas and survived a shipwreck.

After returning to Baltimore, O'Dunne spent nearly two decades as a lawyer and prosecutor. An ardent reformer, he fought corruption in public institutions such as the Baltimore Penitentiary, where his investigations disclosed corruption among prison officials. He was tall, wore stylish clothes, and sported a pair of eyeglasses fastened to a dangling black silk cord. In 1926, Governor Ritchie appointed him to the trial court in Baltimore, where he became known for his independence, sharp wit, and enthusiasm for criminal cases.

O'Dunne gained a reputation among Baltimore's black lawyers as a liberal on racial issues. In 1934, he entertained in his chambers sixty black lawyers attending the National Bar Association convention. During the hour-long event, he made flattering remarks about Charles Houston and some of the other lawyers in attendance.[39]

Marshall, who had tried cases before O'Dunne and had sought his advice in the Kater Stevens matter, took care to ensure that O'Dunne would be the judge who heard the Murray case. Marshall may have also reminded Judge O'Dunne of his own son, who was a lawyer the same age as Marshall and had been on the debate team at the Johns Hopkins University when Marshall was debating at Lincoln. At the time of the Murray case, O'Dunne was also presiding over the receivership of the Baltimore Trust Company, whose empty building stood next to Marshall's office.

THE PRETRIAL STAGE

Before the trial began, several details had to be addressed, and Houston, who had learned from the Hocutt case in North Carolina the dangers of missing documentation, advised Marshall as they proceeded carefully. "Please have Donald send to Amherst College for a transcript of his record under the seal of the College. Further, have the Registrar of the College authenticate the transcript by affidavit before a notary. Attend to this at once so that we may not be caught for time," Houston wrote to Marshall on, June 6, 1935.[40]

Marshall carried out Houston's instructions and sent a memo to LeViness to advise him of the witnesses who would be called and of a list of records from the state of Maryland that might be required for the trial. Leading up to the trial, Marshall developed a cordial working relationship with LeViness, with whom he met to go over pretrial matters, share documents, and discuss the potential admissibility of evidence. Marshall assured LeViness that he would move to dismiss the case if the evidence showed that Murray was academically unqualified for admission to the law school.[41]

THE TRIAL

The trial began on June 18, 1935, with what appeared to be Marshall introducing Houston to O'Dunne. The judge even quipped that it was more customary for the professor to present the student to the court than vice versa. But the introduction was a mere formality. O'Dunne knew Houston, who had tried cases before him, including one long-running case against the estate of former A.M.E. Bishop John Hurst.[42] In his opening argument, Charles Houston explained that Murray, as an honors graduate of Amherst College, exceeded the admissions requirements for the law school, which were two years of undergraduate work and good moral character. Houston pointed out that the Maryland legislature had not appropriated funds for the out-of-state scholarships that were supposed to guarantee "separate but equal" education for blacks.

On direct examination by Marshall, Murray testified that he wished to attend the University of Maryland School of Law because he wanted to study law in his home state, where he could observe the courts and meet Maryland lawyers and judges. The second witness, President Raymond A. Pearson, was questioned by Houston and admitted that Murray's application satisfied the admission requirements and that the only reason for Murray's exclusion was his race. When Houston asked President Pearson why a Mexican, Japanese, or Indian resident of the state would be admitted to the law school but a black person would not, LeViness objected. O'Dunne briskly overruled the objection, stating, "That's just what we are here to find out." After Pearson testified that the scholarships promised for blacks to attend professional schools outside of Maryland would average $200, Judge O'Dunne remarked that the amount was inadequate for tuition, food, and living expenses. "You can't pay the landlady on that," he wryly remarked.[43]

Marshall attacked the state's assertion that Princess Anne Academy was a "separate but equal" facility. He drew out testimony that buildings and equipment were inadequate and that only one faculty member had a master's degree, whereas most faculty members at the University of Maryland had at least a master's degree and many had doctorates.

Obviously building a record for future cases, Marshall and Houston introduced evidence about racial differences in Maryland's elementary and high schools, such as the shorter school year and the lack of bus transportation for black youngsters. Observing that such evidence had little bearing on the case before him, O'Dunne quipped, "Nobody is interested in high schools, but if you want to have that stuff in the record, I will agree to sit here and listen, but I won't guarantee to stay awake."[44]

Marshall and Houston shared the closing arguments. Marshall distinguished Murray's case from prior cases in which the US Supreme Court had permitted "separate but equal" treatment in education. Because there was no separate law school within Maryland where Murray could enroll, Marshall cited *Piper v. Big Pine School District*,[45] in which the California Supreme Court had struck down a lower court ruling prohibiting a Native American girl from attending the only public school in her district.

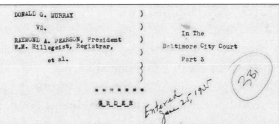

DONALD G. MURRAY)

VS.)

RAYMOND A. PEARSON, President)   In The
W.M. Hillegeist, Registrar,)   Baltimore City Court

et al.)   Part 3

)

)

* * * * * *

O R D E R   Entered
June 25, 1935

The above entitled case coming on for hearing, after full
consideration of all the pleadings, stipulations of record, evidence,
and the arguments of counsel, for the respective parties, it is hereby
ORDERED by the Baltimore City Court this __ day of June 1935, that the
writ of mandamus be issued forthwith requiring the defendants, Raymond
A. Pearson, President, W.M. Hillegeist, Registrar, and George M.
Shriver, John M. Dennis, William P. Cole, Henry Holzapfel, John E.
Raine, Dr. W.W. Skinner, Mrs. John L. Whitehurst, and J. Milton
Patterson, members of the Board of Regents of the University of
Maryland, to admit the said Donald G. Murray, Petitioner, as a first year
student in the Day School of the School of Law of the University of
Maryland for the academic year beginning September 25, 1935, provided
said Donald G. Murray tenders the necessary fees charged first year
students to the Day School of the University of Maryland and completes
his registration in the manner required of qualified and accepted
students to the first year class of the Day School of the School of
Law of the University of Maryland. It is further ORDERED that the
said Donald G. Murray be admitted and permitted to pursue his studies
as a regular first year student of the School of Law of the University
of Maryland pending an appeal from this order if the said appeal is
perfected.

EUGENE O'DUNNE

Judge Eugene O'Dunne's order
that Donald Murray be admitted to the University of Maryland
School of Law was the first court
order in the nation that desegregated a school. *Courtesy of
Maryland State Archives.*

A LANDMARK RULING

After the final arguments, without leaving the bench, Judge Eugene O'Dunne issued his ruling. To stunned silence, he held that the out-of-state scholarship provisions that Maryland was offering to Murray did not afford him equal protection as guaranteed by the Fourteenth Amendment to the Constitution. He signed a writ of mandamus ordering that Murray be admitted to the University of Maryland Law School in September 1935.[46]

The celebrations began immediately. "Court Ends MD. U.'s Color Bar," read the banner headline of the *Afro-American* on June 22, 1935. The paper continued, "The action of the University of Maryland in barring Donald Gaines Murray, Amherst College graduate, from its law school because of his color was declared illegal by a decision of Judge Eugene O'Dunne, white, Tuesday, in the Baltimore City Court."[47] The newspaper displayed a front-page photograph showing Marshall standing at a table and appearing to argue Murray's case, with Murray looking on in apparent admiration and Houston taking notes. The photograph was actually staged in the newsroom of the *Afro-American* immediately after Judge O'Dunne announced his decision. The NAACP national office announced the victory in a press release sent around the nation.[48] For the next several weeks, the *Afro-American* provided extensive coverage of the case, including transcripts of much of the testimony.

THE UNIVERSITY APPEALS

The University of Maryland appealed O'Dunne's decision and asked the Maryland Court of Appeals to advance the argument to an early date[49] and to prevent O'Dunne's order from taking effect until the Court of Appeals had reached a decision.[50] The university's lawyers claimed that Murray's entrance into the school in September would cause scores of white parents to take their children, especially their daughters, out of the university.[51]

Soon after the trial, the University of Maryland entered a period of transition as President Pearson retired and former athletic director and vice president Harry Clifton "Curly" Byrd became the acting president. Hoping to strengthen the case for advancing the appeals hearing, Byrd wrote a letter to Maryland's attorney general Herbert H. O'Connor and Assistant Attorney General LeViness:

> Under the law, I am responsible for all discipline in the University, but if the order of the lower court is carried out, and negro students are admitted in the University, I should not like to be held responsible for what may happen. . . . With five hundred girls on the campus at

Marshall, Murray, and Houston staged this photograph in the *Afro-American* newspaper building after winning the University of Maryland Law School case. *Courtesy of Afro-American Newspaper Archives and Research Center.*

College Park, and with girls entering the Baltimore schools in constantly increasing numbers, the seriousness of the situation for the University, financially and in many other respects, cannot be overestimated. I am convinced that the people of Maryland, because of custom, the State's long standing policy, and laws enacted by the Legislature, will support me in this request.[52]

While Byrd and the University of Maryland prepared to make their case based on racist fears, Marshall went about his work. He prepared and filed a successful brief in opposition to the motion to advance the Court of Appeals hearing.[53] This work required him to cancel plans to attend the 1935 NAACP National Convention in Saint Louis, Missouri, where Walter White had planned to introduce the NAACP's new legal superstar to the delegates from around the country. Marshall would not attend the NAACP convention until the following year.

Marshall did all work on the appeal, while sending some documents to Houston for review. In fact, Marshall devoted so much time to the Murray appeal that the rest of his law practice suffered.

MURRAY BEGINS CLASSES

In mid-September 1936, the Court of Appeals denied the university's request for an expedited hearing. This meant that Murray would begin classes before the appeal was heard. Eight days before Murray was to register for classes, Marshall learned that there was a serious problem with Murray's finances. Marshall urgently telegrammed Houston.

Murray cannot raise money - bad summer for work family cannot raise it - have been trying to raise money in city but without success - could not get a loan - everything looks bad - sister is teaching and could pay back the loan -- Thurgood.[54]

After waging a near-perfect legal battle against the University of Maryland School of Law to force it to open its doors to a black student, Murray almost failed to matriculate because he lacked the money for tuition.

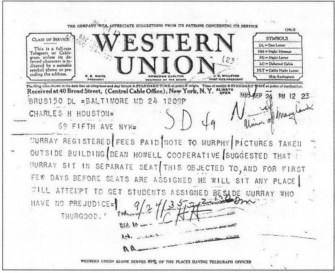

Marshall accompanied Murray to law school to register for classes.
*Courtesy of Afro-American Newspaper Archives and Research Center
and Thurgood Marshall Papers, Manuscript Division, Library of Congress,
Washington, DC.*

The urgency of the situation was reflected in Houston's memo to Walter White, the NAACP's executive secretary:

> A letter from Thurgood Marshall, September 17, confirms the long dis-
> tance conversation I had with him the same day to the effect that Murray
> is unable to raise money for his tuition at the University of Maryland.
> The letter states that we will have to advance $160.00 as a loan. . . . I
> regret sincerely even the temporary expenditure of this money but we
> must get Murray in the University; otherwise our case will become moot
> and you can see what that would do to our plans and program.[55]

Houston then proposed to Marshall that the loan be channeled through *Afro-American* editor Carl Murphy rather than come from the NAACP.[56] Marshall was pleased to inform Houston that the arrangement would work:

> I talked with Carl Murphy and everything is O.K. According to the cata-
> logue, tuition is paid in two installments. One half is paid at the time of
> registration for the first term and one half for the second term, matricu-
> lation fees ten ($10.00) dollars and locker fee three ($3.00) dollars. I
> imagine the cost of books will be about $45.00. Therefore, it seems to
> me, $160.00 should be the minimum. One of his aunts, a school teacher,
> will sign a note for the money.[57]

Amid Marshall's scramble to raise the funds for Murray's tuition, Houston wrote a letter to Marshall admonishing him to tend to his own tenuous finances but also giving him multiple non-income-generating assignments:

> I do not advise that you drop everything for N.A.A.C.P. work. Keep a
> finger on your office practice whatever you do. You can get all the pub-
> licity from the N.A.A.C.P. work but you have got to keep your eye out
> for cashing in. . . .
>   The main thing I want to do now is to get the Murray case in the
> bag. You arrange to have Murray ready to go down on Wednesday. Also,
> arrange to have photographers present to snap Murray when he enters
> and when he comes out. I suggest that you go with him. The *Afro*, of
> course, will want to get the pictures, but we also want to have cuts made
> and distribute them all over the country. There is nothing like a picture

to convince. I will get the money if I have to wire it and beg, borrow, or steal it. This is confidential, but you can assure Carl that I will have $160.00 in his hands the first thing Wednesday morning. In the meantime, you get the notes signed and endorsed. Also, find out in detail the day, hour, and place, and all routine Murray will have to go through in order to register. I suggest that you contact the dean at once."[58]

CONTINUED RESISTANCE

University officials were not eager to comply with the court order desegregating the law school. The law school dean, Roger Howell, thought that the best approach, pending the Court of Appeals decision, would be to accept African American applicants conditionally, reserving the right to cancel their admission if the higher court overturned Judge O'Dunne's ruling. The new university president, Harry Byrd, disagreed. He instructed the registrar not to enroll Donald Murray or any other African American students before conferring with him personally. "Don't give up the ship so easily. We are going to battle the Murray case right down to the last ditch," Byrd wrote to Hillegeist. Byrd insisted that the administration "cannot afford to have Negroes enter the University of Maryland."[59]

A week before Murray was due to register for classes at the law school, Hillegeist wrote a panicked letter to President Byrd, saying, "Registration is on here. What about the Negroes? Unless the Court of Appeals intervenes, we will have to accept Donald Gaines Murray, should he show up on registration day, Wednesday, September 25, 1935. (You know what Judge O'Dunne would do to me, one of the defendants, if I "thumb my nose" at the writ of mandamus to Murray.)"[60]

Byrd tried to lift the spirits of his colleagues and boasted that he was ready to spend time behind bars to defend the school's Jim Crow admissions policy: "Perhaps I shall have to go to jail, but I think we have got to keep the Negroes out. . . . [Governor] Nice tells me he does not mind going to jail provided I go with him, so there is some moral support anyway," Byrd wrote to Howell.[61]

Despite such resolve to keep Murray out, when the registration day arrived, the university officials realized that they had no alternative but to admit Donald Murray.

"AN ETHIOP AMONG THE ARYANS"

The tuition secured, Marshall accompanied Murray to the law school to register. They met with Dean Howell, who was cooperative, although Marshall rejected the dean's proposal that Murray sit apart from the other first-year students so as not to give the impression that he was forcing himself on them. Howell then proposed to assign Murray a seat between two students believed by Howell to be "without prejudice." When Marshall rejected that idea also, they agreed that the best approach for Murray's first day was to be "business as usual," with no special fanfare or assigned seating. The next day, Marshall reported to Houston about the meeting with the dean, writing, "Wonder of wonders! Dean Howell accompanied Murray to register yesterday and came to my office this morning! He had first thought it advisable for him and a representative of the upper class to speak to the first year class relative to the question of Murray's being there. However, he is now of the opinion, and so am I, that it would be better not to focus attention on the matter, but rather to let Murray go in, take a seat, and let the first class start off as usual."[62]

Famous Baltimore author and journalist H. L. Mencken, who had supported Murray's admission, proclaimed in his *Baltimore Evening Sun* column that "there will be an Ethiop among the Aryans when the larval Blackstones assemble next Monday."[63]

As the semester proceeded, Houston asked Marshall to keep in touch with Murray because it was imperative that the subject of the first school victory succeed academically. "Check Murray up and see that he is abstracting and taking good notes. Tell him I want to see him,"[64] Houston wrote to Marshall in a handwritten note just five days after Murray's classes began. Marshall, in addition to all his other responsibilities, now had to monitor Murray's academic progress.

FRATERNITY FLAP

Marshall joined the Baltimore alumni chapter of his college fraternity, Alpha Phi Alpha. In November 1934 he was elected chapter vice president.[65] Near the end of 1935, Belford Lawson and Theodore Berry, general counsel to the fraternity, began to express their displeasure at how the fraternity had been treated by Houston and Marshall in the Murray case. They claimed that the fraternity had been the original motivating force behind the effort to desegregate the University of Maryland and that Marshall and Houston had "hogged the case" and left the fraternity out. There was also a mistaken belief that Alpha Phi Alpha had partially funded the lawsuit.

As the annual fraternity convention, scheduled for December in Nashville, approached, the national president invited Houston to speak for fifteen minutes about the Murray case. Houston decided to send Marshall and persuaded the president to allow Marshall to speak. "Thurgood is the real counsel behind the Murray cases, and I am simply associate counsel, giving it, perhaps, the weight of greater experience," Houston wrote.[66] Houston sent Marshall sixty dollars for travel expenses.[67]

Marshall prepared for the convention speech as he would have for a court appearance. He assembled litigation documents, press materials, and correspondence about the Murray case. He prepared to respond to the notion that in 1934 the fraternity had been the first group to propose challenging Maryland's practice of excluding blacks from its state professional schools. He sought and obtained advice from Houston on fraternity politics.

At the convention, Marshall first met with and briefed a group of fraternity leaders from the Washington, DC, area. He shared with them materials about the aborted North Carolina pharmacy school case that he had worked on while still in law school. Marshall explained that blacks had begun to apply to the University of Maryland professional school in 1933. Marshall also showed them how the fraternity's early interest in desegregating the University of Maryland had been recognized in the press. He assured them that no funds from Alpha Phi Alpha had been used in the case up to that point.[68]

With that core group briefed, Marshall addressed the entire convention. His remarks were so well received that the focus shifted from concern about the past to how the fraternity could be of assistance going forward. Marshall seized the opportunity to solve the persistent problem of Murray's lack of funds to pay his tuition and school fees. Houston and Marshall had arranged a loan for Murray's first year, but funds for the remaining two years were very much in doubt. Even though Murray was not a member of a fraternity, in response to Marshall's presentation, the 1935 national convention of Alpha Phi Alpha voted to provide $550 to cover Murray's tuition for his last two years in law school. Marshall's preparation and diplomacy had once again succeeded. He immediately notified Houston by telegram.[69]

MARSHALL ARGUES BEFORE THE MARYLAND COURT OF APPEALS

In the argument before the appeals court, Assistant Attorney General LeViness cited a Massachusetts case that allowed school segregation based on state policy rather than statutory law. He also argued that the system of scholarships that the Maryland legislature was establishing would provide black students with sufficient opportunities to pursue graduate studies at schools outside the state of Maryland. LeViness suggested that segregation made it easier for blacks in Maryland to attend law school because the state would cover their expenses while white students were on their own. The university counsel asserted that there was not a sufficient demand from blacks for legal education to warrant the construction of a separate black law school. He expressed concern that opening the law school to African Americans would have a domino effect that would result in the eventual desegregation of the University of Maryland's flagship campus at College Park. Finally, LeViness argued that because the law school had been a private institution prior to its merger with the Maryland State College of Agriculture in 1920, it retained the power of a private school to exclude whomever it wished.

Marshall, in his oral argument, attacked the state's claim that the university was a private institution and not a part of state government, pointing out that whenever the university faced civil tort suits, the university raised the defense that it was entitled to governmental immunity as a public institution. Houston's part of the argument took aim at Maryland's out-of-state scholarship program for black students as being no substitute for in-state education. He also argued that black taxpayers should not be forced to fund schools that they could not attend.

AWAITING A DECISION

After oral arguments concluded, the anxious wait for a decision began. Marshall, who had been preparing a high school desegregation suit, decided not to file any new race-related lawsuit until the Court of Appeals had handed down a decision in the Murray case. Although Marshall believed that he and Houston had crafted a strong case against the University of Maryland, he remained concerned that the Court of Appeals might reverse O'Dunne's ruling.

By December, there were tantalizing hints about the outcome of the case. Even though there was still no real news, Marshall passed along whatever rumors or scraps of information he could gather. "I just attended a luncheon of the Junior Bar Association. Judge Soper was one of the speakers. He requested me to tell you that he was seated beside Judge Bond of the Court of Appeals at a dinner, and that Judge Bond was very much impressed with your argument of the Murray case, however, he made no intimation of the probabilities of the case," Marshall wrote to Houston.[70]

In January 1936, Houston insisted that Marshall keep a close eye on Murray, especially with examinations approaching. Donald Murray had to succeed academically, or this landmark case would become a disaster, regardless of the outcome of the appeal. "Since it appears that Murray will be in the School of Law for his first semester examinations, for heaven's sake get hold of him, check up on his notebooks and ship him over to Andy for review," Houston urged Marshall. "Andy" referred to Leon Andrew Ransom, a faculty member at the Howard University School of Law. "If he is absolutely broke and without any money, I will authorize two trips a week for him and pay Andy three dollars a lesson in order to have him properly coached. Start working on this at once because whatever happens, we must not have this boy fail his examinations. We have got to teach him how to answer questions, too." Houston added another instruction for Marshall to deliver: "Impress upon Murray also that from now on, girls are nix until after his examinations."[71]

In a letter dated January 9, 1936, Marshall reported to Houston on Murray and surmised that a decision on the University of Maryland case was near. "I have checked up on Donald and his notebooks, and he is now working on his running reviews. I have also written to Andy to make sure of the appointments to coach him. I shall keep a check on that until after the examinations. The Court of Appeals will convene next Tuesday for consultation and rendering of opinion, so I am again anxiously awaiting the decision in our case."[72]

AN IMPORTANT VICTORY

Finally, on January 15, 1936, the news Marshall, Houston, and many members of Baltimore's black community had anxiously been waiting for finally arrived. "Murray case decided our favor will wire after information checked-Thurgood," read Marshall's telegram to Walter White.[73] The Maryland Court of Appeals had affirmed Judge Eugene O'Dunne's order that the University of Maryland admit Donald Gaines Murray to its law school.[74] The court said that black citizens were being denied the equal protection required by the Fourteenth Amendment to the US Constitution if they were being required to go out of state to obtain law training while a state university was providing such training to white citizens.

This victory, the culmination of more than a year of intense work by Thurgood Marshall, later came to be called "the first step on the road to *Brown v. Board of Education*,"[75] referring to the 1954 school desegregation decision. The Murray case was the first of many court orders throughout the nation ordering the desegregation of schools and other government facilities and activities.

As hard as Marshall had worked to get Murray into the University of Maryland, Pearson and Byrd (the University of Maryland presidents) had worked just as hard to keep Murray out. It is unlikely that Thurgood Marshall ever knew just how determined his opponents had been and how much energy and how many resources they had expended. Certainly, Marshall did not know about the letters that Pearson had written seeking advice from university presidents throughout the South, nor did he know that Byrd had claimed to be willing to go to jail in order to keep the university racially segregated.

Marshall had built a good working relationship with LeViness, and at the conclusion of the Murray trial in the Baltimore City Court, LeViness had shaken hands with Murray and said, "I wish to be quoted as saying that

Donald Murray (second row, far right) reported that his classmates treated him pleasantly. *Courtesy of Afro-American Newspaper Archives and Research Center.*

KKK Note Sent to Attorney in U. of Md. Case

Warned He Is No. 1 Man and Told to Leave Baltimore.

FIRST THREAT SENT TO DONALD MURRAY

Student Now Attending Classes Quietly.

The second of threatening notes in connection with the case of Donald Murray versus the University of Maryland was received today (Friday) by Thurgood Marshall, attorney for the NAACP, who represented Mr. Murray in the case.

The first of these notes was received by Mr. Murray when the case opened and at that time he was warned to give up trying to get into the law school of the University of Maryland.

Mr. Marshall's note reads:

"N - r, if you know what is good for you, you will

The Ku Klux Klan made the first of its many threats to Marshall during the University of Maryland Law School case. *Courtesy of Afro-American Newspaper Archives and Research Center.*

I hope that Mr. Murray leads the class in the law school and graduates as valedictorian."[76] But LeViness's gracious sentiments toward Murray were not shared by his clients. Even after Judge O'Dunne's order, the university administration remained determined to keep the doors of the University of Maryland closed to African Americans.

While Judge O'Dunne's order was being hailed as an important milestone in the fight for civil rights, Houston knew that the war was far from over. He published in the *Crisis*, the official NAACP magazine, an article titled "Don't Shout Too Soon," warning that the fight had just begun. Fifteen years would pass before another professional school of the University of Maryland would admit black students. In 1948, Houston would begin, and Marshall would complete, litigation that allowed Esther McCready to be admitted to the University of Maryland School of Nursing.

Because the Murray case had been won in Maryland state court, it had no binding effect outside of Maryland. Houston and Marshall agreed that it would be necessary to start a new case in a different state and that they would have to lose the case in state court and then go through a round of appeals in order to get it to the US Supreme Court. In 1936, as Marshall was preparing to leave Baltimore, Houston decided to bring a lawsuit on behalf of a law school applicant, Lloyd L. Gaines, against W. W. Canada, the registrar of the University of Missouri. In late 1936 and early 1937, Marshall did much of the research and writing for *Gaines v. Canada*, which did reach the US Supreme Court.[77] But first, the young lawyer had to attend to some matters that he had put off while occupied with the Murray case.

Chapter 13

Becoming a Leader among Lawyers

The regular meeting of the Monumental City Bar Association will be held on March 14, at 8:15 p.m. in the rear of 1201 Druid Hill Avenue. Many items of business must be discussed at this meeting, included therein being the question of "Lawyers Day" for this year, to make an even greater success than that of last year. We trust that each member realizes the business of the Association can be carried on only at regular meetings, and that unless we have a quorum, the activities of the Association are hampered. We, therefore, urge upon you to be present at the meeting, and, in turn, we assure you that we will adjourn at an early hour, providing we are able to open the meeting at the stated time.[1]

S o wrote Thurgood Marshall, secretary of the Monumental City Bar Association (MCBA), the organization of black lawyers in Baltimore. Marshall sent this letter, dated March 5, 1936, to the thirty members of the MCBA four months after he had been re-elected secretary. His first term as secretary had begun in December 1934. The MCBA had existed since 1922, as an unincorporated affiliate of the National Bar Association.[2] One of Marshall's first actions as secretary to the MCBA consisted of drafting and filing incorporation documents with the Maryland Department of Assessments and Taxation.[3] The MCBA had monthly meetings, discussed local and national legal issues, endorsed political candidates, and held an annual banquet. As secretary, Marshall sent out meeting notices, prepared meeting minutes, handled correspondence, and organized a program for Lawyers' Day, the annual, nationwide celebration of the American legal system.[4]

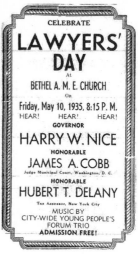

Marshall (upper left corner) served two terms as secretary of the Baltimore black lawyers' association and incorporated the organization that had functioned unincorporated for more than a decade. Marshall organized the group's first Lawyers' Day celebration. *Courtesy of Afro-American Newspaper Archives and Research Center and Thurgood Marshall Papers, Manuscript Division, Library of Congress, Washington, DC.*

A BAR ASSOCIATION OF THEIR OWN

Because the nation's preeminent lawyers' organization, the American Bar Association, remained closed to black lawyers until 1943, black attorneys formed their own bar associations. Formed in Sarasota, New York, in 1878, the American Bar Association did not officially prevent blacks from joining until 1912, when pressure from Southern ABA members led the ABA to adopt an official policy excluding African Americans from its ranks. Soon thereafter, the National Negro Bar Association (NNBA) formed as a branch of Booker T. Washington's National Negro Business League. In 1925, a group of black lawyers who believed that the NNBA was not responsive to the problems faced by African Americans met in Des Moines, Iowa, and created the National Bar Association (NBA).

The NBA became an important forum and voice for black lawyers. At annual conventions held in major cities and through resolutions, correspondence, and by direct lobbying, the NBA aggressively pushed for the appointment of blacks to government positions, lobbied for reapportionment of congressional districts in ways that were more favorable to African Americans, and tried to change substantive and procedural laws that were unfair to blacks.

THE SCOTTSBORO BOYS IGNITE CONTROVERSY

At the seventh annual National Bar Association convention in Cleveland in 1931, the NBA took a big step in establishing itself as an important voice in the black community. Legendary attorney Clarence Darrow also participated in the 1931 convention and urged black lawyers to be more aggressive in fighting for their rights and moving the black community forward. The year 1931 was also the first year of the tragic, racially charged Scottsboro Boys saga. The Scottsboro case became the convention's main focus. Members argued over whether to support the International Labor Defense (ILD), the radical group of white, Communist lawyers defending the accused young men. One group of NBA members believed that Communist lawyers and the ILD had excluded black lawyers from the defense and were exploiting the Scottsboro defendants to advance the ILD's Communist agenda. These NBA members believed that the defendants had suffered because of the unpopular political affiliations of their lawyers. The other camp, led by Charles Houston, believed that the NBA should lend financial and moral support to the ILD defense team.

The floor debate at the convention became so volatile at times that NBA president Raymond Pace Alexander from Philadelphia applied progressively stringent time constraints on the speakers. At the outset, speakers were allowed five minutes to speak about Scottsboro and the ILD. As tempers flared, Alexander reduced the time to one minute per speaker and eventually allowed each speaker just one sentence in which to express his or her views. Ultimately, the NBA passed a rather watered-down and ambiguous resolution that commended the defense team without mentioning the ILD.

The Scottsboro debate continued at the 1932 NBA convention in Indianapolis. Walter White of the NAACP ruffled some feathers when he painted an unflattering portrait of some black attorneys: "The Negro legal profession must weed out of its ranks incompetent, unscrupulous and slothful lawyers who are the greatest hindrance to the Negro legal profession," he said in an address to the delegates.[5] Despite his pointed words, White reached out to NBA members and formed a partnership between the NBA and the NAACP. The two influential organizations decided to work together to fight disenfranchisement, segregation on trains and other mass transit, unequal apportionment of school funds, and employment discrimination. White also announced to the convention that Charles H. Houston had been chosen to head the NAACP's national legal committee. He was the first black lawyer to hold that position.[6]

A second controversy that heightened the tensions between the NBA and the ILD involved Angelo Herndon, a black Communist organizer who was charged with violating a pre–Civil War anti-insurrection law when he led an integrated march of poor farmers and workers in Fulton County, Georgia. When the established black lawyers in Atlanta declined to represent Herndon, Benjamin Davis Jr., a Harvard Law School classmate of William Hastie, who had recently returned home to Atlanta to set up a law practice, volunteered to take the case. Racial tensions were high, and several items of Communist literature were found in Herndon's room after his arrest.

Herndon never had a chance in the contentious trial, as the judge and the prosecutors were very explicit in their racial prejudice. The trial concluded with Davis, at his client's insistence, delivering a final argument that labeled the prosecution part of a scheme to divide white and black workers. Some of the jurors were so enraged by the argument that they turned their chairs around so that Davis argued to their backs. Herndon was convicted of "attempting to incite insurrection" and sentenced to eighteen to twenty years' imprisonment, which in Georgia meant working on a chain gang. Near the end of the trial, Benjamin Davis announced that he had joined the Communist Party of the United States.

Black lawyers at the 1932 and 1933 NBA conventions again debated how to respond to the Scottsboro and Herndon cases, and Houston urged the NBA to get involved. But many black lawyers, especially those from the South, feared that involvement with the Communists would taint them as "red." Finally, during the 1933 convention, the NBA passed a resolution expressing "its appreciation to the International Labor Defense for its unprecedented, courageous and effective fight in the Scottsboro cases."[7] The NBA never took an official position on Herndon, whose conviction was ultimately reversed by the US Supreme Court.

The Scottsboro Boys and the Herndon case underscored a wider conflict among black lawyers and other African American leaders. Some activists believed that fighting injustice required confrontational methods of protest such as marches, boycotts, strikes, and picketing campaigns. Not surprisingly, most black lawyers favored litigation as the best solution. Houston favored a combination of both confrontation and litigation, and he taught his students, including Thurgood Marshall, that, in addition to addressing the specific problems of individual clients, "the Negro lawyer must be trained as a social engineer and group interpreter. Due to the Negro's social and political condition . . . the Negro lawyer must be prepared to anticipate, guide, and interpret his group advancement."[8]

Houston's middle-ground approach to litigation and popular organizing began to mold Marshall's thinking as he finished law school and entered the legal profession. From Houston's combination of litigation and agitation, Marshall learned the importance of raising popular support for civil rights lawsuits through speeches, meetings, and the press.

THE NATIONAL BAR ASSOCIATION
MEETS IN BALTIMORE

In his first year of practice, Marshall had the good fortune of having the 1934 National Bar Association convention held in his hometown of Baltimore. Marshall emerged from the convention with more connections, a leadership role, a better understanding of the issues facing black lawyers, and a clearer sense of his own professional priorities. The 1934 NBA convention in Baltimore was Marshall's introduction to the black legal brotherhood.[9] Marshall did more than just listen to speeches; he eagerly seized the opportunity to get to know other black lawyers from around the country. As Oliver Hill explained, "It was the first time we met Raymond Pace Alexander and several of the big shot lawyers."[10] The delegates noticed Marshall's energy and made him a member of the NBA's publicity committee.

Houston, Marshall, and Oliver Hill arrived at the NBA meeting together. Hill recalled that as they approached the Sharp Street Church Community House, they could hear the powerful voice of veteran lawyer J. Thomas Newsome, from Newport News, Virginia. A respected member of the Virginia bar since 1899, Newsome urged black lawyers attending the convention to stop practicing law for the money and devote themselves to the battle for the rights of colored people.[11] Houston, Marshall, and Hill sat down outside, under a window, and listened for the duration of the speech, captivated by Newsome's powerful voice.[12]

From beginning to end, the convention was rife with conflict. The 1934 Baltimore convention almost did not happen because of conflicts within the Monumental City Bar Association. Some MCBA members thought that their organization was not adequately prepared to host an event of such magnitude. At the previous NBA convention in 1933, MCBA president Josiah Henry invited the NBA to hold its 1934 convention in Baltimore, but he had not adequately consulted with other MCBA members before issuing the invitation. Two weeks before the start of the convention in August 1934, several members of the MCBA publicly threatened to boycott the event.[13] However, a few days before the convention began, the MCBA scrambled to get everything organized in a last-ditch effort to hold a successful convention in Baltimore.[14]

When the National Bar Association held its convention in Baltimore in 1934, Marshall (fourth row, far left) met black lawyers from across the nation. *Courtesy of Afro-American Newspaper Archives and Research Center.*

Minority Groups in Baltimore to Form Alliance

BALTIMORE, Md. — A movement which may institute in Maryland a completely new force to fight for civic, economic and political justice for all minority groups was started Thursday night when a committee comprising several races was formed to make a program for the new organization.

Appoint Committee

At a meeting of the central executive committee of the League Against War and Fascism Thursday evening a special committee, comprising several racial groups, was appointed to make immediate plans for getting together the groups here. Members of that committee include "Thurgood Marshall, Edward S. Lewis, William N. Jones and Gough McDaniels.

Baltimore, Md., ... November 10, ...1936.

Mr. Thurgood Marshall..

.......4 East Redwood Street..............................

To JUNIOR BAR ASSOCIATION OF BALTIMORE CITY, Dr.

Dues for the year 1936-37 . . . . $1.50

Received Payment,

Charles R. Posey Jr.

Make all checks payable to

CHARLES R. POSEY, JR., *Treasurer*, 217 Court House, Baltimore, Md.

The Baltimore City Bar Association excluded black lawyers, but Marshall joined the Junior Bar Association of Baltimore City and attended its events. *Courtesy of Thurgood Marshall Papers, Manuscript Division, Library of Congress, Washington, DC.*

Marshall participated in the organizational meetings of a short-lived coalition of progressive activists. *Courtesy of Afro-American Newspaper Archives and Research Center.*

The seemingly cordial atmosphere at the 1934 convention did not last long. Delegates complained about inadequate preparation of the convention program and arrangements. One visiting lawyer objected to what he called the "down-home, handkerchief-head" principles of the Baltimore attorneys. U. Grant Tyler, president of the MCBA, retorted that "from 1886 to the present day, no colored lawyer in Maryland has been sent to the state penitentiary." He challenged delegates from other states to match that record. He defended Baltimore's black lawyers, proclaiming that "if you don't believe that Baltimore lawyers are good, come to Baltimore and get on the other side of the trial table."[15]

Despite the friction, and with Marshall absorbing every development, the convention approved several important resolutions. The convention's most urgent resolution called for the appointment of black federal judges.[16] The lawyers also vowed to protect freedom of the press for African Americans. They resolved to support full voting rights for blacks, to fight school segregation, and to combat discrimination in President Roosevelt's New Deal public works and farm aid programs. They agreed to fight for the appointment of blacks to positions in federal agencies overseeing New Deal programs. The NBA urged President Roosevelt to appoint black lawyers (not just black social workers) to his group of Negro advisers, known as "the Black Cabinet." The delegates appealed to the governor of Alabama to unconditionally release the Scottsboro Boys and asked the federal government to end segregation at restaurants on government property, including the House and Senate eateries. The lawyers urged the government to appoint a black ambassador to Haiti and to allow Haiti to open a consulate in the United States. The association also called on "the colored lawyers of the country to protest vigorously and courageously, by any and all appropriate legal action, all attempts on the part of public officials to segregate and discriminate [against] colored children in public schools."[17]

This was the convention during which Baltimore Circuit Court judge Eugene O'Dunne entertained the convention delegates in room 131 of the courthouse. Josiah Henry, the former president of the Monumental Bar Association, introduced Judge O'Dunne to the delegates. When Judge O'Dunne addressed the lawyers, he specifically acknowledged Charles Houston and W. Ashbie Hawkins, the two attorneys Marshall admired most.

I see Brother Houston here amongst us, from Washington. He has tried several cases before me, and I have read in the newspaper of the adroit, fearless, splendid defense and presentation he made in the local Federal Court recently, for a client whose interest he espoused, and I believe Brother Hawkins was with him in the case he had before me, and I had great pleasure in seeing the suave, adroit, courteous, and efficient manner in which he handled the litigation.

I do not know that I can say anything more to you except to welcome you, to say that the traditions of the Bar have been the most sacred traditions in American history, and that by your national organization, you have the power and the opportunity of carrying forward into professional life those fine traditions of the Bar which go so far to make the law a living letter.[18]

An editorial in the *Afro-American* commended the convention and encouraged the lawyers in attendance to venture forth and fight for the rights of African Americans. The editorial accurately predicted that most civil rights victories would be won in border states such as Maryland, Missouri, and Kentucky, rather than in the Deep South. It stated, "Where lawyers are needed and where the battle must be waged with unrelenting vigor is the twilight zone between the border states. Here can be won through the courts the battle for the ballot, the battle for equal schools and equal pay for teachers, and the battle for repeal of state Jim Crow car laws. . . . In such a crusade our first line of defense is 1,230 colored lawyers. Our case is in their hands."[19]

JUNIOR BAR ASSOCIATION

With no fanfare—not even a mention in the *Afro-American*—Marshall also joined the white Baltimore City Junior Bar Association. He became a member of the Junior Bar Association two decades before Solomon Baylor, the "first" black man to join the all-white organization, did so in 1955. Marshall paid five dollars in membership dues in 1935 and 1936 and attended the association's luncheon meetings.[20]

The benefits of networking within the broader legal community paid off. At one of the Junior Bar Association's social events, a federal judge told Marshall that the judges of the state's highest court had been favorably impressed with the arguments that Marshall and Houston had made on behalf of Murray.

MARSHALL'S STAR RISES

In 1935, Marshall attended his second NBA convention. He traveled to Nashville with Charles Houston on their third road trip together. The three-day drive each way included many hours of conversation and overnight stops at the homes of Houston's friends. As had the 1934 convention in Baltimore, the 1935 convention included much controversy. The plight of Angelo Herndon continued to cause much debate. Several delegates saw Herndon's efforts to unite poor whites and blacks in a common struggle for justice as too radical. Houston delivered a convention address titled "The Lawyer and His Trust," in which he argued that a lawyer's primary duty is to see that "justice is done between man and man." Some of the lawyers hesitated to become involved with the controversy and called Houston "pink" and "soft on Communism" when he proposed that the NBA provide legal counsel for Angelo Herndon's appeals. Many NBA members feared that the measure would alienate anti-Communist Southern whites who were otherwise sympathetic to the National Bar Association. Those concerns caused many NBA members to vote against direct NBA involvement in Angelo Herndon's case. However, Houston did make some progress in getting NBA support for ILD efforts on behalf of the Scottsboro defendants.[21]

As the 1935 NBA convention drew to a close, the delegates voted for officers. Thurgood Marshall was elected national secretary of the NBA, even though he was only twenty-seven years old and had been a lawyer for less than two years. The most powerful and successful black lawyers in America voted for him. They liked him and had heard from other Baltimore lawyers about his willingness to do organizational work. His status as Houston's confidant and traveling companion added to his prestige.

After Marshall and Houston drove back to Baltimore, Marshall went to work on NBA business. Houston helped Marshall organize and mail the resolutions the convention had adopted. Houston warned the rising leader to be wary of taking on too much at once. Holding an office in a national

NBA national officers, 1937–38. Marshall (far left) served three terms as secretary. Charles Houston's father, William Houston (second from right), became the president. *Courtesy of* Afro-American *Newspaper Archives and Research Center.*

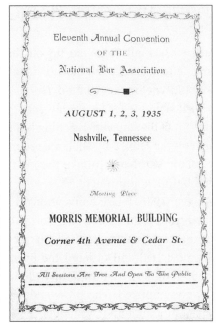

Eleventh Annual Convention

OF THE

National Bar Association

AUGUST 1, 2, 3, 1935

Nashville, Tennessee

Meeting Place

MORRIS MEMORIAL BUILDING

Corner 4th Avenue & Cedar St.

All Sessions Are Free And Open To The Public

In Nashville, the members of the National Bar Association elected Marshall national secretary in 1935, even though Marshall had been a lawyer for less than two years. The NBA re-elected him in Pittsburgh (1936) and in Philadelphia (1937). *Courtesy of Thurgood Marshall Papers, Manuscript Division, Library of Congress, Washington, DC.*

organization was prestigious but of very little remunerative value. Houston feared that Marshall would get too wrapped up in NBA matters and spend too much time and money advancing the organization's cause. "I have had a sad experience in carrying organizations out of my own pocket. . . . Of course, use your own judgment but go as slow as possible," he cautioned Marshall.[22]

When the Angelo Herndon case reached the US Supreme Court, Charles Houston drafted an amicus curiae brief to be filed on behalf of the NAACP. Houston and Marshall attempted to obtain authorization to add the National Bar Association as an official signatory of the brief. Unable to obtain approval from the organization, Marshall and the president of the NBA, George Lawrence, signed the brief as individuals. The Herndon brief became the first document submitted to the US Supreme Court bearing Thurgood Marshall's name.[23] The Court reversed Herndon's conviction.

THE ANTILYNCHING BILL AND THE 1936 CONVENTION

Secretary Marshall followed up on the NBA resolutions he mailed by sending letters and telegrams to members of Congress urging them to support antilynching legislation. His telegram to Senator Robert Wagner of New York stated that "Negro lawyers throughout the country are worried about the fact that the anti-lynching bill is lying dormant in the Senate after passage by the House by such a large majority. . . . We are looking to you and Senator Van Nuys to take the necessary steps to [e]nsure passage of this bill before adjournment."[24]

As the 1936 NBA convention in Pittsburgh approached, Marshall assumed responsibility for most of the convention arrangements. He confirmed the key speakers, mailed out materials, prepared the proposed resolutions, designed and ordered the printed programs, ordered name tags, and undertook a myriad of similar duties. Marshall's efforts for the NBA did not go unnoticed. The press and leaders of other organizations began to contact him about NBA matters.[25]

In addition to Marshall's administrative chores at the convention, he secured the passage of his own resolution that called for the impeachment of a Pennsylvania judge who had told a black defendant in court, "If the

Why the Angelo Herndon Case is So Important

The sentence of from eighteen to twenty years imposed on Angelo Herndon in Atlanta for an attempt at inciting to insurrection by having seditious literature in his possession has just been upheld by the Georgia Supreme Court.

The statute under which Herndon was convicted, which has not been invoked previously for decades, provides for the death sentence as the maximum punishment, but in Herndon's case the jury recommended "mercy."

Herndon was arrested while in the act of opening a postoffice box which he acknowledged as his, and in his room, after his arrest, were found piles of documents, many of them in the original wrappers, which the court termed seditious.

Mere Possession

The case rests so far, therefore, merely on the possession of such documents, and the defense has lain in the contention that mere possession does not in fact constitute the act of inciting to insurrection.

The next move will be application for a writ of certiorari to take the case to the United States Supreme Court, where the constitutionality both of the statute itself and of the Georgia court's application of it will be fought.

As in the Scottsboro case, the appeal in which was argued on May 25 before the Alabama Supreme Court, the International Labor Defense has conducted the defense, and it deserves the interest and support of all those who do not wish to see a man spend two decades in prison on a trumped-up charge which covers the real offense of daring, as Herndon did, to attempt to organize his fellow-workers, white and black, in protest against intolerable conditions.

IN THE SUPREME COURT OF THE
UNITED STATES.

OCTOBER TERM, 1934.

No. 665.

ANGELO HERNDON,

Appellant

vs.

THE STATE OF GEORGIA.

BRIEF OF AMICI CURIAE IN SUPPORT OF MOTION
FOR REHEARING.

I.

Object.

The object of this brief is to support as amici curiae the petition of appellant, Angelo Herndon, for a rehearing in the above-entitled cause, dismissed for want of jurisdiction on May 20, 1935.

II.

Preliminary Statement.

The National Association for the Advancement of Colored People a body corporate with 325 branches i

---

14

mit to this Court that petitioner has conclusively demonstrated that he seasonably and properly presented and saved his federal question in the State Court, and that he is entitled to be heard on his claim that "the statute as construed by the court below, and as applied to appellant, violates the due process clause of the Fourteenth Amendment, and the questions presented are within the jurisdiction of this Court," and that his petition for rehearing should be granted.

Respectfully submitted,

CHARLES H. HOUSTON,
Counsel for National Association for the Advancement of Colored People and National Bar Association, as amici curiae.

GEORGE W. LAWRENCE,
THURGOOD MARSHALL,
JAMES MARSHALL,
of Counsel.

ARTHUR GARFIELD HAYS,
MORRIS L. ERNST,
Counsel for the American Civil Liberties Union, Inc. as amicus curiae.

BETHUEL M. WEBSTER, JR.,
Counsel for the Church League for Industrial Democracy, The Methodist Federation for Social Service, The Justice Commission of the Central Conference of American Rabbis. Rev. W. Russell Bowie, Rev. Allan Knight Chalmers, Rev. Harry Emerson Fosdick, Rev. Hubert C. Herring, Dr. Stephen S. Wise, as amici curiae.

A "friend of the court" brief on behalf of Communist activist Angelo Herndon became the first document filed in the U.S. Supreme Court bearing Marshall's name. *Courtesy of Afro-American Newspaper Archives and Research Center.*

citizens of [Columbia, Pennsylvania] had lynched you, they would have been justified." As the 1936 National Bar Association convention came to a close, Marshall was reelected as secretary.[26] With his reelection again at the 1937 NBA convention in Pittsburgh, Marshall became the only person to serve three consecutive terms in the same office of the National Bar Association. Thurgood Marshall had become a leader among lawyers.[27]

Chapter 14

The Baltimore County
High School Case

As Donald Gaines Murray entered the University of Maryland School of Law under the first court-ordered school desegregation in the nation's history, Marshall did not rest on his laurels or focus on more lucrative criminal and civil cases. He turned his attention to the next major civil rights case of his early career. As hard as Marshall had worked on the Murray matter, he would work even harder in an attempt to desegregate the high schools in Baltimore County.[1] This experience would become the greatest disappointment of Marshall's early career.

BALTIMORE COUNTY

Baltimore County is about six times the size of Baltimore City, and it surrounds the city's northern, eastern, and western boundaries. In 1935, African Americans comprised 10 percent of the county's population and lived primarily in forty small enclaves scattered throughout the county. Some of the county's black communities had just a few families, while others were home to hundreds of people. The three largest black populations were in Towson (to the north of Baltimore), Turner's Station (to the southeast), and Catonsville (a suburb southwest of the city).

Baltimore County had ten public high schools scattered thoughout the county, all of them off-limits to black students.[2] Black youngsters who wished to continue their education beyond the seventh grade had to travel to Frederick Douglass High School in Baltimore City. For some students, the daily journey was twenty miles in each direction. The county paid Baltimore City the tuition of students who passed a qualifying examination administered by the county school system. However, the county gave no money to students for the daily trip to and from Baltimore.

Marshall decided to take on this discriminatory practice and talked with a group of Baltimore County parents about the challenges facing black Marylanders who wanted equal schools. An article in the *Afro-American* gave an account of Marshall's remarks:

> [Blacks in Maryland] have five remedies, he said. . . .
> 1. They could migrate to Northern states, but that is impossible.
> 2. They could start a revolution and fight for what they want, but that would be suicide.
> 3. They can use the ballot and elect colored officials to the several branches of government, but that will take time.
> 4. An appeal to the fairness of white people could be made, but that would not do much good.
> 5. The various matters that irk the people of the State can be carried to the courts for remedy.

Marshall argued the fifth way was the way out of the wilderness for the black community.[3]

Marshall's comments exhibited extraordinary faith in the courts and confidence in the potential of the law.

A BROKEN SYSTEM

Marshall identified two potential plaintiffs, Margaret Williams and Lucille Scott. In 1934, Williams had completed the seventh grade at a one-room schoolhouse in the small black enclave of Cowdensville in southwestern Baltimore County. She had failed the qualifying exam for the county to pay her tuition to attend high school in Baltimore. Of the 128 students who took the exam that year, only 64 had passed. Despite repeating the seventh grade, Margaret failed on her second attempt to pass the examination.[4]

Houston encouraged Marshall to move forward and arranged for the

County Refuses to Accept Petition for High School

Education Head Says Colored People Have Things They Need.

BRANDS EFFORT FOR EQUALITY BAD

Courts Only Recourse, Attorney Declares.

TOWSON—A petition for a high school in Baltimore County, where whites only are now permitted to attend school beyond the seventh grade, was met with a blank refusal from the county board of education, Tuesday.

Thurgood Marshall, attorney for the NAACP, presented the petition, signed by a number of prominent county residents, to Henry M. Warfield, white, president of the board at one of its regular meetings.

Mr. Warfield declared that he would not accept the petition or anything from Mr. Marshall because an attorney had advised him

The Baltimore County School Board refused to accept Marshall's petition signed by African American parents requesting high school education in the county. *Courtesy of Afro-American Newspaper Archives and Research Center.*

Ultimatum to County Board Sent by NAACP

Letter Demands Move to Give Schools by March 12.

SAY TRICKERY OF BOARD IS PLAIN

Only 29 Per Cent Pass Examinations.

An ultimatum, giving the Baltimore County Board of Education until Wednesday to take steps toward providing high school facilities, was issued by the Baltimore branch of the NAACP, this week.

Thurgood Marshall, counsel for the branch, said in a letter to the board:

"We are making a last and final appeal. However, be advised, that if a satisfactory adjustment of this matter is not made on or before March 12, 1936, we shall be forced to avail ourselves of remedies provided by the law."

Survey Completed

Mr. Marshall has just completed a survey of Baltimore County's facilities and he charges:

Marshall sent to Baltimore County officials the demands of the black parents and the NAACP. *Courtesy of Afro-American Newspaper Archives and Research Center.*

NAACP to advance a little financial support. Marshall reported to Houston when he was ready to begin the challenge, "I received the check. Thanks. It will keep the wolf away from the door. . . . Colored pupil will apply to the white high school tomorrow morning."[5]

Marshall drove Margaret, Lucille, and Margaret's father, Joshua Williams, to Catonsville High School, the county high school closest to their home. Marshall remained outside the building while Mr. Williams went inside with the two children. The principal, David W. Zimmerman, refused to admit the students, stating that Baltimore County policy prohibited blacks and whites from attending the same public schools. Zimmerman was pleasant and admitted that Margaret's grades would have qualified her for admission to the school if she were white.[6]

Marshall followed up the school visit by sending Margaret Williams's Catonsville High School application to Clarence G. Cooper, the superintendent of Baltimore County Schools. Marshall wrote that Williams had good grades and desired to attend the Catonsville school but that she could not because the principal had violated her constitutional rights by denying her admission. Cooper refused to take action on the application. A few weeks later, Marshall sent a letter to the Baltimore County Board of Education, urging the board members to accept Williams's application. When the board ignored the application, Marshall felt that he had exhausted all his administrative options and decided to bring suit.[7]

DISCUSSING STRATEGY

Charles Houston suggested that Marshall bring two simultaneous suits. The first suit would be for a court order to have Williams admitted to the white high school and the second suit would be filed on behalf of Scott with the goal of compelling Baltimore County to build a high school for African Americans. Marshall, however, doubted that he could get both suits moving simultaneously and was uncertain which action to pursue first.[8]

The *Afro-American*, which had provided extensive coverage of the Murray case, began to devote attention to the Baltimore County high school matter. Clarence M. Mitchell Jr. again did most of the reporting.

In October 1935, Marshall sent a detailed report on the Baltimore County case to Walter White, executive secretary of the NAACP. In the report, Marshall explained that the planned litigation was aimed at forcing officials to open a high school for black students in a county where there were ten high schools for whites and not a single one for blacks. Marshall concluded by telling White about a meeting of the Baltimore County Board of Education at which he had attempted to present a petition from taxpayers who supported the construction of a black high school. The Board of Education chairman was hostile and told Marshall that his activism was "going to set the Negro race back many years."[9]

Marshall selected Lucille Scott (center) and Margaret Williams (right) as possible plaintiffs. *Courtesy of* Afro-American *Newspaper Archives and Research Center.*

Marshall told White that he had to exhaust one more administrative remedy before filing suit. He would first appeal to the Maryland State Board of Education. If the State Board of Education refused to admit Williams, he would then file two suits at once, per Charles Houston's suggestion.[10]

Marshall, never underestimating the power of good press coverage, arranged with Clarence Mitchell for the *Afro-American* to announce the forthcoming lawsuits.[11] In addition to reaching out to the *Afro-American*, Marshall kept the mainstream white press within his sights and communicated with trusted white reporters.[12]

As planned, Marshall presented two petitions to the State Board of Education, one for the admission of the girls to Catonsville High School and the other one for the establishment of a colored high school in Baltimore County. The board cordially received Marshall. However, Marshall informed Walter White that the State Board of Education would most likely refuse to admit the students. Marshall stood ready to file the suits but hesitated to bring a new civil rights case until the Maryland Court of Appeals had made a decision in the Murray matter.[13] As Marshall had predicted in his report to White, the State Board of Education, through its secretary, Albert S. Cook, declared that decisions about admissions were local matters and that the state education authorities lacked the power to order Baltimore County to accept Williams and Scott.[14]

As a young lawyer struggling to make ends meet, Marshall made no bones about his need for some type of remuneration for all his work in Baltimore County. "Has anything been done on the advancement of my fee?"[15] he wrote to Houston. On December 2, 1935, Marshall received an early Christmas present consisting of a check for fifty dollars from the NAACP.[16]

MULTITASKING

In January 1936, while still waiting for a decision in the Murray case, Marshall began assembling evidence for the Baltimore County high school case. The task quickly became daunting. Marshall feared that because of the county's large size and the NAACP's limited budget, the meticulous investigation he planned to conduct would be difficult, if not impossible.

Marshall began to obtain lists of the black students from the county who attended high schools in Baltimore. He visited past and current students and presented them with a questionnaire about their experiences in Baltimore City schools. Marshall also amassed important statistics, including a systemwide census taken by the Baltimore County school system and data about the Baltimore County students who had completed seventh grade over the past fifteen years.[17]

Despite Marshall's best efforts, the white media's portrayal of the unfolding events in Baltimore County took a turn for the worse. The *Baltimore News*, a Hearst publication, covered the Baltimore County schools matter in a way that portrayed the NAACP and Marshall as troublemakers who sought to disrupt the status quo by advocating for the admission of black students into white schools. The paper wanted to turn moderate whites against the NAACP's goals of desegregation and integration.[18]

As if he did not already have enough irons in the fire, Marshall still kept an eye on Donald Murray's progress in law school. Marshall monitored Murray's studying and notetaking, and he arranged for Professor Ransom of Howard University to prepare Murray for his law school examinations.[19]

Marshall also contemplated a possible school transportation lawsuit in Anne Arundel County, where school buses served only white children. Black children in the county had to arrange for their own transportation to get to the county's only black high school, which was in Annapolis. Marshall considered filming black children trudging along to school while the school buses for white children passed them on the road. This project never materialized, however. By late January 1936, he had completed a draft of the petition for the Baltimore County high school case and had sent it to Houston.

GENERATING PUBLICITY

Houston was adamant about obtaining favorable publicity for Marshall's new cause. He advised Marshall that the Williams case should not be filed without also waging a media campaign to boost public opinion in favor of Williams.[20]

By February, Marshall had developed a media strategy. He wanted to file the suit and publish a press release giving a full account of Baltimore County's refusal to allow Williams to attend Catonsville High School. This press release would be followed by additional press releases and articles as the case progressed. Marshall worked closely with Clarence Mitchell to coordinate the timing of the press releases, and he warned Houston not to give any information about the case to the New York papers before the *Afro-American* had announced the filing of the lawsuit. However, Marshall did give a short press release to other papers explaining that the investigation was almost complete and that he would soon file the Baltimore County suit.[21]

Marshall remained outside of Catonsville High School in his automobile while his client and her father went inside and attempted to register. *Courtesy of Maryland State Archives and Thurgood Marshall Papers, Manuscript Division, Library of Congress, Washington, DC.*

Houston hoped that the investigation would be complete in time for Marshall to travel to New York to strategize for the next phase of the Baltimore County case. Houston asked Marshall to prepare a detailed statement for the NAACP about the educational disparities faced by African Americans in Baltimore County. Houston also wanted the statement to discuss the county's refusal to ameliorate the plight of black students and to recommend litigation as the best solution.[22]

Marshall responded immediately with much of the information that Houston had requested. He informed Houston that the difficulty of traveling throughout Baltimore County remained a significant obstacle to compiling the additional data he needed in order to complete the investigation. Marshall agreed to provide Houston with figures showing that there were enough black children in the county to justify building a separate black high school, and he promised to prepare a questionnaire for a survey designed to determine how far each individual student had to travel from Baltimore County to reach the sole black high school in Baltimore.[23]

Marshall feared that there would not be enough cars available for his team of investigators to survey a sufficient number of students. However, since most of the Baltimore County students attending high school in Baltimore lived within four to eight miles of the city, Marshall's fears were unfounded. He was anxious to begin the survey. Mitchell had started to publicize the investigation and the pending lawsuit in the *Afro-American*, and Marshall wanted to make sure that updates about his progress in the Baltimore County case appeared regularly in the paper.[24]

LOGISTICAL CHALLENGES

A few days later, Marshall prepared to conduct the Baltimore County high school survey. However, Old Man Winter had other plans. A blizzard that wreaked havoc on the greater Baltimore area temporarily delayed Marshall's project, but he pressed on. He recruited Juanita Jackson and attorney Robert McGuinn to assist him. He chose McGuinn for practical reasons. "I am taking Bob McGuinn along with me on my trips so that he will be able to go into the white schools and get information, because I think he looks enough like our white brethren," Marshall wrote to Houston in February 1935. Marshall planned to personally visit and photograph the more dilapidated black schools.[25]

Meanwhile, he requested a copy of Baltimore County's biennial student census. Suspecting trickery on the part of his old nemesis Dr. Cook, he was not swayed by Cook's friendly demeanor and willingness to cooperate with the investigation. Marshall wanted to make sure that the figures he received from Cook were accurate. He planned to have Cook sign the documents he handed over so that Cook could be subpoenaed to testify about their accuracy and authenticity at trial. Despite the early February snowstorm, Marshall and his investigative team were able to venture out and begin collecting information.[26]

A DIFFICULT BALANCING ACT

In the white press, Houston tried to promote the NAACP as seeking a separate high school for black students rather than advocating for outright desegregation. At the same time, Houston knew that the establishment of a separate black high school was inconsistent with the message of racial integration and equality promoted by the NAACP. He knew that he had to strike a balance between achieving quick results while not losing sight of the big picture. Houston suggested to Marshall that he write a letter as a final appeal to the white press on behalf of Baltimore County's black parents and taxpayers, whose wishes for a separate black high school remained unheeded by the county. Houston, wary of sending out mixed messages to the newspapers, did not want Marshall's letter to mention the NAACP, so as to avoid any potential conflicts of interest.[27]

Marshall fully agreed with Houston that black parents and taxpayers, not the NAACP, should be the ones to bring suit demanding a high school for black children. He suggested as potential plaintiffs the United Parent Teacher's Association (UPTA), which had lobbied for a black high school in the past. Marshall had McGuinn draft a letter for UPTA as he resumed his investigation in Baltimore County, just in time for yet another winter storm.[28]

AMASSING EVIDENCE

By February 25, 1936, the information Marshall had collected in the Baltimore County surveys had been organized and presented to Houston and the NAACP leadership.[29] This information served as the foundation for a comprehensive report sent out to the newspapers by UPTA in a press release titled "Need for High School Facilities for Education of Negroes in Baltimore County." The report stated that "according to the 1930 Census the Negroes in Baltimore County form 9.4% of the total population and 8.6% of the school population between the ages of 15 and 19. . . . Last year $336,594.88 was spent for current expenses for the support of [the white] high schools. Not one cent of this was shared by Negro pupils."[30]

It did not take long for the white press to pick up the story and run with it. In fact, Marshall strategically leaked the report to the *Baltimore News Post* before it was officially released. "Seek Colored County School," read the *Baltimore News Post* headline on February 28, 1936. The paper reported that UPTA had charged the Baltimore County authorities with a "flagrant violation of the Fourteenth Amendment" and "demanded the establishment of a high school for Negro students." The article also related how UPTA had claimed that with only a 50 percent passing rate on the high school entrance examination for the black students, either the exam must be inherently unfair or the black elementary schools had failed to adequately prepare their students for the exam.[31] *Baltimore News Post* columnist Louis Azrael also supported Marshall's cause, suggesting that Baltimore County, as only one of two counties in Maryland that did not provide high schools for blacks, should do more to live up to the doctrine of "separate but equal."[32]

By March 1936 both the black and white press had devoted substantial space to the Baltimore County high school dispute, and Marshall was prepared to bring legal action against the Baltimore County Board of Education.

GEARING UP FOR TRIAL

Marshall sued only on behalf of Margaret Williams, intending to bring Lucille Scott's claim later. When Marshall first attempted to file the lawsuit, all the Baltimore County judges were in a joint session in Harford County. The young lawyer now turned to a friend. Marshall approached Judge Offutt of the Court of Appeals, whose local chambers were in Towson, the county seat of Baltimore County. Marshall asked him to sign an emergency order to compel the county to admit Margaret Williams to Catonsville High School. Judge Offutt politely declined and explained that if he were to become involved at the trial level, it would disqualify him from hearing the case if it were to reach the Maryland Court of Appeals. Marshall took this as an encouraging sign that Offutt was on his side and wrote to Houston that "the old boy is still with us."[33]

Marshall then approached Judge C. Gus Grayson of the Baltimore County Circuit Court, who initially declined[34] but then signed an order giving the school officials fourteen days to "show cause" why the court should not order that Margaret be admitted to Catonsville High School.[35]

The *Afro-American* reported that the trial would take place in the Baltimore County Circuit Court in Towson.[36] As with the Murray case, the original petition in the Baltimore County high school case did not mention Williams's race. The petition simply alleged that Margaret Williams was a county resident who had been arbitrarily excluded from admission to the county high school. Marshall and the NAACP would again leave it to the defense to state in their answer that Williams had been denied admission due to her race.

THE COUNTY RESPONDS

Soon after Marshall filed suit, William L. Rawls and Cornelius E. Roe, private attorneys retained by Baltimore County, responded to the petition. They alleged that the plaintiff was not admitted to the high school because she was black and because she had failed the entrance exam. Marshall usually maintained cordial ties with opposing counsel even if he disagreed with their views, but he was never able to develop an informal relationship with Roe or Rawls.

Marshall was surprised that the defense's answer insisted that all the seventh-grade children in Baltimore County, both black and white, were required to take the same examination for admission to high school. Marshall firmly believed that only black students took such an examination.[37]

Houston recommended that Marshall consider filing a second case, one on behalf of a black student from Baltimore County who was already attending the Baltimore City high school. Such a test plaintiff, Houston believed, would bolster Margaret Williams's case. Williams's academic record was not exactly impeccable, and Houston feared that the defense would exploit that potential weakness and argue that Williams did not pass the exam because she lacked sufficient scholastic aptitude. Marshall was caught in a troublesome predicament. He needed a plaintiff who had not passed the high school entrance examination in order to argue that requiring the examination was discriminatory. However, a plaintiff who had already passed the examination and was attending high school in Baltimore City would bolster the defense's argument that the examination was fair and Williams just lacked the skill to pass it.[38]

With the complexity of this situation already weighing on his mind, Marshall received advice from Houston to confer with Carl Murphy from the *Afro-American* and have him write an editorial questioning the quality of education administered by the Baltimore County elementary schools for black children. If Margaret Williams had finished the seventh grade and was still not ready for high school, there must be something lacking in the county's education of its black youngsters. The *Afro-American* was only too willing to oblige, but unfortunately, Marshall could not find a suitable second plaintiff, and he never filed a second suit.

He did find several expert witnesses who were willing to testify that Margaret Williams's grades proved that she was qualified to attend high school. The witnesses included George B. Murphy, a retired Baltimore City elementary school principal, and Jesse Nicholas, a retired Baltimore County elementary school principal and supervisor. Marshall also began to encourage group meetings of black parents in Baltimore County to build support for the case, and he arranged for small leaflets containing information about the white high schools in Baltimore County to be printed and distributed to parents of black students.[39]

After Marshall responded to the defendant's answers, Rawls and Roe fired back with a motion seeking to dismiss the lawsuit on procedural grounds.[40] The case was assigned to Circuit Judge Frank Duncan, who conducted a hearing on the motion. Marshall repeatedly accused the defense lawyers of misrepresenting the facts and threatened to put into evidence photographs he claimed to have that showed the inadequacy of the county's schools for black children.[41] When Judge Duncan denied the defendant's motion, Marshall wrote to Houston and gave his positive assessment of the judge: "At a conference this morning with Judge Duncan at Towson, denied the Motion. . . . He is a pretty decent fellow."[42] Marshall's positive evaluation of the judge proved premature; he would soon conclude that he had drawn the wrong judge.

The defense attorneys made other attempts to throw the case out of court. They filed a motion attacking Marshall for citing Williams's race as the reason why she was not admitted to the school. At the motion hearing before Judge Duncan, Rawls observed that Marshall's original petition did not identify Margaret Williams as "colored," nor did it identify Catonsville High School as an all-white school. Rawls also maintained that the examination system was fair, and he again asserted that both black and white students took the same examination to continue on to high school. Motions filed by the defense accused Marshall of attacking black elementary schools and accused him of interfering with "tradition."[43]

Marshall responded that the defense had first raised the issue of race. However, what proved to be the Achilles' heel of Marshall's strategy was the issue of whether or not white students also had to pass the entrance exam to go on to high school. Marshall was certain that white students who completed the seventh grade moved on to high school automatically and that only black students in Baltimore County had to pass a specific examination to obtain county funds to attend the black high school in Baltimore. The county's lawyers insisted that both black and white students took the same examination. Based on his investigation, Marshall was confident that he could prove in court that only black students took the high school entrance exam. When Judge Duncan ruled against the Baltimore County Board of Education on a demurrer, Marshall believed that he was headed toward another victory.[44]

THE TABLES TURN

After ruling against the county on all of its preliminary motions, Judge Duncan announced what he considered to be the only relevant issue for the trial. Duncan stated that as far as he was concerned, the only important question was whether Margaret Williams had passed the examination. The judge was not interested in other issues raised by the lawyers. This narrow view of the case troubled Marshall. Marshall had selected Williams as the plaintiff exactly because she had not passed the scholarship examination. To Marshall, the point of the litigation was to establish that Williams, a black girl, should not have to pass an examination that only black students took in order to go to high school.

Before the trial began, Marshall attempted to combat Duncan's narrow view of the case.[45] At the trial, Marshall was surprised that Duncan was willing to accept the defendant's uncorroborated assertion that black and white seventh graders took the same examination for admission to high school. Marshall had not anticipated a genuine dispute regarding this issue. School officials testified that they regularly gave the examination to white students, but they were unable to produce a single document that showed that a single white child had taken the test administered to Margaret Williams.[46]

Marshall could see that Judge Duncan had made up his mind. The testimony of Joshua Williams, Margaret Williams's father, did not sway the judge, and neither did Marshall's expert witnesses. To add insult to injury, Superintendent Clarence G. Cooper suggested that Margaret's failure to pass the exam arose from the "fact" that black children were intellectually inferior to white children.[47] Marshall informed Walter White of the negative turn of events. After three long days of testimony, Marshall believed that his only positive achievement consisted in having built a record for the Court of Appeals. He urged the Maryland NAACP branches to start raising funds for an appeal.[48]

Marshall unsuccessfully attempted in this Towson courtroom to get a black student admitted to one of Baltimore County's ten high schools. *Courtesy of Afro-American Newspaper Archives and Research Center and Maryland State Archives.*

Lawyers Clash at Maryland Hearing

N.A.A.C.P. Contends Baltimore County Must Open Catonsville White High School; Says County Can't Violate U. S. Constitution.

TOWSON, Md.—A charge that the lawyers for the county board of education gave erroneous information in the Baltimore County high school case was made Friday by Thurgood Marshall, N.A.A.C.P. counsel, while arguing a demurrer in the circuit court before Judge Frank Duncan.

Mr. Marshall stated that the ard alleges that white pupils must take an examination in order to get high school training in the county. He denied that this is true and added that the board also gave false information as to the number of white children who qualify annually for high school.

William Pawls and Cornelius Roe, the board lawyers, filed the demurrer on the grounds that Mr. Marshall's replication, which is the legal term for a reply to an answer filed in a writ of mandamus, set up a new case. Judge Duncan made no decision at the time of the hearing.

Applied to White High

The case is that of Miss Margaret Williams, county pupil, who applied for admission to the Catonsville High School for whites because there are no high school facilities for colored in Baltimore County.

When Miss Williams was refused admission by the board on the grounds that she was colored, Mr. Marshall and Charles Houston, both NAACP lawyers, filed a petition for a writ of mandamus to require the board to admit her.

The county provides scholarships for colored students to to Douglass High School in Baltimore City, in order to obtain one of these scholarships, however, a pupil must pass an examination and then provide his

U. of Md. Case Used

own transportation to the city. This, the NAACP lawyers contend, is unfair.

A part of the Court of Appeals's decision in the case that gave Donald G. Murray entrance to the University of Maryland law school is applicable in the coun-

"Open Up a High School for Me"

MARGARET WILLIAMS, school girl whose parents are suing Baltimore County to compel officials to open the white high school to colored children. The county has eleven white high schools and no colored high school.

fied for admission to a high school because she had twice failed an examination that is given to colored and white alike.

Replication Sudden

should have contained an allegation showing it. Had the petitioner alleged specifically that there was no colored school in the neighborhood to which she would have conveniently gone . . . different questions might have arisen."

Mr. Rawls argued that counsel for Miss Williams referred to the elementary schools of the county as inadequate. "They also talk about somebody who has to go twenty miles to school in Baltimore from the county," he said, "but they do not give any name or address for that person."

Marshall Follows

Mr. Marshall followed Mr. Rawls with the assertion that everything which the replication he filed contained was in reply to the answer of the lawyers for the board of education.

Mr. Marshall pointed out that when he filed his petition for mandamus the lawyers for the board threw the whole county school system into their answer.

He argued that the recourse he had was to admit or deny the things that the answer to his petition set forth. "And of course," said he, "it is a known fact that I would not admit them."

The whole court action, Mr. Marshall said, was a matter of last resort in that the colored people have for many years been trying to get high school facilities for their children in the county. "We have been unable to obtain them," Mr. Marshall said, "so we take the only avenue open to us and that is an attempt to get into the school for whites."

Color Not Necessary

It was not necessary to say that the girl seeking admission to the Catonsville school was colored, Mr. Marshall said. He challenged anyone in the court to show him that getting Constitutional rights depends on color.

He also challenged the opposition to show him any one item in his replication which was not a legitimate reply to their answer.

He asserted that the board's attorneys struck a path in their answer that he was legally bound to follow. "We have merely gone behind their high sounding facts," said he, "to show what actually exists."

Has Three Experts

Mr. Marshall admitted that he had attacked the county educational system and pointed out that he had three Federal experts in education ready to back him up.

"We have pictures of these schools," Mr. Marshall said, "and moving pictures if anyone wants

DISAPPOINTMENT

Duncan's denial of the plaintiff's petition did not come as a surprise to Marshall and his team. Professor Leon Ransom, who had assisted Marshall with the case, prepared a report for the NAACP national office that was very complimentary of Marshall's efforts. Ransom described how the defendants had done everything within their power to steamroll the NAACP and sideline its agenda of integrating the Baltimore County schools. Ransom complained that many of the judge's rulings were prejudicial and said that he was disappointed with the court's reliance on hearsay evidence. He also found that Judge Duncan had freely admitted questionable "expert testimony" presented by the defense while refusing to admit some of Marshall's expert evidence on the grounds that it was irrelevant to the proceedings. Ransom was also annoyed with the judge's narrow view of the issues but agreed with Marshall that the case had built a good record for the Court of Appeals.[49]

Marshall and Ransom wasted no time in preparing for the appeal. Not surprisingly, Marshall decided that for the appeal, he would hammer away at Judge Duncan's questionable refusal to consider any other issue besides the plaintiff's exam score.[50]

THE SILVER LINING

Thurgood Marshall was disappointed at having lost a case to which he had devoted so much time and effort. The loss, however, did not diminish Thurgood's standing in the eyes of the NAACP. To the contrary, in his report, Professor Ransom made sure that the people at NAACP headquarters in New York understood that Marshall had done a superb job and that he had provided the best possible legal representation for his client. By the time the Maryland Court of Appeals had affirmed Judge Duncan's decision in May 1937, Thurgood Marshall was employed at the NAACP's New York office.[51]

Although the NAACP considered taking the case to the US Supreme Court, that idea quickly faded as other priorities, such as the teacher pay cases, took over. Marshall drafted a press release that pointed to a silver lining in the results of the Baltimore County case. The press release focused on language in the opinion of the Maryland Court of Appeals, which stated that "the existence of a system of separate schools involves allowances of some incidental differences, and some inequalities, in meeting practical problems presented." The NAACP release attempted to spin this ambiguous statement to mean that "for the first time, a court has admitted that certain inequalities are inevitable in a separate school system" and that "it was significant and valuable to have a court recognize and state that the mere existence of a separate system in itself imports inequality." In other words, if it is racially "separate," it will be "unequal."[52]

Despite this encouraging hint from the Maryland Court of Appeals that the "separate but equal" doctrine was showing some cracks, almost two decades would pass before the Supreme Court's decision in *Brown v. Board of Education* marked the legal end of racial segregation in schools and other public facilities in the United States.[53]

Chapter 15

Financial Pressures
and Career Decision

By the middle of 1936, Marshall's financial situation had reached a breaking point, and some solution had to be found. Marshall wrote to Houston:

> The real matter mostly pertains to me. As it stands, things are getting worse and worse, and first of all, I fully realize that the Association has no money and that there is very little left in the Garland Fund. However, I would like for you and Walter to make sure that there is no possibility of helping me out through here. However, if there is a possibility, I would appreciate it very much if I could be assured of enough to tide me over, then in return, I could do more on these cases. For example, to prepare briefs and research, etc. on the other cases or any of the legal matters which you would need assistance on.[1]

The "Garland Fund" to which Marshall referred had been the source of the meager payments that Marshall had received for the law school case and the high school case. While still a student at Harvard College, Charles Garland had inherited more than a million dollars from his father and had used most of it to establish the American Fund for Public Service. The Garland Fund, as it came to be called, supported labor organizing, civil liberties, and "the protection of minorities." The NAACP used money from the Garland Fund to press for antilynching laws, to defend persons accused of crimes, to issue its magazine, the *Crisis*, to prepare reports documenting the inequality of Jim Crow facilities, and to bring litigation for educational equality.

As the money from the Garland Fund became depleted, Marshall was in a desperate financial condition. He was spending around sixty dollars a month on business expenses and bringing in virtually nothing. At home, he was the main breadwinner during most of the summer months. When Marshall wrote that letter, his mother was not teaching and his father had lost his job at Gibson Island and was looking for work.

Dire financial straits were nothing new for Marshall. Lack of money had been a recurring theme early in his life, and by 1936, Marshall was in serious trouble. His letters to Houston in his early years as a lawyer almost always had included a plea for funds, but his May 1936 correspondence carried a tone of desperation that prior letters had lacked. Marshall was begging Houston for help:

> Just to give you an idea of my expenses, the rent is $21.00 per month, $7.00 per week for "Little Bits,"[2] and approximately $8.00 per month for phone bill, besides, there are, of course, the notes on the car and other items including stationary and postage. . . . In conclusion, I am asking that you see what can be done. Of course, you realize that I know you understand the whole situation, and that you can be perfectly frank. But as the "boys" say, "It has arrived at the point where I just can't take it."[3]

In May 1936, Thurgood Marshall was at a true crossroads in his young life. Three years after passing the Maryland bar, he was flat broke. The letter pointed out that as the school year had ended, his mother would not be working and "most of the weight of the house will be on me." Marshall urged Houston to "think this over very carefully and do what you can do for me."[4]

Marshall also did what he could to help other members of the household find work. Marshall drafted a letter for his father to be sent to another country club:

> I am hereby making application for the position of steward at Sherwood Forest for this present year. I have had twelve (12) years of experience as steward of country clubs. For four (4) years I was steward of the Maryland Country Club in Baltimore City, and for eight (8) years I held the position of steward of Gibson Island Club, Gibson Island, Maryland.[5]

Marshall never learned exactly how his father had lost the best job of his life, but Marshall suspected that his father had "got in the way of somebody who was white."[6]

Marshall's wife, Vivian, found only sporadic work and was often unemployed. On March 24, 1936, Marshall wrote to Joseph Evans, one of his Alpha Phi Alpha fraternity brothers in Washington, D.C., seeking employment for his wife:

> My wife, Vivian Marshall, was over to see you last weekend concerning a position in the White Collar Survey or some other Federal Project in Maryland. She was unable to reach you on Saturday because of the fact that she could not locate the office on Vermont Avenue. On Sunday she was told that you were in Baltimore.
>
> On her behalf, I am asking that you, if possible, give us an idea of how one of these positions may be obtained. The handling of positions over here has been quite unsatisfactory from our point of view, and she has been constantly shunted from one to another, and now she is told that there is no possibility of a position in the White Collar Survey. I will more than appreciate anything you may be able to do in this matter, and thanking you in advance. . . .[7]

Evans was of no help.

Like many others who struggled during the Great Depression, the young lawyer was harassed by creditors. He paid his office rent and secretary on time. However, he was chronically late with payments to the Chesapeake and Potomac Telephone Company and to office suppliers such as the Smith Corona Company, from which he rented his well-used typewriter.

Law book publishers were particularly persistent. "We find that the enclosed account, in regard to which we have written you, is still unpaid. Small accounts are expensive to handle in a collection department so we must ask our friends to pay these accounts as promptly as possible," wrote E. Peterson, a credit manager with Prentice-Hall Books.[8] Peterson's inquiry seemed cordial enough initially, but the tone of the letter quickly became more pointed. "In this case you have been favored with an extension of sixty days beyond our regular terms. Are we not therefore entitled to payment now? We think you will agree and feeling certain you will no longer delay the payment, we are enclosing a return envelope for your convenience in sending your check or money-order today."[9]

Prentice-Hall was not the only law book publisher in pursuit of Marshall's elusive, meager earnings. The Washington Law Book Company was another persistent creditor, and it proposed a payment plan.

> You perhaps have delayed remitting until you were in a position to remit the entire amount owing, $108.15. Many of our lawyer friends, who for good reason have been unable to remit in full, have adopted the helpful plan of making small, monthly installment payments. It has been a pleasure to carry your account, and we can and will grant further extension if it is needed.
>
> For your consideration, we enclose a series of checks payable in small amounts at intervals of thirty days. We invite you to sign them, date them the day of the month which you will find most convenient to pay, fill in the name of your bank, and send them back to us with the definite assurance that no check will be deposited until we mail you a notice ten days before maturity.[10]

As if Marshall did not have enough financial problems, his rickety 1929 Ford stopped running. With his characteristic sense of humor, Marshall reported the development to Houston, writing, "'Betsy' has gone up, and I will have to trade her in for another car. I shall invite you to the funeral of 'poor little Betsy.'"[11]

Houston did what he could to get money to Marshall from the NAACP. Marshall's thank-you letter painted the picture: "I received the check. Thanks. It will keep the wolf away from my door."[12]

MARSHALL'S NIGHT JOB

To make ends meet, Marshall worked a night job. Almost the entire time that Marshall was practicing law in Maryland, he also worked for the Baltimore City Department of Heath as a "clinic clerk," keeping records in a clinic that treated sexually transmitted diseases. The severe crowding in Baltimore's black neighborhoods had spawned an epidemic of communicable diseases such as tuberculosis and meningitis as well as sexually transmitted diseases such as gonorrhea and syphilis.

Marshall began working at the clinic in July 1934, nine months after he became a lawyer.[13] His salary was fifty dollars per month. For a few months in 1935, Marshall's brother Aubrey worked at the clinic as a physician. Marshall held down this night job while handling the Stevens, Murray, and Baltimore County high school cases; five death penalty cases; and a wide range of other legal matters.

In October 1936, Marshall requested and was granted a six-month leave without pay from the clinic. Until then, he had worked every weeknight for more than two years, with only three brief vacations. He took fourteen-day breaks to attend the National Bar Association conventions in Nashville in 1935 and in Pittsburgh in 1936. He took a four-day "vacation" to help the Baltimore NAACP branch host the 1936 NAACP national convention.[14]

Marshall's ability to maintain a night job while handling major civil rights cases, tort suits, divorces, and other legal matters required extraordinary stamina. "Nobody cares which twenty-three hours in a day I work," Marshall began to say.[15]

EXPLORING THE TEACHING OPTION

Pushed to the brink, Marshall sought employment at his alma mater, the Howard University School of Law. Charles Houston had resigned as dean to become special counsel to the NAACP. In December 1935, Marshall wrote to the acting dean, William E. Taylor. Always the advocate, Marshall began the letter with a request and an argument as to why he should be considered:

> I do not know whether or not, there is, at present, a vacancy on the faculty of the law school, nor whether there will be one in the near future. I am however, taking this means to make an application for consideration for a position on the faculty whenever a vacancy occurs.
>
> It is my belief that there should be at least one graduate of the Law School as a full-time professor on the faculty. I do not believe that there are, at present, any graduates serving in that capacity.

Marshall's letter then set forth details about his education, including the schools he had attended, the academic honors he had received, and his extracurricular activities. Finally, Marshall described his first two years as a lawyer.[16]

Receiving no response to this letter, four months later Marshall sent a similar letter to a member of Howard's Board of Trustees, George W. Crawford, a Connecticut judge.[17] In his reply, Judge Crawford told Marshall to contact Howard University president Mordecai Johnson and Acting Dean William Taylor.[18] Having already written to Taylor, Marshall wrote to Johnson.[19] The same day, Marshall also wrote to Walter W. Cook, one of his former professors at Howard, to ask for a letter of recommendation. Cook agreed and sent the letters to Johnson and Crawford.[20]

Soon, there emerged another teaching candidate, Edward Lovett, who had graduated from Howard University Law School a year ahead of Marshall. Lovett was another protégé of Charles Houston. He had spent a year in a graduate law program at Harvard (a program that Marshall had turned down), after which he had been working at the Washington, DC, law firm headed by Charles Houston's father, William Houston.

The competition between the two young lawyers for the Howard teaching job made the pages of the *Afro-American*, which reported, "The law alumni are backing Eddie Lovett for a vacancy in the Howard Law School faculty. Thurgood Marshall, the Baltimore lawyer, is the choice of Charley Houston, former dean."[21] On the surface, the newspaper's assessment seemed logical, given Marshall and Houston's productive relationship. However, Houston had a closer personal relationship with Lovett, who had worked with Houston's father. A couple of days after the *Afro-American* published the story, Houston contacted Lovett and set the record straight, calling the idea that Houston would support Marshall over Lovett "foolish." Houston told Lovett to feel free to correct any mistaken impression people might have, unless Lovett believed that having Houston appear to be against him would help his chances. Houston was aware that he had some adversaries at the university. "Truth is," Houston wrote to Lovett, "I hope both of you make it, but I told Thurgood I would have to give you first choice."[22]

Houston's slight preference for Lovett over Marshall was consistent with a view Houston had previously expressed. When Lovett applied for a position with the Social Security Board in Washington, DC, Houston's recommendation letter stated, "I have known Mr. Lovett since 1929. . . . He is the best student graduated from the Law School between 1929 and 1936, the period of my service."[23] That time frame included Marshall's years at Howard. Yet it was Marshall, not Lovett, who worked so arduously beside Houston on Murray's victory over the University of Maryland. Marshall was the workhorse during the Bernard Ades case, and Marshall succeeded Houston as special counsel at the NAACP. In Houston's eyes, Lovett may have been the superior scholar, while Marshall was the more effective advocate. Houston may have based his decision on the old proverb "Those who can, do. Those who can't, teach."

Ultimately, neither Marshall nor Lovett got the teaching position, largely due to internal (and somewhat anti-Houston) politics at Howard University. Marshall continued to scramble to make ends meet.

MARSHALL CONSIDERS OTHER OPTIONS

Marshall briefly entertained the idea of running for elected office. He reported to Houston about being approached by a left-leaning group that was encouraging him to make a run for Congress under the banner of a new political party.

> The gang that has been trying to get me to run for Congress has just left the office. The fellow whom I thought was a Communist has turned out not to be. One of them is a Socialist, the other is Jones, of the *Afro*, and the other is a professor at Johns Hopkins University.
>
> They intend to call the party something similar to the Independent Voters' League, with the idea of getting endorsements from both the Republican and the Democratic Parties for the individual candidate. This will, perhaps, be impossible, yet, on the other hand, there are some members of both parties who will be unable to refuse as individuals.
>
> I am going to talk the matter over with Carl Murphy tomorrow. I have not decided finally as yet and want you to advise me once and for all as to just what you think is best. Of course, your advice will be confidential."[24]

A run for office was not far-fetched, and Marshall's political instincts were undeniable. Blacks were beginning to make strides in Congress in the 1930s. In 1929, Oscar De Priest became the first post-Reconstruction black member of Congress, representing the South Side of Chicago as a Republican. Arthur Mitchell, also an African American, succeeded De Priest in the 1934 elections. Several of Marshall's predecessors in the Monumental Bar Association had run for political office. Baltimore lawyer Harry Sythe Cummings and Marshall's current officemate, Warner T. McGuinn, had served multiple terms in the Baltimore City Council. Maryland's first great civil rights lawyer and Marshall's personal hero, W. Ashbie Hawkins, had made a serious bid for the US Senate. Even Thurgood's Uncle Fearless had tested the political waters as a Republican candidate.[25]

Several black lawyers in Baltimore threw their hats into the political ring in 1934. Marshall's friend Josiah Henry, former president of the Monumental City Bar Association, ran for the Maryland legislature on the Democratic ticket. Clarence Mitchell, the *Afro-American* reporter who had worked so closely with Marshall, ran as a Socialist candidate for Maryland's House of Delegates. Robert McGuinn, the young attorney (and nephew of Warner T. McGuinn) who had helped Marshall investigate the Baltimore County schools, ran as a Republican for a seat in the state legislature. In 1934, eighteen blacks ran for political office in Maryland. None of them was elected.[26]

As the 1936 national elections approached, both the Republicans and the Democrats sought Marshall's involvement. Marshall received a letter from the local Republican Party seeking Marshall's support and the names of other prominent leaders who might help the Republican Party gain black votes in Baltimore.[27] The Democratic National Campaign Committee asked Marshall to speak at upcoming events. Ralph Robinson, chairman of the Maryland Democratic Campaign Committee's Speakers Bureau, arranged for Marshall to speak before an audience of between two hundred and three hundred blacks at an Anne Arundel County church.[28]

Marshall sought advice from his two closest advisers as to how he should respond to the invitation to run for Congress with a new party. He got conflicting advice from Charles Houston and Carl Murphy. Houston's reply by telegram was succinct, saying, "Accept candidacy but avoid communism and personal expense."[29] Murphy, whose newspaper had helped launch Marshall's career as a civil rights attorney, told the young man that he almost certainly would not win the election and that he should not run. Marshall decided against becoming a candidate and would never run for political office.

Labor unions also wanted Marshall. Although involvement with unions in the 1930s carried risks because of organized labor's ties to leftist movements, Marshall explored some union options. In July 1936, the Maryland director of the Steel Workers Organizing Committee invited Marshall to a meeting with the committee's eastern regional director.[30] The next month, Marshall spoke at a rally attended by seven hundred steel workers in Baltimore. The *Afro-American* reported afterward that the organization had considered retaining Marshall as legal counsel. In September 1936, the Agricultural Workers Union, based in Bridgeton, New Jersey, also approached Marshall for help in organizing farm workers on the Eastern Shore.[31] None of these forays had matured into major involvement before Marshall left Baltimore to pursue his true passion, civil rights.

THE BALTIMORE BRANCH OF THE NAACP

Despite offers from numerous groups, only one organization captured Marshall's interest and sustained involvement—the National Association for the Advancement of Colored People, or NAACP. Most of Marshall's early civil rights work was coordinated with the NAACP's national office through Walter White, Roy Wilkins, and Charles Houston. When Marshall first became a lawyer, the Baltimore branch of the NAACP had been moribund for two decades and was just beginning to become active again.

The NAACP's Baltimore branch was chartered in 1912, three years after the national organization was founded. In its early years, the Baltimore branch was one of the most active branches. Lawyers Harry Sythe Cummings, W. Ashbie Hawkins, and Warner T. McGuinn had joined forces with church leaders such as Reverend Harvey Johnson and Reverend William Waller, under the banner of the NAACP. Their initial goal was to fight disenfranchisement and housing segregation laws. After Maryland voters had rejected the Poe, Digges, and Strauss amendments that would have disenfranchised black voters, and after the US Supreme Court had struck down mandatory housing segregation laws, the Baltimore branch of the NAACP slowly slipped into inactivity. In a 1927 letter to Walter White, the then-president of the Baltimore branch, attorney Linwood Koger, acknowledged the comatose state of the branch:

Your letter of April 15 is before me and with shame and embarrassment, I now make answer. I am embarrassed because I was foolish enough to accept the presidency of the local branch a second time, and am now unable to muster a sufficient number of the executive committee or members at-large to be relieved of this very great honor. I can appreciate the noble work the National organization is doing and esteem it an honor to be considered worthy of being the president of any Branch of this great body, yet I think I have met my waterloo in Baltimore. I have never let anything die before, while in my charge. Hence the shame.[32]

Through this period, Carl Murphy, who was on the national board of the NAACP, tried almost singlehandedly to keep the branch alive.

In 1932, Walter White wrote to Murphy about the sad condition into which the Baltimore branch had fallen:

The Baltimore Branch is doing nothing so far as we know. I shall be in Washington on October 16th and I asked that a conference be arranged in Baltimore on the 18th and if possible a mass meeting on the 19th with the idea of reviving the Branch and organizing for some activity.

It is a shame that a city of the size of Baltimore should lay down absolutely on the job which the Association is designed to do.[33]

Although Murphy declined White's suggestion that he take over as president of the branch, Murphy agreed to help find someone who would inject new life into it. Thurgood Marshall was still in law school, but Murphy told White about another young lawyer who had recently joined the Maryland bar and had solid Baltimore connections. "I am wondering if we would not be better off with an exceedingly young person, man or woman, at the head of the local branch. W. A. C. Hughes, Jr., is a likely local attorney. He would make a good president if we could land him. Drop him a line and put a bee in his bonnet," Murphy wrote to Walter White on October 12, 1932.[34]

White agreed with Murphy's suggestion of placing a young lawyer in charge and thought that Hughes was a good pick for the job:

It may be that some young man might bring to the Branch the energy and enthusiasm which is needed and which would go far towards building up a successful Branch in Baltimore. Mr. W. A. C. Hughes, Jr., may be just the person.

I shall probably be in Baltimore on Tuesday and shall make it a point
to have a talk with him. I hope that we may be able to have an alert
Branch there shortly.[35]

Although Hughes declined to take on the presidency of the Baltimore
branch, he did agree to serve as its legal counsel. The Reverend C. Y. Trigg
became the branch president in December 1932 and began to revive it.

Between 1933 and 1934, the Baltimore branch resumed regular meetings, although membership remained below two hundred members. The
branch encouraged qualified blacks to apply for admission to the University
of Maryland's graduate programs, promoted voter registration, and intervened
on behalf of some defendants in criminal cases. Operating out of the same law
offices as Marshall, Hughes represented the local branch, while Marshall
continued to focus on matters of special interest to the national office.

In 1935, Baltimore leaders and national NAACP staff developed plans
to conduct a major membership drive for the Baltimore branch. Aware of
the NAACP's importance, Marshall agreed to help with the membership
drive and became the membership committee's legal adviser. The membership drive for the Baltimore branch officially began in October 1935.
The membership drive had its own letterhead, emblazoned with the slogan
"You Can't Win By Yourself! Join the N.A.A.C.P.!" Thousands of orange
leaflets showed George Armwood under arrest the day before he was
lynched. They also included the photograph that Marshall, Houston, and
Murray had staged in the *Afro-American* newsroom. The national NAACP
sent its assistant field secretary, Daisy I. Lampkin, to assist the membership drive. Marshall's high school teacher and debate coach, Gough
McDaniels, organized a "flying squad" that held street-corner rallies with
a microphone mounted on a flatbed truck. Lillie Jackson and her daughter
Juanita played leadership roles, as did attorney Robert McGuinn.

The membership campaign was a major success, adding two thousand
new members to the Baltimore branch. By the next year, membership had
climbed to three thousand. In December, the branch elected new officers,
with Lillie Jackson as president. She held that position for the next thirty-
five years, during which time the Baltimore branch became one of the
largest NAACP branches in the nation. At Jackson's request in December
1935, Marshall for the first time became the lead attorney for the Baltimore
branch of the NAACP. William Hughes remained a member of the branch's

legal redress committee, which included another person quite familiar to Marshall—his uncle Fearless Williams.[36]

MARSHALL CONTINUES TO DO CIVIL RIGHTS WORK

As counsel for the Baltimore branch, Marshall in 1936 carried on an intense four-month letter-writing campaign aimed at convincing Baltimore's congressional delegation to vote for the pending antilynching legislation. In March 1936, Lillie M. Jackson began the campaign with a series of telegrams to US representatives William P. Cole Jr., Vincent L. Palmisano, Ambrose J. Kennedy, and Stephen W. Gambrill. She urged the legislators to sign a petition to bring the sixteen pending antilynching bills to the floor of the House of Representatives for a vote. Marshall followed up with a long series of letters and telegrams sent throughout the spring and summer of 1936, pressuring the legislators to help move the antilynching legislation forward. Marshall sent Walter White copies of the congressional correspondence. He also asked for White's advice on what he should do on the antilynching campaign as a leader in the National Bar Association.

Rep. Cole was the first to respond to Marshall's follow-up letter. Cole wrote that he was unaware of the antilynching petition and that even if twenty-five lawmakers were to sign the petition, it would not guarantee the support of the Democratic caucus. Cole neither supported nor opposed the antilynching legislation but balked at the petition because it was not prepared by a member of the House.

Still lacking a response from the rest of Baltimore's congressional delegation, Marshall sent each of them a letter, urging them to sign the antilynching petition. Rep. Kennedy responded next. He said that he was in favor of antilynching legislation but refused to sign a petition. Marshall quickly responded to Kennedy, thanking him for his support and pushing again for his signature. Marshall explained that a petition was the only way to get the House to act on the proposed bill.

By April 18, 1936, Marshall was exasperated that half of Baltimore's congressional delegation had not responded. He sent off another salvo of letters. To Rep. Palmisano, he wrote, "I cannot understand your reason

Juanita Jackson and Gough McDaniels lead a street corner rally for the NAACP membership campaign in 1935. *Courtesy of Afro-American* Newspaper *Archives and Research Center and Clarence and Juanita Mitchell family.*

The flyer distributed in the NAACP membership campaign highlighted the Armwood lynching and Marshall's law school case. *Courtesy of Afro-American* Newspaper *Archives and Research Center.*

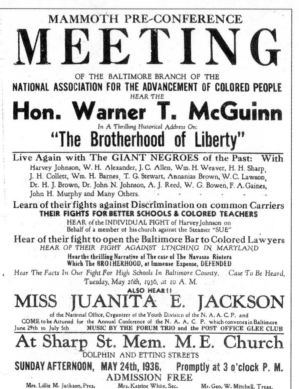

Marshall helped organize a massive rally in preparation for the 1936 NAACP
National Convention in Baltimore. *Courtesy of Afro-American Newspaper Archives
and Research Center.*

for not replying unless it is that you intend to absolutely ignore and to
refuse to extend even the courtesy of a reply to more than 2,000 of your
constituents."[37]

Marshall sent a similar note to Rep. Gambrill, who issued an ambivalent reply: "No discourtesy was intended by my failure to reply at an earlier date to your communications and no discourtesy is intended if my reply is not sufficiently comprehensive. It should be sufficient for me to say the subject requires careful thought and study."[38]

Marshall provided copies of all the correspondence to the *Afro-American*, which published most of it. Walter White in New York enjoyed the exchange and encouraged Marshall to "keep up the pressure and publicity." White suggested that Marshall use his position as secretary of the National Bar Association to start lobbying politicians beyond the Maryland delegation, including the chairman of the House Rules Committee, the speaker of the house, and President Roosevelt. Marshall followed White's suggestion by sending off a new set of letters. To Roosevelt, Marshall wrote:

> Dear President Roosevelt:
> The Baltimore Branch of the National Association for the Advancement of Colored People urgently solicits your cooperation toward granting favorable action in the Democratic Caucus of the House on Anti-lynching legislation.[39]

Marshall's letter-writing campaign appeared to have some effect. Democratic caucus reports revealed that all the members of the Baltimore delegation were prepared to vote in favor of the antilynching legislation. However, winning that battle did not win the war. President Roosevelt hesitated to publicly endorse the legislation in an election year, and the bill ultimately died in the Senate, following a filibuster led by Southern Democrats.

BALTIMORE HOSTS THE NAACP CONVENTION

As Marshall's role in the antilynching campaign wound down, the Baltimore branch prepared to host the twenty-seventh national convention of the NAACP. With 530 delegates registered, the convention, held at the Sharp Street Church Community House from June 29 through July 5, 1936, was the largest-ever NAACP convention.[40] Also, for the first time, 200 NAACP youth delegates held a separate, concurrent conference with Juanita Jackson, who had joined the national NAACP staff as a coordinator of youth activities. At the B&O Railroad station, Marshall had arranged with the stationmaster to create a welcoming booth for arriving delegates.[41]

The NAACP convention opened with addresses by Baltimore mayor Howard Jackson, Maryland governor Harry W. Nice, and NAACP Baltimore branch president Lillie M. Jackson. The keynote address, delivered by US Secretary of the Interior Harold L. Ickes, was broadcast nationwide. Marshall served as the local staff person responsible for coordinating the broadcast. Ickes had briefly been secretary of the Chicago NAACP and was the principal administrator of Roosevelt's New Deal program. Before becoming interior secretary, Ickes had directed the Public Works Administration (PWA) and had issued orders prohibiting racial discrimination in its programs.

In his convention speech, Ickes observed that, despite opposition from labor unions, the PWA had provided substantial employment for blacks by establishing numerical targets based on the percentage of black workers residing in locales per the 1930 census. A contractor who failed to meet the target had the burden of proving that the failure was not due to the company practicing discrimination. It was probably the first time that Marshall had heard a high-level defense of affirmative action.[42]

Also at the convention, Thurgood Marshall and Enolia Pettigen, the president of the Maryland State Colored Teachers' Association, jointly addressed the delegates on the subject of "Educational Problems: Methods of Fighting Educational Inequalities."[43] Immediately after the convention, the national office of the NAACP sent Marshall twenty-five dollars for his "valuable assistance during the sessions of our recent conference in Baltimore."[44]

MARSHALL BROUGHT ON TO NAACP STAFF

The NAACP convention in Baltimore gave Marshall opportunities to meet NAACP board members and leaders from around the country. A month after the convention, Marshall's constant pestering of Charles Houston finally bore fruit, and he was offered a position at the NAACP headquarters in New York.

Marshall (third row, fifth from the left) met NAACP leaders from around the country at the 1936 NAACP National Convention in Baltimore. *Courtesy of* Afro-American *Newspaper Archives and Research Center.*

Please Preserve This Program

Twenty-Seventh Annual

CONFERENCE

of the

NATIONAL ASSOCIATION

FOR THE

ADVANCEMENT

OF

COLORED PEOPLE

BALTIMORE, MARYLAND

JUNE 29–JULY 5, 1936

•

REGISTRATION BUREAU
and
CONFERENCE HEADQUARTERS
Sharp Street Memorial M. E.
Church Community House
1206 Etting Street

BALTIMORE BRANCH OFFICERS

President	Mrs. Lillie M. Jackson
Vice Presidents	Gough McDaniels
	Robert P. McGuinn
	Dr. Jesse B. Weaver
	Mrs. Julia Jackson
	Mrs. Sarah Diggs
	Miss Enolia Pettigen
Secretary	Mrs. Katrine N. White
Assistant Secretary	Mrs. Frances Madden
Treasurer	George Mitchell
Chaplain	Rev. C. Y. Trigg

CONFERENCE COMMITTEE CHAIRMEN

Housing	Mrs. Bertha Proctor
Publicity	Clarence M. Mitchell
Entertainment	Mrs. Sarah F. Diggs
Registration	Mrs. Lillian Lottier
Membership	Miss Enolia Pettigen
Church	Mrs. Howard E. Young
Welcome and Transportation	John W. Haywood, Jr.
Interracial	Mrs. Augusta T. Chissell
Broadcasting	Thurgood Marshall, Esq.
Sale of Literature	Miss Marion Jackson
Ushers	Mrs. Florence Snowden
Music	Mrs. Katrine N. White
Finance	George W. Mitchell
Governor's Reception	Dr. Ulysses G. Bourne
Caterer Service	Bailey Conway
Marshal of Parade	Linwood Koger, Esq.

USHERS

June 29—Bethel A. M. E. Church, John Snowden,
President

June 30—Enon Baptist Church, John Curry, President

July 1—Baltimore Youth Council, Maceo Howard,
Chairman

July 2—Faith Baptist Church, Warren Harris,
President

July 3—Metropolitan M. E. Church, Joseph Kennard,
President

July 5—Morning Star Baptist Church, George Swift,
President

Marshall coordinated the nationwide broadcast of a keynote speech by US Secretary of the Interior Harold Ickes. *Courtesy of Clarence and Juanita Mitchell family.*

Houston had convinced Walter White that the NAACP needed another full-time lawyer in its national office. Houston's responsibilities called for frequent travel, which left him little time to actually work on cases. Between the NAACP legal matters, office correspondence, consultation, and research, there was plenty of work to justify the NAACP's hiring another lawyer.

Houston left no doubt that Marshall was his first choice to fill the position. "I don't know of anybody I would rather have in the office than you or anybody who can do a better job of research and preparation of cases," Houston wrote to Marshall. "You have been more than faithful in giving your time to the Association and I know this has meant a sacrifice of private practice."[45] Houston recommended to Walter White and Roy Wilkins that they hire Marshall for a six-month stint, with a salary of two hundred dollars per month.

Marshall readily accepted the offer. He immediately made arrangements with McGuinn and Hughes to handle his open cases and asked the Baltimore City Department of Health for a six-month leave of absence without pay from his clinic clerk job. The NAACP's magazine, the *Crisis,* announced, "Thurgood Marshall of Baltimore, Maryland, chief counsel of the successful suit against the University of Maryland (the Donald Gaines Murray case), joined the N.A.A.C.P. legal staff October 15. Mr. Marshall will work with Charles H. Houston, special counsel, on the campaign for educational equality. He has been engaged for a period of six months to do special research work."[46]

Marshall and Buster joined Aunt Medi and her husband Boots Dodson in their New York apartment. Marshall spent the next several months traveling back and forth between New York and Baltimore, handling a series of Maryland lawsuits that led to a national campaign that spawned the births of hundreds of new NAACP branches. The lawsuits also resulted in rulings that doubled the salaries of the largest professional group in the African American community at the time—school teachers.

Chapter 16

Commuting Back for Equal Teacher Pay

"Between 1936 and 1938, I commuted practically, between Baltimore and New York . . . and there was considerable practice in the period. . . . I was based in New York, but I maintained an office in my mother's house in Baltimore," Marshall testified in 1962 before the Senate Judiciary Committee considering his nomination to become a judge on the US Court of Appeals for the Second Circuit.[1] The most consequential part of the "considerable practice" that kept him returning to Maryland dealt with the problem of racial discrimination in schoolteacher pay.

Throughout the South, black public school teachers were paid significantly less than their white counterparts with comparable education and experience. In Maryland, state law set the minimum pay for black teachers at substantially less than the minimum for white teachers. Article 77 of the Maryland Code provided, "No white teacher regularly employed in a public school of the State of Maryland shall receive a salary of less than $600 per school year." The same statute stated that "no teacher regularly employed in the public schools for colored children in the State of Maryland shall receive a salary of less than $40 per month."[2] With schools for colored children open nine months of the year, the minimum pay for a black teacher was $360 per year.

Each of Maryland's twenty-three counties paid its public school teachers more than the state required minimum, and each county maintained a racial differential. In 1932, Montgomery County black teachers were paid 48 percent of the salary of white teachers, or $655 compared to

Local Attorney Gets NAACP Post

OCT 2 4 1936

BALTIMORE—Thurgood Marshall, local attorney, left here, Sunday for New York to assume temporary duties as a special assistant counsel for the national office of the N.A.A.C.P.

The attorney, who was counsel for the local branch of the N.A.A.C.P., won distinction while assisting Dr. Charles H. Houston, special counsel of the association, in the defense of Bernard Ades, white, and the successful suit of Donald G. Murray, for admission to the University of Maryland.

Mr. Marshall — T. Marshall supervised the suit of Margaret Williams against the Baltimore County Board of Education for admittance to the Catonsville white high school, which is still pending in the circuit court at Towson.

A native of Baltimore, Mr. Marshall is the son of Mr. and Mrs. William C. Marshall of 1838 Druid Hill Avenue. He is a graduate of the Douglass High School, Lincoln University and the Howard University law school.

In 1937, the NAACP national staff became William Pickens, Juanita Jackson, Daisy Lampkin, Roy Wilkins, James Weldon Johnson, Walter White, Thurgood Marshall, and Charles Houston. *Courtesy of Clarence and Juanita Mitchell family and Afro-American Newspaper Archives and Research Center.*

$1,362. In Queen Anne's County, the situation was slightly worse, with black teachers making 47 percent of what white teachers made, or $561 compared to $1,191.[3]

Every year starting in the early 1920s, bills had been introduced in the Maryland General Assembly to equalize the salaries of black and white teachers, but none had become law. Only in Baltimore, an independent city, were black and white teachers paid the same rates, following an aggressive political campaign and litigation between 1920 and 1925.

PLAINTIFF FOUND, BUT CASE DELAYED

By the middle of 1935, Marshall was very busy. He was handling the Stevens and Murray cases and had his sights set on the Baltimore County high school case. Marshall began discussing possible teacher pay litigation with Charles Houston and Warner T. McGuinn, the senior lawyer in Marshall's law offices who had filed a teacher pay lawsuit in Baltimore in 1925.

Houston advised Marshall to hold off on the teacher pay cases. "O.K. postponing the teachers salary case in order to work on the Murray case. I think it is much more important to have the Murray case in good shape," Houston wrote to Marshall in August 1935.[4] Yet Marshall was eager to start. "Since the University of Maryland appeal will most likely not be up by then, would it be possible to file the teachers' salary case about that time? I have my work on the brief far enough advanced to drop it for a few days," Marshall wrote to Houston in September 1935.[5] "Go ahead on the teachers' salary case and the high school case," Houston replied.[6]

Both Marshall and Houston knew that *Afro-American* publisher Carl Murphy was particularly interested in the teacher pay issue. The newspaper had supported the teacher pay cases filed by McGuinn in the mid-1920s. Murphy would again be a steadfast ally in the current teacher pay fight. However, Marshall's challenge was finding a plaintiff, which was no small task since black teachers hesitated to bring suit for fear of losing their jobs. Anne Arundel County appeared to be a good place to find one because after two years of service, schoolteachers acquired tenure and, with it, job security.

Marshall and Houston discussed the potential teachers' salary litigation through September and October. Finally, Marshall believed that he had found the right plaintiff. "Located plaintiff for teachers salary case. Teacher in Anne Arundel County. Enolia Pettigen,[7] recommends him as all right. Well liked in community. Believe you should talk to him as soon as possible to clinch it. He lives in Baltimore and commutes can see him any night or Sunday. Give notice," Marshall informed Houston in a telegram sent on November 15, 1935.[8]

Houston advised Marshall to obtain a letter from the prospective client so that the record would show that the client initially contacted the lawyer and not vice versa. Civil rights lawyers feared reprisal for "stirring up litigation" in violation of lawyer ethics rules against "champerty and maintenance."

Howard Pindell, a Morgan College graduate and an officer of the City-Wide Young People's Forum, taught at the black high school in Annapolis, the state capital and county seat of Anne Arundel County. He sent a letter to Marshall explaining his plight:

> This is my fifth teaching year in the State of Maryland. During this period I have served as Science Instructor in the Wiley H. Bates High School of Annapolis, Anne Arundel County. I entered the system with the sincere hope of furthering my studies by doing graduate work in a northern university in either summer courses or on a leave of absence. The small, unjust, and incommensurate salary that has been paid me blasted my hopes and many times has driven me to seek loans in order to "make essential ends meet."
>
> I understand that the differential between the salaries of White and of Colored teachers of this State has been a problem which has confronted the Negro citizenry of the State for many exasperating years. Efforts by Negro leaders of the State to secure justice or any degree of satisfaction through the Maryland State Legislature have been disappointingly in vain. The courts seem the only alternative.
>
> I am, personally, interested in seeing if this deplorable injustice can be removed by a fair and just decision of the courts of this State. Your capability as an attorney was concretely proven by your triumphant success in the University of Maryland case. In view of this fact I should like to rest my case in your hands. Let me know at your earliest convenience, if you will take it.[9]

Marshall forwarded Pindell's letter to Walter White. "Enclosed please find copy of letter written by a prospective plaintiff for the teachers' salary case in Maryland. Charlie and I have, both, talked to him and we have requested this letter as a means of protection for the Association as well for ourselves," he wrote to White.[10]

Later in January 1936, Marshall met with a group of black Anne Arundel County teachers at the home of Philip and Rachel Brown, both Morgan graduates and Anne Arundel County teachers.[11] They provided information about the county schools and the pay scales. Marshall told Clarence Mitchell at the *Afro-American* about the meeting, and by the first week in February, the *Afro-American* publicity machine was in full gear, even though ten months would pass before Marshall filed the first teacher pay case. "Teacher Ready to File Suit for County Salary," read the headline. "One teacher is ready to file suit against a county for failing to pay a salary equal to that given white teachers, according to Thurgood Marshall, NAACP lawyer," reported the paper.[12]

As the newspaper brought the issue publicity, the young potential plaintiff became anxious. "It happens that I am, personally, financially unable to supply any of the funds necessary to fight this case. Having some knowledge of the platform of the NAACP, I am taking this opportunity to find out if you would be interested in investing a sum in the case and in supplying the necessary legal counsel," Pindell revealed to Houston in a letter he had originally sent to Marshall.[13]

Pindell also sent Houston a handwritten note, just in case he had not made himself perfectly clear. "So far as I am personally concerned the sooner you and Mr. Marshall file this case the better. My decision has been made and the shorter the delay, the better—for many reasons which I'll not take time to write," he confided to Houston.[14]

Marshall and Houston strategized about the best way to set up the teachers' salary case in Anne Arundel County. When Houston suggested that Pindell refuse his monthly salary check and use that as a basis for filing suit, Marshall expressed some concerns about that approach, responding, "In regard to the question of having Pindell refuse his salary check, the only question in my mind at present is that [it] would, of course, certainly exclude him from the payroll, whereas, on the other hand, if some other form of action were taken, although it is quite possible that he would be fired, this is more certain than too, if he is fired we would have an opportunity to, at least, put up a fight to keep him in."[15]

Houston agreed with Marshall, writing, "In answer to your letter of March 23, I suggest that you advise Pindell to accept his check for March. . . . I will be in Baltimore the first of next week and will stay there long enough to work out all matters with you in the Pindell case and also to work on any reply which has to be made in the Baltimore County high school case.[16]

Marshall and Houston were no longer professor and student. They now operated as equal partners.

As the lawyers handled other matters while continuing to discuss the pay case, the *Afro-American* kept the cause alive. The newspaper reported that janitors in white Anne Arundel County schools earned more than black teachers in the county's black schools.[17] Carl Murphy, whose brother George B. Murphy was a Baltimore school administrator and officer of the Maryland State Colored Teachers' Association, wanted the black community to understand that a victory for teachers' salaries could have an immediate and dramatic economic impact.

In January 1936, the victory in Murray's law school case was finally sealed when the Maryland Court of Appeals affirmed Judge O'Dunne's order. Marshall spent some time catching up on matters in his private practice and then turned his attention to the Baltimore County high school case. He again placed the teacher pay matter toward the top of his priorities.

LOSING PINDELL

In September 1936, an unexpected development forced Marshall to change his plans. "You remember Pindell, in the teachers' salary case, well, he has been appointed principal of one of the county schools and is, therefore, out as a plaintiff in the case. Miss Pettigen has another prospective plaintiff whom we will interview within the next two weeks," Marshall wrote to Houston.[18]

Pindell had discussed with Marshall whether to leave his tenured job in Anne Arundel County and to accept an offer to become the principal of the black high school in neighboring Frederick County. Marshall had advised him not to pass up the opportunity for promotion.[19] Two years later, the Frederick County school administration released Pindell from his position as the principal of Lincoln High School. Decades later, Pindell was still not certain whether the Frederick County promotion had been a setup to entice him to relinquish his teacher tenure in Anne Arundel County. Marshall had no doubts and stated his conclusion emphatically:

> In 1938 Howard Pindell was a high school teacher in Anne Arundel County with five years' tenure. At the beginning of our fight to equalize salaries he was the first prospective plaintiff. At the end of the school year, 1936, he was informed that he had been offered a position as principal in Frederick County which was a better job and worth more pay. He applied for this position and told the Superintendent he did not have a principal's certificate. He was assured by the Superintendent that he could obtain his certificate within four years and this would be agreeable with the Board of Education. He started in his duties as principal in Frederick County. By moving from Anne Arundel County to Frederick County he lost his tenure and became a probationary principal. His second year as a probationary principal ended last week; and he was told that he would be released.
>
> This to my mind was the most traitorous trick. The authorities wanted to get rid of him for his activities in the teachers' salary cases but could not do so as long as he had tenure. By offering him a better job he lost his tenure and now he has no job. This is a roundabout way of putting a man out "legally."[20]

MONTGOMERY COUNTY

By November 1936, Enolia Pettigen had identified an alternate plaintiff, William B. Gibbs Jr., the acting principal of an elementary school in Montgomery County. "I have your letter of October 27th. Mr. Gibbs and I had the conference as planned. I am favorably impressed with him and believe that he will make a desirable client. He is really interested too," Pettigen wrote to Marshall.[21] Gibbs's salary was $612 per month, while the average salary for white principals was $1,475 per month.

As Marshall and Houston put the pieces in place to move forward with the litigation on behalf of Gibbs, the *Afro-American* did its part to keep the story alive in the press.[22] The NAACP organized a letter-writing campaign in an effort to compel the Maryland General Assembly to address the issue of teacher pay equalization. As in several years prior, a bill was crafted to give black teachers pay equal to their white counterparts. As in previous years, the legislature failed to pass a law equalizing teacher salaries.

By December 1936, two months after Marshall had relocated to New York, the *Afro-American* published an even bolder article, even though no litigation had yet been filed. "Opening Gun Fired in War to Equalize Teachers' Pay," read the *Afro-American* headline on December 12, 1936. The article summarized what Marshall had told the reporter about his plans for the teachers' pay cases:

> Their petition to the Montgomery County board of education being curtly denied, Tuesday, NAACP attorneys are now preparing briefs for the State's first suit to enforce equalization of teachers' salaries. The action was determined after Edward P. Lovett of Washington and Thurgood Marshall of Baltimore, NAACP attorneys, presented a petition to the board in behalf of William B. Gibbs, Jr., acting principal of the Rockville Elementary School, for back pay and equalized schedule. Prior to the presentation of Gibbs' claims, Messrs. Marshall and Lovett conferred with Edwin W. Broome, white, superintendent of Montgomery County schools. Informed of their mission, he asserted that the matter could be settled before the board in just a "couple of minutes." The board refused to grant the petition.[23]

Finally, in January 1937, Marshall, Houston, and cocounsel Edward Lovett filed a petition in Montgomery County Circuit Court for a writ of mandamus against the Montgomery County Board of Education. The attorneys requested equal pay for black teachers and back pay for previous years in accordance with a new, equalized scale.[24]

Circuit Judge Charles W. Woodward signed an order giving the defendants until February 6 to show cause why the petition should not be granted. The *Afro-American* continued to highlight the teachers' pay case in its pages.[25]

AVERAGE ANNUAL SALARIES IN THE COUNTIES OF
THE STATE ELEMENTARY SCHOOLS FOR 1932

County	White	Colored	Percentage
Baltimore........................	$1541	$1227	79
Montgomery....................	1362	655	48
Allegany	1287	1172	90
Prince George's..............	1221	730	59
Cecil	1210	717	59
Anne Arundel	1200	660	55
Queen Anne's	1191	561	47
Kent	1170	587	50
Washington	1167	795	68
Harford	1146	695	60
*Garrett	1131		
Frederick	1129	574	50
Wicomico	1127	580	51
Talbot	1127	553	49
Calvert	1114	566	50
Somerset	1109	536	48
Worcester	1102	557	50
Howard	1101	560	50
Carroll	1097	587	53
Caroline	1096	553	50
Dorchester....................	1090	559	51
Charles	1088	558	51
St. Mary's	1077	554	51
State Average by Counties....	$1230	$ 653	53.9

*Note:—There are no Colored Schools in Garrett County.
   The following table may be noted for comparison:

Marshall introduced this chart as an exhibit in each of the Maryland teacher pay cases. *Courtesy of Library of Congress, NAACP Papers.*

A LANDMARK RULING

By February, attorneys for the defense had responded to the petition with a demurrer that challenged the legal basis of the case. The case then took an unusual turn. In a long-distance telephone conversation, Judge Woodward informed Marshall that he was asking the other two circuit judges to join him in hearing and deciding the demurrer.

Three judges presiding over a noncapital case at the circuit court or trial level was highly unusual. Woodward understood the significance of the cases, and this worked in Marshall's favor. Marshall had encountered all three judges during the trial of William Carter in 1934, a trial Marshall deemed fair. Marshall had also conferred with Woodward during his assessment of the James Poindexter case in 1935. Again, Marshall concluded that the defendant, Poindexter, had been treated fairly. As a result of his prior work, Marshall had established credibility with these judges, and they treated the teachers' salary case with deference and respect.

Houston, Marshall, and Lovett argued in opposition to the demurrer in Rockville, the Montgomery County seat. On June 20, 1937, the judges overruled the demurrer and asked the school board to respond to the factual allegations of the petitions. This landmark decision marked the first time that any court in the nation had found that black professionals with the same experience and credentials as white professionals had the right to equal pay. In ruling for the plaintiff on the demurrer, the court assumed the truth of the facts alleged in the petition and gave the defendants twenty days to respond.

"NAACP Wins Opening Round In Md. Case," raved the *Afro-American* in its opening headline on July 3, 1937. "The circuit court of Montgomery County awarded the NAACP first blood in the fight to equalize teachers' salaries in the rural schools."[26]

THE FIRST SETTLEMENT

Immediately after the court's decision overruling the demurrer, the attorney for the school board wrote to Marshall that he was prepared to negotiate a settlement on behalf of the Montgomery County Board of Education:

> You are aware, of course, of the result of the demurrer in the above case and I congratulate you on the skill with which you handled the matter. . . . I have had several conferences since then with Dr. Broome and certain changes of personnel in the Board of Education having occurred, it seems that the disposition of the Board as now constituted is to give further consideration to the possibility of an adjustment of the matters in issue.

Maryland State Colored Teachers' Association

ENOLIA V. PETTIGEN
PRESIDENT

FRANK B. BUTLER
TREASURER

OFFICE OF
1515 ~~Druid~~man St.
2502 McCULLOH STREET.
BALTIMORE. MD.

THERESA A. S. DOUGLAS
CORRESPONDING SECRETARY

JOSEPH C. PARKS
EXECUTIVE SECRETARY

Nov. 5, 1936

Attorney Thurgood Marshall
69 Fifth Ave.
New York City

Dear Mr. Marshall:

I have your letter of October 27th. Mr. Gibbs
and I had the conference as planned. I am favorably impressed
with him and believe that he will make a desirable client. He
is really interested, too.

I have had word from each of the other prospective
clients. All except one have declined for one reason or another.
The remaining one desires a conference before his final decision.
He is on the Eastern Shore, but he plans to attend our session
next week. I believe Mr. Gibbs is the best when all is considered.

What are the prospects for filing the case
now? The State Teachers' Association holds its annual session on
next week, Nov. 13th and 14th. I wish it were possible to take
some action by then. I should like to have the Association endorse
the plans made, select the committee to collect the fund, and decide
upon the amount of the contribution to be asked for. Would such
a plan meet your approval?

Kindly let me hear from you before next Friday.

Yours truly,

Enolia Pettigen
Enolia Pettigen

~~glad~~ to have you attend the business session
if you think it best.

White Janitors Get More Than County Teachers

ANNAPOLIS, Md. — Janitors in white schools of Anne Arundel County earn more than most teachers in one-room schools for colored children, according to Robert A. Brooks, who presided at the opening meeting of the spring campaign of the local branch of the NAACP, Monday, in Asbury ME Church.

Miss Juanita E. Jackson, special assistant to Walter White, executive secretary of the NAACP, and Robert P. McGuinn, executive secretary of the Governor's commission on higher education, were the main speakers.

According to Mr. Brooks, the salary scale for white school custodians is one and one-third times that of colored teachers in the single-room schools.

Mr. Brooks made his statement by way of convincing the audience that the county educational system is fraught with inequalities that the NAACP can remedy.

Necessary to Fight

In Maryland, black teachers were paid approximately half of that paid to white teachers with similar education and experience. *Courtesy of Betha McMillan and Afro-American Newspaper Archives and Research Center.*

William Gibbs, the plaintiff in Marshall's first teacher pay case, taught school in Montgomery County. *Courtesy of Afro-American Newspaper Archives and Research Center.*

In order to ascertain whether or not this can be done, not only does the Board of Education feel that it needs a little time to go into the question but conferences with the Board of County Commissioners of Montgomery County would also be essential. In this situation I would like to have the Court grant us a reasonable extension of time before proceeding further with the litigation, in the hope that a just and satisfactory solution can be arrived at without proceeding further with the pending suit.[27]

The negotiations were quick and decisive. With Marshall and Leon Ransom representing Gibbs, and with newspaper publisher Carl Murphy present, the Montgomery County school superintendent signed on behalf of the school board an agreement to equalize the pay of black and white teachers within a year. Fifty African American teachers in Montgomery County immediately had their salaries increased, and thousands more school teachers around the nation would soon benefit from this development. The teacher pay cases would dominate Marshall's time for the next four years.

The *Afro-American*'s coverage of the teachers' salary victory in Montgomery County was nearly as comprehensive as its reporting on the Murray case. "County Agrees to $30,000 in Back Salaries," read the headline. "The NAACP won a sudden and sensational victory in its suit to equalize teachers' salaries in Montgomery County, Md., Friday, when the case was settled out of court," the *Afro-American* reported.[28] The newspaper printed a banner headline across the top of the front page, a timeline of the case, an editorial, and the full text of the agreement between the black teachers and the Montgomery County school board. Years later, a historical roadside marker about the teacher pay case was installed where the Montgomery County court had met.

CALVERT COUNTY

With this major ruling under his belt, Marshall urged the Colored Teachers' Association to find plaintiffs in other counties. The plan was to move around the state, county by county, to strike down the unequal pay for black teachers.[29]

In August 1937, there came forward a second plaintiff, Harriet Elizabeth Brown, an elementary school teacher in Calvert County. Marshall

Opening Gun Fired in War to Equalize Teachers' Pay

ROCKVILLE, Md.—Their petition to the Montgomery County board of education being curtly denied, Tuesday, NAACP attorneys are now preparing briefs for the State's first suit to enforce equalization of teachers' salaries.

The action was determined after Edward P. Lovett of Washington and Thurgood Marshall of Baltimore, NAACP attorneys, reveal that the average annual salary of white elementary teachers in Montgomery County is $1362, for colored, $612. It was stated that 98.4 per cent of the whites have at least first-grade certificates; colored, 97.9 per cent, or less than one degree of difference.

Gibbs's petition requested that he be paid the difference between the salary he has been receiving and the salary provided for white

Marshall, Houston, and Lovett won, in Montgomery County, a key court ruling that led the county officials to equalize the salaries of black and white teachers. *Courtesy of Afro-American Newspaper Archives and Research Center.*

made several trips from New York to Calvert County, two hours south of Baltimore, to meet with his potential client, other teachers, and school officials. His preliminary work convinced him that the appointed Calvert County Board of Education was willing to end the pay disparities but that the elected county commissioners who appropriated the school budget needed a push.

As Marshall prepared to file the second teachers' salary action in Maryland, the *Afro-American* again broke the story first. "New Teacher Salary Case May Be Filed," read the headline.[30] In November, the paper reported, "The National Association for the Advancement of Colored People renewed its legal offensive against differentials in salaries of white and colored teachers in Maryland counties this week. The court action, begun by Miss Elizabeth Brown, teacher in the Mount Hope elementary school in Calvert County, asks that a mandamus be granted compelling the board of education of Calvert County and H.R. Hughes, county superintendent of education, to pay her the same salary paid white teachers of the same grade who do the same work."[31]

The case was not in court for long. One month after the suit was filed, the Calvert County Board of Education and the Calvert County Commissioners agreed to equalize salaries between black teachers and white teachers, and the suit against the county was dropped. Meetings with county school officials and the success of the Montgomery County case had paved the way for a relatively easy win.

This second victory was a huge boost to the NAACP and the teachers' equalization movement, not just in Maryland but throughout the South. The teachers' salary cases resulted in the establishment of thousands of new NAACP branches in cities and towns throughout the country. The NAACP spread from the cities to the vast rural areas of America. These victories showed that significant change could be achieved through litigation and the cooperation of the community.

Several other Maryland counties adopted equal pay for teachers in 1938. In Cecil, Kent, and Queen Anne's counties, Marshall negotiated equal pay agreements with school officials. Baltimore County and Washington County reached agreements with their black teachers to keep Marshall and the NAACP away. By the end of 1938, nine of Maryland's twenty-three counties had agreed to equalize teacher pay.[32]

However, some counties resisted change. In Charles County, black teachers did not press for equalization of pay and did not provide a potential plaintiff. School officials in Prince George's County and Anne Arundel County refused to change, and additional litigation was required.

In Prince George's County, where the third suit was filed, Nicholas Orem, the school board superintendent, refused to allow Marshall to inspect the minutes of the board of education. Marshall had to file a writ of mandamus to force Orem to give him access to the records. Orem took the extreme step of firing all the black probationary teachers in the county in an effort to intimidate the NAACP and the black community.[33] The lawsuit became bogged down in the Prince George's County Circuit Court.

MARSHALL GOES TO FEDERAL COURT

As the Prince George's County lawsuit stalled, Marshall grew impatient with the slow and expensive county-by-county approach. He informed the statewide committee of teachers supporting the litigation that he was considering a statewide solution to the issue of pay equalization:

> You are all aware of the fact that most of the counties in Maryland operate under the Equalization Fund. I have been informed that the Equalization Fund is based upon the salary schedule of the Maryland Code. I am also informed that under these provisions the money is sent from the State to the Counties on the basis of this schedule whereby more money is sent for white teachers than is sent for Negro teachers.
>
> We are now working on the theory of bringing a case against the State Board of Education to raise the question of the payment of the State Board to the counties of the discriminatory amounts for salaries. We will work on this over the summer in the hope that we will be able to file the case in early fall."[34]

In his fourth teacher pay lawsuit, Marshall sued the Maryland State Board of Education on behalf of Walter Mills, principal and teacher at an elementary school in Anne Arundel County. The earlier lawsuits in Montgomery, Calvert, and Prince George's counties were filed in the respective counties' circuit courts, but this time Marshall sued in federal court. The complaint in the US District Court for the District of Maryland alleged that state laws requiring different pay scales for black and white teachers were unconstitutional under the Fourteenth Amendment's equal protection clause.[35]

Marshall sought a federal injunction to have the statute stricken, and counsel for the State Board of Education Charles T. LeViness III, Marshall's old opponent from the law school cases, filed a federal version of a demurrer called a motion to dismiss.

School Law of Maryland

Governing the Salaries of White and Colored Teachers

(From Article 77—Maryland Code of Law)

Elementary White Teachers
(Third-Grade Certificate)

No white teacher regularly employed in a public school of the State of Maryland shall receive a salary of less than $600 per school year.

Provided, if such teacher holds a third grade certificate of the first class and has taught in the public schools of the State of Maryland for a period of three years, such teacher shall receive a salary of not less than $650 per school year.   Sec. 90, Acts 1922, ch. 382.

(Second-Grade Certificate)

No white teacher regularly employed in a public school of the State of Maryland, holding a second grade certificate, shall receive a salary of less than $750 per school year.

Provided, if such a teacher holds a second grade certificate of the first class and has taught in the public schools of the State of Maryland for a period of three years, such teacher shall receive a salary of not less than $800 per school year.

Provided, further: if such teacher holds a high school teacher's certificate of the first class and has taught in an approved high school of the State of Maryland for a period of seven years, such teacher shall receive a salary of not less than $1,350 per school year. Sec. 195, Acts 1927, ch. 121.

Elementary Colored Teachers
(Third-Grade Certificate)

No teacher regularly employed in the public schools for colored children in the State of Maryland shall receive a salary of less than $40 per month.

Provided that if such teacher holds a third grade certificate of the first class and has taught in the public schools for colored children in the State of Maryland for a period of three years, such teacher shall receive a salary of not less than $45 per month.   Sec. 202, Acts 1922, ch. 382.

(Second-Grade Certificate)

No teacher regularly employed in the public schools for colored children in the State of Maryland, holding a second grade certificate, shall receive a salary of less than $50 per month.

Provided that if such teacher holds a second grade certificate of the first class and has taught in the public schools for colored children in the State of Maryland for a period

NAACP Begins New Pay Suit

The National Association for the Advancement of Colored People renewed its legal offensive against differentials in salaries of white and colored teachers in Maryland counties this week.

The court action, begun by Miss Elizabeth Brown, teacher in the Mount Hope elementary school in Calvert County, asks that a mandamus be granted compelling the board of education of Calvert County and H. R. Hughes, county superintendent of education, to pay her the same salary paid white teachers of the same grade who do the same work.

Follows Montgomery Case

The case follows the proceedings taken in the successful Montgomery County action whereby the NAACP attorneys brought about an adjustment which added $30,000 per year to the salaries of teachers in that county.

Miss Brown holds a first

for eight years. She is now receiving a salary of $75 per month for eight months, or $600 per year.

The petition sets forth that white teachers holding first grade certificates similar to that held by Miss Brown and performing

Continued on page 2, col. 1

NAACP WINS OPENING ROUND IN MD. CASE

Court Overrules Demurrer and Orders State to Answer Petition

ROCKVILLE, Md. — The circuit court of Montgomery County awarded the NAACP first blood in the fight to equalize teachers' salaries in the rural schools.

Salaries in public schools of Baltimore City are already equalized.

The court ordered the county attorney to answer the NAACP petition within ten days and overruled a demurrer filed by County Attorney William F. Prettyman, who has said that the

NAACP's case was not properly filed and was suing the wrong parties.

The court's ruling is a virtual command to the county's lawyers to quit bluffing and do some legal work.

The suit was filed by William B. Gibbs, of West Chester, Pa., a Rockville principal, who says the county is paying him $612 a year while it pays white principals of the same rank, $1125 a year.

This is the first time in the history of U.S. Courts that a case

Marshall brought teacher pay lawsuits in five Maryland counties and negotiated salary equalization agreements in three other counties without lawsuits. *Courtesy of Afro-American Newspaper Archives and Research Center.*

The motion to dismiss was argued before US District Court Judge W. Calvin Chesnut.[36] Judge Chesnut dismissed the injunction and informed Marshall that in suing the State Board of Education, the plantiffs had pursued the wrong entity. Judge Chesnut said, "To redress this grievance on behalf of himself and others of his race in the same class he has filed this suit, not against the County Board by which he is employed, but against the State Board of Education, the State Superintendent of Education and the Treasurer and Comptroller of the State, all general State officers. In Maryland since 1865, the county has been the unit for most local governmental functions including that of public education."[37]

What initially looked like a major defeat proved to be only a temporary delay of victory. Chesnut invited Marshall to refile his lawsuit against the county board instead of the state board. Two months later, Marshall filed a new lawsuit on behalf of Mills against the Anne Arundel County Board of Education.

This time, Judge Chesnut ruled in Marshall's favor and ordered equal pay for black and white public school teachers in Anne Arundel. In his ruling, Judge Chesnut said, "As already stated, the controlling issue of fact is whether there has been unlawful discrimination by the defendants in determining the salaries of white and colored teachers in Anne Arundel County solely on account of race or color, and my finding from the testimony is that this question must be answered in the affirmative, and the conclusion of law is that the plaintiff is therefore entitled to an injunction against the continuance of this unlawful discrimination."[38]

The Mills victory was the first federal court decision in the nation that declared unequal pay scales for black and white teachers to be unconstitutional. In 1941, after decades of failed attempts, the Maryland General Assembly finally passed a statute equalizing pay for the state's black and white teachers.

Chesnut's ruling provided the foundation for teacher pay litigation throughout the South. Marshall's involvement in the battle to equalize salaries between black and white teachers, which had begun with letters from Howard Pindell in 1935, would ultimately take him to Virginia,[39] Florida, Tennessee, Arkansas, Georgia, South Carolina, Alabama, North Carolina, Kentucky, and Texas. Using the knowledge, litigation experience, and negotiation skills that he had refined in Maryland, Marshall sued, organized, negotiated, and won lawsuits that dramatically increased the income of black educators and expanded the reach and credibility of the NAACP. Marshall saw the teacher pay equalization suits as a major tool to "build interest in the Association" because the suits "[gave] a material benefit to Negroes in general." Teachers with more money could spend more, and this benefited "[black] physicians, dentists, lawyers, and other professional[s] and businessmen."[40] Marshall often insisted, as a condition of his involvement in a case, that there be a local coordinating committee consisting of teachers and members of a local branch of the NAACP. In his relentless and successful campaign to obtain equal pay for black teachers, Thurgood Marshall became the nation's leading civil rights lawyer—"Mr. Civil Rights."

Conclusion

As a young person, Thurgood Marshall studied the art of verbal persuasion. The substantive issues of his arguments were secondary to the process of debating them. Marshall practiced being an effective speaker years before he decided to use his oratorical skills to promote civil rights.

Marshall was born into a family of articulate and assertive people, with both sets of grandparents being business owners and community leaders. His mother spoke with polished diction and precision and was determined that her sons would go to college and professional schools. His father led vigorous dinner table discussions about current events and challenged his sons to support their positions with sound information. Thurgood Marshall would frequently claim that his father influenced him to become a lawyer without ever proposing it directly. With several nearby aunts and uncles also providing guidance, Marshall's extended family expected him to succeed.

Marshall's elementary school classmates and teachers were fascinated by the disputatious boy who sought to win arguments by assembling facts. Formal training in verbal persuasion began in the ninth grade, when he joined his high school debate club. The history teacher who directed the debating program became the first of several influential mentors. He taught Marshall how to weave information into persuasive arguments and how to deliver effective rebuttals. When Marshall graduated from high school at the age of sixteen, he was already comfortable speaking before large audiences.

Marshall's advocacy training intensified in college, when he became the first freshman to survive the stiff competition for a slot on the Lincoln University debate team. The sociology and anthropology professor who advised the debate team introduced Marshall to new research sources and verbal techniques. As he participated in historic debates against teams of national and international stature, Marshall grew in rhetorical skill and confidence.

Marshall's vocal control became a powerful and flexible instrument. Emulating his father, Marshall learned to change the accent and tone of his voice, the pace of his speech, and even the pronunciation of specific words to fit different situations. Discussions at home, four years of college dormitory bull sessions, eight years of formal debating, and eight summers as a waiter had enhanced his verbal dexterity. Marshall also enjoyed the advantages of some valuable genetic inheritances—a commanding physical presence, a handsome face, a facile mind, a loud voice, and a storyteller's sense of timing.

By the time Marshall graduated from Lincoln University, he had taken formal courses in public speaking, rhetoric, logic, ethics, the Bible, Virgil, Milton, Plato, and Shakespeare. He had studied Latin, Greek, and French, and had acquired extraordinary command of the English language. Thurgood Marshall entered law school a proficient and experienced public speaker.

Although extremely successful as a law student, Marshall did not initially display any special interest in civil rights matters. But the civil rights advocate almost certainly lurked just under the surface. Marshall had grown up around people who openly fought against racial discrimination, his grandparents being nineteenth-century leaders, organizers, and fighters for fairness. His father ridiculed racism and taught his sons to confront it directly. His mother's social clubs raised money for the NAACP, years before Thurgood got involved. Richard Kluger, in his book *Simple Justice*, called Thurgood "Uncle Fearless' nephew," referring to the favorite uncle who organized a savings bank, owned a real estate company, and fought discrimination in the Catholic church.[1] Marshall's high school mentor was an intrepid "race man," and his favorite college professor took special interest in advising bright young black men who showed potential for leadership.

Marshall's civil rights work began in his last law school semester, when first a professor and then the dean involved him in cases they were developing. At Charles Houston's request, Marshall assembled a research memorandum on options to help George Crawford, a black man who had been arrested in Massachusetts and accused of committing murder in Virginia. The NAACP had solicited Houston's assistance to prevent the defendant from being extradited back to Virginia to face a possible lynching or an unfair trial. Marshall learned that he could make a difference and even save a man's life.

As Marshall awaited his bar examination results, he accompanied Houston on a trip to the Deep South and observed for the first time its overt suppression of black people. They drove in Houston's car to New Orleans and back, gathering along the way information about public schools in the states they passed through. Marshall recalled that they never saw a school for white youngsters in as poor a condition as the best school they saw for blacks. As they traveled, Houston explained to his young protégé his philosophy that black lawyers either were "social engineers" or "parasites." Marshall would often speak about this trip and Houston's philosophy.

The trip to New Orleans might have remained an isolated event had George Armwood not been lynched in October 1933, one week after Marshall became a lawyer. This tragedy on the Eastern Shore of Maryland brought Marshall and Houston together in the office of Maryland's governor and launched Marshall's lifelong campaign for criminal justice.

As Marshall began law practice, civil rights matters arose that drew his immediate attention. The Buy Where You Can Work campaign, the representation of an activist white lawyer, and the aftermath of a policeman killing an unarmed motorist consumed the first several months of Marshall's career, with other civil rights matters soon to follow. As civil rights and fee-producing law practice competed for Marshall's attention, the former inevitably received priority, producing both Marshall's first major victory—the University of Maryland Law School case—and his first major defeat—the Baltimore County high school case.

By early 1936, Marshall realized that he had become and wished to remain a civil rights advocate. He was not driven to this choice by a lack of options. The range and quantity of clients Marshall acquired as a beginning lawyer in the Great Depression suggest that, if he had chosen to focus on building a fee-producing law practice, he could have earned a very comfortable living. But, as he told Houston in March 1936, he decided that he would not give up the civil rights work "for anything in the world." Yet, the automobile accident cases, divorces, wills, contracts, business deals, and criminal defense cases gave Marshall valuable experience.

Marshall had also developed work habits, attitudes, and personal traits that would characterize his legal career. Colleagues marveled at Marshall's almost superhuman capacity to work long days for weeks and months without breaks. His industrious character become apparent early in life, when as a child he never missed school, participated in extensive extracurricular activities, and still had an after-school job. During college years, Marshall worked in the campus bakery and on the railroad. While in law school, he worked in the school library and as a country club waiter. While practicing law during the day, he also worked nights as a clerk in a health clinic. In later years, Marshall became fond of saying, "Isn't it nice that no one cares which twenty-three hours of the day I work?"[2]

Optimistic and resilient, Marshall invariably found a silver lining in the results of his court cases, even those that might be regarded as failures. Marshall's client in his first serious criminal case got the death penalty and was hanged. Yet Marshall thought it important that a black lawyer had handled a major criminal case in southern Maryland. Marshall's letter to Charles Houston the day after George Armwood was lynched predicted that "something will come out of it" because the incident would increase support for antilynching legislation. Although the monetary judgment that Marshall obtained for a widow was not likely to be collectible, Marshall saw benefit in requiring a police officer to defend himself against a claim of police misconduct. Following Marshall's most dramatic early loss—the Baltimore County high school case—he highlighted one line in the Maryland appeals court decision that seemed to recognize, eighteen years before *Brown v. Board of Education*, that racially separate schools would never be equal.

A gregarious person and a natural politician, Marshall enjoyed conversing with persons of all economic levels. As a lawyer he was diplomatic and collegial, disarming adversaries and defusing tense situations with personal charm and humor. Eight summers as a waiter had cultivated tact and skill in quickly assessing people and situations, and these interpersonal skills helped him greatly during his early career. Marshall's direct negotiations with Baltimore's police commissioner cleared the way for the Buy Where You Can Work picketing to begin smoothly. His collegial relationship with opposing counsel in the Bernard Ades case helped him to avoid traps set by a dangerous federal judge. Marshall's political deal with a rural prosecutor led to the manslaughter indictment of a police officer and averted the indictment of four reform-school youths falsely accused of rape. Marshall's negotiations with judges and school boards in rural counties led to historic rulings and agreements in teacher pay cases. His carefully cultivated personal relationship with the trial judge produced the court order that historians call "the first step on the road to *Brown v. Board of Education*." Conversely, Marshall believed that his failure to create better relationships with the lawyers and the judge in the Baltimore County high school case worked to his detriment.

One of Marshall's special assets was his appreciation for opposing views. Classmate Oliver Hill spoke of Marshall's "extraordinary talent of being reasonable with those who disagreed with him." Judges and attorneys were impressed by his willingness to try to understand their positions, even if he ultimately disagreed with them. Marshall's inclination to see both sides of issues was a direct consequence of his experience as a competitive debater in high school and college, where teams typically prepared to argue both the affirmative and negative sides of propositions. Furthermore, Marshall genuinely liked and identified with other lawyers, viewing them as fellow travelers who, at the moment, happened to be on different teams.

Even though Marshall was a forceful advocate for his settled positions, he was a good listener who sought and received advice. Marshall seldom conveyed the impression that he thought he knew it all and had every answer. Others have described him as a "sponge" and a "brain picker" because of how he absorbed ideas from those around him. Because Marshall obviously valued the opinions of others, people gave him thoughtful advice. Marshall consulted a Baltimore City trial judge on how to handle the police shooting case in rural southern Maryland. Marshall discussed with an appellate judge how to proceed in the Baltimore County high school case. Marshall frequently sought advice from his officemate, veteran attorney Warner T. McGuinn. *Afro-American* publisher Carl Murphy was an important sounding board. Marshall stayed in constant contact with Charles Houston, leaving behind a treasure trove of the letters and memoranda that had passed between them over the years.

Marshall was pragmatic and no "Don Quixote." Focusing on obtainable goals and promising tactics, he refused to embark on futile missions or tasks that he regarded as wastes of time. As his cousin Cyrus Marshall Jr. described him, "Thurgood disliked busywork. If there was nothing important to do, he wouldn't do anything. But, if there was something important to do, he would stay on the task until the job was done."[3]

Marshall had no hobbies, eschewed exercise, and exhibited no interest in the arts. He never developed an interest in cars or clothes. His reading was utilitarian and rarely just for pleasure. Even money seemed unimportant to Marshall. Good food and drink, chain smoking, western movies, and talking—especially storytelling—were good enough for him.

Marshall's pragmatism could on occasion lead to a lack of candor, such as his claim to be a Presbyterian on his college application, his misstated date of birth when he began working for the railroad, his semester off from college working on the railroad when he supposedly was sick, and a few deceptions he engaged in to move law cases forward.

Another element of Marshall's pragmatism, developed early in life, was his preference in difficult situations to directly approach the person who had the most authority to address the situation—whether that person be a governor, a judge, a prosecutor, a school superintendent, or a local police chief. A person's status or power did not intimidate him. His well-documented communications with FBI director J. Edgar Hoover were extensions of his meeting with Governor Ritchie during his first month as a lawyer and his negotiations with the Baltimore police commissioner two months later. His visits to judges and his letter-writing exchanges with members of Congress provide other examples. When Marshall met Great Britain's Prince Edward, His Highness asked Marshall, "Do you care to hear my opinion of lawyers?" to which Marshall reportedly responded with a smile, "Only if you care to hear my opinion of princes."[4] The informality went both ways, as Marshall never seemed to be impressed with his own importance.

Marshall's insistence on careful development of factual evidence, a hallmark of his approach to litigation and negotiations, developed from his at-home discussions, his preparation for current-events talks in school, his years of competitive debating, and the influence of Charles Houston, who repeatedly reminded Marshall of Justice Brandeis's comment to Howard University's President Johnson that black lawyers often left the factual record too incomplete for even a sympathetic Supreme Court to help their clients. The Cheltenham investigation, the Lucas murder case, the Murray law school case, the teacher pay cases, and the Poindexter inquiry all exemplify Marshall's careful development of the facts to foster success. Conversely, Marshall would identify his failure to nail down with evidence the fact that a certain examination was administered only to black eighth graders as one of the main reasons why he lost the Baltimore County high school case. Over the years that followed, whenever Marshall lost a case, it was seldom due to an inadequate factual record.

Marshall's careful adherence to the facts in litigation did not extend to his storytelling. When it came to verbal entertainment, this scion of a family of raconteurs did not let the truth stand in the way of a good story.

The apocryphal tale about Marshall's slave ancestor being set free by his master because he was too uncooperative to be a slave grew in detail over the years but does not withstand scrutiny. Likewise, Marshall's story about his learning the US Constitution when he was sent to the basement of his elementary school or high school for punishment is doubtful. On the other hand, his story about Grandmother Annie Marshall sitting down over a hole to prevent a utility pole from being installed in front of her store comports with the evidence.

Marshall's humorously insightful remarks about race became legendary. As a lawyer, and later as a judge, he used humor to make points about the absurdities of race relations in America. This practice was a direct echo of his father. Even though he undoubtedly experienced racial discrimination, Marshall did not generally distrust white people. His attitudes about race were person-specific because he had encountered many decent white people. He repeatedly said, "I never had any hatred of white people as such, because there were some that touched my life, whom I considered to be very good."[5] Whites and blacks interacted constantly in his neighborhood. One of his father's best friends was a white police officer. Marshall had supportive white employers. All of his college professors were white. Marshall's first full trial as a lawyer was on behalf of a white attorney being persecuted for asserting rights on behalf of black defendants.

Marshall became a lawyer in a city with a tradition of courageous and effective black lawyers who provided him solid role models. Everett Waring, the first African American to argue before the US Supreme Court, fought for black people on many fronts but received criticism for also defending white clients. Harry Cummings, who brought high school education to Baltimore's black community and resisted disenfranchisement efforts, seconded the nomination of Theodore Roosevelt for president. W. Ashbie Hawkins, the first lawyer for the Baltimore branch of the NAACP, spent decades as the indefatigable adversary of racial discrimination and became Marshall's personal hero. Warner T. McGuinn, with whom Marshall began his law practice, fought for the rights of women as well as blacks.

Waring, Cummings, Hawkins, and McGuinn not only showed Marshall how to be a civil rights lawyer but also defined for Marshall a precise civil rights agenda—demand criminal justice, protect voting rights, reduce housing discrimination, eliminate Jim Crow transportation, and fight for equal educational opportunity. Less than two decades after relocating to

New York, Marshall had argued each item of that agenda before the US Supreme Court in several criminal cases, in *Smith v. Allwright* (voting rights),[6] *Morgan v. Virginia* (transportation),[7] *Shelly v. Kraemer* (housing),[8] and *Brown v. Board of Education*.[9] Maryland had prepared Thurgood Marshall well.

At age thirty, Thurgood Marshall became the special counsel of the NAACP and the nation's leading civil rights lawyer. Maryland had prepared him for the challenges that lay ahead. *Courtesy of Afro-American Newspaper Archives and Research Center.*

Acknowledgments

Exploring Thurgood Marshall's life has been a privilege and an adventure filled with fascination and discovery. I have received help from many people along this journey that began when I first went to Marshall's home late one night in July 1975.

After that encounter, I decided to learn more about Thurgood Marshall directly from people who knew him in his early years. During the 1980s, I interviewed Marshall's contemporaries living in Baltimore—relatives, classmates, neighbors, friends, and even two of his high school teachers. Among those who generously shared with me their recollections were Cyrus Marshall, Oliver Hill, Essie Hughes, Nellie Buchanan, Charles Burns, Juliet Carter, James Murphy, Carrie Jackson, Charlotte Shervington, Howard Pindell, Harold Seaborne, William H. Murphy Sr., Herbert Frisby, Philip Brown, and Rachel Brown. Helen Ramia, a law school secretary, transcribed the tapes before personal computers and word processing were available.

Having satisfied my initial curiosity about Marshall, I turned my attention to other matters. But the research and writings of my colleague, Professor David Bogen, and his enthusiasm for the history of civil rights in Maryland were infectious. I resumed my inquiries. Drawing on a special interest in photography, I produced some exhibits about civil rights and black lawyers in Maryland, including Thurgood Marshall.

Karen Rothenberg, then dean of the University of Maryland School of Law, urged me to dig deeper and to produce a substantial product. She then took steps to provide me with important resources. The law school acquired microfilm collections of the *Afro-American* newspaper, the NAACP Papers, the William Hastie papers, and other publications on civil rights.

As I began ten years of in-depth research into Thurgood Marshall's life, the staff of the Thurgood Marshall Law Library, under director Barbara Gontrum, became my steady partners. William Sleeman, now on the staff of the US Supreme Court's library, introduced me to the wide world of electronic databases. Pamela Bluh obtained books, doctorial dissertations, and master's theses from libraries around the nation. Nathan Robertson designed a database to manage voluminous documents and individual bits of information.

Dr. Edward Papenfuse, Maryland's state archivist, with whom I teach a seminar titled "Race and the Law: The Maryland Experience," made available to me records stored at the Maryland State Archives and the Baltimore City Archives. No search was too challenging, as he and his assistant, Owen Lourie, retrieved court records, birth and death certificates, photographs, legislative materials, property records, old newspapers, and myriad other items. Archivists in charge of other collections made important contributions, including Seth Kronemer at the Howard University School of Law, Tracey Hunter Hayes at the Langston Hughes Memorial Library of Lincoln University, J. Rodney Little and Mary Louise de Sarran at the Maryland Historical Trust, Kathleen Kotarba and Eric Holcomb at the Baltimore Commission for Historical and Architectural Preservation, Vivian Fisher and Jeff Korman at the Enoch Pratt Free Library, Eben Dennis at the Maryland Historical Society, David Shakelford at the B&O Railroad Museum, Catherine Scott at the Baltimore Museum of Industry, and the staff at the Manuscript Collection of the Library of Congress.

The *Afro-American* newspaper and its archives are national treasures. I shudder to think what we would not know about our history were it not documented and preserved by the *Afro*. Publisher John Oliver and *Afro* archivist John Gartrell facilitated my exploration of this mother lode of history.

Close friends pitched in to assist me. Michael Bowen Mitchell and Dr. Keiffer Mitchell shared important family photographs and original documents about the early years of the NAACP. Dwight Taylor helped me obtain important records from Marshall's college years. Anne Sherrington Davis gave me materials collected by her mother, Marshall's classmate, that highlighted Marshall's high school years. Kurt Schmoke paved the way for me at the Moorland-Spingarn Research Center of Howard University. Jacques Kelly of the *Baltimore Sun* provided insight into Baltimore history and shared valuable photographs from his bountiful collection. James Morrison and Jean Fox Crunkleton helped me understand Marshall's four summers working on Gibson Island. Thurgood Marshall's nephew, William Aubry Marshall Jr.; cousin, Norma Anderson; and cousin, Marsha Jordan gave me family photographs that appear in this book.

I am indebted to many scholars who created a rich body of literature from which I have drawn information and inspiration, including Genna McNeal's biography of Charles Houston, J. Clay Smith's books about black lawyers, Mark Tushnet's writings about Marshall, and autobiographies by Langston Hughes and Clarence Mitchell. My understanding of Maryland's distinct racial experience was enhanced by the writings of Sherilyn Ifill, Garrett Power, C. Fraser Smith, Louis Diggs, and Antero Pietila.

I am profoundly grateful to Bennett Beach, who turned over to me his entire set of notes and drafts from years of research about Thurgood Marshall. I also wish to thank the unknown person who, several years ago, left in my mailbox a file containing original 1930s correspondence to and from black applicants seeking admission to the University of Maryland.

Thurgood Marshall's family has been fully supportive. Cecilia Marshall, Thurgood's wife, graciously and patiently tolerated my intrusions into her home, family photo albums, and personal mementos. Thurgood Marshall Jr. sent letters to Lincoln University and Howard University that opened up to me his father's academic records, which otherwise would have been unavailable. I am honored by his foreword to this book.

I have benefited from association with two strong institutions. The University of Maryland Francis King Carey School of Law was home base, where I did most of my writing. I thank the administration, the faculty, the information technology staff, the audiovisual team, and my assistant, Myra Carter-Hickman. At my law firm, Shapiro, Sher, Guinot & Sandler, managing partner William Carlson and administrator Renee Lane-Kunz saw that I had space to work, store things, make copies, send out mailings, and whatever else I needed. I especially thank my assistant, Earlene Croxton, the office services staff headed by William Gross, and McKinley Thomas.

Joseph Yoor at New World Graphics did excellent photograph retouching and graphic design work. Robert Cronan, an accomplished cartographer, produced the original maps in the center of the book.

When the time arrived to begin converting the extensive research into a single document of reasonable brevity and clarity, Sean Yoes, a gifted writer, helped me organize the material, define the chapters, and begin writing. Paul Jaskunas also gave valuable advice.

As portions of the manuscript took shape, law school colleagues Oscar Gray, Donald Gifford, and Peter Quint read portions and gave valuable feedback. My former student Sarah Garrett, now a college administrator, helped edit the manuscript. Pulitzer Prize–author Taylor Branch took time from his demanding schedule to read the entire manuscript and make suggestions. My friend and neighbor Walter Eversley, a brilliant man with a phenomenal mastery of the English language, read multiple drafts of the manuscript and was the source of many improvements. My wife came to insist that nothing went forth that had not been duly "Walterized."

Student research assistants have made valuable contributions at each step. Rebecca Tabb and Mary Louise Preis were present for the early interviews. Charles Madden and Munachi Nsofor performed major research assignments. More than two thousand documents were digested and entered into a database by Melanie Barr, Phillip Hummel, Owen Jarvis, Alikbar Esfahani, Megan McDermott, and Rick Hellings. Kate DeAngelis, Laila Said, and Claire McLemore helped manage documents and checked citations. As I completed the writing and editing, Miroslav Nikolav was exceptionally productive. Other student research assistants in the final phase were Andrew Bennett, Adam Spiers, Allysa Rodriguez, Heidi Mun, Tsehauti Retta, and Rory Parks.

During periods of stress and doubt about whether I would ever finish this book and whether I should have undertaken a less arduous task, friends provided needed encouragement. My best friend, Ronald Shapiro, himself a bestselling author, has been in my corner for more than forty years and was a constant source of advice, energy, and optimism. My law partner Paul Sandler, a prolific author, closed off all escape routes to a less ambitious product. He insisted that instead of merely a law review article, a series of short pieces, or a website, I write a full-length book, what he called "one of mankind's few enduring art forms." Paul gave advice about the tone of the book, the book cover, the book length, the title, and the subtitle. And he was usually right. At the law school, Professor Taunya Banks was a constant presence and a conscience, also insisting that I cut no corners. My dean for the last three years, Phoebe Haddon, made only two demands: "get it done" and "get it right." She then saw that I had whatever I needed in order to finish, including a deadline.

Obtaining a national publisher is a challenge for a first-time author. My literary agent, Elizabeth Evans of Jean V. Naggar Literary Agency, helped me reshape my concept, fine-tune the book proposal, and get published. I am grateful to Steven Mitchell at Prometheus Books for immediately appreciating the potential of this book. His keen editorial comments on my first draft had a dramatic impact. The team at Prometheus Books, editorial assistant Melissa Shofner, production editor Catherine Roberts-Abel, and copyeditors Paula Fleming and Brian McMahon, worked efficiently and pleasantly to transform the manuscript into an attractive finished book.

My most consistent and versatile assistant through the years has been Delores Mack, a retired school teacher. She has been dedicated to this book since its inception. During the research years, she was at the law school so much that many people assumed she was on the staff. Delores Mack reviewed many reels of microfilm, scanned thousands of documents, organized stacks of materials, and proofread hundreds of pages.

My life and this book have been fueled and replenished by a network of love and support, at the center of which are my beautiful wife Diana Gibson, my amazing son Dr. Steven Gibson, my brilliant daughter-in-law Cicely Germain Gibson, and the apple of all of our eyes, my grandson, Gavin Larry Gibson. Diana endured my periods of absorption and obsession with this book. Through it all, she sustained me with her love and steadfast belief in my work.

Notes

PREFACE

1. Richard Kluger, *Simple Justice: The History of* Brown v. Board of Education *and Black America's Struggle for Equality* (New York: Knopf, 1976); Bob Woodward and Scott Armstrong, *The Brethren: Inside the Supreme Court* (New York: Simon and Schuster, 1979).

2. Carl T. Rowan, *Dream Makers, Dream Breakers: The World of Justice Thurgood Marshall* (Boston: Little, Brown, 1993); Michael D. Davis and Hunter R. Clark, *Thurgood Marshall: Warrior at the Bar, Rebel on the Bench*, updated and rev. ed. (New York: Carol, 1994); Howard Ball, *A Defiant Life: Thurgood Marshall and the Persistence of Racism in America* (New York: Crown, 1998); Juan Williams, *Thurgood Marshall: American Revolutionary* (New York: Times Books, 1998).

CHAPTER 1: IS THERE AN INVESTIGATION TAKING PLACE?

1. "Lawyers Want Federal Action about Lynching," *Afro-American*, October 28, 1933. For a comprehensive history of Maryland, including its physical structure, economics, politics, and demographics, see Robert J. Brugger, *Maryland: A Middle Temperament* (Baltimore: Johns Hopkins University Press 1988). See also George H. Calcott, *Maryland & America 1940–1980* (Baltimore: Johns Hopkins University Press, 1985).

2. "Maryland Prisoner Snatched from Eastern Shore Mob," *Afro-American*, October 23, 1933; "Armwood Quit School in the 5th Grade, Says Pal," *Afro-American*, October 28, 1933.

3. "Is Sped to Baltimore from Jail in Snow Md, After Confession That He Murdered Davis Family," *Baltimore Sun*, October 14, 1941; "Held for Murder of George Davis and Family at Berlin, Md.," *Baltimore Sun*, October 13, 1931.

4. "Nov. 3 Likely Date for Lee Execution," *Baltimore Sun*, October 10, 1933; "Euel Lee's Plea Before Ritchie Late Today," *Baltimore Sun*, October 19, 1933; "Rush Suspect to City for Safe Keeping," *Afro-American*, October 21, 1933.

5. "Eye Witness to Lynching Tells How Mob Acted," *Afro-American*, December 12, 1931; "Mob Lynches Negro Seized in Hospital," *New York Times*, December 5, 1931; "Mob Hangs Wounded Negro in Maryland; Burns Body," *New York American*, December 5, 1931; "Maryland Mob Storms Hospital and Kills Negro," *New York Herald Tribune*, December 5, 1931; "Matthew Williams, Negro, Murderer of Danial J. Elliott, Lynched at Salisbury, Md," *Baltimore Sun*, December 5, 1931.

6. "Godfrey Child Blames Lynching of Matthew Williams on International Labor Defense League," *Baltimore Sun*, December 5, 1931.

7. "Police Squads Escort Negro Back to Shore," *Baltimore Sun*, October 18, 1933.

8. "Police Captain Urges Moving of Accused Negro," *Baltimore Evening Sun*, October 18, 1933.

9. Ibid.

10. "Rush Suspect to City for Safe Keeping," *Afro-American*, October 21, 1933.

11. "Police Squads Escort Negro Back to Shore," *Baltimore Sun,* October 18, 1933; "Armwood Taken in Darkness to Princess Anne," *Baltimore Evening Sun*, October 18, 1933.

12. "Maryland Mob Lynches Negro after Battling State Police," *Richmond Times-Dispatch*, October 19, 1933; "Lynchers Hang Prisoner and Burn His Body," *Philadelphia Public Ledger*, October 19, 1933; "2 State Policemen Badly Hurt," *Baltimore News*, October 19, 1933; "Mob of 3,000 Routs Police, Lynches Negro," *Washington Herald*, October 19, 1933; "Victim Beaten Hanged to Pole Then Burned," *Philadelphia Record*, October 18, 1933; George Ruark, "Witness Describes Lynching," *Washington Daily News*, October 19, 1933; "People of Town Discuss Lynching," *Baltimore Sun,* October 20, 1933. Through every case, incident, controversy, campaign, and challenge discussed in this book, the *Afro-American* newspaper was the main chronicler, communications instrument, and voice of Maryland's black communities. See Hayward Farrar, *The Baltimore Afro-American 1892–1950* (Westport, CT: Greenwood Press, 1998).

13. "Burn," *Afro-American*, October 21, 1933; "Fire Alarm Signals Shore Mob to Gather," *Afro-American*, October 21, 1933; "Mob Members Knew Prey was Feeble Minded," *Afro-American*, October 21, 1933; "Roman Holiday as Armwood is Hanged, Burned," *Afro-American*, October 21, 1933.

14. *Lynching* means punishment, usually causing death, inflicted by a mob or vigilantes without due process of law for a presumed criminal offense.

15. See Robert L. Zangrango, *The NAACP Crusade against Lynching: 1909–1950* (Philadelphia: Temple University Press, 1980); Ralph Ginzburg, *100 Years of Lynchings* (Baltimore: Black Classic Press, 1996); James H. Chadbourn, *Lynching and the Law* (Chapel Hill: University of North Carolina Press, 1933).

16. "Maryland Lynchings Since 1882 Now Increased to 33," *Afro-American*, October 28, 1933; "31 Lynchings in Maryland Since the Year 1882," *Afro-American*, December 12, 1931; "Lynching of Matthew Williams, Negro, at Salisbury Breaks 20 Year Record for Maryland,"

Baltimore Sun, December 5, 1931; Sherrilyn A. Ifill, *On the Courthouse Lawn: Confronting the Legacy of Lynching in the Twenty-First Century* (Boston: Beacon Press, 2007).

17. "Ritchie Ouster Urged: Lynch Probe Widens," *Washington Post*, October 20, 1933; "Interracial Group Demands Governor Oust Duer, Robbins," *Baltimore Sun*, October 21, 1933; "State Blamed for Lynchings by Ministers," *Baltimore Sun*, October 22, 1933; "Ministers in City Deplore Lynching," *Baltimore Sun*, October 23, 1933; "Plan Protest Meeting Here Friday," *Afro-American*, October 28, 1933; "Ainslee Hears Anti-Lynch Body Here," *Afro-American*, November 11, 1933; "Liberals Here Saturday for Lynch Tribunal," *Afro-American*, November 18, 1933.

18. "Baltimore Boy Finishes Law," *Afro-American*, June 17, 1933; "Admitted to Bar," *Afro-American*, August 12, 1933; "Marshall Opens Law Office," *Afro-American*, November 11, 1933.

19. McGuinn and Hughes created a partnership. Marshall became a solo practitioner.

20. Marshall to Houston, October 19, 1933, Charles Houston Papers, Moorland-Spingarn Research Center, Howard University, Washington, DC.

21. "Governor Blames Judge Duer and State's Attorney Robbins," *Afro-American*, October 21, 1933.

22. "Blame in Lynching Placed on Judge by Gov. Ritchie," *Baltimore Evening Sun*, October 19, 1933; "False Safety Pledge Blamed by Governor for Shore Horror," *New York Times*, October 19, 1933; "Ritchie Places Mob Guilt on Judge and State's Attorney: Orders Probe," *Washington Daily News*, October 19, 1933; "Robbins and Daugherty Told Armwood Would Be Lynched," *Afro-American*, October 28, 1933; "Eyewitness Says Police Might Have Halted Mob," *Baltimore Evening Sun*, October 21, 1933. The day after Armwood was murdered, Houston had written to Walter White at the NAACP headquarters in New York and urged him, "For heaven's sake, swing the whole NAACP against Maryland in the Armwood lynching. Get down to Baltimore yourself if necessary and interview Ritchie"; Houston to White, October 19, 1933. Houston appears to have followed his own advice.

23. "Governor Ritchie Assailed by Law Group," *Washington Tribune*, October 26, 1933. Leon Andrew Ransom was born in Columbus, Ohio, and graduated from Ohio University School of Law. Charles Houston recruited him to join the law faculty at Howard University. Edward Lovett was born in Fayetteville, North Carolina, and graduated from Howard University Law School a year ahead of Thurgood Marshall. James Tyson was born in Smithfield, Pennsylvania, and also graduated from Howard University Law School in 1932.

24. "Memorandum for His Excellency, Albert C. Ritchie, Governor of Maryland," October 25, 1933, Charles Houston Papers, Moorland-Spingarn Research Center, Howard University.

25. "Lawyers Want Federal Action about Lynching," *Afro-American*, October 28, 1933.

26. Nevertheless, the arrests infuriated many local whites and led to a "Never Ritchie Again" campaign, which later took credit for defeating Ritchie's 1934 reelection bid.

27. See Ifill, *On the Courthouse Lawn*. Professor Ifill's book presents an in-depth analysis of the Armwood and Williams lynchings and their aftermaths. See also "Hold Mob Control Effort Was Lacking," *Baltimore Evening Sun*, October 27, 1933; "Officials Blamed in Mob Hanging," *Washington Post*, November 11, 1933; "Lynch Inquiry to Have List of Eyewitnesses," *Baltimore Sun*, October 23, 1933; "$1,000 Reward Offered for Md. Lynchers," *Pittsburgh Courier*, November 11, 1933; "9 Face Arrest in Lynching at Princess Anne," *Washington Herald*, November 17, 1933; "Nine Named as Lynchers in Maryland," *Washington Post*, November 17, 1933; "Text of Ritchie's Disregarded Plea to Judge Duer for Re-arrest of 4 Men," *Washington Herald*, November 30, 1933; "The State v. The Shore," *Afro-American*, December 2, 1933; "Maryland Mob Routs Soldiers Arresting Lynch Suspects," *Afro-American*, December 2, 1933; "Lynch Suspects Released in Md. Arrested in Mo.," *Norfolk Journal and Guide*, December 9, 1933; "Cop Suspected in Md. Lynching Goes Back to Job," *Pittsburgh Courier*, December 9, 1933.

28. A Bill to Assure to Persons Within the Jurisdiction of Every State the Equal Protection of the Law, and to Punish the Crime of Lynching, S. 1978, 73rd Cong. (1934).

29. "Alphabetical List of Witnesses to Appear at Hearings on the Costigan-Wagner Anti-Lynching Bill, before the Senate Subcommittee on the Judiciary," February 20–21, 1934, NAACP Papers; "City to Send Ten to Lynch Hearing," *Baltimore Sun*, February 20, 1934; "All Sections Join in Fight for Federal Anti-Lynch Bill," NAACP Press Release, February 23, 1934.

30. S. 24, 74th Cong. (1935)

31. "Tydings Stand on Anti-Mob Bill Not Yet Cleared," *Afro-American*, March 30, 1935; see also "Stay in District for Anti-Lynching Bill, Tydings Told," *Afro-American*, April 13, 1935.

32. Thurgood Marshall to Millard Tydings, March 28, 1935, NAACP Papers, Library of Congress.

33. Thurgood Marshall to Millard Tydings, April 13, 1935, NAACP Papers, Library of Congress.

CHAPTER 2: THE BALTIMORE GROCERS' GRANDSON

1. Thurgood Marshall, interview with Ed Edwin, Columbia University Oral History Research Office, February 15, 1977.

2. "Obituary of Thorney Marshall," *Afro-American,* July 16, 1915.

3. Advertisement for T. G. Marshall Grocery Store, *Afro-American,* August 29, 1908 and August 26, 1916.

4. Advertisement for T. G. Marshall Grocery Store, *Afro-American*, January 3, 1914. A list of the goods sold in 1913 included 15,600 loaves of bread, 177 barrels of flour, 60 barrels of sugar, 3,370 gallons of oil, 563 pounds of tea and coffee, 150 bushels of potatoes, 730 gallons of milk, and 23,576 pounds of meat.

5. The earlier store was on Somerset Street, near Sharp Street. The church that the Thorney Good Marshall family attended was originally located on Sharp Street. After moving to Etting Street in Old West Baltimore, the church retained its original name, Sharp Street United Methodist Church.

6. "The Marshall family had the most successful grocery store owned by blacks in Baltimore, and we were all, in a sense, raised out of it," boasted Thurgood's first cousin, Charles Burns. In 1917 and 1918, directories listed Annie Marshall, Cyrus Marshall, Thomas R. Marshall, and Thoroughgood Marshall as residents of 535 Dolphin Street, where the family grocery was located.

7. Thurgood's uncle, Thoroughgood, never changed his name.

8. Thorney and Annie's children were Mary Elizabeth (b. 1880), William C. (b. 1882, Thurgood's father), Thoroughgood (b. 1884), Anne B. (b. 1888), Cyrus W. (b. 1891), Thomas R. (b. 1896), and Margaret B. (b. 1897).

9. Anne and Sandy Burns were the parents of Charles Burns, Juliet Burns Carter, Norma Burns Anderson, and Dorothy Burns Randall.

10. "Helped in Movement to Raise First Flag over Colored School," *Afro-American*, July 23, 1915.

11. "Obituary of Thorney Marshall."

12. Cyrus Marshall Jr., interview with the author, June 25, 1981; Juliet Carter, interview with the author, July 2, 1981.

13. Deed, Mary E. Marshall to Jeanne M. Watkins, Baltimore City Superior Court (Land Records), 1930, SCL 5121, p. 567–569 MCA CE168-5129.

14. US Navy pension application 28387, certificate 17884; US Navy pension application 14302, certificate 11218. Isaiah Williams and his brother James enlisted in the US Navy in October 1861 and served on the USS *Santiago de Cuba*, a brigantine-rigged side-wheeler, supporting the naval blockade of the South. He was the steward to Captain Daniel B. Ridgley. Discharged in 1865, Williams reenlisted a year later and served another three years as steward to Ridgely, now a commodore. This tour was on the USS *Powhatan* in the Pacific Ocean.

15. Assignment, Richard M. Johnson to Isaiah O. B. Williams, 1881, Baltimore County Circuit Court (Land Records) 1881, Liber 120, p. 618–619 MSA CE 62-120.

16. Thurgood Marshall, interviews with Ed Edwin, February–April 1977, Columbia University Oral History Office, in Mark Tushnet, *Thurgood Marshall: His Speeches, Writings, Arguments, Opinions, and Reminiscences* (Chicago: Lawrence Hill Books, 2001), pp. 413–516.

17. Baltimore City Directories: Woods 1875, p. 739; Woods 1880, p. 987; Woods 1881, p. 1060; Woods 1882, p. 1098; Woods 1883, p. 1066; Woods 1886, p. 1437; Killam and Maffitt 1887, p. 1250; Killam and Maffitt 1890, p. 1300; Killam and Maffitt 1892, p. 1313.

18. "The Colored People's Mass Meeting," *Baltimore Sun*, August 6, 1875; "The Colored People's Mass Meeting: Not a Question of Class," *Baltimore Sun*, August 7, 1875; "The Cake Walk Homicide: Trial of Ex-Policeman Patrick M'Donald for the Murder of Daniel Browne, Colored," *The Sun*, November 16, 1875; "The Cake Walk Homicide," *Baltimore Sun*, November 20, 1875; "The Cake Walk Homicide: End of Trial of Patrick M'Donald for the Murder of Daniel Brown, Colored—Verdict of Manslaughter," *Baltimore Sun*, November 25, 1875.

19. "Alleged Damage from Tunnel," *Baltimore Sun*, December 1, 1892; "Damages of $100 for Mr. Williams," *Baltimore Sun,* December 6, 1892; *Williams v. Ryan et al.* (Baltimore City Court, 1892).

20. Obituary of Isaiah Williams, *Baltimore Sun*, March 22, 1894.

21. Assignment, Mary E. Williams, admin. Isaiah O. B. Williams to Charles J. Bonaparte, 1895, Baltimore City Superior Court (Land Records) 1895, JB 1578, p. 393–394 MSA CE168-1586. Charles J. Bonaparte was the grandson of Jerome Bonaparte, the brother of Napoleon Bonaparte. After graduating from Harvard Law School, he led a lifelong crusade for clean government and racial equity. He was cocounsel in *Myer v. Anderson*, 182 F. 223 (Cir Ct D. Md 1910), which struck down a statute that deprived black citizens of the right to vote in Annapolis municipal elections. He rose to become the secretary of the Navy and the attorney general of the United States in the Theodore Roosevelt administration. For the career and politics of Charles Bonaparte, see James B. Crooks, *Politics & Progress: The Rise of Urban Progressivism in Baltimore 1895–1911* (Baton Rouge: Lousiana State University Press, 1968).

Mary Williams's application for a widow's pension had been rejected on the grounds that she was not "dependent," presumably because of her ownership of the store, although her application claimed that the store was not profitable. See Application for Widow's Pension 14302, Notice of Rejection, February 20, 1886, Bureau of Pensions, US Department of the Interior.

22. Much of the information about William Marshall and Norma Marshall in this chapter is from the author's interviews of Norma Burns Anderson (2012), Nellie Buchanan (1981), Charles Burns (1981), Juliet Carter (1981), Essie Hughes (1981), Carrie Jackson (1981), Cyrus Marshall Jr. (1981), William Aubrey Marshall Jr. (2011–2012), James H. Murphy (1985), William H. Murphy Sr. (2001), and Charlotte Shervington (1985).

23. Charles Burns, interview with the author, July 2, 1981.

24. Ibid.

25. The manager was Albert Fox, the secretary of the Gibson Island Club. William

Marshall stopped working at Gibson Island in 1935 but resumed working for Albert Fox in 1940, when Fox became the manager of the Belvedere Hotel in Baltimore. There, William Marshall served as the headwaiter in the John Eager Howard Room, a highly regarded restaurant in the hotel.

26. Burns, interview with the author.

27. Thurgood Marshall, interview with Ed Edwin for the Columbia University Oral History Project, 1977.

28. "Thurgood Marshall Takes a 'Tush-Tush' Job," *New York Times Magazine*, August 22, 1965.

29. Burns, interview with the author.

30. William H. Murphy was a member of the family that owned the *Afro-American* newspaper. He had a distinguished career as a judge in Baltimore.

31. William H. Murphy, interview with the author, October 4, 2001.

32. "Mother Considered Power behind Spingarn Medalist," *Afro-American*, July 13, 1946.

33. "17 Playgrounds Open Season," *Afro-American*, July 4, 1925.

34. "12,416 Pupils Start Work in Public School," *Afro-American*, September 11, 1926.

35. Nellie Buchanan, interview with the author, June 27, 1981.

36. Burns, interview with the author.

37. B. M. Phillips, "Remembering Norma Marshall," *Afro-American*, August 23, 1961.

38. Irvin Shaw, "Thurgood Marshall," *Afro-American*, August 13, 1960.

39. "Mother Considered Power behind Spingarn Medalist."

40. Juliet Carter, interview with the author, July 2, 1981.

41. Arnold de Mille, "Thurgood Marshall—Two Women Figure in Life of Great Lawyer," *Chicago Defender*, May 8, 1954.

42. Marshall, interview with Ed Edwin.

43. Ibid.

44. Ibid.

45. Avon Williams, a railroad dining car waiter, had five children, three of whom—Hayden, Ravine, and Velaine—were born in Baltimore and were close to Thurgood Marshall's age. The other two, Lee Livingston and Avon Jr., were born in Knoxville, Tennessee. Avon Williams Jr. had a distinguished career as a lawyer and political leader, becoming the first African American elected to the Tennessee Senate. He worked with Thurgood Marshall on the teacher pay cases in the 1940s.

46. Fearless Williams and Wallis Lansey were married to sisters. Lansey owned the Druid Laundry, whose largest customer, thanks to Williams, was the B&O Railroad.

47. "Provident Hospital Board Elects Three," *Afro-American*, July 18, 1925.

48. "To Defy St. Gregory Ouster Order," *Afro-American*, April 4, 1925.

49. "McGuinn, Briscoe and Callis Win Berths on G.O.P. Ticket," *Afro-American*, September 22, 1934; "700 at Opening of 4th District G.O.P. Club," *Afro-American*, June 10, 1933.

50. "But the Question Is: Was That Which Went into the Paper True?" *Afro-American*, July 9, 1932; "In the Matter of the Desecration of the Graves of Our Parents at Laurel Cemetery," *Afro-American*, April 18, 1931.

51. After selling the store in 1930, Annie Marshall and Mary Marshall moved above North Avenue to 2452 McCulloh Street.

52. Born in 1921, the fourth child of Avon and Carrie Williams, Avon Jr. obtained his law degree from Boston University in 1947. He became the leading civil rights lawyer in Tennessee and served in the Tennessee State Senate.

53. For a history of racial housing patterns in Baltimore and the laws, people, and events that shaped them, see Antero Pietila, *Not in My Neighborhood: How Bigotry Shaped a Great American City* (Chicago: Ivan R. Dee, 2010). See also Roberick N. Ryon, "Old West Baltimore," *Maryland Historical Magazine* 77, no. 1 (1982): 54–69.

54. *Convention Souvenir Book*, National Negro Business League, 1908. In the 1920 US Census, the cities with the five largest black populations were Washington, DC (84,446), New York City (91,708), New Orleans (89,292), Baltimore (84,740), and Philadelphia (84,459).

55. *The First Colored Professional, Clerical, and Business Directory of Baltimore City, 3rd Annual Edition*, 1915, published by William Coleman and commonly called "The Coleman Directory."

56. de Mille, "Thurgood Marshall—Two Women Figure in Life of Great Lawyer."

57. Carrie Jackson, interview with the author, July 6, 1981.

58. Ibid.

59. Baltimore City Health Department, Bureau of Vital Certificates (Birth Record), Certificate No. A39924, July 2, 1908.

60. Charlotte Watson Shervington, interview with the author, July 10, 1985.

61. Thurgood's teachers were Francis Holler (fifth grade), Ella Hayes (sixth grade), and Kate Sheppard (seventh grade).

62. "284 Pupils Finish 8th Grade in City School," *Afro-American*, June 24, 1921. Marshall's classmates were Jean Alexander, Gertrude Bennett, Vivian Bowman, Edna Brown, Earl Campbell, James Carr, Carrie Dorsey, Dorothy Dow, Rosa Hance, Charlotte Harris, Catherine Hill, Dorothy Jones, Laura Jones, Monistella Jones, Bessie Lake, Margaret Loudon, Mary Mendezes, Dorothy Newby, Thomas Pennington, Thelma Press, Ethel Rusk, Roberta Scott, Anita Short, Consuelo Smith, Bertha Tilghman, George Thomas, Charlotte Watson, Edna Watty, and Julia Woodhouse.

CHAPTER 3: MARSHALL'S HIGH SCHOOL YEARS

1. Thurgood Marshall's Application for Admission, 1925, Langston Hughes Memorial Library Archives, Lincoln University, Pennsylvania.

2. Board of School Commissioners, *Annual Report*, 1867, p. 70. For a history of the school from it inception to 1927, see Mason A. Hawkins, "Frederick Douglass High School: A Seventeen Year Period Survey" (PhD diss., University of Pennsylvania, 1933).

3. Baltimore City Council, Ordinance No. 113 (1896).

4. This became the third location of the Colored High School. It was first located in downtown Baltimore on Holliday Street, across from the old city hall. It soon outgrew that building and was moved to another downtown building on Saratoga Street, near Charles Street.

5. From 1840 to 1889, greenhouses occupied the northeast corner of Pennsylvania Avenue and Dolphin Street. The city bought the land and, in 1892, completed a two-and a-half-story brick building intended to serve as a new home for the German-American School #1, which had been languishing in unsuitable quarters four blocks away. However, in the summer of 1892, the façade of Baltimore's elite male high school, called the Baltimore City College, was undermined by the construction of a railroad tunnel. The school board decided to move City College into the new building at Pennsylvania and Dolphin while the high school building was repaired. The German-American School was forced to sit tight. In 1899, the German-American School finally moved into the building it had expected to occupy seven years earlier. But it enjoyed its new home for only two years. In 1901, it moved to a smaller building, and the newly created Colored High School took its place at Pennsylvania Avenue and Dolphin Street.

6. Neighboring Baltimore County and Howard County had no high school that African American youngsters could attend. See chapter 14.

7. The Colored High School, later renamed Frederick Douglass High School, was the only public high school in Baltimore that blacks could attend until Paul Laurence Dunbar High School opened its doors in 1937.

8. "Half Time Classes Create School Problem," *Afro-American*, September 23, 1923.

9. Mason A. Hawkins, "Frederick Douglass High School: A Seventeen Year Period Survey" (PhD diss., University of Pennsylvania, 1933).

10. Essie Hughes, interview with the author, July 1, 1981.

11. Cyrus Marshall Jr., interview with the author, June 25, 1981.

12. "Baltimore Boy Gets Gaston Medal at Brown: Gough McDaniels, Graduate of Colored High School Makes Good Record as Orator," *Afro-American*, May 28, 1910. The article stated, "For the first time in the history of Brown University, a colored student, Gough Decatur McDaniels, of Baltimore, won the Gaston Medal for excellence in oratory last night. The medal is the most valuable prize offered by the university."

13. "A mass meeting was held at Union Baptist Church, Thursday, in the interest of a new high school for colored children. Gough McDaniels, president of the alumni association, presided," the *Afro-American* reported in February 1915. As early as 1913, McDaniels was secretary of the Baltimore Branch of the NAACP and secretary of the Forum, a group of educators, lawyers, and other leaders that held organized public informational lectures. See *Coleman Directory*, First Edition, 1913.

14. Essie Hughes, interview with the author, July 2, 1981. Gough McDaniels also coached the participants in the school's annual Declaration Contest, the winner of which was given the prized H. S. McCard Medal.

15. "Balto. Teacher-Poet Gets Recognition: Verse of Gough McDaniels Is Accepted by Magazines. Will Contribute to Nationally Known Book," *Afro-American,* August 31, 1929; "McDaniels and Edmonds Write Winning Plays," *Afro-American*, June 3, 1939; "Last Rites for Gough McDaniels," *Afro-American*, February 15, 1941; "Throng Attends McDaniels Rites," *Afro-American*, February 22, 1942.

16. "Will Dedicate Park Swimming Pool Saturday: Gough McDaniels in Charge, Will Have Twenty-Five Employees," *Afro-American,* June 10, 1921.

17. Essie Hughes, interview with the author, July 2, 1981.

18. Charlotte Watson Shervington, interview with the author, July 10, 1985.

19. Carrie Dorsey Jackson, interview with the author, July 12, 1985.

20. Mary Anita Short later attended Morgan College, where she was on the debate team along with Frances Male, another of Marshall's high school debate teammates.

21. McDaniels was a leader in the three main community-mobilization efforts in which Marshall became involved: the antilynching campaign, the Buy Where You Can Work campaign, and the NAACP membership drive. See "Anti-lynching Body Hears a Secret Report," *Afro-American*, November 25, 1933; "Hail Costonie as Hero after Chain Victory," *Afro-American*, December 2, 1933.

22. Several biographies repeat Marshall's story about being disciplined by a school administrator who banished him to the school basement to memorize sections of the US Constitution. Marshall became fond of saying that "before it was over, I knew the whole thing." Some accounts describe these events as occurring in high school, and other times they are placed in elementary school. None of Marshall's classmates recalled such occurrences, and most doubted the story. Young Marshall was an orderly child; his parents would not have tolerated repeated misbehavior in school.

23. Arnold de Mille, "Thurgood Marshall—Two Women Figure in Life of Great Lawyer," *Chicago Defender*, May 8, 1954.

24. Ibid.

25. Confirmation Book, St. Katherine of Alexandria Episcopal Church, Baltimore, Maryland.

26. Hawkins, "Frederick Douglass High School."

27. "The Groundbreaking of the New Colored Junior-Senior High School," *Afro-American*, April 27, 1923.

28. "Minutes of the Board of School Commissioners," July 13, 1923, p. 23, Baltimore City Archives; "New High School Named for Douglass," *Afro-American*, July 20, 1923.

29. "Douglass High School Wins Annual Debate," *Afro-American*, May 23, 1925.

30. "Dates Set For Final School Exercises," *Afro-American*, May 16, 1925; "Douglass High Graduates Largest Class in History," *Afro-American*, June 20, 1925; "Commencement Program, Frederick Douglass High School," June 12, 1925.

31. "Commencement Program, Frederick Douglass High School."

32. Ibid.

33. Essie Hughes, interview with the author, July 2, 1981.

34. Cyrus Marshall, interview with the author, June 25, 1981.

35. Juliet Carter, interview with the author, July 2, 1981.

36. Charles Burns, interview with the author, July 2, 1981.

CHAPTER 4: LINCOLN UNIVERSITY

1. W. W. Walker to W. Hallock Johnson, Acting President of Lincoln University, June 17, 1925, Langston Hughes Memorial Library Archives, Lincoln University. William W. Walker, an 1897 graduate of Lincoln University, was the pastor of Madison Street Presbyterian Church in Baltimore, Maryland.

2. The costs at Lincoln University for one year were as follows: tuition $110, textbooks $15, room $25–$75, library fee $5, medical fee $3, YMCA fee $5, athletic fee $5, board $144, laundry $10.

3. Registrar of Lincoln University to Norma Marshall, June 24, 1925, Langston Hughes Memorial Library Archives, Lincoln University.

4. Norma Marshall to William Hallock Johnson, June 22, 1925, Langston Hughes Memorial Library Archives, Lincoln University.

5. Registrar of Lincoln University to Norma Marshall, June 24, 1925, Langston Hughes Memorial Library Archives, Lincoln University.

6. The school was founded by the Reverend John Miller Dickey and his wife, Sarah Emlen Cresson. They named it after Jehudi Ashmun, a religious leader and social reformer. In 1866, Ashmun Institute was renamed Lincoln University. The tenured faculty members as of 1923 who were ministers were W. H. Johnson, professor of mathematics; W. P. Finney, professor of English; E. J. Reinke, professor of English Bible; Paul DeLattre, professor of French; James Carter, professor of history; W. T. L. Keiffer, professor of archeology; and R. M. Labaree, professor of sociology. The non-ministers were W. L Wright, professor of mathematics, and H. F. Grim, professor of biology.

7. "No Lincoln U. President for Past 2 Years," *Afro-American*, May 22, 1926; "L. U. Trustees Meet June 23 with Alumni," *Afro-American*, June 19, 1926; "Wright Quits as Head of Lincoln U.," *Afro-American*, August 14, 1926; "Alumni Ask Investigation of Lincoln University," *Afro-American*, November 6, 1926. After a series of acting presidents, William Hallock Johnson was inaugurated as Lincoln's president in October 1927, during Marshall's junior year. See "President Johnson Inaugurated Lincoln Head," *Afro-American*, October 29, 1927.

8. "Agreement for Payment of College Bill," signed by Thurgood Marshall on August 10, 1925, Langston Hughes Memorial Library Archives, Lincoln University.

9. "Varsity Debate Team," *Lincoln News*, November 1925; "Debating," *Lincoln News*, March 1926. Until two years earlier, only juniors and seniors had been permitted to be on the varsity team. In 1923, two sophomores were on the varsity team. In 1924, the year before Marshall arrived, sophomores held all the team positions, according to the March 1925 *Lincoln News*.

10. "Debating."

11. Several writers have repeated Marshall's recollection that he went to college planning to be a dentist but changed his mind after failing a science course, identified either as chemistry or biology. No record indicates that Marshall planned to become a dentist. On his admissions application, he wrote that he planned to be "a lawyer." He took no biology courses. He got a C in General Chemistry and a B in Qualitative Chemistry.

12. Arnold Rampersad, *The Life of Langston Hughes*, vol 1: 1902–1941 (New York: Oxford University Press, 2002), p. 126.

13. Denton L. Watson, *Lion in the Lobby: Clarence Mitchell, Jr.'s Struggle for the Passage of Civil Rights Laws* (Lanham, MD: University Press of America, 2002), p. 74.

14. Irvin Shaw, "Thurgood Marshall," *Afro-American*, August 13, 1960; James H. Murphy, interview with the author, May 6, 1985.

15. B&O Employee Card for Thurgood Marshall, 1926–1929, B&O Railroad Museum and Archives, Baltimore, Maryland.

16. Ibid.

17. Norma Marshall to Registrar of Lincoln University, summer 1926, Langston Hughes Memorial Library Archives, Lincoln University.

18. "20 Lincoln Students Fired," *Afro-American*, October 2, 1926.

19. James H. Murphy, interview with the author. Some biographers, encouraged by Marshall, have grossly exaggerated Marshall's role in this incident, which was Marshall's sole disciplinary encounter at Lincoln.

20. "Freshman and Sophomore Trial Debate," *Lincoln News*, February 1927.

21. "Official and Faculty News," *Lincoln News*, November 1926.

22. Five major black newspapers covered African American news on the East Coast. The *Afro-American* was the most widely circulated black newspaper in the east. The

Chicago Defender had a broad reach, with more than two-thirds of its readership outside of the Chicago area. The *New York Amsterdam News* reached its peak in the 1940s and covered the historically important Harlem Renaissance. *The Philadelphia Tribune* served the fifth-largest black community in the United States and constantly fought against racial discrimination. The *Pittsburgh Courier* was one of the most nationally circulated black newspapers; it challenged the misrepresentation of African Americans in the national media and advocated social reforms.

23. "Negro Debating Team Defeats Trio from Oxford University," *New York Amsterdam News*, December 22, 1926; "Oxford Wins, But Loses Debate with Lincoln U.," *Pittsburgh Courier*, December 25, 1926; "Lincoln Debaters Defeat Oxford University Team by a Popular Decision," *Philadelphia Tribune*, December 26, 1926.

24. "Lincoln Loses to Penn State Debating Team," *Philadelphia Tribune*, March 5, 1927; "Another Inter-Racial Debate," *Lincoln News*, March 1927; "Phillygrams," *Pittsburgh Courier*, March 12, 1927; "Penn State Wins," *Afro-American*, March 12, 1917.

25. See Hobart Jarrett, "Adventures in Interracial Debates," *Crisis*, August 1935. The phenomenon of debates between black and white colleges first received national attention with the success of the debating team from Wiley College in Marshall, Texas. In 1935, the team from the small, historically black Methodist Episcopal college, coached by Lincoln graduate Melvin Tolson, toured the South, breaking racial barriers. Ultimately, the Wiley debaters met and defeated the team from the University of Southern California (USC). Their story was told in a motion picture, *The Great Debaters*, directed by and starring Denzel Washington. In the film, Harvard University stands in for USC.

26. "Homines Honorees for the Past Year," *Lincoln News*, October 1928.

27. Norma Marshall had obtained a full-time teaching position almost a year earlier, in September 1926. "12,416 Pupils Start Work in Public School," *Afro-American*, September 11, 1926.

28. Norma Marshall to Business Manager of Lincoln University, September 12, 1927, Langston Hughes Memorial Library Archives, Lincoln University.

29. "Big International Debate," *New York Amsterdam News*, November 23, 1927.

30. "Lincoln U. Meets Britons in Debate," *Afro-American*, December 24, 1927. See also "Applause Given Lincoln U. Victory," *New York Amsterdam News*, December 21, 1927; "Negro Debaters Face British Team," *Pittsburgh Courier*, December 24, 1927; "Lincoln-British Debate Draws 3,000 Persons," *Philadelphia Tribune*, December 27, 1927; "Our Debaters Face British Union Team," *Chicago Defender*, December 24, 1927.

31. "*Ku Klux* Warned Lincoln Men to Change Subject," *Afro-American*, March 31, 1928.

32. "Lincoln-Harvard Debate to Be Used to Raise Funds," *Afro-American*, March 17, 1928.

33. "Klan Threats Fail to Stop Boston Debate," *Chicago Defender*, March 24, 1928; "Race Intermixture is Discussed without Vote," *Harvard Crimson*, March 16, 1928.

34. "Lincoln-Harvard Club Debate Grossed Over $1,000," *Afro-American*, April 7, 1928; "Race Intermixture is Discussed without Vote."

35. "Lincoln-Harvard Debate to Be Used to Raise Funds."

36. Thurgood Marshall, R. D. Certificate 734465, employment records of the Baltimore and Ohio Railroad, Baltimore, Maryland.

37. Letters between Norma Marshall and the Registrar of Lincoln University, September 1928, Langston Hughes Memorial Library Archives, Lincoln University.

38. "Debating High Lights," *Lincoln News*, January 1929.

39. "Lincoln Meets Oxford Team Here Tuesday," *Afro-American*, November 24, 1928.

40. "Lincoln Given Debate Decision over Oxford," *Afro-American*, December 1, 1928.

41. "Negro Debaters Win over Oxford," *Baltimore Sun*, November 28, 1928.

42. "No Lincoln U. President for Past 2 Years," *Afro-American*, March 22, 1926; "Lincoln Graduates May Teach Elsewhere, But Never at Home," *Afro-American*, July 17, 1926.

43. "Lincoln U. Students Oppose Colored Members of Faculty," *Afro-American*, April 6, 1929; "Explaining Lincoln's Scandal," *Afro-American*, July 6, 1929; Francis J. Grimke, letter to the editor, "Poison in Lincoln U. Color Bar," *Afro-American*, April 20, 1929; Thomas E. Miller, "Pres. Rendell Said Lincoln Is for White Profs Only," *Afro-American*, April 27, 1929; "Put Ban on Lincoln University, Urges Dr. DuBois," *Afro-American*, June 1, 1929.

44. "Lincoln Students Do Not Speak for University." *Afro-American*, April 13, 1929.

45. Business manager of Lincoln University to Norma Marshall, August 26, 1929, Langston Hughes Memorial Library Archives, Lincoln University.

46. Arnold de Mille, "Thurgood Marshall—Two Women Figure in Life of Great Lawyer," *Chicago Defender*, May 8, 1954.

47. "Thurgood Marshall: The Brain of the Civil Rights Movement," *Time*, September 19, 1955.

48. "To Wed Philly Belle," *Afro-American*, August 24, 1929.

49. Vivian Burey was born on February 11, 1911. The formal name of the church was First African Baptist Church; because of its location at 1025 Cherry Street, it came to be called Cherry Memorial Baptist Church and Cherry Street Baptist Church.

50. Acting registrar and dean of Lincoln University to Thurgood Marshall, January 30, 1930, Langston Hughes Memorial Library Archives, Lincoln University.

51. de Mille, "Thurgood Marshall—Two Women Figure in Life of Great Lawyer."

52. "Lincoln University Graduates Sixty-one," *Pittsburgh Courier*, June 14, 1930.

53. "Honor Men for 1929–1930," *Lincoln News*, October, 1930.

54. "Quiet Greet[s] Queer Remark at Lincoln Univ. Graduation," *Afro-American*, June 7, 1930.

55. Official transcript of Thurgood Marshall, Office of the Dean, Howard University School of Law, Washington, DC.

CHAPTER 5: EDUCATING A SOCIAL ENGINEER

1. Irvin Shaw, "Thurgood Marshall," *Afro-American*, August 13, 1960. Marshall repeated this statement many times, including when interviewed seventeen years later for the Columbia University Oral History Project. "But, we were trained, and were part of the program which Houston called the program of making lawyers, social engineers, instead of somebody going out to make a dollar practicing law."

2. Marshall to William Taylor, acting dean of Howard University School of Law, published in J. Clay Smith, *Supreme Justice: Speeches and Writings; Thurgood Marshall* (Philadelphia: University of Pennsylvania Press, 2003), pp. 8–9.

3. Many writers have repeated the mistaken belief that Marshall applied to and was rejected by the University of Maryland School of Law, even though Marshall and the law school administration attempted to correct this false impression. Had he applied, he most certainly would have been rejected. See Kluger, *Simple Justice: The History of* Brown v. Board of Education *and Black America's Struggle for Equality* (New York: Knopf, 1976); Williams, *Thurgood Marshall: American Revolutionary* (New York: Times Books, 1998); Thurgood Marshall, interview with Ed Edwin, Columbia Oral History Office, February 15, 1977.

4. "Howard President Cites Race's Need of Great Lawyers," *Afro-American*, October 12, 1929; Genna McNeil, *Groundwork: Charles Hamilton Houston and the Struggle for Civil Rights* (Philadelphia: University of Pennsylvania Press, 1983), p. 76.

5. Oliver W. Hill, interview with the author, July 20, 2004.

6. Charles Houston, "Report on the Status of Black Lawyers," 1928, Charles Houston Papers, Moorland-Spingarn Research Center, Howard University, Washington DC. Houston reported his findings to the press. See, for example, "Lawyers Few Pastors Many, Down in Dixie," *Afro-American*, June 11, 1932. See also Charles H. Houston, "Need for Black Lawyers," *Journal of Negro Education* 49 (1935).

In 1928, Houston sent the clerk of court in several counties throughout the South a letter that stated, "The Howard University Law School is trying to determine how many Negro lawyers are practicing law in the United States. . . . Would you be so kind as to give us this information about the Negro lawyers in your jurisdiction?" Houston included a self-addressed, stamped return envelope.

Houston received responses from twenty-seven court clerks. Their verbatim responses were as follows: Dade County, Fla.: One attorney identified "This is the only Negro lawyer that we have any record of."; Duval County, Fla.: Six attorneys identified; Putnam County, Fla.: "None Thank the Lord"; Taylor County, Fla.: "No Negro lawyer in this county now nor as ever been. A Negro lawyer would be as much out of place here as a snowball would be in Hades."; Page County, Va.: "None—nor have been nor hope ever will be in our Court."; Marion County, Ala.: "This Co. Is a white Co. No coons here"; Dickinson County, Va.: "Replying to the above I beg to advise that we have no negro Attorneys at our bar, of which we feel very proud"; Carlise County, Ky.: "We haven't any Nig Negro lawyers in this District."; Lafayette County, Mo.: "None. Better spend your time on more profitable questions. Who ever heard of negroes practicing law. They can't even read it. We make the laws, all they have to do is to obey them and clean up the trash we may when making them. You are wasting money and stamps. Negroes practicing law, outrageous."; Habersham County, Ga: "Replying to above, there is no negro lawyer or negro lawyers in this, Habersham County, Georgia. I never knew or heard of any negro with nerve enough to come to this County Board Court House to practice law from any other county or section."; Laurens County, Ga.: "Thank the Lord, There are None."; Howard County, Mo: "None So far we have been fortunate enough not to be bothered with such things."; Manatee County, Fla.: "None and never has been."; Calcasieu County, La.: "We have none and don't anticipate any very soon. There ain't no such animal 'round here."; Live Oak County, Tex.: "None in this district. P.S, those Black Bur Heads can't practice in this District."; Hamilton County, Tex.: "There is not a Negro of any kind in this, Hamilton County. He is not even allowed to camp here."; Howard County, Tex: "No Negro lawyers in this County, Thank God."; Stoddard County, Mo.: "None, thank God."; Francis County, Tex.: "None & never will be in this Dist."; Mills County, Tex: "There is not a Negro man woman or child in this Mills County Texas nor has not been for 20 odd years."; Parker County, Tex.: "will state that we have no Negro lawyers in Parker County, Texas. (as our Negroes all just make 'Crap Shooters')"; Throckmorton County, Tex.: "None. Negroes have not been allowed to live in Throckmorton County for over 40 years. Few coming in now with our first railroad, but no lawyers."; Randolph County, Mo.: "We are free. Non est."; Catoosa County, Ga.: "The negroes of North Georgia and no member of their race practicing law in this Court. They are too busy raising cotton to bother about law, but leave the administration of justice to their white bretheren."; Lynn County, Tex.: "None, We're still nearly white out here.": Hillsborough County, Fla.: One lawyer listed. Jefferson County, Ga.: "None." [response included photograph of an old slave market building].

7. "Three New Deans Named by Howard Trustees," *Afro-American*, June 8, 1929; "Howard Gives Deanships to Former Grads," *Philadelphia Tribune*, June 6, 1929.

8. "Dean Booth Resigns from H.U. Law School," *Afro-American*, August 9, 1930. Those who resigned were former deans Fenton W. Booth (chief judge of the US Court of Claims), Dion Scott Birney, Charles Vernon Imlay, Edward Stafford, Dale David Drain, and Gilbert Lewis Hall. See "New Instructor at Howard Law School," *Philadelphia Tribune*, January 29, 1931.

9. "Law School Quizzed by Bar Association," *Afro-American*, October 18, 1930.

10. "Body Suggests Naming Law School Dean," *Afro-American*, October 17, 1932; "Howard University Trouble Is Seen as War between the Old and the New by Observers," *Norfolk New Journal and Guide*, April 18, 1931; "Lines Drawn Tight for Ouster," *Afro-American*, April 11, 1931; "Public Wonders What Started H.U. Eruption," *Afro-American*, April 4, 1931.

11. "Howard Law School Standards Raised," *Afro-American*, May 16, 1931.

12. Oliver W. Hill, interview with the author, July 20, 2004. See also "H.U. Students See Va. Reformatory," *Afro-American*, May 15, 1931; "H.U. Law Students See Va. Reformatory," *Afro-American*, May 16, 1931; "Law Students to Learn of Finger Printing," *Afro-American*, February 7, 1941.

13. In 1911, President William Howard Taft appointed William H. Lewis as an assistant attorney general of the United States. He was confirmed by the Senate.

14. Oliver W. Hill, interview with the author, July 20, 2004; McNeil, *Groundwork*; "Darrow Concludes Lecture Series to Students," *Pittsburgh Courier*, January 17, 1931; "Darrow at Howard," *Chicago Defender*, January 16, 1931. See also "At Law School," *Afro-American*, February 14, 1931; "$3,000,000 Attorney to Address Law Students," *Afro-American*, March 17, 1931; "Speaks at Law School," *Afro-American*, April 2, 1932; "Lewis, ex-U.S. Lawyer to Speak at Law School," *Afro-American*, February 27, 1932.

15. "Survey of Howard Law School Completed," *Afro-American*, October 25, 1930.

16. "Howard U Law School OK'ed by Am. Bar Ass'n," *Norfolk New Journal and Guide*, May 9, 1931; "Howard University's Law School Put on Approved List by American Bar Assn.," *Chicago Defender*, May 9, 1931.

17. The black professors were Charles Houston, William Hastie, William H. Houston, Leon Andrew Ransom, James Adlai Cobb, George E. C. Hayes, and William E. Taylor. The white professors were Nathan Cayton, Walter Wheeler Cook, Alfred Joseph Buschek, Theodore Cogswell, and Milton A. Kallis. See "Howard University Bulletin, the School of Law, 1932–34," pp. 13–14.

18. McNeil, *Groundwork*.

19. Thurgood Marshall's student file, Howard University School of Law, Washington, DC; Irvin Shaw, "Thurgood Marshall," *Afro-American*, August 13, 1960. William Hastie received his law degree from Harvard in 1930, the year that Marshall began law school. He was only four years older than Marshall. He later became dean of Howard University School of Law. In 1937, he became the first African American federal judge, serving in the Virgin Islands. He was later promoted to the US Court of Appeals for the Third Circuit.

20. See "Departments of Howard All on Quarter System," *Norfolk New Journal and Guide*, May 16, 1931. Marshall was a member of the Webster Club, which lost to the Clay Club, with judges from Washington, DC, New York, and Philadelphia presiding.

21. "Heard and Seen at the Howard Commencement," *Afro-American*, June 13, 1931.

22. "The Law: The Tension of Change," *Time*, September 19, 1955. Hastie graduated from Harvard Law School in 1930.

23. Oliver W. Hill, interview with the author, July 20, 2004.

24. Marshall's direct supervisor was A. Mercer Daniel, law professor and librarian. See "Howard University Bulletin, the School of Law, 1932–1933."

25. James Adlai Cobb had been a municipal court judge in the District of Columbia since 1926.

26. "Howard University Bulletin, the School of Law, 1932–34"; Thurgood Marshall's Student File; Oliver W. Hill, interview with the author, July 20, 2004.

27. "Howard Law Class Split in Factions," *Afro-American*, October 17, 1931.

28. Oliver W. Hill, interview with the author, July 20, 2004.

29. Oliver W. Hill, "A Classmate's Recollections of Thurgood Marshall in the Earlier Years," *Howard Law Journal* 35, no. 1 (1991): 49–51.

30. Louisa B. Reynolds, *Gibson Island Hearsay* (Baltimore: Gibson Island Historical Society, 1968).

31. Jean F. Crunkleton, interview with the author, May 20, 2012. She was nine months old in June 1931, when Marshall returned to work at Gibson Island following his first year in law school.

32. Thurgood Marshall, interview with Ed Edwin, Columbia University Oral History Office, 1977.

33. Oliver W. Hill, interview with the author, July 20, 2004.

34. The president of Hocutt's undergraduate college refused to forward the transcript that was needed to complete Hocutt's application.

35. The original memorandum is with NAACP papers at the Library of Congress, Washington, DC, in the Manuscript Department.

36. "To Associated Negro Press," NAACP press release, April 25, 1933, NAACP Papers, Library of Congress; "To the Editors of the Weekly Press," press release by Walter White, April 28, 1933, NAACP Papers, Library of Congress.

37. A former Marshall law clerk and distinguished scholar warns against unquestioning reliance on Marshall's recollection of events: "Marshall is a great raconteur, and his reconstructions of what happened thirty or forty years before must be accepted with a skepticism born of knowledge that he is at least as much concerned about telling a good story as with telling the true one." Mark V. Tushnet, *The NAACP's Legal Stategy against Segregated Education, 1925–1950* (Chapel Hill: Unversity of North Carolina Press, 1986). For example, not all of Marshall's recollections about his law school involvements with Houston are accurate. When interviewed by Ed Edwin for the Columbia University Oral History Office in 1977, Marshall described his supposed participation and arrest in a picketing demonstration that Houston had organized at an anti-crime conference headed by US Attorney General Homer Cummings in Washington, DC. Houston did hold a demonstration to protest the fact that the subject of lynching was not an agenda item. Marshall mistakenly believed that the conference had been held in 1932, while he was still student at Howard Law School. Marshall told Edwin that there had been twenty demonstrators and that, after Houston and other picketers had filled two police wagons, Marshall and two other students had hailed a taxi and followed the wagons to the police station to be arrested. Marshall's recollection is mistaken. Actually, the anti-crime conference, the demonstration, and the arrests occurred on December 11, 1934, more than a year after Marshall had graduated from law

school. Four demonstrators were arrested, including Roy W. Wilkins of the NAACP, George B. Murphy of the *Afro-American* newspaper, Howard University political science professor Emmett Dorsey, and attorney Edward Lovett. Charles Houston led the demonstration but was not arrested. Marshall did not participate in this demonstration and was not arrested. See "NAACP Protests U.S. Conference Which Does Not Discuss Lynching, *Afro-American*, December 15, 1934; "Lynching Is Crime Too," *Afro-American*, December 15, 1934.

38. *Hale v. Crawford*, 65 F.2d 739 (1st Cir. 1933), cert. denied, 220 U.S. 674 (1933).

39. Walter Francis White, *A Man Called White: The Autobiography of Walter White* (Athens: University of Georgia Press, 1995), p. 154.

40. Crawford expressed complete satisfaction with his legal representation. See "Statement of George Crawford, Witnessed by George B. Murphy," February 16, 1935, Charles Houston Papers, Moorland-Spingarn Research Center, Howard University.

41. The International Labor Defense (ILD) was formed in 1925 to serve as the legal arm of the Communist Party of the United States. See Martha Gruening, "The Truth about the Crawford Case: How the NAACP 'Defended' A Negro into a Life Sentence," *New Masses*, January 8, 1935. Houston published his detailed account of the George Crawford case in the April and May 1935 editions of the *Crisis*.

42. "Howard University Bulletin, the School of Law, 1932–1933." The other seven graduates were Otho D. Branson, Lorenzo Henderson, Oliver W. Hill, Onette W. Johnson, Leslie S. Perry, L. Edward Sanders, and Henry M. Sweet Jr. Also see "Sun Broils 2,000 at H.U. Commencement," *Afro-American*, June 17, 1933.

43. Marshall to Houston, December 18, 1934; "Strike at Howard Law School Is Called Off," *Afro-American*, December 22, 1934, Charles Houston Papers, Moorland-Spingarn Research Center, Howard University.

44. Marshall had turned down a graduate fellowship at Harvard Law School that Houston had obtained through his friendship with Dean Roscoe Pound. Edward Pharoah Lovett, the top student from Howard University Law School's class of 1932, accepted the fellowship.

CHAPTER 6: A NEW LAWYER JOINS THE BROTHERHOOD

1. Marshall to Houston, October 19, 1933, NAACP Papers, Library of Congress.

2. "Marshall Opens Law Offices," *Afro-American*, November 11, 1933.

3. Statistics compiled and published by Charles H. Houston in 1932, Charles Houston Papers, Moorland-Spingarn Research Center, Howard University.

4. Charles H. Houston, "Tentative Findings Re Negro Lawyers" (unpublished man-

uscript, 1928), p. 2, Charles Houston Papers, Moorland-Spingarn Research Center, Howard University. See "Lawyers Few, Pastors Many, Down In Dixie," *Afro-American*, June 11, 1932. The most complete history of early African American lawyers in the United States continues to be J. Clay Smith, *Emancipation: The Making of the Black Lawyer 1844–1944* (Philadelphia: University of Pennsylvania Press, 1993). For an insightful analysis of the complicated and conflicting pressures and expectations faced by early black lawyers, see Kenneth W. Mack, *Representing the Race: The Creation of the Civil Rights Lawyer* (Cambridge, MA: Harvard University Press, 2012).

5. Azzie Briscoe Koger, *The Negro Lawyer in Maryland* (Baltimore: Clarke, 1948).

6. Maryland Code, Article 11, Section 3, reenacted in Act of 1876, Chapter 264.

7. *In re Charles Taylor*, 48 Md. 28 (1877). The court relied on a decision of the US Supreme Court upholding an Illinois statute that excluded women from practicing law. See *Bradwell v. State* 83 U.S. (16 Wall) 130, 139 (1872).

8. David Skillen Bogen, "The First Integration of Maryland School of Law," *Maryland Historical Magazine* 88 (1989); *Strauder v. West Virginia*, 100 U.S. 303 (1880).

9. Ibid.; Elaine K Freeman, "Harvey Johnson and Everett Waring: A Study of Leadership in the Baltimore Negro Community, 1880–1900" (master's thesis, George Washington University 1968); "Lawyer Waring's Career," *New York Age*, November 14, 1891.

10. "Bar Association Holds Its Banquet," *Afro-American*, September 27, 1922; Koger, *The Negro Lawyer in Maryland*.

11. "Lawyer Waring's Career."

12. Ibid.

13. William M. Alexander, *The Brotherhood of Liberty, or, Our Day in Court: Including the Navassa Case* (Baltimore: Weishampel, 1891), pp. 14–15.

14. Soon after Waring's case ended without an appeal being filed, a white defendant challenged his prosecution on the grounds that the bastardy law was unconstitutional because it did not apply to all women. The Maryland Court of Appeals rejected the argument and upheld the law. See *Plunkard v. State*, 67 Md. 364, 10 A. 225 (1887). However, in a codification of Maryland statutes in 1887, the word *white* was omitted, bringing an end to the racial distinction in the law.

15. Alexander, *The Brotherhood of Liberty*, p. 15.

16. Jeffrey Brackett, *Notes on the Progress of the Colored People of Maryland Since the War* (Baltimore: Johns Hopkins University, 1890), pp. 29–39.

17. "The Prisoners from Navassa," *New York Age*, November 9, 1889.

18. "The Navassa Murder Cases," *New York Age*, April 19, 1890.

19. "National Capital—The Navassa Cases before the Supreme Court," *New York Age*, November 15, 1890. See also "Tales of Hardship at Navassa, Negroes Testify in Baltimore," *New York Herald Tribune*, July 15, 1890. Although Waring was the first black

lawyer to argue before the US Supreme Court, he was not the first black lawyer admitted to the bar of the Supreme Court. That distinction went to John Swett Rock, a Massachusetts lawyer, who was admitted to the Supreme Court bar in 1865. Rock's admission to the Supreme Court bar is documented in detail in J. Clay Smith, *Emancipation*.

20. "An Historical Event," *New York Age*, November 15, 1890.

21. *Jones v. United States*, 137 U.S. 202 (1890). See also *United States v. Key*, 137 U.S. 224 (1890). John S. Davis died soon after the Supreme Court decided *Jones v. United States*. See also "Last Act in the Navassa Tragedy," *New York Age*, May 30, 1891; "Baltimore Topics—Re-Sentencing of the Navassa Prisoners," *New York Age*, March 28, 1891.

22. Statement by President William Harrison, printed in the *New York Age*, May 30, 1891.

23. "Separation Not Distinction—Judge Bond's Opinion in a Suit against Steamboat Owners in Baltimore," *New York Age*, May 10, 1890.

24. "Lawyer Waring's Career," *New York Age*, November 14, 1891; "Baltimore Republicans—Popular Feeling Increasing against Lawyer Waring," *New York Age*, October 10, 1891; "Dastardly White Ruffians Retain an Afro American Lawyer to Defend Them," *New York Age*, October 3, 1891.

25. In addition to the law and politics, Waring became involved in real estate and business ventures. He was a founder and the president of the Lexington Savings Bank, one of the first black-owned banks in the nation. Thurgood Marshall's grandfather, Thorney Good Marshall, became one of the bank's stockholders. When the bank failed, Waring was charged with embezzlement but acquitted by a jury. Soon thereafter, Waring moved back to Ohio, where he served as a judge on the Municipal Court. He later moved to Philadelphia, where he practiced law and worked for the state government.

26. See chapter 12 for a discussion of *Pearson v. Murray*, 169 Md. 478 (1936).

27. Cummings was a much sought after orator. See "Fighting Senator Gorman," *New York Age*, February 21, 1891 (address to a veteran's group about the life of Abraham Lincoln).

28. In 1891, Cummings was elected to represent the 11th Ward, which had 2,300 white voters and 2,000 black voters. In 1887, lawyer T. Arrington Thompson was elected as an alderman in Annapolis, becoming the first African American to hold elected office in Maryland. See Jean R. Russo, *City Officers: 1720–1989* (Annapolis, MD: Historic Annapolis Foundation, 1989).

29. Cummings said of Theodore Roosevelt, "He is a just man, and believes that a man should be judged on merit, and merit alone, and that the just rewards of faithful and patriotic service should be withheld from no one, for any cause whatever. With a vision unclouded by bias or prejudice he sees through the outer clay, clad in different hues, the man within, and therefore beholds the image of the Divine Master indicating the Fatherhood of Good and the Brotherhood of Man." See *Addresses of the Republican Convention, 1904* (New York: I. H. Blanchard,1904).

30. Cummings introduced on February 1, 1892, an ordinance to establish a Manual Training School for Colored Youth. Mayor Latrobe signed the ordinance on February 16, 1892. For the early intiatives for public schools, see Bettye C. Thomas, "Public Education and Black Protest," *Maryland Historical Magazine* 71, no. 3 (1976): 318–91.

31. "Republican Union Restored—A Victory at the Maryland Institute," *New York Age*, September 26, 1891.

32. The first eleven black lawyers in Maryland were Everett J. Waring, Joseph S. Davis, Harry Sythe Cummings, Charles W. Johnson, George M. Lane, Warner T. McGuinn, Richard E. King, John L. Dozier, William H. Daniels, Malachi Gibson, and W. Ashbie Hawkins.

33. "Baltimore Brevities," *New York Age*, January 17, 1891.

34. See *Jackson v. State*, 132 Md. 311 (1918), *State v. Jenkins*, 124 Md. 376 (1914), *State v. Gurry* 121 Md. 534 (1913), *Clark v. Maryland Institute*, 87 Md. 653 (1898).

35. *Rother v. Trustee of Sharp Street Station*, 37 A. 24 (Md. 1898).

36. "McGuinn—Poor Lad Who Worked Way Up," *Baltimore Sun*, July 11, 1937.

37. "A Little Help from Twain," *Baltimore Sun*, February 17, 2001; "McGuinn—Poor Lad Who Worked Way Up."

38. "At Baltimore—Cummings Re-nominated for the City Council," *New York Age*, October 17, 1891.

39. Most of the information in the section is documented in Margaret Law Callcott, *The Negro in Maryland Politics: 1870–1912* (Baltimore: Johns Hopkins Press, 1969), p. 155.

40. In the 1888 election in Baltimore City, out of 100,009 Republicans voting, 50,000 were African Americans. See "Mixed Maryland Politics—Political Daggers Drawn in Baltimore," *New York Age*, July 18, 1891.

41. Callcott, *The Negro in Maryland Politics*, p.115; Louis R. Harlan, *Booker T. Washington* (New York: Oxford University Press, 1983), p. 25; August Meier, *Negro Thought in America, 1880–1915: Racial Ideologies in the Age of Booker T. Washington* (Ann Arbor: University of Michigan Press, 1963), pp. 338, 350.

42. *Smith v. Allwright*, 321 U.S. 649 (1944).

43. "Hawkins Makes Masterful Argument," *Afro-American*, June 28, 1913.

44. *State v. Gurry*, 121 Md. 534, 88 A. 546 (1913).

45. *Buchanan v. Warley*, 245 U.S. 60 (1917). The NAACP was founded in 1909. *Buchanan* was argued on behalf of the NAACP by Moorfield Storey, a former president of the American Bar Association.

46. These covenants were typically placed in the sections of the deeds that excluded from residential areas manufacturing plants, warehousing, livestock grazing, and other "nuisances."

47. *122th Annual Report of the Department of Health of Baltimore City*, 1936, Baltimore City Archives.

48. *Shelley v. Kraemer*, 334 U.S. 1 (1948).

49. Racial discrimination in public accommodations began to take a hold around the turn of the century. See "Colorphobia In Baltimore—Recent Instances of Prejudice and Discrimination," *New York Age*, November 1, 1908.

50. The "Jim Crow" law, Annotated Code of Maryland, Article 27, Section 438, provided, "All persons running operating cars or coaches by steam on any railroad line track in the State of Maryland, for the transportation of passengers, are hereby required to provide separate cars or coaches for the travel and transportation of white and colored passengers on their respective lines or railroad; and each compartment of a car or coach, divided by good and substantial partition, with a door or place of exit from each division, shall be deemed a separate car or coach within the meaning of this section, and each separate car, coach or compartment shall bear in some conspicuous place appropriate words, in plain letters, indicating whether it is set apart for white or colored passengers."

51. In *Hawkins v. Baltimore, Chesapeake & Atl. Ry. Co.*, 3 Md. Pub. Serv. Comm'n 49, 52 (1912), the Maryland Public Service Commission dismissed the claim on the grounds that Hawkins could not prove that the differences in the facilities were due to racial discrimination. In *Turner v. Baltimore, Chesapeake & Atlanta Railway Co.*, 4 Md. Pub. Serv. Commission 101 (1913), the Commission dismissed the charge but recommended to the railroad that it implement changes to address the disparities raised by Hawkins.

52. *Joseph P. Evans v. Chesapeake and Ohio Railway Co*, 92 I.C.C. 713 (1924).

53. *State v. Jenkins*, 124 Md. 376 (1914).

54. *Morgan v. Commonwealth of Virginia*, 328 U.S. 373 (1946).

55. *Boynton v. Virginia*, 364 U.S. 454 (1960). This ruling was an important catalyst for the Freedom Rider movement, as it gave activists the legal right to desegregate restaurants within bus terminals even though local law in many states continued to require segregation.

56. For example, see *Burton v. Wilmington Parking Authority*, 365 U.S. 715 (1961).

57. Marshall was not motivated to address teacher pay disparities because his mother had received lower pay than white teachers, as some other authors have alleged. The teacher pay scales in Baltimore City had been equalized by statute before Norma Marshall began teaching. Marshall's teacher pay lawsuits, beginning in 1936, attacked disparities in Maryland counties outside of Baltimore City. See chapter 16.

58. Harold Alfred Lett, *How Unemployment Affects Negroes* (New York: National Urban League, Department of Industrial Relations, 1931); Joseph L. Arnold, "The Last of the Good Old Days: Politics in Baltimore, 1920–1950," *Maryland Historical Magazine* 71, no. 3 (1976): 443–48.

59. Jo Ann E. Argensinger, *Toward a New Deal in Baltimore* (Chapel Hill: University of North Carolina Press, 1988). Marshall joined protests against Mayor Jackson's persistent reliance on private relief efforts rather than goverment programs. "600 Unemployed

Denounce ECA: Want Relief Administered By City Department of Public Welfare," *Baltimore Sun*, June 13, 1936.

60. Dorothy Brown, "The Election of 1934: The 'New Deal' in Maryland," *Maryland Historical Magazine* 68, no. 4 (1973): 404–21; Charles M. Kimberly, "The Depression and the New Deal in Maryland" (PhD diss., Washington, DC, American University, 1974); Nancy J. Weiss, *Fairwell to the Party of Lincoln: Black Politics in the Age of FDR* (Princeton, NJ: Princeton University Press, 1983); Lois Rita Heimbold, "Making Choices, Making Do: Black and White Working Class Women's Lives and Work During the Great Depression" (PhD diss., Palo Alto, CA: Stanford University, 1982).

61. "Lawyers Buy Building," *Afro-American*, November 28, 1919.

62. Ginsberg was active in Jewish charities. "Sidney Lansburgh Elected," *Baltimore Sun*, January 19, 1926; "Jewish Charities Plans Completed," *Baltimore Sun*, November 9, 1928; "Palestine Appeal Will Open Tonight," *Baltimore Sun*, January 8, 1928; "Real Estate Deals and Building News," *Baltimore Sun*, June 6, 1925.

63. *Baltimore Address Telephone Directory*, Chesapeake and Potomac Company of Baltimore City, 1934–1936. Their offices occupied the entire front part of the top floor. In 1935 and 1936, three other black lawyers rented offices on other floors in the building—Robert McGuinn, J. Howard Payne, and Karl F. Phillips. By 1938, no black lawyers remained in the building. In 1943, the building was converted to a hotel. See "Downtown Office Building Becomes a Successful Hotel," *Baltimore Sun*, June 6, 1943. The building was demolished in the early 1950s.

CHAPTER 7: BUY WHERE YOU CAN WORK

1. *Samuelson v. Green*, Md. Cir. Ct. Balt. City (1934), Transcript of Record at 834.

2. For a detailed account of the Buy Where You Can Work campaign, see Andor D. Skotness "The Black Freedom Movement and the Workers' Movement in Baltimore, 1930–1939" (PhD diss., Rutgers University, 1991); Bruce A. Thompson, "The Civil Rights Vanguard: The NAACP and the Black Community in Baltimore, 1931–1942." (PhD diss., University of Maryland, 1996).

3. See "Love Advisor, Healing Seer, Loses Own Wife," *Afro-American*, June 17, 1933.

4. Ralph Matthews, "This Man Costonie," *Afro-American*, August 24, 1935.

5. In 1929, Costonie married Emma Stewart, the niece of Judge Albert S. George. "Women Irked by Prophet's Cotton Underwear Sermon," *Afro-American*, July 22, 1933; "Love Adviser, Healing Seer, Loses Own Wife"; "Prophet Denies 500 Will Go on Pilgrimage," *Afro-American*, June 3, 1933. The *Afro-American* was smitten with the handsome "Prophet," describing him as "the suave, immaculately dressed seer" and reporting regularly on his life and activities in Baltimore.

6. For a history of the City-Wide Young People's Forum and the Buy Where You Can Work campaign, see Thompson, *The Civil Rights Vanguard.*

7. Several publications mistakenly identify the NAACP as the leading organization in this campaign, but there were others. In 1933, the Baltimore branch of the NAACP was just beginning to become active after being moribund for a decade. In the years that followed, some of the leaders of the boycott, particularly Lillie M. Jackson and her family, played major roles in reviving the NAACP.

8. Thompson, "The Civil Rights Vanguard," p. 109. Marshall's high school teacher and debate coach, Gough McDaniels, made the public announcement of the A&P success. Harold A. Seaborne was one of those hired. Earlier in the year, Seaborne had been the first black to apply to the University of Maryland School of Law in the twentieth century. See "Boycott Here Is Not Necessary, Say Two Firms," *Afro-American*, October 7, 1933; Harold Seaborne, interview with the author, November 11, 2003.

9. "Hail Costonie as Hero after Chain Victory," *Afro-American*, November 25, 1933.

10. The family describes the lineage as follows: Charles Carroll of Carrolton, Maryland, was the last surviving signer of the Declaration of Independence. He was reputed to be the largest slave owner in Maryland, with more than eight hundred slaves. One of his sons was of mixed race. Daniel married a black woman named Rachel. One of the sons of Daniel and Rachel was Charles Henry Carroll. He married Amanda Bowen. Lillie Mae Carroll Jackson was the daughter of Charles Henry Carroll and Amanda. Thus, Charles Carroll of Carrollton was Lillie's great-grandfather.

11. A son, Bowen, was born after they returned to Baltimore.

12. The other stated goals of the Forum were (1) "To inform the people of Baltimore about the political, social, and economic problems which confront them, and upon the resultant understanding, to afford an opportunity for organized, united action on some of the important issues; (2) To develop an intelligent, militant youth leadership engaged in a constructive program with city-wide community influence; (3) To discover and develop the talents of youth who have not the means of helping themselves; and (4) To stimulate a consciousness of values in life which are not found in material things alone."

13. City-Wide Young People's Forum, "Meeting Minutes," November 14, 1933.

14. *Samuelson v. Green*, Transcript of Record at 859.

15. "Discourteous Officer Is Transferred," *Afro-American*, December 2, 1933.

16. *Samuelson v. Green*, Transcript of Record at 840–41.

17. "Tommy Tucker Clerk Is Picket," *Afro-American*, December 16, 1933.

18. The authorized sign read, "Don't Buy Where You Can't Work, This Store Does Not Hire Any Colored Help." See photograph in *Afro-American*, December 2, 1933. The unauthorized signs read, "Don't Buy Where You Can't Work, This Store Does Not Hire All-Colored Help." See photograph in *Afro-American*, December 16, 1933.

19. "Store Pickets Assail Cleric; Fight Averted," *Afro-American*, December 16, 1933.

20. "Pickets Made Business Drop 60 Per Cent," *Afro-American*, May 5, 1934.

21. "Ave. Merchants Halt Picketers by Injunction," *Afro-American*, December 23, 1934; "'Go to Jail If Necessary'—Walter White," *Afro-American*, December 23, 1934. The merchants seeking the injunction were the following: Aaron Samuelson, trading as Tommy Tucker Five & Ten Cent Stores; Samuel Cohen, trading as Capital Five & Ten Cent Stores; Isaac Goodman, trading as Goodman's; Max Meyers, trading as Meyers Shoe Store; and Samuel and Harry Silverman, trading as Silverman Brothers. The individual defendants were Kiowa Costonie, Lillie Carroll Jackson, Elvira Bond, Sara Boling Mason, Juanita Jackson, Rev. Robert F. Coates, Rev. Charles Trigg, Harriet Jones, Leah Clark, Mary Grant, Anna Parker, Margaret Woods, Thelma Beale, John Lake, Virginia Jones, Frances Marshal, Catherine Colman, Hilda Robinson, Miss Jordan, Margaret Roberts, Matthew Roberts, William Valentine, H. Diggs, E. Wilson, Grace Turner, Ruth Brown, Virginia Banks, and Irma Gouch. For reasons that are unclear, neither Thurgood Marshall nor his wife, Vivian Marshall, were named as defendants.

22. The assertions by some writers that Charles Houston served as legal counsel to the demonstrators in court are not correct. Also mistaken are descriptions of Marshall as the trial lawyer for the demonstrators. He advised the demonstrators before the injunction was granted, but during the litigation, McGuinn and Hughes emphasized that they were the only lawyers of record for the defendants. Marshall's role became that of witness for the defense. See "Local Lawyers to Make Fight Alone, They Say," *Afro-American*, December 31, 1933. Assertions that the NAACP was one of the defendants are also incorrect. The named defendant organizations were the National Housewives League, the Housewives League, and the City-Wide Young People's Forum.

23. "Pickets Made Business Drop 60 Per Cent."

24. *Samuelson v. Green*, Cir. Ct. Balt. City (1934) *aff'd*, *Green v. Samuelson*, 168 Md. 421, 178 A. 109 (1935).

25. "Judge Makes Jurisdiction Permanent," *Afro-American*, May 26, 1934.

26. *Green v Samuelson*, 168 Md. 421 (1935). The written opinion began by identifying the question before the court as "Can a race, in this case a group of negroes, by picketing impose their will on a white merchant and compel him to employ colored instead of white clerks?" A 1938 US Supreme Court decision found in favor of the Buy Where You Can Work campaign in Washington, DC, and overturned a lower court's injunction against a similar picketing effort. See *New Negro Alliance v. Sanitary Grocery Co.*, 303 U.S. 552 (1938).

27. "The Avenue Pickets," *Afro-American*, December 16, 1933; "Lesson in Economics," *Afro-American*, May 5, 1934.

28. Charles T. Burns, interview with the author, July 2, 1981. Burns was the son of Thurgood's Aunt Annie, his father's sister. Charles's middle name was originally "Thoroughgood." He changed it to "Thurgood."

CHAPTER 8: BLACK AND WHITE
AND RED ALL OVER

1. "Inquiring Reporter," *Afro-American*, February 3, 1934.

2. "Bethel Bars Ades at Lynch Protest Meet," *Afro-American*, November 11, 1933.

3. "First Day of Trial Found Lee a Mile from Murder Scene," *Afro-American*, January 23, 1932; "Found Guilty of Killing Green K. Davis," *Baltimore Sun*, January 21, 1932; "Negro is Found Guilty in Maryland Slayings, *New York Times*, January 21, 1932.

4. "Negroes as Jurors," *New York Times*, July 12, 1932; "Negroes Kept off Jury, Lee Wins New Trial," *Baltimore Sun*, July 6, 1932.

5. "Lee again Found Guilty at Second Trial," *Afro-American*, October 8, 1932; "State Blocks Naming of 3 Colored Men," *Afro-American*, October 1, 1932; "Jones Is Found Guilty of First-Degree Murder by Second Trial Jury," *Baltimore Sun*, September 29, 1932.

6. "Hanged a Few Minutes after Midnight This Morning," *Baltimore Sun*, October 27, 1933; "Supreme Court Denies Euel Lee Review of Case," *Baltimore Evening Sun,* October 9, 1933. For a compelling review of the Euel Lee case, see Joseph E. Moore, *Murder on Maryland's Eastern Shore: Race, Politics, and the Case of Orphan Jones* (Charleston, SC: History Press, 2006).

7. "Ades Not Alone," *Afro-American*, March 10, 1934.

8. "News Summary," *Afro-American*, October 28, 1933.

9. *In re Ades*, 6 F. Supp. 467, 469 (D. Md. 1934).

10. Ibid.

11. Statement by the ILD on the Ades Case Decision, April 2, 1934.

12. "Ades Retains H.U. Law Head as Counsel," *Afro-American*, December 19, 1933.

13. Neither Leibowitz nor Pollak were Communists or members of the ILD. In 1934, when some members of the ILD were caught trying to pay money to one of the alleged victims for having recanted her accusations against the Scottsboro defendants, Leibowitz broke off his relationship with the ILD. Thereafter, he defended the case with the assistance of the broader-based American Scottsboro Committee.

14. "New Stage Is Set for Boys at Scottsboro," *Afro-American*, March 18, 1933.

15. "Question for This Week," *Afro-American*, July 15, 1933.

16. "Local N.A.A.C.P. to Back Reds in Fights Here," *Afro-American*, March 18, 1933.

17. Houston to White, October 17, 1933, Charles Houston Papers, Moorland-Spingarn Research Center, Howard University.

18. "Ades Retains H.U. Law Head as Counsel." The article noted, "The selection of Mr. Houston came as a surprise because Mr. Houston is one of the chief attorneys for the N.A.A.C.P., and the feeling between this organization and the I.L.D. has not been the best since the Scottsboro case disagreement."

19. "Ades Fight Here Becomes National," *Afro-American*, February 3, 1934.

20. Marshall to Houston, January 8, 1934, Charles Houston Papers, Moorland-Spingarn Research Center, Howard University.

21. Marshall to Houston, February 7, 1934, Charles Houston Papers, Moorland-Spingarn Research Center, Howard University.

22. Houston to Marshall, February 10, 1934, Charles Houston Papers, Moorland-Spingarn Research Center, Howard University. Marshall was admitted to the bar of the federal court when Josiah Henry sponsored the admission of Marshall, Leon Ransom, and Edward Lovett; "Ades Lawyers Presented Here," *Afro-American*, December 30, 1933.

23. Marshall to Houston, February 13, 1934, Charles Houston Papers, Moorland-Spingarn Research Center, Howard University.

24. Marshall to Houston, February 20, 1934, Charles Houston Papers, Moorland-Spingarn Research Center, Howard University.

25. Ades to Houston, January 10, 1934, Charles Houston Papers, Moorland-Spingarn Research Center, Howard University.

26. "Negro Lawyer Scored," *Evening Sun*, June 22, 1928. However, when an effort was made to suspend him at the state level, Warner T. McGuinn and W. Ashbie Hawkins, representing the Monumental City Bar Association, came to his defense and prevented the discipline. See "Two Attorneys Will Defend Pendleton," *Afro-American*, August 4, 1928.

27. "Ades Papers Were Tampered With, Says Houston," *Afro-American*, January 20, 1934.

28. "Houston May Force Court to Open Records," *Afro-American*, January 27, 1934; "Who Changed the Records?" *Afro-American*, January 27, 1934; "Ades' Counsel Denied Use of Clerk's Notes," *Baltimore Sun*, January 20, 1934.

29. "Ades Hearing Set by Judge Soper," *Afro-American*, February 10, 1934.

30. Houston to Marshall, January 25, 1934, Charles Houston Papers, Moorland-Spingarn Research Center, Howard University.

31. Houston to Dr. Mordecai Johnson, president of Howard University, February 18, 1934, Charles Houston Papers, Moorland-Spingarn Research Center, Howard University.

32. "Large Crowd in Court During Ades' Trial," *Afro-American*, February 28, 1934. The newspaper reported among those in attendance lawyers E. Everett Lane, W. A. C. Hughes Jr., George W. F. McMechen, Linwood Koger, A. B. Koger, Gregory Hawkins, Peter Woodbury, Cornelius C. Fitzgerald, and George Pendleton (who years earlier had been suspended by Judge Coleman).

33. Stenographic Transcript, In the Matter of Barmard Ades, No. 291, U.S District Court for the District of Maryland, March 1, 1935.

34. Houston to Marshall, March 12, 1934, Charles Houston Papers, Moorland-Spingarn Research Center, Howard University. Marshall also kept the press apprised of developments. See "No Decision in Ades Case," *Afro-American*, March 10, 1934: "Thurgood Marshall, attorney, who associated with Dr. Charles Houston, defense counsel, informed the *Afro-American* that a decision was expected on Friday or Saturday."

35. Judge Soper's written opinion found that "Ades published from time to time in the public press in Maryland false statements embodying criticism of certain state judges and other officials of the state of Maryland." The opinion also stated that "Ades on the day before the execution of Lee, and without his request, had visited him in the death house of the Maryland penitentiary, and caused him to execute a will, making Ades his beneficiary; and after his death, Ades sought by legal proceedings in the circuit court No. 2 of Baltimore City to secure the body of Lee in order that he might take it to New York and hold a memorial meeting over it in order to incite race prejudice."

36. *In re Ades*, 6 F. Supp. 467 (D. Md. 1934); "Bernard Ades Is Reprimanded by Court," *Afro-American*, March 24, 1934.

37. Houston to the editor of the *Afro-American*, telegram, March 19, 1934, Charles Houston Papers, Moorland-Spingarn Research Center, Howard University.

38. "Bernard Ades Calls Bar Group Inconsistent and Says Dr. Houston is a 'Tent Sulker,'" *Afro-American*, May 12, 1934.

39. Houston to the Editor of the *Afro-American*, May 14, 1934, Charles Houston Papers, Moorland-Spingarn Research Center, Howard University.

40. "Bernard Ades Calls Bar Group Inconsistent . . ." *Afro-American*, May 12, 1934.

41. Statement by the International Labor Defense on the Ades Case Decision, April 2, 1934, Charles Houston Papers, Moorland-Spingarn Research Center, Howard University. See also "Reds Make Comment on Court Decision Reprimanding Ades," *Afro-American*, March 31, 1934.

42. Ades to Houston, May 9, 1934, Charles Houston Papers, Moorland-Spingarn Research Center, Howard University.

43. Houston to the Editor of the *Afro-American*, May 14, 1934, Charles Houston Papers, Moorland-Spingarn Research Center, Howard University.

44. "Renew Ades Ouster—New Move on by Bar Group to Disbar Ades," *Afro-American*, April 21, 1934.

45. "Pot Can't Call Kettle Black, Ades Tells Bar," *Afro-American*, May 12, 1934.

46. "I am well aware that under ordinary circumstances a bar association represents the bar and can request the court to institute such proceedings. But the Bar Association of Baltimore City does not represent the bar of Baltimore City. On the contrary, by its set and well-known policy of excluding from its membership all Negro members of the bar, it forfeits its right to act as the representative of the entire bar." Ades to George R. Veazy, June 6, 1934, Charles Houston Papers, Moorland-Spingarn Research Center, Howard University.

47. Houston to Ades, May 1, 1934, Charles Houston Papers, Moorland-Spingarn Research Center, Howard University.

48. Ades to Houston, May 9, 1934, Charles Houston Papers, Moorland-Spingarn Research Center, Howard University.

49. Marshall to Houston, May 12, 1934, Charles Houston Papers, Moorland-Spingarn

Research Center, Howard University; "Bernard Ades Calls Bar Group Inconsistent and Says Dr. Houston Is a 'Tent Sulker,'" *Afro-American*, May 12, 1934. See also "Houston Won't Represent Red Lawyer," *Afro-American*, May 19, 1934.

50. "Monumental Bar Prexy under Fire: Lawyers Rap Tyler for Ades Action," *Afro-American*, June 23, 1934. See also "Tyler Is for Jim Crow, Says Bernard Ades," *Afro-American*, June 16, 1934.

51. "Ades Suspended for Three Months by Local Court," *Afro-American*, December 15, 1934. The complaint against Ades was prosecuted on behalf of the Baltimore City Bar Association by Robert B. Carman, Wendell D. Allen, and Moses W. Rosenfeld. The disciplinary hearing was held before eight of the eleven judges on the Supreme Bench of Baltimore City. At the hearing, Ades and his lawyers continued to challenge the bar association's exclusion of black lawyers from its membership. The court did not issue a written opinion or explanation but only a brief order suspending Ades for three months. See "Bar Group Hit as Ades Disbarment Hearing Begins," *Afro-American*, December 8, 1934.

52. Moore, *Murder on Maryland's Eastern Shore*, p. 212.

CHAPTER 9: THE CIVIL CASES

1. *Howard v. Gaither et al.*, Docket No. 1782, (Md. Cir. Ct. of Balt., 1934). The judges of the trial courts with general civil and criminal jurisdiction in Baltimore were called the Supreme Bench of Baltimore City. Marshall represented clients before at least seven of the eleven judges, Albert S. J. Owens, Duke Bond, Charles F. Stein, Samuel K. Dennis, Robert F. Stanton, Eli Frank, and Eugene V. O'Dunne. For history of the Baltimore courts, see *Histories of the Bench and Bar of Baltimore City* (Baltimore: Baltimore Courthouse Foundation, 1997).

2. Such an arrangement is known as working on a contingency fee. This arrangement is typical in many civil cases because the plaintiff cannot otherwise afford to hire an attorney to pursue a legal claim. The attorney and client agree to a fee, typically one-third of any recovery, before a claim is filed. If the client prevails, the attorney receives the contingency fee specified. If the client does not prevail, the attorney receives no compensation.

3. Marbury, Gosnell, and Williams became Piper and Marbury, the largest law firm in Maryland.

4. The judge told the jury, "The Court instructs the Jury that if they find that the accident complained of was caused partly by the negligence of the Defendant and partly by the negligence of the Plaintiff then the verdict of the Jury must be for the Defendant without regard as to whose negligence was the greater." See *Howard v. Gaither et al.*, Court's Instruction No. 3. The defense of contributory negligence arose out of the common law. Today, only four states and the District of Columbia maintain the defense of contribu-

tory negligence. The other forty-six states permit the defense of comparative negligence, wherein a plaintiff's negligence reduces recovery but is not of itself a bar to recovery.

5. *Barkley v. Norris et al.,* Docket No. 116 (Md. Cir. Ct. of Balt., 1934).

6. *Tiller v. Snowden,* Docket No. 1804 (Md. Cir. Ct. of Balt., 1934).

7. *Haley v. Rainer,* Docket No. 158 (Super. Ct. of Balt., 1934).

8. *Clark v. Kellert,* Docket No. 2032 (Md. Cir. Ct. of Balt., 1934).

9. *Metropolitan Finance Corp. v. Andrews et al.,* Docket No. 1877 (Md. Cir. Ct. of Balt., 1935).

10. *The Afro-American Co. v. Schoonmaker,* Docket No. 1898 (Md. Cir. Ct. of Balt., 1935).

11. *Penn v. The Progressive Grand Ancient United Supreme Host of Israel of the U.S.A.,* Docket No. 21438a (Md. Cir. Ct. of Balt., 1936).

12. *Matthews v. Matthews,* Docket No. B38606 (Md. Cir. Ct. of Balt., 1934).

13. *Arnold v. Arnold,* Docket No. 1206 (Md. Cir. Ct. for Anne Arundel Co., 1934).

14. *Loyse Trigg v. Frank Trigg,* Docket No. B138/1934 (Md. Cir. Ct. of Balt., 1934).

15. *McGuinn v. McGuinn,* Docket No. B36776 (Md. Cir. Ct. of Balt., 1935).

16. Marshall's other divorce cases in Baltimore City Circuit Court were *Franklin v. Franklin,* Docket No. B41784 (1936); *Jones v. Jones,* Docket No. B41403 (1936); *Garcia v. Garcia,* Docket No. B41207 (1936); and *Gordon v. Gordon,* Docket No. B39816 (1934). Marshall also had a divorce case in Anne Arundel County Circuit Court, *McKamey v. McKamey,* Docket No. 1246 (1934).

17. *Moses v. Marshall,* Docket No. 2047 (Md. Cir. Ct. of Balt., 1936).

18. In *Baker v. Hurst,* Docket No. 1890 (Md. Cir. Ct. of Balt., 1936), Marshall represented the defendant's estate in a case where the plaintiff claimed $3,060 for various expenses related to the care, maintenance, and minor modification of a property. Marshall filed a bill of particulars and, upon receiving no response within the specified time period, submitted a motion for a judgment of *non pros.* The plaintiff did not pursue the claim. Judge O'Dunne granted that motion, resulting in a victory for Marshall. In *Yeager v. Smothers,* Docket No. 1896 (Md. Cir. Ct. of Balt., 1936), the plaintiff filed suit on August 27, 1936, for an automobile tort in the amount of $10,000. Marshall, the attorney for the defendant, issued a Demand for Bill of Particulars. When the plaintiff did not properly respond, Marshall filed a motion for judgment of *non pros.* The plaintiff filed the Bill of Particulars a few days after the expiration of the time limit and asked the court to accept the complaint. Judge O'Dunne ultimately granted the plaintiff's motion. The case, however, was ultimately settled out of court by McGuinn, who had taken over the case because Marshall had gone to work in New York for the NAACP.

19. "Bowie Registrar Appeals Blanket Dismissal Charge," *Afro-American,* July 10, 1935. Bowie Normal School, a historically black teacher's college, is today known as Bowie State University and is part of the University System of Maryland.

20. Marshall to Houston, July 10, 1935, NAACP Papers, Library of Congress.

21. Houston wrote Walter White, the secretary of the NAACP, on July 11, 1935, saying that "I do not think the Association should go into this case unless it can be shown that a personal injustice is being done to Taylor. James, the principal of the trade school, is a Negro. It is a fight between a Negro principal and one of his teachers. Rather dangerous to go into a case which cannot stand on its own merits. . . ."

22. Houston to Marshall, July 11, 1935, NAACP Papers, Library of Congress.

23. Marshall, in his letter to Houston of July 11, 1935, recognized that "Bill [Taylor] has very little money. Only makes about $90 a month." The letter also indicated Marshall wasn't very confident he could save Taylor's job, but again for the young lawyer, the issue was one of principle.

24. "Bowie Registrar Wins Fight to Keep Position," *Afro-American*, August 3, 1935.

25. While it is unclear why Marshall believed that the Taylor case was worthy of national attention, the Taylor matter was still very important because it was a forerunner of the Donald G. Murray case, which would consume the majority of Marshall's efforts in 1935.

CHAPTER 10: THE CRIMINAL CASES

1. Marshall to Wilkins, June 7, 1935, NAACP Papers, Library of Congress.

2. See "Gallows Holds No Fear for Condemned Imbecile," *Afro-American*, June 29, 1935.

3. James Poindexter to the NAACP National Office, May 20, 1935, NAACP Papers, Library of Congress.

4. Wilkins to Marshall, June 3, 1935, NAACP Papers, Library of Congress.

5. Marshall Houston, May 25, 1935, NAACP Papers, Library of Congress; Marshall to Wilkins, June 7, 1935, NAACP Papers, Library of Congress.

6. Marshall to Wilkins, June 7, 1935, NAACP Papers, Library of Congress. Between 1930 and 1939 Maryland executed sixteen individuals. Twelve were executed for murder and four for rape. Out of the sixteen executed, fourteen were black and two were white. See William J. Bowers, Glenn L. Pierce, and John F. McDevitt, *Legal Homicide: Death as Punishment in America, 1864–1982* (Boston: Northeastern University Press, 1984).

7. Ibid.

8. Wilkins to Marshall, June 20, 1935, NAACP Papers, Library of Congress.

9. "Trio in Terror Reign Confess Holdup Murder," *Washington Post*, June 11, 1934; "Self Styled 'Black Dillingers' to Meet Same Fate as Their White Prototype; Await Doom Heavily Guarded," *Norfolk New Journal and Guide*, August 4, 1934.

10. "Prince George's Man Is Shot as Terrorists Strike Again," *Washington Post*, May 31, 1934.

11. "Bandit Team's Victim Is Dead," *Washington Post*, June 3, 1934.

12. "Trio in Terror Reign Confess Holdup Murder," *Washington Post*, June 11, 1934; "'Dillinger' Trio Scares Police," *Washington Post*, June 30, 1934.

13. *Maryland v. Gordon Dent, James A. Gross and Donald Parker*, No. 6-7 Special Term July 1934 (Md. Cir. Ct. for Prince George's, Charles, Calvert, and St. Mary's Counties), July 11, 1934; "Three Sentenced to Death For Geary Murder," *Enquirer-Gazette*, July 27, 1934.

14. "2 Are Hanged in Maryland Pen on Good Friday," *Afro-American*, April 20, 1935; "Last Hope Fades for Pair Convicted in Holdup Murder," *Afro-American*, March 9, 1935; Death Warrant, signed by Governor Albert C. Ritchie, Case #13,816, January 3, 1935, Ritchie Papers, Special Collections, Hornbake Library, University of Maryland.

15. "Ritchie Orders Colored Killers to Be Hanged," *Washington Post*, January 3, 1935.

16. "Perfecting Case Against Negro," *Frederick Daily News*, November 3, 1934.

17. "Police Make New Arrest in Park Assault," *Frederick Post*, November 5, 1934; "Officials Say Negro Admits Attack Charge," *Frederick Post*, November 6, 1934; "Mahammit Returned to Frederick Jail," *Frederick Daily News*, November 7, 1934.

18. "12 Indictments Are Returned by Local Grand Jury," *Frederick Daily News*, November 21, 1934.

19. "Carter Given Life Term for Attack on Girl," *Frederick Daily News*, December 17, 1934; "Carter Taken to MD State 'Pen,'" *Frederick Daily News*, December 18, 1934.

20. Marshall to Houston, December 18, 1934, NAACP Papers, Library of Congress. Marshall also asked Houston for help with his penurious condition that had been made worse by the Frederick matters: "I haven't heard from Walter on the University of Maryland case. Can I get any of that money before Christmas? I am about broke from paying traveling expenses, etc. That Carter case about finished my huge bank role."

21. "Life Term for Man in Frederick, Md., Assault Case," *Afro-American*, December 22, 1934.

22. Marshall to Wilkins, December 18, 1934, NAACP Papers, Library of Congress.

23. Roy Wilkins, assistant secretary of the NAACP, expressed interest in founding a Frederick branch of the NAACP in his return letter. See Wilkins to Marshall, December 20, 1934, NAACP Papers, Library of Congress. The Frederick branch was established in late 1934.

24. *Maryland v. Everett A. Ball*, No. 2398 Indictment Docket (Md. Crim. Ct. of Balt.), August 8, 1935.

25. *Maryland v. George Clark*, No. 3504 Indictment Docket (Md. Crim. Ct. of Balt.), November 13, 1935.

26. *Maryland v. James E. Dudley*, No. 102 Indictment Docket (Md. Crim. Ct. of Balt.), January 15, 1936.

27. "Lucas Boy Is Held on Freak Police Theory," *Afro-American*, February 22, 1936.

28. Early newspaper articles on the issue stated Lucas was fifteen years old, but later documents refer to Lucas as being seventeen years old.

29. "Baltimore NAACP Takes Up Case of Shooting Suspect," *Afro-American*, January, 11, 1936.

30. Coroner's Investigation at the Northeastern (Baltimore) Police Station in the Matter of the Death of Hyman Brilliant, February 20, 1936, NAACP Papers, Library of Congress.

31. "Negro Boy Faces Shooting Charge," *Baltimore Sun*, February 20, 1936.

32. *Maryland v. Virtis Lucas*, No. 515-16 Indictment Docket (Md. Crim. Ct. of Balt.), February 21, 1936.

33. Ibid.

34. Ibid.

35. "Gets 6 Months Sentence in Slaying of Youth, 17," *Baltimore Sun*, March 25, 1936; "Mystery Still Shrouds Brilliant Killing as Youth Gets Six Months," *Afro-American*, March 28, 1936.

36. *Maryland v. Linwood Dorsey*, No. 2821 Indictment Docket (Md. Crim. Ct. of Balt.), September 3, 1936.

37. *Maryland v. Earl Carter*, No. 163 Indictment Docket (Md. Crim. Ct. of Balt.), January 16, 1936.

38. *Maryland v. Shedrack Turner*, No. 1778 Indictment Docket (Md. Crim. Ct. of Balt.), May 7, 1936.

39. *Maryland v. Schalley Webb*, No. 6629 Indictment Docket (Md. Crim. Ct. of Balt.), May 22, 1935.

40. *Maryland v. Florence Cooper*, No. 2593 Indictment Docket (Md. Crim. Ct. of Balt.), August 13, 1936.

41. "Baltimore Has Its 'Scottsboro' Farce," *Norfolk New Journal and Guide*, February 8, 1936.

42. Marshall, "Four Boys from Cheltenham Held for Questioning at Upper Marlboro," Memorandum for the NAACP, January 26, 1936.

CHAPTER 11: THE MURDER OF KATER STEVENS

1. Marshall to White, September 10, 1934, NAACP Papers, Library of Congress.

2. His name may have actually been Decater Stevens. Stevens had moved from North Carolina to Washington, DC, six years earlier. He worked as a laborer in a garage in the District of Columbia. He and his wife, Mildred, had no children.

3. Belford Lawson to White, August 11, 1934, NAACP Papers, Library of Congress; Mildred Stevens, Affidavit, July 27, 1934, NAACP Papers, Library of Congress; Prince

George's County Coroner's Inquest into the Death of Kater Stevens, July 27, 1934, NAACP Papers, Library of Congress.

4. Edward Smallwood, Affidavit, August 25, 1934, NAACP Papers, Library of Congress.

5. Lawson to Alan Bowie, July 27, 1934, NAACP Papers, Library of Congress.

6. Robert S. Jason held an AB degree from Lincoln University and a PhD from the University of Chicago. He had 5 years of experience as a pathologist, had performed 288 autopsies, and had been teaching at Howard University School of Medicine for 3 years. Lawson to White, August 11, 1934. Dr. Robert S. Jason, Autopsy Report of Kater B. Stevens (No. X285), July 28, 1934,

7. Dr. Robert S. Jason, Autopsy Report of Kater R. Stevens (No. X285), July 28, 1934; Marshall, "State of Maryland vs. Charles Flory," Memorandum, May 7, 1935.

8. Marshall to Houston, October 17, 1935, NAACP Papers, Library of Congress.

9. Jason, Autopsy No. X285, July 28, 1934.

10. Dr. Robert Jason, "Coroner's Inquest into the Death of Kater Stevens," Testimony, July 27, 1934.

11. "Citizens Want Bailiff Held as Man's Slayer," *Afro-American*, August 18, 1934.

12. Lawson to Rev. Charles Y. Trigg, July 30, 1934; Lawson to Virginia McGuire, August 2, 1934, NAACP Papers, Library of Congress.

13. White to Ritchie, August 8, 1934, NAACP Papers, Library of Congress.

14. White to W. Preston Lane Jr., August 7, 1934, NAACP Papers, Library of Congress.

15. Lawson to White, August 2, 1934; Walter White to Charles Y. Trigg, president of the Baltimore Branch of the NAACP, August 8, 1934; Marshall to White, September 10, 1934; White to Marshall, September 13, 1934, NAACP Papers, Library of Congress. Marshall appears to have entered the case at the request of Reverend Trigg of the Baltimore branch. Walter White also urged Carl Murphy, the publisher of the *Afro-American* newspaper, to "give us strong editorial support in our demand for investigation and action. We are going to follow the case up vigorous and will need all the public support possible." White to Murphy, August 9, 1934, NAACP Papers, Library of Congress.

16. Marshall to White, September 10, 1934, NAACP Papers, Library of Congress.

17. Upper Marlboro, the Prince George's County seat, where the Stevens cases was heard, is ninety miles south of Baltimore.

18. Marshall to White, September 10, 1934, NAACP Papers, Library of Congress.

19. Marshall to White, September 11, 1934, NAACP Papers, Library of Congress.

20. Marshall to Lawson, September 11, 1934, NAACP Papers, Library of Congress.

21. Marshall to White, September 11, 1934, NAACP Papers, Library of Congress.

22. White to Marshall, September 13, 1934, NAACP Papers, Library of Congress.

23. Ibid.

24. Marshall to Ritchie, September 10, 1934, NAACP Papers, Library of Congress. Marshall wrote, "A committee composed of citizens of Prince George's County, members of the District of Columbia and Baltimore City branches of the National Association for the Advancement of Colored People and attorneys for Mrs. Kater Stevens urgently request an audience with you for the purpose of briefly presenting certain facts concerning the killing of Kater Stevens at Bladensburg, Maryland."

25. Ritchie to Marshall, September 17, 1934, NAACP Papers, Library of Congress.

26. Marshall to Ritchie, September 21, 1934, NAACP Papers, Library of Congress. See Md. Const. art. V, § 3, cl. 2. Maryland's attorney general William Preston Lane Jr. interpreted the Maryland Constitution differently. In response to a letter from Walter White, he wrote that "under the Constitution, this office has no jurisdiction in criminal matters, except upon appeal before the Court of Appeals, and except where requested to participate by the State's Attorney concerned and directed by the Governor." Lane Jr. to White, August 14, 1934, NAACP Papers, Library of Congress.

27. Ibid.

28. Marshall to Bowie, September 21, 1934, NAACP Papers, Library of Congress. Marshall wrote in part, "This killing appears to strike at the very roots of law enforcement agencies of the state and has caused many people to be interested in it. The citizens of Prince George's County and the citizens of the entire state have focused their attention on this matter. Consequently they are looking to you to carry out your duty and to investigate this matter."

29. Marshall to Ritchie, September 24, 1934, NAACP Papers, Library of Congress.

30. Marshall to White, September 26, 1934, NAACP Papers, Library of Congress.

31. Marshall to Bowie, September 28, 1934, NAACP Papers, Library of Congress. The memorandum stated: "Unless it be in cases of riots, it is not lawful for an officer to kill a party accused of a misdemeanor, if you fly from the arrest, though he cannot be otherwise overtaken. Under such circumstances (the deceased only being charged with a misdemeanor) killing him intentionally is murder, but the offense will amount only to manslaughter if it appear that death was not intended."

32. Lawson to White, October 12, 1934, NAACP Papers, Library of Congress.

33. "I am happy to advise you that the Grand Jury of Prince George's County Maryland indicted Charles Flory for manslaughter. The citizens of Prince George's County consider this a great victory." Lawson to Marshall, October 15, 1934, NAACP Papers, Library of Congress. Marshall prepared a press release giving credit to Bowie: "Steven Slaying to Be Submitted to Grand Jury," press release, September 28, 1934.

34. Marshall to Bowie, October 20, 1934, NAACP Papers, Library of Congress.

35. Marshall to White, November 2, 1934, NAACP Papers, Library of Congress.

36. Marshall to White, December 10, 1934, NAACP Papers, Library of Congress. Marshall kept the press, particularly the *Afro-American*, up to date with press releases, for example, "Slayer of Autoist to Be Tried in February," press release, December 14, 1934.

37. Florey's attorney was Robert W. McCullough, whose law office was in Washington, DC. A defendant filing a demurrer moves that the court dismiss the plaintiff's complaint. In the demurrer, the defendant alleges that even if the facts in the complaint are completely true, the defendant cannot win as a matter of law. A demurrer is often referred to as a "motion to dismiss."

38. Marshall to Lawson, April 2, 1935, NAACP Papers, Library of Congress.

39. Marshall, "State of Maryland vs. Charles Flory," Memorandum, May 7, 1935.

40. "Begins New Duties," *JET*, March 18, 1954, p. 9; Hon. John Carroll Byrnes, "Commemorative Histories of the Bench and Bar: In Celebration of the Bicentennial of Baltimore City 1797–1997," *University of Baltimore Law Forum* 30, no. 1 (Summer/Fall, 1999).

41. Marshall prepared a press release stating that "Bladensburg is notorious for its prejudiced attitude toward colored people and Negro motorists in particular, and the outrage aroused great indignation both here and in Washington." Marshall said that the civil case would go forward. "Rural Policeman Who Slew Unarmed Motorist 'Not Guilty.'" press release, May 12, 1935.

42. Marshall to Lawson, June 10, 1935, NAACP Papers, Library of Congress.

43. Lawson to Marshall, July 9, 1935, NAACP Papers, Library of Congress. Lawson had previously given Marshall payments of $12 and $5; Lawson to Marshall, September 10, 1934; Lawson to Marshall, November 14, 1934. According to Lawson, he gave to Marshall half of what he had collected. Lawson to Marshall, September 10, 1934; Lawson to White, September 10, 1934. There is no evidence to the contrary.

44. Marshall to Houston, October 4, 1935, NAACP Papers, Library of Congress. Lawson had in fact reviewed and edited Marshall's first and second drafts of the complaint. See Lawson to Marshall, September 17, 1934; Marshall to Lawson, September 20, 1934; Lawson to Marshall, September 21, 1934, NAACP Papers, Library of Congress. Houston advised Marshall that "I agree with you that it is probably better for you to steer clear of Lawson, consider the $22.00 paid you as compensation for your side of the case, and that we pay you your out of pocket expenses. We are not in position to pay a fee." Houston to Marshall, November 1, 1935. Marshall and Houston did "steer clear" of Lawson in their next big case.

45. Lawson to Marshall, October 9, 1935, NAACP Papers, Library of Congress. Lawson to Marshall, October 15, 1935, NAACP Papers, Library of Congress.

46. Marshall to Houston, October 17, 1935, NAACP Papers, Library of Congress.

47. Ibid. Marshall also drafted a press release that cast the result in the most positive light and complimented the two judges who presided over the case, William L. Loker and Joseph Mattingly, for having been "eminently fair in both the criminal and civil actions." "Maryland Jury Awards $1,200.00 for Killing of Motorist by Policeman," press release, October 18, 1935.

48. "The Cake Walk Homicide: Trial of Ex-Policeman Patrick M'Donald for the

Murder of Daniel Browne, Colored," *Baltimore Sun*, November 16, 1875; "The Cake Walk Homicide," *Baltimore Sun*, November 20, 1875; "The Cake Walk Homicide: End of Trial of Patrick M'Donald for the Murder of Daniel Brown, Colored—Verdict of Manslaughter," *Baltimore Sun*, November 25, 1875.

CHAPTER 12: THE FIRST STEP ON
THE ROAD TO *BROWN*

1. Marshall to Houston, January 25, 1935, NAACP Papers, Library of Congress. At Amherst College, Murray was awarded the John Franklin Genung Prize for excellence in prose composition. "Baltimoren Wins Award at Amherst," *Afro-American*, June 9, 1934.

2. Donald Gaines Murray was the twenty-one-year-old grandson of A. L. Gaines, DD, a prominent bishop of the African Methodist Episcopal Church.

3. Marshall to Houston, January 25, 1935, NAACP papers, Library of Congress

4. "N.A.A.C.P. to Declare War on Univ. of Md.," *Afro-American*, December, 31,1932, NAACP Papers, Library of Congress.

5. "Local N.A.A.C.P. to Start Fight on Color Bar in State-Supported Institution, *Afro-American*, January 14, 1933.

6. "Two Apply at Md. U," *Afro-American*, January 21, 1933. "First steps of the local N.A.A.C.P., in its newly organized program to test the legality of the laws that prohibit colored students from attending the University of Maryland, were taken this week when Clarence Mitchell, 712 Carrollton Avenue, filed application for admission. Mr. Mitchell, who is a graduate of Lincoln University, where he majored in sociology, seeks to continue his course and obtain a master's degree in the graduate school of the institution. Harold A. Seaborne, 1127 Carrollton Avenue, also a graduate of Lincoln, sought admission to the law department of the same institution."

7. Hillegeist to Pearson, March 6, 1933, file labeled "Miscellaneous Important: In Re Colored Applicants to the Baltimore Schools," University of Maryland School of Law.

8. Hillegeist to Roger Howell, July 13, 1933, file labeled "Miscellaneous Important: In Re Colored Applicants to the Baltimore Schools," University of Maryland School of Law.

9. Hillegeist to Pearson, March 6, 1933, file labeled "Miscellaneous Important: In Re Colored Applicants to the Baltimore Schools," University of Maryland School of Law. The University of Maryland operated on two campuses. The undergraduate colleges and central administration were located in College Park, Maryland, outside Washington, DC. The professional schools for law, medicine, nursing, dentistry, and pharmacy were located in downtown Baltimore.

10. Ibid.

11. Harold A. Seaborne, interview with the author, November 11, 2003.

12. Julian A. Burruss to Pearson, February 16, 1933, file labeled "Miscellaneous Important: In Re Colored Applicants to the Baltimore Schools," University of Maryland School of Law.

13. H. A. Morgan to Pearson, March 22, 1933, file labeled "Miscellaneous Important: In Re Colored Applicants to the Baltimore Schools," University of Maryland School of Law.

14. Pearson to William P. Lane, March 11, 1933, file labeled "Miscellaneous Important: In Re Colored Applicants to the Baltimore Schools," University of Maryland School of Law.

15. Harold A. Seaborne, University of Maryland application, July 12, 1933, file labeled "Miscellaneous Important: In Re Colored Applicants to the Baltimore Schools," University of Maryland School of Law.

16. Hillegeist to Howell, July 13, 1933, file labeled "Miscellaneous Important: In Re Colored Applicants to the Baltimore Schools," University of Maryland School of Law.

17. Howell to Hillegeist, July 15, 1933, file labeled "Miscellaneous Important: In Re Colored Applicants to the Baltimore Schools," University of Maryland School of Law.

18. Pearson to Seaborne, July 26, 1933, file labeled "Miscellaneous Important: In Re Colored Applicants to the Baltimore Schools," University of Maryland School of Law.

19. The other law school applicants were Rufus W. Cooper, William W. Proctor, Ethelbert Cordery, Charles L. Tarter, Olin Thaddeus Thompson, and Benjamin Price. University of Maryland file labeled "In Re: Colored Applicants for Admission to the Baltimore Schools." Additionally, applications by Juanita Jackson and Clarence Mitchell to non-law graduate programs at the University of Maryland were returned. University of Maryland file labeled "Miscellaneous Important: In Re Colored Applicants to the Baltimore Schools." See also Raymond Pearson to Juanita Jackson, January 26, 1934; William A. C. Hughes to Walter White, February 16, 1933, NAACP Papers, Library of Congress.

William A. C. Hughes, who later became Marshall's law office mate, was the attorney for the Baltimore branch of the NAACP during these applications and advised some of the applicants. Hughes, Marshall, and Walter White originally expected that Hughes would be one of the attorneys in any lawsuit against the University of Maryland. See Marshall to White, December 4, 1933, NAACP Papers, Library of Congress; Hughes to White, December 6, 1933, NAACP Papers, Library of Congress; White to Hughes, December 8, 1933, NAACP Papers, Library of Congress. However, Marshall and Houston did not invite Hughes to participate in *Murray v Pearson*.

20. Donald G. Murray, University of Maryland Application, January 24, 1935, NAACP Papers, Library of Congress.

21. Pearson to Murray, January, 1936, NAACP Papers, Library of Congress.

22. Murray to the Board of Regents of the University of Maryland, March 6, 1935, NAACP Papers, Library of Congress.

23. Pearson to O'Connor, April 24, 1935, file labeled "Miscellaneous Important: In Re Colored Applicants to the Baltimore Schools," University of Maryland School of Law. Marshall supplied a copy of the complaint to the *Afro-American* a few days before it was filed. The front page of the *Afro-American* of April 20, 1935, contained stories about two Marshall cases—one about the law school case, "To Sue University of Maryland: Bill to Break up U. of Md. Jim Crow Is Prepared," and one about the execution of Marshall's client James Gross, "2 Are Hanged in Maryland Pen on Good Friday."

24. Pearson to O'Connor, April 24, 1935, file labeled "Miscellaneous Important: In Re Colored Applicants to the Baltimore Schools," University of Maryland School of Law.

25. Marshall to Houston, October 11, 1934, NAACP Papers, Library of Congress.

26. Marshall to Alpha Phi Alpha Fraternity, May 3, 1935, NAACP Papers, Library of Congress.

27. Marshall to Houston, May 9, 1935, NAACP Papers, Library of Congress.

28. Marshall to Pearson, April 24, 1935, NAACP Papers, Library of Congress.

29. Marshall to George M. Shriver, April 15, 1935, NAACP Papers, Library of Congress.

30. Pearson to Marshall, April 25, 1935, NAACP Papers, Library of Congress.

31. Marshall to Houston, Memorandum, May 3, 1935, NAACP Papers, Library of Congress.

32. Marshall to Houston, undated letter handwritten between May 11 and May 29, 1935, NAACP Papers, Library of Congress. The head of Princess Anne Academy was Calvin Kiah, whom Marshall frequently referred to as an "Uncle Tom." The academy was located in Princess Anne, Maryland, eighteen miles from Salisbury.

33. *Murray v. Pearson*, Replication, May 20, 1935, NAACP Papers, Library of Congress.

34. Ibid.

35. LeViness to Pearson, June 8, 1935, file labeled "Miscellaneous Important: In Re Colored Applicants to the Baltimore Schools," University of Maryland School of Law.

36. Marshall to Houston, telegram, June 3, 1935, NAACP Papers, Library of Congress.

37. "Lawyer for State Would Postpone U. of Md. Case," *Afro-American*, June 15, 1935.

38. Marshall to Houston, telegram, June 14, 1935, NAACP Papers, Library of Congress.

39. "Meeting of National Bar Assn.," *Baltimore Daily Record*, August 27, 1934.

40. Houston to Marshall, June 6, 1935, NAACP Papers, Library of Congress. As public awareness expanded, Marshall reported to Houston, "Colored people beginning to get interested. All 'barbershop' lawyers are sure we will win." Houston to Marshall, May 26, 1935, NAACP Papers, Library of Congress.

41. Marshall to Charles T. LeViness, June 8, 1935, NAACP Papers, Library of Congress. Marshall's initial assessment of LeViness was positive: "Been in touch with LeViness III. He will handle the case, Service is OK. Does not need any copies of the bill. Will answer on Monday. Says he is working on the case. Very agreeable." Marshall to Houston, June 3, 1935.

42. "Heirs to Hurst Estate Victors in Suit," *Afro-American*, February 6, 1932; "Mrs. F. B. Hurst Wins Suit in Annapolis," *Afro-American*, December 10, 1932.

43. This remark by Judge O'Dunne does not appear in the official stenographer's record. It does appear in the detailed account of the hearing printed in the *Afro-American* on June 22, 1935.

44. Stenographer's Record, *Murray v. Pearson*, Baltimore City Court, Part III, June 18, 1935, Maryland State Archives, pp. 116–17.

45. 193 Cal. 664 (1924).

46. *Murray v. Pearson*, Writ of Mandamus.

47. "Court Ends MD. U.'s Color Bar," *Afro-American*, June 22, 1935.

48. "Maryland U. Color Bar Smashed By N.A.A.C.P. Lawyers," NAACP press release, June 21, 1935. The press release stated in part, "This is the first case in the Association's recently accelerated campaign to force open tax-supported higher educational institutions to colored students through legal action. It is thus of far-reaching significance, since a practice that is illegal in the tax-supported institutions of one state is doubtless illegal elsewhere."

49. *Pearson v. Murray*, 169 Md. 478 (1936), Petition to Advance Case for an Immediate Hearing, August 6, 1935.

50. *Pearson v. Murray*, Defense Motion to Expedite the Court of Appeals Hearing. On September 16, 1935, Houston received notice that the motion to advance the case had been denied.

51. "U. of Md. Petitions to Keep School for Whites Only," *Afro-American*, August 24, 1935.

52. Harry Clifton Byrd to Herbert H. O'Connor and Charles T. LeViness, undated copy of letter incorporated into Petition to Advance Case for an Immediate Argument filed in the Maryland Court of Appeals on August 6, 1935, Maryland State archives

53. *Pearson v. Murray*, Appellee's Answer to Petition to Advance. This long and detailed response was drafted entirely by Marshall. Houston had told White about his plans to showcase Marshall at the NAACP convention: "Also advance travel requistion for $35.00 for Marshall. I think it would be good publicity to have him at St. Louis, to acquaint him with the work and to let the Conference and public see more young Negro lawyers who are working for the Association." Houston to White, June 19, 1935, NAACP Papers, Library of Congress.

54. Marshall to Houston, telegram, September 17, 1935, NAACP Papers, Library of Congress.

55. Houston to White, September 19, 1935, NAACP Papers, Library of Congress.

56. Houston to Marshall, September 21, 1935, NAACP Papers, Library of Congress.

57. Marshall to Houston, September 17, 1935, NAACP Papers, Library of Congress.

58. Houston to Marshall, September 21, 1935, NAACP Papers, Library of Congress.

59. Byrd to Hillegeist, July 15, 1935, file labeled "Miscellaneous Important: In Re Colored Applicants to the Baltimore Schools," University of Maryland School of Law. A week earlier, Byrd had made an ominous prediction to the law school dean: "Confidentially and personally, if negro students are allowed to enter College Park, it will come pretty close to ruining us." Byrd to Howell, July 9, 1935, Byrd Papers, Special Collections, Hornbake Library, University of Maryland.

60. Hillegeist to Byrd, September 18, 1935, file labeled "Miscellaneous Important: In Re Colored Applicants to the Baltimore Schools," University of Maryland School of Law.

61. Byrd to Howell, July 16, 1935, Byrd Papers, Special Collections, Hornbake Library, University of Maryland.

62. Marshall to Houston, September 25, 1935, NAACP Papers, Library of Congress.

63. H. L. Mencken, *Baltimore Evening Sun*, September 23, 1935.

64. Houston to Marshall, September 30, 1935, NAACP Papers, Library of Congress.

65. "Gadabouting in Baltimore," *Afro-American*, November, 11, 1934.

66. Charles Houston to Charles H. Wesley, national president of Alpha Phi Alpha, December 7, 1935. Belford Lawson had repeatedly indicated to Marshall and Houston that he expected to participate as cocounsel in the lawsuit to be brought against the University of Maryland Law School. Marshall and William I. Gosnell had met in Washington, DC, in November 1934 to discuss the university matter. On three subsequent occasions—December 16, 1934, January 22, 1935, February 4, 1935—Lawson came to Baltimore to discuss the university matter with Marshall. In letters addressing other matters, Lawson repeatedly inquired about the status of the plans to sue the University of Maryland. See, for example, Lawson to Marshall, September 1, 1934; Lawson to Marshall, October 1, 1934. Marshall assured Lawson that "you will be advised of whatever action is contemplated. I understand you are to be associated in the case as of counsel and we will let you know further developments." Marshall to Lawson, January 20, 1935, file labeled "Miscellaneous Important: In Re Colored Applicants to the Baltimore Schools," University of Maryland School of Law.

Marshall did not keep that commitment. After he and Houston had proceeded without Lawson, Marshall wrote to Houston, "Suggest you write to Lawson and tell him case is filed, so that it will be a matter of record." Marshall to Houston, April 21, 1935, file labeled "Miscellaneous Important: In Re Colored Applicants to the Baltimore Schools," University of Maryland School of Law.

Belford V. Lawson enjoyed a distinguished career as a lawyer and civic leader. His argument before the US Supreme Court secured the right to use picketing to support economic boycotts like the "Buy Where You Can Work" campaign. He served as president of the District of Columbia Chamber of Commerce and became the national president of Alpha Phi Alpha fraternity.

67. Houston to Marshall, December 23, 1935, NAACP Papers, Library of Congress.

68. Marshall to Houston, December 21, 1935, NAACP Papers, Library of Congress.

69. Marshall to Houston, telegram, December 31, 1935, NAACP Papers, Library of Congress

70. Marshall to Houston, December 6, 1935, NAACP Papers, Library of Congress. A month earlier Marshall had written Houston that "everyone here is sitting on pins and needles waiting for the Court of Appeals." Marshall to Houston, November 11, 1935, NAACP Papers, Library of Congress.

71. Houston to Marshall, December 7, 1936; Marshall to Houston, December 23, 1936; Houston to Marshall, December 24, 1935; Houston to Wesley, January 3, 1936; "Alphas Vote to Ban Brutality in Initiations," *Afro-American*, January 11, 1936; "Alpha Silver Convention is Successful," *Norfolk New Journal and Guide*, January 11, 1936. Back in Baltimore, Marshall coordinated the scholarship payment arrangements between the fraternity and the university. Marshall to Rayford W. Logan, January 17, 1936, NAACP Papers, Library of Congress.

72. Marshall to Houston, January 9, 1936, NAACP Papers, Library of Congress.

73. Houston to Marshall, January 3, 1936, NAACP Papers, Library of Congress.

73. Marshall to White, telegram, January 15, 1936, NAACP Papers, Library of Congress.

74. *Pearson v. Murray*, 169 Md. 478 (1936).

75. The inscription on the Thurgood Marshall Memorial in Annapolis, Maryland, reads: "Thurgood Marshall's first major victory in his lifelong struggle for equality under the law for all Americans took place in the Maryland Court of Appeals which then stood near this memorial. In 1935, Marshall successfully argued for the admission of Donald Murray to the University of Maryland School of Law. This was the first step on the road to *Brown v The Board of Education of Topeka* in which the United States Supreme Court in 1954 overturned the doctrine of 'separate but equal' established by *Plessy v Ferguson* (1896). Thurgood Marshall fought to fulfill the promise held within the quotes above the entrance of the United States Supreme Court Building in Washington, D.C., 'Equal Justice Under Law.'"

76. "Court Ends MD. U.'s Color Bar." Although he was not the valedictorian, Murray experienced no problems with his classmates and completed law school in the regular three years.

77. *Missouri ex rel Gaines v. Canada*, 305 U.S. 337 (1938).

CHAPTER 13: BECOMING A LEADER AMONG LAWYERS

1. The letter is dated March 5, 1936. I found it among the papers of one of the lawyers to whom Marshall sent the letter, Azzie B. Koger. Those papers are now in the possession of the Maryland State Archives.

2. Several publications state incorrectly that Marshall was a founder of the Monumental City Bar Association (MCBA). Marshall was one of the incorporators in 1934, and he did pay the incorporation fee (see note 3), but the association had existed since at least 1917. Some of the early presidents of the MCBA were Cornelius C. Fitzgerald (1917), Ephraim Jackson (1922), Roy Bond (1925–1927), U. Grant Tyler (1927–1929, 1933–1935), and Josiah Henry (1929–1933). In 1930, the MCBA cohosted with the Washington Bar Association the National Bar Association convention in Washington, DC. See "Capital Is Ready for Bar Association," *Afro-American*, July 26, 1930.

3. The incorporators of the Monumental City Bar Association Inc. were Emory Cole, George Evans, W. Ashbie Hawkins, Thurgood Marshall, Robert McGuinn, Warner T. McGuinn, and Karl F. Phillips. Warner T. McGuinn, at 4 East Redwood Street, was listed as the resident agent. See Certificate of Incorporation, Maryland State Department of Assessments and Taxation, April 2, 1935, liber 128, folio 68. Marshall paid the incorporation fee.

4. The 1936 Law Day celebration in Baltimore featured Maryland governor Harry Nice and James A. Cobb, a District of Columbia judge who had taught Marshall constitutional law at Howard University Law School. Marshall, as national secretary of the National Bar Association, also issued a call to lawyers around the country to observe Law Day. "Lawyers Asked to Observe Bar Day," *Afro-American*, May 16, 1936.

5. "NAACP Bar Asso. United for Action, *Afro-American*, August 13, 1932.

6. "Howard Law Dean Joins NAACP Staff," *Pittsburgh Courier*, July 16, 1932.

7. "Resolutions of the National Bar Association, 1933," Charles Houston Papers, Moorland-Spingarn Research Center, Howard University.

8. Genna McNeil, *Groundwork: Charles Hamilton Houston and the Struggle for Civil Rights* (Philadelphia: University of Pennsylvania Press, 1983), p. 71, quoting from an unpublished manuscript by Houston labeled "Personal Observation on the Studies in Legal Education as Applied to the Howard University School of Law," Charles Houston Papers, Moorland-Spingarn Research Center, Howard University.

9. Although all of the black lawyers practicing in Baltimore were men, at least four out-of-town female lawyers attended the 1934 NBA convention.

10. Oliver W. Hill, interview with the author, July 20, 2004. Raymond Pace Alexander was a prominent lawyer in Philadelphia who became a close friend of Marshall. See David A. Canton, *Raymond Pace Alexander: A New Negro Lawyer Fights for Civil Rights in Philadelphia* (Jackson: University Press of Mississippi, 2010).

11. "U.S. Court Posts Goal of National Bar Association," *Afro-American*, September 1, 1934.

12. Oliver W. Hill, interview with the author, July 20, 2004; "U.S. Court Posts Goal of National Bar Association." J. Thomas Newsome practiced law for more than forty years. See "Has Been Lawyer for 40 Years," *Norfolk Journal and Guide*, January 27, 1940. Newsome was followed by Robert L. Vann of Pittsburgh, who urged the lawyers to protest against all legislation that harmed their clients and their business practices. Fitzhugh Styles, a Philadelphia lawyer, spoke about the special contributions of black lawyers and estimated that there were 2,130 black lawyers practicing in the United States. Ibid.

13. "Local Bar Chilly as Convention Nears," *Afro-American*, August 11, 1934.

14. "National Bar Group Assured Full Welcome," *Afro-American*, August 18, 1934.

15. "Lawyers Row over Conduct of Conv. Program," *Afro-American*, August 25, 1934.

16. "U.S. Court Posts Goal of National Bar Association."

17. "Lawyers Urge Government Changes at Recent Meet," *Afro-American*, September 1, 1934.

18. "Meeting of National Bar Assn.," *Baltimore Daily Record*, August 27, 1934.

19. "The Lawyers Are Here," *Afro-American*, August 8, 1934.

20. Receipt from Junior Bar Association, 1935.

21. "Official Program: Eleventh Annual Convention of the National Bar Association, Nashville, Tennessee, August 1–3, 1935"; "National Bar Association a Little Pink but Refuses to Turn Red," *Afro-American*, August 17, 1935.

22. Houston to Marshall, August 22, 1935, NAACP Papers, Library of Congress. Marshall's principal responsibility after the convention was to distribute copies of the adopted resolutions to the press, government officials, and other interested persons and organizations. He reported to Houston on his progress. Marshall to Houston, October 22, 1935. Marshall also coordinated meetings between national conventions. See, for example, "Memorandum to the Officers and Chairmen of Committees of the National Bar Association," February 13, 1936, NAACP Papers, Library of Congress.

23. "Herndon Case Brief Filed by NAACP," press release, October 4, 1935; "Supreme Court Urged to Take up Herndon Case," *Afro-American*, November 12, 1935. Herndon spent twenty months on a Georgia prison chain gang before his release.

24. Marshall gave special attention in his correspondence to US senators and representatives from Maryland.

25. As the 1936 NBA convention in Philadelpha approached, Marshal complained to his friend Juanita Jackson that "everything has fallen on me." Marshall to Juantita Jackson, July 20, 1936, NAACP Papers, Library of Congress.

26. Upon taking a position on the staff of the NAACP, Marshall attempted unsuccessfully to extricate himself from his NBA office and duties. See Marshall to George W. Lawrence, president of the NBA, October 27, 1936, NAACP Papers, Library of Congress.

27. Roster of National Bar Association Officers, 3. N.B.A. J. 302, September 1945.

CHAPTER 14: THE BALTIMORE COUNTY HIGH SCHOOL CASE

1. "The people of Baltimore County are organizing a local branch of the NAACP and will fight the high school case as such, providing they get cooperation from the Baltimore City branch. Carl Murphy considered this a better idea than having the parent teachers' association of the Baltimore County back the suit. As a matter of fact, the two groups will be identical in personnel. Yet, at the same time, we will have this NAACP for future work in the County." Marshall to Houston, September 12, 1935, NAACP Papers, Library of Congress.

2. The schools were located in Catonsville, Randallstown, Reisterstown, Parkton, Sparks, Towson, Baldwin, Dundalk, Kenwood, and Sparrows Point. See *Seventieth Annual Report of the State Board of Education Showing Condition of the Public Schools of Maryland for the Year Ending July 31, 1936* (Baltimore, MD: State of Maryland Department of Education, 1936).

3. "Jelly-Back Era Ended, NAACP Speakers Avow," *Afro-American*, September 15, 1935.

4. Marshall to Houston, September 12, 1935, NAACP Papers, Library of Congress.

5. Marshall to Houston, September 9, 1935, NAACP Papers, Library of Congress.

6. "NAACP Wades into Problem of MD County Schooling," *Afro-American*, September 21, 1935.

7. Marshall to Clarence Cooper, September 13, 1935; Marshall to Baltimore County Board of Education, September 27, 1935; "County Officials Sent a Letter on School Question," *Afro-American*, October 5, 1938.

8. Houston to Marshall, September 14, 1935, NAACP Papers, Library of Congress.

9. Marshall to White, October 8, 1935, NAACP Papers, Library of Congress.

10. Ibid.

11. "NAACP Wades into Problem of Md. County Schooling," *Afro American*, September 21, 1935.

12. Marshall to Houston, October 15, 1935, NAACP Papers, Library of Congress.

13. Marshall to White, November 22, 1935, NAACP Papers, Library of Congress.

14. Marshall strongly disliked Dr. Cook and referred to him as a "Negro hater."

15. Marshall to Houston, November 26, 1935, NAACP Papers, Library of Congress.

16. Ibid.

17. Marshall to Houston, January 22, 1936, NAACP Papers, Library of Congress.

18. Ibid.

19. Ibid.

20. Houston to Marshall, January 31, 1936, NAACP Papers, Library of Congress.

21. Marshall to Houston, February 3, 1936, NAACP Papers, Library of Congress.

22. Houston to Marshall, February 4, 1936, NAACP Papers, Library of Congress.

23. Marshall to Houston, February 5, 1936, NAACP Papers, Library of Congress.

24. Ibid.

25. Marshall to Houston, February 7, 1936, NAACP Papers, Library of Congress.

26. Marshall to Houston, February 10, 1936, NAACP Papers, Library of Congress.

27. Houston to Marshall, February 11, 1936, NAACP Papers, Library of Congress.

28. Marshall to Houston, February 12, 1936, NAACP Papers, Library of Congress. Marshall carefully planned press coverage: "As to the idea of publicity, I believe the best way to handle this is to do so after the suit is filed. We have been informed that pressure has already been put on the County Board, and they are waiting to see whether or not we mean business. It, therefore, seems to me that the correct way to take up the publicity in this step is to file the suit along with the press release, and to follow this up with additional publicity." Marshall to Houston, February 3, 1936.

29. Marshall to Houston, February 25, 1936, NAACP Papers, Library of Congress.

30. "Need for High School Facilities for Education of Negroes in Baltimore County," United Parent-Teachers Association, press release, March 2, 1936.

31. "Seek Colored County School," *Baltimore News Post*, February 28, 1936.

32. Louis Azrael, "Louis Azrael Says: Tip to Baltimore County," *Baltimore News Post*, March 3, 1936.

33. Marshall to Houston, March 12, 1936, NAACP Papers, Library of Congress.

34. Ibid.

35. Marshall to Houston, telegram, March 14, 1936, NAACP Papers, Library of Congress.

36. "County School Case Goes to Towson Court," *Afro-American*, March 14, 1936.

37. Houston urged Marshall to ask *Baltimore News Post* columnist Louis Azrael to confirm that only black students took the examination. See Houston to Marshall, March 30, 1936, NAACP Papers, Library of Congress. Marshall corresponded with Azrael as the case proceeded. See Marshall to Louis Azrael, September 10, 1936, NAACP Papers, Library of Congress (transmitting a copy of Marshall's replication).

38. Ibid.

39. Marshall to Houston, April 1, 1936, NAACP Papers, Library of Congress.

40. Marshall to Houston, May 8, 1936, NAACP Papers, Library of Congress.

41. "Lawyers Clash at Maryland Hearing," *Afro-American*, July 18, 1936.

42. Marshall to Houston, June 22, 1936, NAACP Papers, Library of Congress.

43. Marshall, memorandum titled "Statement re: Baltimore County High School Case," July 10, 1936, NAACP Papers, Library of Congress.

44. "County High School Verdict Favors NAACP," *Afro-American*, August 8, 1936.

45. "NAACP Attorney Files Exception in County Case," *Afro-American*, August 22, 1936.

46. Marshall to Houston, September 16, 1936, NAACP Papers, Library of Congress.

47. "Demands Md. School Admit His Daughter," *Afro-American*, September 19, 1936.

48. Marshall to White, September 21, 1936, NAACP Papers, Library of Congress.

49. Ransom to Houston, "Confidential Report: re Baltimore County High School Case," September 20, 1936, NAACP Papers, Library of Congress.

50. Marshall to Houston, September 29, 1936, NAACP Papers, Library of Congress.

51. *Williams v. Zimmerman*, 172 Md. 563 (1937).

52. "Maryland Court Declares Inequalities Inevitable in Segregated School," NAACP press release, May 28, 1937, NAACP Papers, Library of Congress. A more tangible consequence of the litigation is that it prompted the Baltimore County government to begin providing high school education in the county for its African American population. By 1941, high school programs had been established in three locations in the county—Towson, Catonsville, and Sparrows Points. The schools were named for George Washington Carver, Benjamin Banneker, and George F. Bragg.

53. For an excellent work that positions the Maryland law school case and the Baltimore County high school case in the continuum of litigation that preceeded *Brown v. Board of Education*, see Mark V. Tushnet, *The NAACP's Legal Strategy against Segregated Education, 1925–1950* (Chapel Hill: Unversity of North Carolina Press, 1986).

CHAPTER 15: FINANCIAL PRESSURES AND CAREER DECISION

1. Marshall to Houston May 25, 1936, NAACP Papers, Library of Congress. Between Garland Fund payments, Houston occasionally loaned money to Marshall. Acknowledging a $25 loan in early 1935, Marshall wrote, "Received the check. You cannot imagine how much I needed it nor how much I appreciate it. I had a terrible month and everything has been in a jam." Marshall to Houston, January 14, 1935.

2. "Little Bits" was Marshall's nickname for his secretary, Madeline Tilghman. Before he left Baltimore, Marshall persuaded his friend and client at the *Afro-American*, John Murphy, to hire Tilghman. She remained at the newspaper for more than thirty years. Bettye M. Moss, "If You Ask Me," *Afro-American*, June 17, 1967.

3. Marshall to Houston, May 25, 1936, NAACP Papers, Library of Congress.

4. Ibid.

5. William O. Marshall to W. G. Murray, May 15, 1936. Marshall's wife, Vivian, was energetic and charismatic. One of her temporary store jobs involved demonstrating packaged sliced bread, then a new product. In April 1935, she had been elected national president of a women's social organization called the Girl Friends at the national convention in Philadelphia. She was reelected the next year in Boston.

6. Charles Burns, interview with the author, July 2, 1981.

7. Marshall to Joseph H. B. Evans, March 24, 1936, NAACP Papers, Library of Congress.

8. E. Peterson to Marshall, July 17, 1936, NAACP Papers, Library of Congress.

9. Ibid.

10. L. Church to Marshall, January 29, 1937, NAACP Papers, Library of Congress.

11. Marshall to Houston, March 23, 1936, NAACP Papers, Library of Congress.

12. Marshall to Houston, September 9, 1935, NAACP Papers, Library of Congress.

13. Employee record, Thurgood Marshall, Health Department, Reel BAC 728, SC 5636-B73, 0/57/7/33, BRG 7, 1934–1937, Baltimore City Archives.

14. Ibid.

15. "High Court's Tenth Member," *Baltimore Sun*, February 20, 1966.

16. Marshall to William E. Taylor, December 5, 1935, NAACP Papers, Library of Congress.

17. Marshall to George W. Crawford, April 23, 1936, NAACP Papers, Library of Congress.

18. George W. Crawford to Marshall, April 26, 1936, NAACP Papers, Library of Congress.

19. Marshall to Mordecai Johnson, May 9, 1936, NAACP Papers, Library of Congress.

20. Marshall to Walter W. Cook, May 9, 1936, NAACP Papers, Library of Congress; Walter W. Cook to Marshall, May 14, 1936, NAACP Papers, Library of Congress.

21. Louis Lautier, "Capital Spotlight," *Afro-American*, June 13, 1936.

22. Houston to Edward P. Lovett, telegram, June 17, 1936, NAACP Papers, Library of Congress.

23. Houston to William C. Bowen, NAACP Papers, Library of Congress.

24. Marshall to Houston, January 21, 1936, NAACP Papers, Library of Congress.

25. "Williams Is Candidate," *Afro-American*, June 10, 1933.

26. "Files as Democrat," *Afro-American*, August 11, 1934; "Eighteen Candidates Aspire to Political Posts in Maryland," *Afro-American*, October 27, 1934; "Local Men Lose," *Afro-American*, November 10, 1934.

27. Turman L. Dodson and Henry Lincoln Johnson Jr. to Marshall, August 19, 1936, NAACP Papers, Library of Congress.

28. Houston to Marshall, September 28, 1936, NAACP Papers, Library of Congress.

29. Houston to Marshall, telegram, January 23, 1936, NAACP Papers, Library of Congress.

30. Robert B. Kimble to Marshall, July 28, 1936, NAACP Papers, Library of Congress.

31. Letter from officials of Agricultural Workers Union to Thurgood Marshall, September 10, 1936, NAACP Papers, Library of Congress; "700 Gather for Steel Rally on Street Corner," *Afro-American*, August 22, 1936. The Committee of Industrial Organzations (CIO) was attempting to become the bargaining representative of the Baltimore steel workers and was appealing for support from black steel workers who faced severe racial discrimina-

tion at the steel plants; see Roderick N. Ryon, "An Ambiguous Legacy: Baltimore Blacks and the CIO, 1936–1941," *Journal of Negro History* 65, no. 1 (1980): 18–33.

32. Linwood Koger to White, May 11, 1927, NAACP Papers, Library of Congress.

33. White to Murphy, October 8, 1932, NAACP Papers, Library of Congress.

34. Murphy to White, October 12, 1932, NAACP Papers, Library of Congress.

35. White to Murphy, October 25, 1932, NAACP Papers, Library of Congress.

36. "New Officers of the Baltimore Branch of the NAACP—1935–1936," NAACP Papers, Library of Congress. The list of new officers included Gough McDaniels, Marshall's high school debate coach, as one of the vice presidents. Many writers incorrectly state that Thurgood Marshall became the lawyer for the Baltimore branch of the NAACP immediately after passing the bar. Marshall was the legal counsel for the Baltimore branch only from December 1935 until he moved to New York in October 1936. Before December 1935 and after October 1936 until 1960, W. A. C Hughes was the attorney for the Baltimore branch. Most of Marshall's early NAACP work in Maryland was directly with the national office and not with the local branch.

37. Marshall to Rep. Palmissano, April 18, 1936, NAACP Papers, Library of Congress.

38. Rep. Gambrill to Marshall, April 10, 1936, NAACP Papers, Library of Congress.

39. Marshall to President Roosevelt, telegram, April 22, 1936, NAACP Papers, Library of Congress.

40. "500 NAACP Delegates in Session," *Afro-American*, July 11, 1936. In addition to coming from Maryland, delegates came from California, Florida, Georgia, Illinois, Indiana, Kansas, Minnesota, Missouri, New Jersey, North Carolina, Ohio, Rhode Island, Tennessee, and Texas. "15 States Represented," *Afro-American*, July 11, 1936. The Sharp Street Church Community House, where the NAACP convention met, was the same building where the National Bar Association convention had met a year earlier and where Marshall had participated in debates.

41. Marshall to station master of Union Station, June 11, 1936, NAACP Papers, Library of Congress.

42. Harold L. Ickes, "Message to NAACP Annual Conference," June 30, 1935, NAACP Papers, Library of Congress. See also Mark W. Kruman, "Quotas for Blacks: The Public Works Administration and the Black Construction Worker," *Labor History* 16 (Winter 1975): 37–49. Of the four major New Deal programs, only the PWA provided significant help to blacks. The Agricultural Adjustment Administration actually reduced the number of blacks working in agriculture by a third. The CCC camps were highly discriminatory. The NRA was openly hostile to blacks.

43. "Official Program: Twenty-Seventh Annual Conference of the National Association for the Advancement of Colored People, Baltimore, Maryland, June 29–July 5, 1936."

44. Roy Wilkins to Thurgood Marshall, July 9, 1936, NAACP Papers, Library of Congress.

45. Houston to Marshall, September 17, 1936, NAACP Papers, Library of Congress.

46. "Thurgood Marshall Joins NAACP Staff," *Crisis*, November 1936. See also "Local Attorney Gets NAACP Post," *Afro-American*, October 24, 1936.

CHAPTER 16: COMMUTING BACK FOR EQUAL TEACHER PAY

1. US Congress, Senate Committee on the Judiciary, *Nomination of Thurgood Marshall: Hearings Before a Subcommittee of the Committee on the Judiciary, United States Senate, Eighty-Seventh Congress, Second Session, on Nomination of Thurgood Marshall, of New York, to be United States Circuit Judge for the Second Circuit, May 1, July 12; August 8, 17, 20, and 24, 1962* (Washington, DC: US Government Printing Office, 1962).

2. "School Law of Maryland: Governing the Salaries of White and Colored Children" (quoting Article 77, Sec.202, Acts 1922, ch. 382), *Afro-American*, January 2, 1937.

3. Marshall, "Average Annual Salaries in the Counties of the State Elementary Schools for 1932," memorandum, 1932, NAACP Papers, Library of Congress.

4. Houston to Marshall, August 21, 1935, NAACP Papers, Library of Congress.

5. Marshall to Houston, September 9, 1935, NAACP Papers, Library of Congress.

6. Houston to Marshall, September 10, 1935, NAACP Papers, Library of Congress.

7. Enolia Pettigen, later Enolia McMillan, was the president of the Maryland State Colored Teachers' Association. She lived in Baltimore but taught in Charles County in southern Maryland. In 1941, she became the first president of the Maryland State Conference of NAACP Branches.

8. Marshall to Houston, telegram, November 15, 1935, NAACP Papers, Library of Congress.

9. Pindell to Marshall, January 25, 1936, NAACP Papers, Library of Congress.

10. Marshall to White, January 27, 1936, NAACP Papers, Library of Congress.

11. Marshall to Houston, January 22, 1936, NAACP Papers, Library of Congress.

12. "Teacher Ready to File Suit for County Salary," *Afro-American*, February 1, 1936.

13. Pindell to Houston, February 4, 1936, NAACP Papers, Library of Congress.

14. Ibid.

15. Marshall to Houston, March 23, 1936, NAACP Papers, Library of Congress.

16. Houston to Marshall, March 24, 1936, NAACP Papers, Library of Congress.

17. "White Janitors Get More Than County Teachers," *Afro-American*, May 23, 1936.

18. Marshall to Houston, September 29, 1936, NAACP Papers, Library of Congress.

19. Howard Pindell, interview with the author, January 2004.

20. Marshall, "Teachers' Salary Cases in Maryland," memorandum, June 25, 1938, NAACP Papers, Library of Congress.

21. Pettigen to Marshall, November 5, 1936, NAACP Papers, Library of Congress.

22. "Plan Court Fight for Md. Teachers: Loss Due to Salary Differential Estimated at $500,000 a Year," *Afro-American*, November 21, 1936.

23. "Opening Gun Fired in War to Equalize Teachers' Pay," *Afro-American*, December 12, 1936.

24. "Teacher Sues for Equal Pay," *Afro-American*, January 9, 1937.

25. "The Cookies Run," *Afro-American*, January 30, 1937.

26. "NAACP Wins Opening Round In Md. Case," *Afro-American*, July 3, 1937.

27. William Prettyman to Marshall, June 29, 1937, NAACP Papers, Library of Congress.

28. "County Agrees to $30,000 in Back Pay," *Afro-American*, July 31, 1937. The *Afro-American* printed in this edition the entire text of the Montgomery County agreement.

29. Marshall to George Murphy, August 30, 1937, NAACP Papers, Library of Congress.

30. "New Teacher Salary Case May Be Filed," *Afro-American*, September 25, 1937.

31. "NAACP Begins New Pay Suit," *Afro-American*, November 13, 1937.

32. "Balto. County Equalizes Its Teachers' Pay," *Afro-American*, December 18, 1937.

33. Marshall, "Teachers' Salary Cases in Maryland."

34. Marshall to Maryland Teachers' Committee, "Proposed Case Against the State Board of Education," memorandum, July 13, 1938, NAACP Papers, Library of Congress.

35. See "Maryland Teacher's Salaries" in NAACP, *Racial Inequalities in Education* (New York: National Association for the Advancement of Colored People, 1938).

36. Clerk of US District Court for the District of Maryland to Marshall, January 5, 1938, NAACP Papers, Library of Congress.

37. *Mills v. Lowndes*, 26 F. Supp.792, 795 (D. Md. 1939).

38. Judge Chestnut's unpublished opinion, November 22, 1939, NAACP Papers, Library of Congress.

39. *Alston v. School Board of City of Norfolk*, 112 F2d. 992 (4th Cir. 1940).

40. Marshall to Charles Todd, August 30, 1937, NAACP Papers, Library of Congress.

CONCLUSION

1. Richard Kluger, *Simple Justice: The History of* Brown v. Board of Education *and Black America's Struggle for Equality* (New York: Knopf, 1976), chapter 8.

2. "High Court's Tenth Member," *Baltimore Sun*, February 20, 1966.

3. Cyrus Marshall, interview with the author, June 25, 1981.

4. Elena Kagan, "In Memoriam: For Justice Marshall," *Texas Law Review* 71 (May 1993): 1125–27.

5. Marshall, interviewed by Ed Edwin for the Columbia Oral History Project (1977).

6. 321 U.S. 649 (1944).

7. 328 U.S. 373 (1948).

8. 334 U.S. 1 (1948).

9. 347 U.S. 483 (1954).

Index